RELIGION AND AMERICAN FOREIGN POLICY, 1945–1960

The Cold War was in many ways a religious war. Presidents Truman and Eisenhower and other American leaders believed that human rights and freedoms were endowed by God, that God had called the United States to defend liberty in the world, and that Soviet communism was especially evil because of its atheism and its enmity to religion. Along with security and economic concerns, these religious convictions helped determine both how the United States defined the enemy and how it fought the conflict. Meanwhile, American Protestant churches failed to seize the moment. Internal differences over theology and politics, and resistance to cooperation with Catholics and Jews, hindered Protestant leaders domestically and internationally. Frustrated by these internecine disputes, Truman and Eisenhower attempted instead to construct a new civil religion. This public theology was used to mobilize domestic support for Cold War measures, to determine the strategic boundaries of containment, to appeal to people of all religious faiths around the world to unite against communism, and to undermine the authority of communist governments within their own countries.

William Inboden is currently the Senior Vice President of the Legatum Institute. He previously served as Senior Director for Strategic Planning on the National Security Council at the White House. He has also worked at the State Department as a member of the Policy Planning staff and in the Office of International Religious Freedom, and at the American Enterprise Institute as a Civitas Fellow.

Religion and American Foreign Policy, 1945–1960

The Soul of Containment

WILLIAM INBODEN

Legatum Institute

CAMBRIDGE
UNIVERSITY PRESS

CAMBRIDGE UNIVERSITY PRESS
Cambridge, New York, Melbourne, Madrid, Cape Town, Singapore,
São Paulo, Delhi, Dubai, Tokyo, Mexico City

Cambridge University Press
32 Avenue of the Americas, New York, NY 10013-2473, USA

www.cambridge.org
Information on this title: www.cambridge.org/9780521156301

First published 2008
Reprinted 2009
First paperback edition 2010

A catalog record for this publication is available from the British Library.

Library of Congress Cataloging in Publication Data

Inboden, William, 1972–
Religion and American foreign policy, 1945–1960 : the soul of containment /William Inboden.
p.   cm.
Includes bibliographical references and index.
ISBN 978-0-521-51347-0 (hbk.)
1. United States – Foreign relations – 1945–1953. 2. United States – Foreign relations – 1953–1961.
3. Cold War. 4. Christianity and politics – United States – Protestant churches – History –
20th century. 5. Religion and politics – United States – History – 20th century. 6. Civil religion –
United States – History – 20th century. 7. Truman, Harry S., 1884–1972 – Political and
social views. 8. Eisenhower, Dwight D. (Dwight David), 1890–1969 – Political and social views.
9. Truman, Harry S., 1884–1972 – Religion. 10. Eisenhower, Dwight D. (Dwight David),
1890–1969 – Religion. I. Title.
E813.I54   2008
973.91 – dc22   2008020176

ISBN 978-0-521-51347-0 Hardback
ISBN 978-0-521-15630-1 Paperback

For Rana

Contents

Preface and Acknowledgments

In recent years, when friends and acquaintances would inquire about the topic of my book, their responses almost invariably included some version of "well, that is certainly quite relevant these days." I think they are right. As a factor in international relations, religion has acquired – or perhaps re-acquired – a new salience that before had been neglected in the years preceding "the eleventh of the ninth," 2001. Whether as the declared motivation for those who attacked the United States on that day, or in the personal convictions and public statements of recent British Prime Minister Tony Blair, or likewise in the worldview of the American President whom I worked under at the National Security Council, George W. Bush, religion cannot be ignored.

Yet historians sometimes risk tripping into anachronism or even inanity when trying to make political judgments on the present day from their study of the past. In some cases that can well be an appropriate and helpful exercise, one in which I at times participate myself. But it is also a path fraught with methodological peril. Excavating the origins of the Cold War is a sufficient challenge in its own right. To speculate here on what the early Cold War's religious dimension means for current events would, I believe, do justice neither to the past nor the present. The point is more basic: not only is religion a major factor in foreign policy today, it was a major factor in the early Cold War as well, and in many other eras besides. Readers are welcome, of course, to draw their own further applications from the story that follows.

Though I did not realize it at the time, this book had its beginnings almost a decade ago in a research paper written under the supervision of Jon Butler. I am grateful to him, and to John Lewis Gaddis and Harry Stout, for exceedingly helpful guidance throughout the entire process. Many thanks also to Paul Kennedy, Jonathan Spence, John Demos, and Robert Johnston for their support and wisdom during my graduate school years. And I am forever indebted to David Kennedy, whose mentorship of an eager undergraduate helped set the course for much of my subsequent studies.

For generous grants that made possible much of the research and writing, I am grateful to the Mustard Seed Foundation, the Pew Foundation, the Smith Richardson Foundation, the Earhart Foundation, International Security Studies, the Institute for the Advanced Study of Religion at Yale, and the Civitas Program in Faith and Public Affairs. The Rivendell Institute at Yale, particularly Jon Hinkson, Dave Mahan, and Greg Ganssle, also provided support of the most enduring kind. And while numerous archivists made research more often a joy than a trial, special thanks are due to Martha Smalley of the Yale Divinity School Archives, Dwight Strandberg of the Eisenhower Presidential Library, and Randy Sowell, Dennis Bilger, and Liz Saffly of the Truman Presidential Library.

I had the great privilege to spend one year on a fellowship at the American Enterprise Institute, where much of this writing was accomplished. AEI's reputation for supporting innovative thinking in a collegial environment is well deserved. I particularly benefitted from the insights of Michael Novak, James Lilley, Walter Berns, Michael Greve, Kim Hendrickson, and the late Jeanne Kirkpatrick. A special measure of thanks to Chris DeMuth, Keith Pavlischek, and Jim Skillen, whose collective vision made the fellowship possible.

In the process of preparing for publication, Heather Morton lent her exceptional talents to the editing of the manuscript. Jeremi Suri and Leo Ribuffo provided extensive feedback, much of which I was wise to incorporate. Andy Beck and Bonnie Lee provided capable, encouraging, and especially patient editorial guidance throughout the process. Other valued conversation partners in the small but growing field of religion and foreign policy include Timothy Shah, Tom Farr, Joe Loconte, Mike Cromartie, Chris Seiple, Scott Flipse, and Charlie Edel.

Though research and writing are solitary endeavors, I have been helped along the way by the friendship, encouragement, and support of many. During my time at the State Department and the National Security Council, I had the honor of participating in the practice of foreign policy with some exceptional colleagues and supervisors. Working with them on present-day issues helped enhance my reading of the past. Seeing firsthand the singular pressures that policy-makers labor under, and the complexities of the process from writing memos to conducting negotiations to making decisions, gave me a new perspective and empathy as a historian for those policy-makers who have gone before, including those whose archives provided the material for this book. I make particular mention of Steve Hadley, J. D. Crouch, Jim Jeffrey, Peter Feaver, Mike Gerson, Pete Wehner, Steve Krasner, Mitchell

Reiss, Barry Lowenkron, John Hanford, Paula Dobriansky, Todd Deatherage, Lisa Disbrow, John Tsagronis, Rebekah Rein, Sarah Gelinas, Tony Harriman, Jean Geran, Elliott Abrams, Juan Zarate, Mike Kozak, Mike Magan, Paul Lettow, Mike Green, Dennis Wilder, Mike Doran, Dan Markey, Matt Waxman, Emilie Kao, Lou Marchetti, Dick Sokolsky, Nicole Bibbins Sedaca, Mark Lagon, Samantha Ravich, Ryan Streeter, Chris Brose, Christian Whiton, Meghan O'Sullivan, Brett McGurk, and Mark Busse.

I am currently privileged to work with an incomparable team at Legatum, whose patience and support helped see this book through its final stages. Christopher Chandler, Mark Stoleson, Alan McCormick, Hamish Banks, Derek Sheeler, and Philip Vassiliou in particular are models of wisdom, generosity, and integrity.

And then there are those friends who contributed in so many intangible ways, which are hard to measure but impossible to disregard. To include all of their names would fill its own book, yet special mention must be made of Brian Lee, Ben Sasse, Sebastian Traeger, Paul Vinogradov, Bill Behrens, Andrew Cuneo, Keith Carlson, Kevin Prestwich, Hunter Powell, Alan Hanson, Duncan Rein, Timothy Jackson, Terry Taylor, Hartwell Brown, Rod Macleod, Andrew Rein, Franklin Cate, Matthew Woelbern, Alan Philp, Kent Weber, Dan Bryant, Jeff Hendrickson, Stewart Davenport, David Legg, James Smith, Eric Gregory, Marc Allen, Randy Heinig, Jon Baer, John Folmar, Mack Stiles, Mark Dever, and Michael Lawrence.

My parents, Bill and Connie, encouraged my love of history from a very young age, and they along with my siblings Brian and Jennifer provided a foundation for me that continues to this day.

When I first set out on the path that led to this book, I had not yet met the woman who would become my wife. Along the way I came to know, to love, and to marry Rana, who is a living display of Solomon's wisdom: "An excellent wife who can find? She is far more precious than jewels. The heart of her husband trusts in her, and he will have no lack of gain." In everything from inspiration to the index, she was indispensable. It is to her that I dedicate this book.

Introduction

I

Upon appointing Andrei Gromyko as the Soviet Ambassador to the United States, Josef Stalin urged Gromyko to attend an American church each Sunday. Why this unusual advice from the Soviet dictator, a committed atheist? Stalin informed Gromyko that listening to the sermons preached by American ministers would provide the new ambassador with unique insights into the American mindset and value system.[1]

American churches, Stalin believed, helped define America's understanding of itself and its place in the world. One way to consider this book is as a test of Stalin's conviction: how did religion influence American foreign policy in the early Cold War years?

Harry S. Truman, America's first Cold War president, saw the conflict as nothing less than a religious war. Assessing both the nature of the foe and the need for an American response, he warned in an address at a Presbyterian Church that "the danger that threatens us in the world today is utterly and totally opposed to [spiritual values]. The international Communist movement is based on a fierce and terrible fanaticism. It denies the existence of God, and wherever it can it stamps out the worship of God. . . . God has created us and brought us to our present position of power and strength for some great purpose."[2] Consider also the language of the Truman Administration's

---

[1] This anecdote was related by Gromyko to former Soviet Ambassador Anatoly Dobrynin, as described by Dobrynin in his memoir *In Confidence: Moscow's Ambassador to America's Six Cold War Presidents, 1962–1986* (New York: Random House 1995), 22. Stalin also told Gromyko that listening to American sermons would help Gromyko improve his English skills.

[2] Truman, address at New York Avenue Presbyterian Church, April 3, 1951. *Public Papers of the Presidents: Harry S. Truman, 1951* (Washington: United States Government Printing Office 1965), 210–213. Also quoted in Walter A. McDougall, *Promised Land, Crusader State: The American Encounter with the World Since 1776* (New York: Houghton Mifflin 1997), 169.

policy directive known as NSC-68. One of the seminal manifestos of the Cold War, NSC-68 was drafted largely by State Department official Paul Nitze, under the direction of the Secretary of State and the Secretary of Defense, and was approved by Truman. Its importance can hardly be overstated. It articulated the strategic framework and ideological foundations for American Cold War policy, and it directed a massive increase in defense spending and all-out diplomatic and military mobilization to defeat communism. It remained classified for more than two decades, until 1975, and was intended to be read only by policy-makers at senior levels – not by the general public. Yet it reads in parts more like a sermon than a policy blueprint. These were years in which the lines between homily and strategy often blurred. NSC-68 warned that the Soviet Union "is animated by a new fanatic faith, antithetical to our own, and seeks to impose its absolute authority over the rest of the world." In contrast, America's "fundamental purpose is to assure the integrity and vitality of our free society, which is founded upon the dignity and worth of the individual."[3] That such a document was drafted by and directed at only policy-makers at the highest levels of government indicates that appeals to the American "faith" were intended not merely for marshaling – or manipulating – domestic support. They reflected the genuine convictions of many policy-makers.[4]

II

How was the Cold War a "religious war"? Religion functioned in two distinct yet related ways in the great conflict: as a cause and as an instrument. As a cause, it helped determine *why* the United States opposed the Soviet Union in the Cold War. After all, in many ways it made little sense for the United States in the late 1940s, just after World War II, to step into yet another cataclysmic global conflict. The puzzle has been observed widely and studied exhaustively, and yet it persists. In the immediate aftermath of victory over the Axis powers, in a world shattered by the most catastrophic war history had ever known, in a time when the American people would seem to want nothing more than

---

[3] NSC-68, from Thomas H. Etzold and John Lewis Gaddis, eds., *Containment: Documents on American Policy and Strategy, 1945–1950* (New York: Columbia University Press 1978), 385. For more on NSC-68, see also Ernest R. May, ed., *American Cold War Strategy: Interpreting NSC-68* (Boston: Bedford Books 1993).

[4] See in particular Bruce Kuklick's essay on NSC-68 in *American Cold War Strategy*, in which Kuklick compares NSC-68 to seminal civil-religious documents in American history, such as John Winthrop's "city on a hill" sermon. "The synthesis of righteousness, pride in *patria*, and sense of the evil in other polities, as well as the belief in the spiritual potency of American ideas, places NSC-68 in a long line of similar documents." In May, 158.

respite and recovery, why did the United States find itself so soon after 1945 mobilizing to confront yet another foe?

There is no single reason, of course. Almost as soon as the Cold War began, scholars began debating its causes, a debate that continued unabated through the Cold War's end, and a debate that this book has no pretense of attempting to resolve. What this book *does* do is introduce a significant factor that has been almost wholly ignored in the debate: religion. Yet as much as this book will argue for the prominence of religion in determining the causes and contours of the Cold War, it by no means seeks to disregard the other factors that sparked the conflict, factors that have been elucidated by many other scholars. For one, basic security concerns played a significant part. Following World War II, the strong and growing military power of the Soviet Union, so welcome and even indispensable in the Allied victory over Nazi Germany, appeared to many Americans in a different, more malevolent light. The Soviet role in securing communist governments in several Eastern European nations only added to this sense of foreboding, as did the communist threats to governments in places such as Greece, Turkey, Iran, and China. Perhaps communist expansion would stop at the borders of central Europe, but perhaps it would not; would capitals in Paris, London, even Washington, DC, be the next to be enveloped in the Soviet sphere of influence?

Related to these security concerns was the geopolitical reality of the balance of power. It has long been a truism of international relations theory that the collection of nations that form the international system will not tolerate the emergence of one hegemonic state power. If such a nation begins to emerge – as was the case with the United States immediately after World War II, possessing unrivaled economic might, a global military presence, and a monopoly on nuclear weapons – it is almost inevitable that at least one if not several other nations will seek, together or separately, to increase their own strength as a counterweight. By virtue of its own considerable military strength and its span from Europe to the Pacific, the Soviet Union was best positioned to balance American power in the international system.

Then there were the ideological fears of many in the United States that authoritarian communism threatened democracy and free markets. Communism was inimical to both, and wherever it expanded, whether in Asia or Latin America or the Middle East or Europe, political and economic liberty necessarily would diminish. Capitalism in particular found its most formidable opponent in communism. While the contention of a previous generation of revisionist historians – that an unholy alliance of American corporate interests and political opportunists initiated the Cold War in order to secure

access to new markets for the capitalist barons of the American empire –
now seems more conspiratorial than credible, it also has at least a shadow of
truth. American capitalism was threatened profoundly by communism, and
American captains of industry did exert considerable influence on American
foreign policy. Finally, the role of individual leaders and personality cannot
be discounted. As John Lewis Gaddis and others have argued, the singular
combination of aggression, paranoia, ideology, and avarice in the person of
Josef Stalin made the Cold War almost inevitable.[5] Stalin was determined
to secure as much power and territory as possible after World War II, and
the only way conflict could have been averted would have been if Western
leaders acquiesced to Stalin's designs. Individual leadership made a crucial
difference in the United States as well. Following Franklin Roosevelt's death
in 1945, had Henry Wallace become president – which came within a very
few secret ballots and backroom clouds of smoke from happening during
the 1944 Democratic Convention's selection of Roosevelt's running mate –
Stalin would have faced an American leader with little appetite to resist
Soviet expansion. But the delegates in Chicago in 1944 selected instead a Missouri haberdasher-turned-Senator, and when the United States gained Harry
Truman as president following Roosevelt's death in April 1945, Stalin gained
a determined opponent.

   As important as each of these factors may have been in causing the Cold
War – balance of power realities, security concerns, political and economic
ideology, individual leadership – taken apart or even together they are still
insufficient. They ignore God. And though Cold War historians may neglect
the spiritual factor, Americans in the 1940s and 1950s did not. As Truman's
speech to the church illustrates, many American political leaders believed
that their nation had a divine calling to oppose the Soviet Union, and to
reshape the world according to the divine design. This mission came in
general because they perceived communism to be evil, and in particular
because of communism's dogmatic atheism. It would be hard to conceive a
more stark division in the world than between those nations who believed in
God and those nations who outlawed such belief. Americans found it even
more ominous that not only were the communists attempting to exterminate
religious faith in their own orbit, but they also were seeking to spread their
godless materialism around the world. Differences over political structures
and economic systems and even national interests, though important in their
own right, paled in comparison with the prospect of a world ruled by evil, a

---

[5] See, for example, John Lewis Gaddis, *We Now Know: Rethinking Cold War History* (New York:
    Oxford University Press 1997), 292–294.

world devoid of spiritual values, a world without God. If ever there was cause to fight, this was it.

And yet how could America contend with such an enemy? The conflict certainly called for military force, as America's eventual massive mobilization demonstrated. Economic productivity, diplomacy, and ideological combat all took prominent places in the American arsenal as well. Here the second role of religion emerges. In addition to being a cause, it was an instrument in America's Cold War effort, a factor in *how* the United States fought the Soviet Union. If faith in God was as important and powerful as many Americans believed, and if communism sought to control and even extinguish religious belief, then it only followed that religion could serve as a potent tool for strengthening anticommunist resolve at home and undermining communism abroad.

The American government certainly tried to use religion in this way. Presidents Truman and Eisenhower, along with many other political and religious leaders, constantly reminded Americans of the centrality of religious faith in their national heritage, of the connection between faith in God and human rights and freedoms, of the special responsibility to which God had called America, and of communism's atheism and hostility to religion. Only by summoning the American people to a religious crusade could U.S. leaders maintain domestic support for the extraordinary measures needed to fight the Cold War. Beyond just rhetoric, this use of religion included deliberate measures to construct the institutions and rituals of a new American civil religion. Cultural Protestantism now reached out to Catholics, Jews, and others to unite against the common foe of militant irreligion.

Religion did not just serve as a Cold War instrument within the United States. The American government, led by Truman and Eisenhower, also employed religion in a number of ways – often creative and sometimes effective – to undermine communism abroad. From efforts to forge a common alliance of world religious leaders against communism, to covert funding for clergy behind the Iron Curtain, to broadcasts of sermons and other religious programming into communist nations, to calls for worldwide days of prayer "for peace" (and implicitly, against communism), the United States made religion an integral weapon in its anticommunist arsenal.

The importance of religion in the American government's Cold War policy underscores an emerging irony during these years. While religion maintained its influence in American diplomacy, American churches became less influential in shaping public culture. The American Protestant leadership probably reached the zenith of its foreign policy influence during its campaign of 1945 and 1946 to craft the postwar international order and to mobilize popular support for the United Nations. This only somewhat masked American Protestantism's ongoing internal conflicts, and as Cold War tensions mounted, American Protestantism degenerated into ambivalence, confusion, and sometimes bitter divisions over precisely how the United States should act in the world. Though most Protestant leaders agreed that communism was at best unpalatable, they differed on just how pernicious a threat it posed, and how and where and to what extent America should oppose it. Frustrated over these internal church squabbles, political leaders such as Truman and Eisenhower built their own pulpits in place of the clergy. They developed their own diplomatic theology and proclaimed it to their national congregation.

The American civil religion was not entirely new. Earlier versions can be found in the nineteenth century, and its roots can be traced all the way back to before the nation's founding. Yet while Eisenhower may not have invented the American civil religion, he did create a new incarnation. His chief innovation, perfecting themes developed by Truman, was combining the nineteenth century's domestic merger of "God and country" with Woodrow Wilson's belief in America's international mission. Moreover, Eisenhower institutionalized his civil religion and made it more doctrinally inclusive so that Catholics, Jews, and Mormons were welcome guests and even at times full adherents.

III

The influence of religion on American foreign policy in the early Cold War years is just one incarnation of a longer tradition. From the earliest European settlements in North America, American leaders had long been shaped by religious convictions in developing their posture towards the rest of the world. From the Puritan John Winthrop's "City on a Hill" sermon aboard the *Arbella* to the Declaration of Independence's assertion to the world that divinely endowed rights would determine the new nation's identity, to the nineteenth century's calling of "Manifest Destiny" for the United States to extend its frontiers, America's definition of itself and its place in the world had an irreducibly religious cast. More explicitly and directly, for at least a half century before the Cold War, the religious principles and policies that would so inform American Cold War policy were already at work, as the American people heard from their leaders (political and religious) consistent appeals to God's will and even the cause of Christ in calling for interventions abroad. The late nineteenth century witnessed the widespread flourishing in the United States of the conviction that American values and Christian (read: Protestant) values were virtually one and the same. God was directing history in a linear progression, with America at the vanguard, and it only remained for God's people to play their parts in advancing this progress.

Some theological conservatives in the day dissented from progressivism's optimistic union of God and country. Concerned that the leaders of the largest Protestant denominations had embraced a theological liberalism that ignored or even disavowed traditional Christian tenets such as original sin, biblical authority, the need for personal redemption, the imperfectibility of human beings, and the judgment of a transcendent God, these conservatives looked askance at the focus of mainline Protestants on equating the Christian mission with reforming and even perfecting society. Nevertheless, conservatives functioned in the early decades of the twentieth century largely as fundamentalist dissenters from the sidelines and would only later begin to emerge as neo-evangelicals in the early Cold War years as a significant force shaping – instead of resisting – the broader culture. Meanwhile, the ideal of a "Christian America" initially inspired many progressive reform movements at home; it only followed in the progressive mind that since the Kingdom of God was being realized in America it should extend its ideals abroad as well.

America's very emergence as a global power – and arguably its first taste of imperialism – in 1898 stemmed in part from the clamor of many Protestant clergy for the United States to intervene in Cuba and stop Spain's oppression. "And if it be the will of Almighty God that by war the last trace of this inhumanity of man to man shall be swept away from this Western hemisphere, let it come!" thundered one Protestant journal, while another proclaimed "should we now go to war our cause will be just. Every Methodist preacher will be a recruiting officer." If these were the sentiments emanating from houses of worship, an even more dramatic moment came in the White House itself. Following the swift defeat of Spain in Cuba, President William McKinley faced the hard choice of whether the United States should take possession of the Philippines, Spain's erstwhile colonial territory. McKinley spent an evening in prayer, and the next morning had his answer: "there was nothing left for us to do but to take them all, and to educate the Filipinos, and uplift and Christianize them, and by God's grace do the very best we could by them, as our fellow-men for whom Christ died." McKinley's divine revelation received a proverbial "Amen" from some in the United States Senate as well, such as Senator Albert Beveridge of Indiana, who defended the American annexation of the new territories with a similar appeal: "Fellow citizens, it is a noble land that God has given us.... Have we no mission to perform, no duty to discharge to our fellow man? Has the Almighty Father endowed us with gifts beyond our deserts and marked us as the people of his peculiar favor, merely to rot in our own selfishness, as men and nations must, who take cowardice for their companion and self for their Deity? . . . William McKinley plants the flag over the islands of the seas, outposts of commerce, citadels of national security, and the march of the flag goes on!"[6] It is no exaggeration to say that the Spanish–American War and the American acquisition of new territories in its aftermath would not have happened the way they did – indeed, might not have happened at all – without the influence of Protestant religion.

The optimistic early years of the new century saw this vision continue to grow, in both support at home and aspirations abroad. In November 1905, several hundred church leaders representing virtually every major Protestant denomination in America gathered at Carnegie Hall in New York for the "Inter-Church Conference on Federation," a conference on world missions that was also a precursor to the formation of the Federal Council of Churches three years later. President Theodore Roosevelt, who had just finished leading the Treaty of Portsmouth negotiations ending the Russo–Japanese War, sent a greeting highlighting a new opportunity in Japan. Roosevelt expressed his regrets at not being in attendance and assured the delegates that he had "the very highest sympathy with [your] movement . . . in addition to the great good it will do here, it is perfectly possible that the movement may have a very considerable effect in the Christianizing of Japan." The other goals of the conference were at least as ambitious. In what could serve as the manifesto of mainline Protestantism of the day, according to the *New York Times* one conference leader described its mission as "giving impulse to all great movements that make for righteousness" and that "questions like those of marriage and divorce, Sabbath desecration, social evils, child labor, the relation of labor and capital, problems created by foreign immigration, and the moral and religious training of the young, demanded united and concerted action which the conference sought to afford."[7]

The conference also heard plenary addresses from two Supreme Court Justices and several college presidents, including the president of Princeton University, Woodrow Wilson, who was the son of a Presbyterian minister. Wilson summoned the convention to the "mighty task set before us [that] welds us together. It is to make the United States a mighty Christian nation,

---

[6] Quotations from journals, McKinley, and Beveridge cited in McDougall, 112, 101–102.

[7] "Roosevelt Encourages Christianizing Japan; Declares the Federation of Churches Will Aid the Cause," *New York Times*, 16 November 1905, 11. Roosevelt quote also cited in Richard M. Gamble, *The War for Righteousness: Progressive Christianity, the Great War, and the Rise of the Messianic Nation* (Wilmington, DE: ISI Books 2003), 55–56.

and to Christianize the world." Wilson's charge well embodied the spirit of the age. In the words of historian Richard Gamble, "the church was no longer seen as a refuge from the world, as an enclave of the redeemed within Augustine's City of Man, but rather as a conquering army liberating the world and rebuilding the City of Man into the City of God."[8]

On being elected President of the United States seven years later, Wilson could advance this vision of a new City from the most powerful pulpit in the land. While in his first term he would pursue a broad program of domestic reforms, Wilson believed that his own country was already far along on the path towards the Christian ideal. In the words of one historian, Wilson held that "the American experience witnessed the fullest manifestation of public Christian values in human history."[9] Wilson in turn saw the presidency as a divine mandate to extend these values across the globe. In December 1915 he again addressed the Federal Council of Churches (FCC) and sounded a familiar theme: "we have got to save society... by the instrumentality of Christianity in this world." Moreover, just as Christianity and patriotism both appealed to the same high virtues, so did America have a similar calling. Its "object in the world, its only reason for existence as a government, was to show men the paths of liberty and mutual serviceability." Wilson elaborated on these themes in another speech the next day to a local civic group. "I believe... that the interests of America are coincident with the interests of the world, and that, if we can make America lead the way of example along the paths of peace and regeneration for herself, we shall enable her to lead the whole world along those paths of promise and achievement."[10] Remarkably, Wilson did not deliver these hopeful speeches during a time of peace, but rather while war had already been consuming Europe for more than a year, and after Wilson had delivered two stern warnings to Germany in the aftermath of the torpedoing of the *Lusitania*, and in the midst of the growing possibility that the United States might enter the war.

In casting his vision, Wilson enjoyed considerable support from – even embodied the hopes and prayers of – many of the nation's most prominent Protestant ministers. That same year, in *The Fight for Peace* Sidney Gulick of the FCC called for American Christians to be "ready to suffer with [Christ] in the redemption of the world, transforming it from what

---

[8] Gamble, 56–58; also includes Wilson quote.

[9] Mark Noll, *A History of Christianity in the United States and Canada* (Grand Rapids, MI: Eerdmans 1992), 302.

[10] Cited in Gamble, 128–130.

it is into what it ought to be." Likewise in 1916, the Rev. Frederick Lynch wrote in his book *The Challenge: The Church and the New World Order* that churches needed to "preach a new patriotism, a patriotism that is not so much concerned with saving the nation as it is in having the nation be a Christ-nation to the other nations of the world" because "those who are truly Christian are anxious to have the United States become the savior of impoverished, distracted, disrupted, groaning Europe, after the war is over."[11]

Yet Wilson did not maintain the support of all of the nation's Christians, or even the most renowned Christian in his own cabinet. William Jennings Bryan, the three-time Democratic presidential nominee and Wilson's Secretary of State, is best known to history, perhaps unfairly, for his later role as a prosecuting attorney in the 1925 trial of John Scopes for teaching evolution in a Tennessee public school. In his own day, however, Bryan was a revered populist, conservative Presbyterian, and advocate for nonviolence committed passionately to ending war. On taking office in 1913 as Secretary of State, Bryan promoted a series of bilateral treaties between the United States and eventually 30 other nations in which each committed to resolve disputes peacefully, through international arbitration. Appalled at the outbreak of war in Europe the next year, Bryan repeatedly urged Wilson to offer to mediate peace with all belligerent parties. Bryan appealed to their common faith: "the Lord never had a better opportunity or reason than now to show his power." Wilson shared most of Bryan's spiritual commitments and hopes for peace, but tempered those with a growing sympathy for the Allies and skepticism towards the utility of Bryan's arbitration treaties. This initial disagreement over tactics erupted the next year into a crisis of conscience for Bryan, who feared that Wilson's strong protests to Germany over its attacks on American ships meant an abandonment of neutrality and a march to war. Ever faithful to his higher calling, on June 8, 1915, Bryan resigned in protest. He remained loyal to his party, however, and the next year gave a stirring speech at the Democratic convention reminding delegates (and presumably President Wilson as well) that "God, in his Providence" called on the United States to apply the Golden Rule in its relations around the world, and that the Democratic party was most fit to bring world peace because it is "the party that preaches the brotherhood of man as next in importance to the fatherhood of God."[12]

---

[11]   Quoted in Gamble, 130–132.
[12]   Quoted in Michael Kazin, *A Godly Hero: The Life of William Jennings Bryan* (New York: Knopf 2006), 234, 251.

In one sense anticipating the debates that would consume American Protestantism decades later in the Cold War, Wilson and Bryan illustrated how a common theological framework (though not identical, Bryan being more theologically conservative) did not necessarily lead to a common position on the most pressing foreign policy issues of the day. Meanwhile, though evident to all observers, Wilson's religious devotion was not appreciated by all. At one point a disgruntled British Ambassador noted acerbically that Wilson "believes that God has sent him here to do something and that God knows what. This may be pleasing to God but not to Congressmen or ambassadors."[13]

Wilson, for his part, while still hoping for continued American neutrality and a mediated peace in Europe, was becoming convinced by both events on earth and a mandate from heaven that the United States would have to enter the war. "I believe that God planted in us the vision of liberty. . . . I cannot be deprived of the hope that we are chosen, and prominently chosen, to show the way to the nations of the world how they shall walk in the paths of liberty."[14] Many progressive Protestants had long believed that God called America to promote both peace and freedom in the world. As ideals, peace and freedom are hardly incompatible. But achieving them could pose a conflict; sometimes peace would have to be set aside to protect and promote freedom. And so it was in early 1917, as a coalition of more than 60 eminent church leaders issued a remarkable statement directed at Wilson. Urging the United States to enter the war immediately on the side of the Allies, the letter declaimed that "peace is the triumph of righteousness and not the mere sheathing of the sword." Going to war was nothing less than a spiritual imperative. "The just God, who withheld not his own Son from the cross, would not look with favor upon a people who put their fear of pain and death, their dread of suffering and loss, their concern for comfort and ease, above the holy claims of righteousness and justice and freedom and mercy and truth."[15] A few weeks later, Germany resumed unrestricted submarine warfare, and the interception of the infamous "Zimmerman telegram" revealed Germany's purported plans to ally with Mexico against the United States. Wilson and many other American

---

[13] Quoted by McDougall, 130.
[14] Quoted by McDougall, 136.
[15] Quoted in Gamble, 142–143. Signers included Harry Emerson Fosdick, Lyman Abbott, Gifford Pinchot, and Billy Sunday – the last was the popular evangelist who had more conservative, almost fundamentalist, theological convictions than the other signers, but shared in their support for war.

Protestants cast aside any lingering hopes they had for negotiations and prepared instead for a war that they intended to secure freedom and eventual world peace.

Wilson's speech to Congress on April 2, 1917, summoning the nation to war is remembered most famously for his call to "make the world safe for democracy." His message also attempted to bring together the principles of peace and freedom. "We shall fight for . . . a universal dominion of right by such a concert of free peoples as shall bring peace and safety to all nations and make the world at last free." Wilson concluded with a stirring peroration that managed to combine echoes of the Declaration of Independence, the sacrifice of Christ, and Martin Luther's call to conscience in defending the Reformation: "To such a task we can dedicate our lives and our fortunes. . . . America is privileged to spend her blood and her might for the principles that gave her birth and happiness and the peace that she has treasured. God helping her, she can do no other."[16]

Upon entering the war, Wilson's thoughts turned almost immediately to the end of the war and the new international order he hoped to help build. The victorious revolution of Vladimir Ilyich Lenin and the Bolsheviks in Russia in November 1917 brought a new challenge to Wilson's vision for the world. As John Lewis Gaddis observes, Wilson

> quickly found himself waging two wars, one with military might against Imperial Germany and its allies, the other with words against the Bolsheviks. Wilson's Fourteen Points speech of January, 1918, the single most influential statement of an *American* ideology in the 20th century, was a direct response to the ideological challenge Lenin had posed. There began at this point, then, a war of ideas – a contest among visions – that would extend through the rest of World War I, the interwar years, World War II, and most of the Cold War.[17]

Though Wilson could hardly have known it, his religious and political principles would be adopted, modified, and advanced by American leaders for decades to come.

As American churches commemorated the end of the war, Manhattan's venerable Episcopal Cathedral of St. John the Divine invited Elihu Root to deliver a message at the Sunday service following Armistice Day. Root, the

---

[16] Text of Wilson speech at: http://historymatters.gmu.edu/d/4943/. I am indebted to David Kennedy for pointing out the Martin Luther reference.

[17] John Lewis Gaddis, *The Cold War: A New History* (New York: Penguin Press 2005), 87. Emphasis original. Note that Gaddis in turn credits Arno Mayer with first developing this line of argument.

quintessential elder statesman, had been Secretary of War under McKinley, Secretary of State under Roosevelt, a Republican Senator, and the leader of a delegation (which included missionary leader John Mott) appointed by Wilson to travel to Russia in 1917 and take account of the revolution. Ascending the pulpit that November morning, Root exulted in victory and made clear its author. "God Himself was on our side. And so today, thanks to the Lord, Christian civilization triumphs." Looking ahead, Root was no less hopeful. "America can meet and solve all the great problems that will be hers as a result of the war and its sudden ending." Yet Root, who in his time had seen firsthand the dangers of nationalism, militarism, and communism, also sounded a note of political and spiritual caution. "The public has no conception of how great and how difficult our task will be" and "no man can frame the timetable of the Almighty." And in words that through the lens of history now appear ominous, he observed that "from [the war] will flow consequences to all the nations . . . which we cannot yet begin to understand or with any certainty to prophesy."[18]

Root essentially shared Wilson's vision for the postwar order and held considerable influence with many Republicans in the Senate and across the nation, whose support would be crucial for ratifying the Treaty of Versailles, including Wilson's great hope, the League of Nations. Sending the League of Nations Covenant to the Senate in 1919, Wilson proclaimed "the stage is set, the destiny disclosed. It has come about by no plan of our conceiving but by the hand of God, who led us into the way."[19] The FCC trumpeted its full support for the League, and more than 17,000 ministers signed petitions to the Senate urging its adoption.[20] However, the Covenant's encroachments on American sovereignty and freedom of action and Wilson's own dogmatic refusal to compromise – borne in part from his perceived divine mandate – proved to be too much even for progressive internationalists such as Root, and Wilson's grand vision perished in the Senate.

Into the postwar years – which we now know to be the interwar years – many Protestant clergy continued to hold to the progressive theology that America embodied Christian civilization and had a divine calling to reshape the world. However, somewhat chastened by the war's carnage, they shifted tactics to focus on ending the possibility of war itself, through disarmament and non-intervention. Prompted in part by the FCC, in 1921 more than 20,000

---

[18] "Root Says America Will Lead the Nations; From St. John's Pulpit He Declares We Will Solve the War's Problems," *New York Times*, 18 November 1918, 15. Root address also cited in Gamble, 210.

[19] Quoted in MacDougall, 142.

[20] Gamble, 228–231.

Protestant ministers sent letters and petitions to President Warren Harding urging an international disarmament conference. Harding, facing fiscal and other political pressures, agreed, and with nine other nations convened the Washington Naval Conference in November 1921. On the eve of the conference, Harding gave an address on Armistice Day at Arlington National Cemetery, in which, echoing Wilson's political theology, he called on his nation to put "mankind on a little higher plane . . . with war's distressing and depressing tragedies barred from the stage of righteous civilization." An enthusiastic FCC mobilized a massive campaign in support of the Conference, printing more than a half million brochures to educate its members, and helping generate more than 12.5 million letters urging passage of the disarmament treaties.[21] The Conference itself produced landmark commitments by the major naval powers to make dramatic reductions in their fleets. The peace movement continued to gather momentum, culminating in the negotiation and ratification of the Kellogg–Briand Pact of 1928, which quite literally secured the agreement of every major world power to outlaw war.

Into the 1930s, many mainline Protestant clergy continued to embrace what they saw as the lesson of World War I: war is never a legitimate instrument to advance the cause of peace and justice. They still maintained their progressive hopes for a new international order and the realization of the kingdom of God on earth. Many also still identified the United States as the best embodiment of this ideal, while others, chastened by America's absence from the League of Nations and then by the Great Depression, diminished their exaltation of America and focused instead on the international community. Harry Emerson Fosdick perhaps best illustrates this shift. One of the nation's most eminent liberal churchmen, Fosdick served for decades as the pastor of New York's First Presbyterian Church and then, with the sponsorship of John D. Rockefeller, as pastor of the Riverside Church. Looking back on World War I, Fosdick confessed he had used his ministry "in the support and sanction of war" and was "ready to declare war . . . even before the nation was. I, a minister of Christ, went all out for the backing of the fray." Now, as a professing pacifist, he knew that "only a federation of the nations, a unified world order, can present an ultimate substitute for war." Notably, Fosdick wrote these words in January 1941, as the German and Japanese militaries advanced across Europe and Asia, and Americans wrestled with whether they should enter the war to defend the Allied cause. On this, Fosdick was unequivocal: "for the United States to become a belligerent in this conflict would be a colossal and futile

---

[21] Quote and figures from Gamble, 241–243.

disaster" and "I will not prostitute the ministry of Jesus Christ to the sanction and support of war." He reached back to the end of World War I and found a telling lesson. The democracies "had the world in our hands and could do what we would. As to what we did and did not do... we, the democracies, are just as responsible for the rise of the dictatorships as the dictatorships themselves, and perhaps more so."[22]

While Fosdick spoke for many Protestant leaders, he did not speak for all of them. At this same time Reinhold Niebuhr was summoning his fellow Protestants – and his nation – to take up arms against Axis tyranny. Compared with Fosdick, Niebuhr drew similar lessons but different conclusions from World War I. "A simple Christian moralism... is senseless when, as in the World War, it seeks uncritically to identify the cause of Christ with the cause of democracy." Yet Niebuhr worried that too many church leaders were drawing the wrong conclusion in their opposition to American intervention in the current war. Christian moralism "is just as senseless when it seeks to purge itself of this error by an uncritical refusal to make any distinctions" between tyranny and democracy. Just over two weeks after Fosdick's essay appeared in the *Christian Century*, Niebuhr wrote the lead editorial in the inaugural issue of *Christianity and Crisis*, the new journal he founded in a break with the pacifism of the *Christian Century*. "We feel that American Christianity is all too prone to disavow its responsibilities for the preservation of our civilization against the perils of totalitarian aggression." After all, "there are times when our hopes for the future, as well as contrition over past misdeeds, must be subordinated to the urgent, immediate task... the defeat of Nazi tyranny."[23]

The debate between Fosdick and Niebuhr and their respective theological partners, impassioned as it was leading up to American entry into World War II, also anticipated the similar debates that would continue among Protestant leaders after the war, as new international institutions were built in the midst of rising tensions between the United States and the Soviet Union. The merits and flaws of democracy, the nature of the communist threat, the possibility of international cooperation and peace, the question of nuclear weapons, and the role of the United States in God's plan would all be fiercely

---

[22] Harry Emerson Fosdick, "Keeping Christ Above the Strife," *Christian Century*, 22 January 1941, reprinted in Joseph Loconte, ed., *The End of Illusions: Religious Leaders Confront Hitler's Gathering Storm* (Lanham, MD: Rowman and Littlefield 2004), 115–121.

[23] Reinhold Niebuhr, "Why the Christian Church Is Not Pacifist" in *Christianity and Power Politics* (New York: Scribners 1940), and "Christian Faith and the World Crisis," *Christianity and Crisis*, 10 February 1941, reprinted in Loconte, 147–152.

contested. And just as American political leaders such as Truman, Eisenhower, and Dulles would try to lead the nation with their own views on God's plan for America and the world, so did Franklin Roosevelt make his appeal to the American people. On October 27, 1941, President Roosevelt delivered a radio address warning of the Nazi threat to the United States. In one remarkable passage, he announced that he had acquired a

> document made in Germany by Hitler's government . . . which they are ready to impose a little later on a dominated world – if Hitler wins. It is a plan to abolish all existing religions – Protestant, Catholic, Mohammedan, Hindu, Buddhist, and Jewish alike. The property of all churches will be seized by the Reich and its puppets. The cross and all other symbols of religion are to be forbidden. The clergy are to be forever silenced under penalty of the concentration camps, where even now so many fearless men are being tortured because they have placed God above Hitler. In the place of the churches of our civilization, there is to be set up an international Nazi church – a church which will be served by orators sent out by the Nazi government. In the place of the Bible, the words of *Mein Kampf* will be imposed and enforced as Holy Writ. And in place of the cross of Christ will be put two symbols – the swastika and the naked sword. A god of blood and iron will take the place of the God of love and mercy.

Roosevelt concluded that the calling was clear. "Today in the face of this newest and greatest challenge of them all we Americans have cleared our decks and taken our battle stations. We stand ready in the defense of our Nation and the faith of our fathers to do what God has given us the power to see as our full duty."[24] Little did he know how these themes – the threat of totalitarianism to religion, the particular danger to Christianity, the divine mandate for America to defend freedom around the world – would soon return after the war as a new challenge emerged from Soviet communism.

[24] "President Roosevelt's Navy Day Address on World Affairs," *New York Times*, 28 October 1941, 4. The document in question, apparently an internal German Government memo, described the Third Reich's plan to establish the "National Reich's Church of Germany." The U.S. Department of State had acquired a copy of the document through Swiss channels, and Assistant Secretary of State A.A. Berle had given a speech on the document to a YMCA dinner in Columbus, Ohio, two days before Roosevelt's radio address. Roosevelt also sent copies of the document to American religious leaders such as Archbishop Edward Mooney of Detroit and Archbishop Francis Spellman of New York, whom he was attempting to cultivate in support of American entry into the war. See Stone to Tully letter with attachments, October 24, 1941; Folder: Diplomatic Correspondence: Germany; President's Secretary's File. See also October 25, 1941, Press Release; Folder: Speeches 1941; Box 144; Berle Papers Collection. Franklin Delano Roosevelt Library, Hyde Park, NY.

IV

On a fall Sunday in 1953, parishioners at the First Presbyterian Church in Princeton, New Jersey, witnessed one of their own step onto the pulpit to deliver a layman's sermon. His homily expounded in theological terms why the United States stood unalterably opposed to the Soviet Union. The lay preacher began with the admission that "it is hard, in our day, to be a Christian." The alternative, however, horrified him. "But it is still harder to embrace totalitarian outlooks that go the whole hog on the path of Godlessness; that deny the Christian truth and values; deny the existence of any supreme being, deny all individual salvation; and deny all individual moral law." More than merely a political or economic system, it was a religious worldview that distinguished the United States from the Soviet Union. The preacher then warned of the diabolical nature of communism. "Evil is a force in this world of no mean quality, with its own pride and even its own desperate self-respect. . . . Whatever the effective response to communism may be, I can say with assurance that it does not lie in any smug temporizing or opportunism with respect to the overriding moral issues." Americans must not quail in the face of this threat. They could draw strength and resolve and hope from their history, and from on high. "We are not to be spared the fire of conscience and decision in which our fathers' faith was forged." He closed with a prayer: "Almighty God, who hast found it fitting that our lives here on earth should be lived in this particular context of time and of place, grant us, now . . . the power of penetration to discern the peculiar dangers and delusions with which our age is replete, and the strength to meet them."[25]

The lay preacher was the American diplomat George Kennan. At the time of his sermon he had just retired from a distinguished career in the State Department, where several years earlier, while posted at the U.S. Embassy in Moscow, he had developed the strategic doctrine of "containment." Containment in various incarnations would define American foreign policy throughout the Cold War. Kennan first articulated containment in his famous "Long Telegram," later described by Henry Kissinger as "one of those rare embassy reports that would by itself reshape Washington's view of the world."[26] Kennan premised his doctrine on a shrewd analysis of the Soviet worldview, motivations, and expansionist designs, holding that there was an irreconcilable set of differences between the values and goals of the United States and the Soviet Union. Because the USSR could not be appeased, nor defeated by anything

---

[25] Kennan, "To Be or Not to Be a Christian," *Christianity and Crisis*, May 3, 1954, 51–53.
[26] Henry Kissinger, *Diplomacy* (New York: Simon and Schuster 1994), 447.

less than a catastrophic global war, Kennan contended that the United
States instead should "contain" the USSR by applying calculated pressure
at strategic points, while waiting patiently for the Soviet system to collapse internally from the burden of its own internal contradictions and
dysfunctions.

Conventional historical wisdom regards Kennan as a calculating realist,
unencumbered by sentiment or ideology, let alone religious faith. Indeed,
Kennan was quite critical of the foreign policy moralism he saw exemplified
by his fellow Presbyterian and Princetonian, Woodrow Wilson. But this gloss
overlooks the religious dimension of Kennan's own thought and the religious
aspects of containment as a strategic doctrine. For Kennan and many other
American leaders, religious faith provided a stark dividing line between the
spiritual United States and the atheistic USSR. In other words, although
religion did not call for an American effort to remake the entire world, it did
help determine the very boundaries of containment. On one side, the coalition
of nations led by the United States that would work together to contain Soviet
communism all had vibrant religious communities and political leaders who
largely believed in God. On the other side, the coalition of nations controlled
by the Soviet Union who would be contained from further expansion all
adopted atheism as an official tenet and worked to suppress any independent
religious belief.

Kennan later described his "Long Telegram" as having the structure of "an
eighteenth-century Protestant sermon."[27] He further developed this "sermon"
in an anonymous article the following year in *Foreign Affairs*. In his closing
prescription for American policy, he urged the United States to maintain
"a spiritual vitality capable of holding its own among the major ideological currents of the time." And his conclusion echoed Truman's own provi-
dentialist convictions about America's role in history. Kennan declared his
"gratitude to a Providence which, by providing the American people with
this implacable challenge, has made their entire security as a nation depen-
dent on . . . accepting the responsibilities of moral and political leadership
that history plainly intended them to bear."[28] Not only did religion determine the lines of containment, but in Kennan's formulation, containment
also depended on the United States maintaining its own religious strength
and answering its divine calling to lead in the world.

The homiletical exhortations of Truman, Kennan, and others for the United
States to follow its divine calling to oppose Soviet communism and to maintain its religious strength raise in turn a vital question: what type of "religion"

---

[27] George Kennan, *Memoirs: 1925–1950* (Boston: Little, Brown, and Co. 1967), 293.
[28] Kennan, "The Sources of Soviet Conduct," in *Foreign Affairs*, July 1947, 566–582.

did they mean? Almost every national American political leader during this era was Protestant and generally affiliated with one of the historic mainline Protestant denominations. Moreover, Protestantism still exerted a dominant influence on American culture and public religion. Because of its cultural and political hegemony, this book will focus on Protestantism, usually the mainline Protestantism of elite leaders. However, there are two important qualifications to this. First, American Protestantism itself during these decades became increasingly wracked by internal divisions, as leaders and denominations fractured over theological and political disputes. One of the themes of this book concerns the fierce contests among American Protestants to determine who they were, who spoke for them, what they stood for – and what they stood against. Second, Catholic and Jewish leaders play important roles in this story as well, though most often as cultural and political "outsiders" either attempting to shape the dominant Protestant culture on foreign policy or as potential sources of influence being solicited by American Protestant political leaders to embrace the American civil religion and resist communism.

It was the Jewish thinker Will Herberg who most perceptively distilled these trends and tensions. In his 1955 classic *Protestant, Catholic, Jew: An Essay in American Religious Sociology*, Herberg wrestled with the increasing yet evolving levels of religious observance in America. Internal developments within mainline Protestantism – particularly the preponderance of theological liberalism, the focus on morality in this world rather than salvation in the next, and an affirmation that other religions contained significant measures of truth – combined with the external pressures of the Cold War to move much of American Protestantism beyond its own parochial perspective into a broader religious movement. Herein lies the paradox: the new American civil religion did not arise *sui generis*, but grew directly out of American Protestantism. As Herberg put it, "from the very beginning the American Way of Life was shaped by the contours of American Protestantism; it may, indeed, be best understood as a kind of secularized Puritanism."[29] Having identified itself so closely with American culture, American Protestantism now found itself needing to evolve in response to changes within that culture – not only a growing pluralism at home, but the sinister foe abroad that threatened all religion.[30]

[29] Herberg, 81. For a discussion on earlier efforts by scholars and the U.S. military during World War II to construct a "Judeo-Christian" identity and values, see also Jeremi Suri, *Henry Kissinger and the American Century* (Cambridge, MA: Belknap Press 2007), 59–64.

[30] For a thoughtful discussion on how the broader American civil–religious culture that included a variety of faith traditions grew directly out of American Protestantism, see David Hollinger,

Yet this new level of religiosity was accompanied by a "new secularism," defined not by unbelief but by the diminished authority of religion over people's lives. "The religion which actually prevails among Americans today has lost much of its authentic Christian (or Jewish) content. Even when [Americans] are thinking, feeling, or acting religiously, their thinking, feeling, and acting do not bear an unequivocal relation to the faiths they profess."[31] Instead, Herberg argued that while Americans at one level affirmed the theological distinctives of their respective faiths, these distinctives gave way to a more transcendent new faith that trumped all else: "The American Way of Life."

Herberg's "American Way of Life" was moralistic, idealistic yet pragmatic, fiercely democratic, and fervently anticommunist. It was not just an amalgamation of beliefs common to different religions, however. Rather, it was "an organic structure of ideas, values, and beliefs that constitutes a faith common to all Americans and genuinely operative in their lives, a faith that markedly influences, and is influenced by, the 'official' religions of American society." This new faith genuinely valued traditional religion and sincerely believed in God. However, in a profound teleological shift, no longer was Jesus Christ (for Christians) or even God (for Christians and Jews) the final object of faith. "Religion" and "faith" were now taken to be ends in themselves, as objects of devotion, as indispensable for society's foundations.[32]

Even a civil religion such as "The American Way of Life" needs a high priest, and to Herberg, it was President Eisenhower who "in many ways exemplifies American religion." Religion was indispensable to the American identity in the 1950s, an identity actively shaped by the president. Herberg quoted Eisenhower's 1955 address commencing the American Legion's "Back to God" campaign: "Recognition of the Supreme Being is the first, the most basic expression of Americanism. Without God, there could be no American form of government, nor an American way of life."[33] And Americans, whether returning to or newly embracing their faith, clung to it all the more tenaciously in the face of the Soviet menace. Communism, after all, threatened far more than just their nation's physical security or economic prosperity. It threatened their very identity as God's people – even if they were God's people on their own terms.

Science, Jews, and Secular Culture: Studies in Mid-Twentieth Century American Intellectual History (Princeton, NJ: Princeton University Press 1996), 17–41.

[31] Will Herberg, *Protestant, Catholic, Jew: An Essay in American Religious Sociology* (New York: Doubleday and Company 1955), 3.

[32] Herberg, 77–84.

[33] Herberg, 79, 258.

Though a sociologist, Herberg was no reductionist. He did not dismiss the faith of those he studied as merely functional, as just an effort at social conformity or a contrived emotional escape from a tenuous existence in a tense nuclear age. Neither did he deny the partial truth of these factors. "Ultimately," he wrote, "the crisis of our time is a crisis of faith. The secular faiths of our culture have ignominiously collapsed under the shattering impact of the events of our time. . . . We can no longer look to science, to 'progress,' to economics, or to politics for salvation." Into the void brought by this collapse had come a renewed turn to religion. And "religion, touching as it does man's ultimate relation, in the end escapes all explanatory categories."[34]

Nor was Herberg merely a removed critic. Like Reinhold Niebuhr, he alternated between raising a prophetic voice against the complacency and self-indulgence of American religion and raising the spiritual banner against Soviet communism. In 1954, the year before he published *Protestant, Catholic, Jew*, Herberg gave an address to an Eisenhower Administration–supported forum on the spiritual stakes of the Cold War. His speech, titled "The Biblical Basis of American Democracy," contended that "the conflict between Soviet Communism and the free world is a religious conflict . . . a struggle for the soul of modern man." To combat "the self-deifying state that prevails under every form of totalitarianism," Herberg called for a more biblically grounded understanding of democracy, one that both affirmed democracy as the highest political ideal and yet resisted the temptation to idolatry. "Democracy may not, therefore, be made the object of a religious cult, as so many secular-minded Americans are trying to make it in the hope of developing a spiritual dynamic with which to meet Communism on the ultimate level."[35] A religious war, in other words, needed to be fought by an authentically religious people.

Without this theological context, the Cold War cannot be understood. "Theology" is by no means the exclusive preserve of seminaries or theologians. This is not to say that American political leaders self-consciously embraced academic theological tenets. "Theology" in this book merely refers to a basic set of beliefs about God, humanity, and how the world should work. In this sense, virtually every person has a set of "theological" beliefs, even those who would be unfamiliar with the term itself. While academic theologians play some role in this book, it is the broader and very basic theological

---

[34] Herberg, 63–64.

[35] Herberg, "The Biblical Basis of American Democracy," paper delivered at FRASCO conference, November 8–10, 1954, Washington DC; Evangelical Foreign Missions Association Collection, Box 68, Folder 11; Billy Graham Center Archives, Wheaton, IL. For more on this conference, see chapter seven of this book.

convictions of American political leaders that form the bulk of the argument. After all, arguments over matters such as God's will for the United States and the world, the divine mandate for human rights and freedoms and for international justice and peace, or the role of religious values in government, are at their core theological disputes.

Having identified their nation with God's kingdom and their American identity with a generic, nonsectarian faith in God, Americans looked in horror at what appeared to be an expanding, encroaching communism. To be sure, it threatened their nation's security, economic system, and political ideals. But before and above that, it threatened their faith in God. Their faith in God, in turn, called them to resist.

V

This book looks at how religious ideas and values shaped the worldview of American leaders, and the lens through which they viewed the world beyond American shores. It also explores the debates in America – whether among church leaders, among political leaders, or often between church and political leaders – over who determined and spoke for these religious ideas, and what they meant for America. This does not mean that there are always direct connections between a particular religious belief and a particular policy pursued by American leaders, but rather that religion helped shape the basic worldview of many American elites. Their actions in turn grew out of this worldview.

This argument will be made through a series of profiles demonstrating different – though interwoven – ways in which religion played various roles in American foreign policy. In part one, before the profiles, chapters one and two survey developments within American Protestantism from 1945 to 1960, particularly relating to international relations. These chapters survey the religious context that American political leaders encountered in their own efforts to define the Cold War in religious terms. From its confident heights at the end of World War II, when America's Protestant leadership enjoyed considerable public influence and shared a common foreign policy vision of international cooperation, foreign assistance, and multinational institutions, the churchmen (as they widely were known) began a precipitous decline into intramural squabbling, theological disputes, political disagreements, and diminishing public relevance. Liberals differed with realists, evangelicals with the mainline, and clergy with politicians. At the end of the day, their own divisions prevented Protestant leaders from forging a united religious front against communism – which American political leaders so desperately wanted.

Yet despite their differences, the churches did succeed in giving Cold War concerns prominence in both pulpits and pews across the country.

American Protestantism may have been divided on God's will for America in the world, but American political leaders did not necessarily entertain such hesitations. Part two looks at American political leaders through five profiles. To begin, chapter three focuses on the religious faith of President Harry Truman and how it motivated his decision to mobilize against Soviet communism. In particular, this chapter tells the curious story of Myron Taylor, Truman's personal envoy to Pope Pius XII, whom the president tasked with forging an alliance of world Christian leaders against communism. Chapter four explores the role of American missionaries in the debate over U.S.–China relations during the Chinese Civil War and the immediate aftermath of the communist victory. Did containment include opposing communist expansion in Asia? The missionary community split deeply over this question; both sides desired to "save" China, but they differed over whether that meant supporting or abandoning the Chinese Nationalists, and whether it meant recognizing or ostracizing Mao Zedong's new communist regime.

Chapter five addresses a vexing methodological question. How do historians account for an elusive factor like prayer – and more particularly, with a public leader who believes that he receives daily divine guidance, for his own personal life as well as for American foreign policy? Senator H. Alexander Smith, a subcommittee chairman on the Foreign Relations Committee and an active participant in the Moral Re-Armament spiritual movement, kept a daily prayer journal that recorded God's direction for America's role in the world, particularly in the struggle against communism. Chapter six looks at the person who is most often associated with the religious dimension of the Cold War: Secretary of State John Foster Dulles. This chapter traces the evolution of Dulles's theological conception of America's role in the world and how that vision related to both the challenges of public office and the Eisenhower Administration's construction of a new civil religion. This serves in turn as the subject of the final chapter, an exploration of President Eisenhower's use of religion as an ideological weapon against communism. Like Truman, Eisenhower believed the Cold War to be a religious war, and his newfound faith in God invigorated his desire to oppose the Soviet Union. Eisenhower also employed religion in his efforts to forge closer ties with Islamic political leaders in the Middle East, in his propaganda campaign against the communist world, and domestically in bolstering the fortitude of the American people for a costly, prolonged international struggle.

The informed reader will no doubt wonder at the relative paucity of references to Dean Acheson. After all, the State Department stalwart who rose to become arguably the most consequential Secretary of the century occupies a singular place in the pantheon of Cold War luminaries. Moreover, he inherited a formidable theological pedigree: son of the Episcopal Bishop of Connecticut and schooled at Groton in headmaster Endicott Peabody's ideals of service to God and country.[36] And he conceived his task as a quasi-religious duty. Thus Acheson titled his State Department memoirs "Present at the Creation," and described the Truman Administration's challenge as "just a bit less formidable than that described in the first chapter of Genesis. That was to create a world out of chaos; ours, to create half a world, a free half, out of the same material without blowing the whole thing to pieces in the process."[37]

One searches in vain through the record of Acheson's public life, however, for an extensive conceptualization of the Cold War in religious terms – at least in the same manner as Truman, Eisenhower, or Dulles. This left Truman to pursue his grandiose plan for a united religious front against communism without Acheson's involvement, and this found Acheson holding in contempt Dulles's public spiritual moralizing. Acheson's comparative reticence does not mean that he lacked a public theology, even if he may not have practiced a personal faith. His convictions stemmed more from his stoic duty to preserve the free world and its roots in both the classical and Judeo–Christian traditions. In the midst of the increasingly fervent crusade on which his nation embarked, he saw himself as a dispassionate realist, more comfortable with power than with piety. Both were needed, he believed, but with so many of his fellow Americans focusing on piety in world affairs, it fell to him to focus on power. Thus he recalled giving a 1950 address to the National Conference of Christians and Jews, in which he urged on his audience a "wholeness of view" of America's role in the world that saw the need for "a union between moral purpose and physical power." Acheson saw this balance in the practical American wisdom of the admonition to "put your faith in God and keep your powder dry." After quoting Reinhold Niebuhr and the Apostle Paul, he concluded that the "'wholeness' we sought included not only the shield of faith but also dry powder and the will to pass it."[38]

Yet Acheson's proud realism did not blind him to the Cold War's religious dimension. In a 1952 speech on "The Role of the Bible in Our National Life,"

---

[36] James Chace, *Acheson: The Secretary of State Who Created the American World* (New York: Simon and Schuster 1998), 17–24.

[37] Dean Acheson, *Present at the Creation: My Years in the State Department* (New York: W.W. Norton 1969), xvii. For more on Acheson's religious background and beliefs, see Robert L. Beisner, *Dean Acheson: A Life in the Cold War* (New York: Oxford University Press 2006), 101–102.

[38] Acheson, 461.

Acheson reverently described the unique roots of the American character, in which "the idea of God-fearing . . . meant a voluntary and militant submission to a moral order overriding the wills of the lowly and the great and the state itself." This led, in turn, to a great contrast, between the ideal of love in the Christian moral universe and the "hatred" cultivated by the Soviet system.[39] Here again was the basic outline of America's diplomatic theology. God had endowed humankind with basic rights and freedoms, and had endowed the world with a transcendent moral order. The Soviet Union – atheistic, naturalistic, totalitarian – set itself in mortal opposition to these principles. Though the United States was not perfect, it was blessed – not only with liberty, but with power. And God called America to use its liberty and its power for a higher purpose, a purpose that included resisting the Soviet Union and remaking the world.

[39] Acheson, 692–693.

PART ONE

ɷ

Hopes Deferred: Protestants and Foreign Policy, 1945–1952

I

The approaching end of World War II brought to the American people a sense of relief, joy, and anticipation. For America's Protestant leadership, the end of the war also brought a dilemma. The international system lay in chaos and urgent need of repair. Meanwhile, Protestantism stood at its zenith of cultural influence in American life. But translating that cultural hegemony into concrete action posed a considerable challenge. Moreover, Protestantism's predominance in shaping American values only lightly glossed over serious internal differences wracking the churches. The dilemma confronting Protestant leaders was twofold. How could they channel their cultural influence into specific policy initiatives? And how could they resolve their own growing differences over the nature of God, man, and America's place in the world?

Ultimately, they failed at both tasks. Despite concerted efforts over the next fifteen years, the mainline Protestant churches were unable to shape decisively American foreign policy or the international order. Furthermore, the theological divisions simmering in 1945 soon developed into massive rifts, further fracturing American Protestantism into diffuse voices and diluted influence.

Failures often reveal as much as successes, however. The story of the mainline leadership's inability to implement a common foreign policy vision in turn points to the triumph of an alternative diplomatic theology developed by America's political leadership. This public theology, which strongly influenced the strategic doctrine of containment, drew on many resources in the American Protestant tradition. In the midst of this, the U.S. government maintained an ambivalent relationship with the Protestant churches, alternately embracing and resisting them, as it tried to develop a new public faith for confronting communism.

The American people, meanwhile, found themselves bombarded by a caco-phony of religious voices offering various pronouncements on their nation's role in the world. Some pulpits proclaimed a peaceful vision of world cooper-ation and unity, while others thundered a call to arms against the "communist menace." And the White House, perhaps the most prominent of pulpits, urged all faithful Americans – Protestant, Catholic, and Jew – to mobilize spiritually for the great crusade against communism.

The outlook for the Protestant churches initially had seemed much bet-ter. America's mainline Protestant leaders, or the "churchmen" as they were widely known, enjoyed considerable success during the war years in gen-erating popular support for the United Nations. While the Allied military campaign against Germany and Japan dominated the headlines from 1943 to 1945, the churchmen instead focused on shaping the world that would emerge after the war. They gave early and enthusiastic support for a postwar order centered on the United Nations organization. Beginning in 1943, the Fed-eral Council of Churches' (FCC) Commission on a Just and Durable Peace, chaired by John Foster Dulles, began distributing copies of its "Six Pillars of Peace" to ministers and churches throughout the nation and to every chap-lain in the armed forces. Various denominations, including the Methodists, Presbyterians, Congregationalists, and Northern Baptists, mobilized massive numbers of churchgoers to write letters to Congress and the White House urging "international cooperation" in organizing the post-war world. The laity eagerly responded by subjecting Washington to a deluge of mail. Dis-pensing with the customary form letter format, most of these epistles were hand-written originals, indicating the earnest and abiding hopes held by so many Americans for a new world order. For these American Protestants, hor-rified at the violent world seemingly wrought in – and by – America's absence, isolationism had gone the way of the frontier circuit preacher.[1]

Besides generating grassroots support, the Commission on a Just and Durable Peace also attempted to influence directly the United Nations charter. Of nine proposed amendments offered by the FCC at the UN's organizing con-ference in San Francisco in April, 1945, four were incorporated into the final document. These included language in the preamble stating the moral pur-poses of the UN, a commitment to developing customary international law, the formation of a Trusteeship Council to assist colonial peoples' transition

---

[1] Heather A. Warren, *Theologians of a New World Order: Reinhold Niebuhr and the Christian Realists, 1920–1948* (New York: Oxford University Press 1997), 101–108. See also Robert A. Divine, *Second Chance: The Triumph of Internationalism in America During World War II* (New York: Atheneum 1967), 88–89 and 161–163; Robert Moats Miller, *Bishop G. Bromley Oxnam: Paladin of Liberal Protestantism* (Nashville, TN: Abingdon Press 1990), 259–268.

to democratic rule, and a declaration of universal human rights.[2] Meanwhile, thousands of Protestant churches commemorated April 22 as "United Nations Sunday," offering their prayers and support on the eve of the conference. The FCC even threatened to have the UN Charter read aloud from every Protestant pulpit in the country if the Senate delayed its ratification.[3]

Within weeks of Japan's surrender, the FCC's Department of International Justice and Goodwill proclaimed a new beginning and a new world. In a message to Christians across the globe, the FCC announced that the end of the war brought "a clarion call for Christians to achieve in the here and now a righteous world order." The United Nations bore the brunt of the FCC's hopes. The UN promised to "displace the anarchy of competing and unrestrained sovereign states" with "a true community of nations."[4] In other words, the UN incarnated a new international reality – at least in the minds of the churchmen. Competition would give way to cooperation; nationalism would surrender to internationalism.

Affirming these hopes, the Nobel Committee the next year awarded the 1946 Peace Prize to John Mott, the legendary American Protestant leader in world missions and the ecumenical movement. This was doubly symbolic, signifying both the dreams of the world community for a new order, and the primacy of American churchmen in shaping it. Mott affirmed as much in his Nobel address. As he surveyed this moment in history from his vantage point of 81 years, he envisioned a "truly international" generation, one that would lead the "constructive forces of the world . . . into a triumphant stage." Mott did not offer a precise plan for shaping this new world, but only called time and again for "leadership."[5] In the year or two immediately following World War II, the American churchmen saw a major opportunity, and struggled to seize it.

They saw a major problem as well. The war had ended, after all, not with a rainbow but with two mushroom clouds over Japan. The dawn of the nuclear age threatened to obliterate American Protestantism's dreams for "a world made new."[6] The churchmen's high hopes for the UN were tethered uneasily

---

[2] Warren, 107.

[3] Divine, 303; Miller, 265, 268.

[4] September 10, 1945 Message from Department of International Justice and Goodwill; National Council of Churches Collection (hereinafter NCC Papers), Record Group 18, Box 24, Folder 16; Presbyterian Historical Society, Philadelphia, PA (hereinafter PHS).

[5] Mott, "The Leadership Demanded in this Momentous Time," December 13, 1946 Nobel Peace Prize Address. John Mott Papers, Record Group 45, Box 136, Folder 2194; Yale Divinity School Archives; Yale University, New Haven, CT (hereinafter YDSA).

[6] The phrase "a world made new" is drawn from Eleanor Roosevelt's nightly prayer, which closed: "Save us from ourselves and show us a vision of a world made new." For more on

to their fears of atomic energy's awful potential. Like many other Americans, they reacted initially to the atomic bombing of Japan with a mixture of triumph, fear, and bewilderment. On August 9, 1945, Methodist Bishop G. Bromley Oxnam, President of the FCC, and John Foster Dulles issued a statement in response to Hiroshima and Nagasaki. Steeped in ambivalence, Oxnam and Dulles pronounced themselves both "proud" at the "scientific miracle" of atomic energy, yet "concerned" over its potential misuse. They called twice for "self-restraint" on the part of the U.S. government, further development of the United Nations, and the suspension of further attacks on Japan until the Japanese government had responded to the American ultimatum.[7] Notably, the statement raised no qualms about the bombings as a direct assault on Japanese civilians – even though forbidden by the cardinal tenets of the Christian just war tradition.

At least one church leader dissented from even a qualified approval of the bombing. Rev. Samuel McCrea Cavert, General Secretary of the FCC, sent a letter to President Truman on August 9 (the same day as Oxnam and Dulles's statement) announcing that he was "deeply disturbed" over the use of the atomic bombs. Truman, with characteristic bluntness, rejected Cavert's criticism, protesting that "nobody is more disturbed over the use of Atomic Bombs than I am but I was greatly disturbed over the unwarranted attack by the Japanese on Pearl Harbor and their murder of our prisoners of war. The only language they seem to understand is one we have been using to bombard them. When you have to deal with a beast you have to treat him as a beast."[8] Truman's sharp reply reveals the skepticism of official Washington towards some of the Protestant churchmen. The president suffered neither fools nor blind idealists gladly – whom he often regarded as one and the same.

this, particularly Roosevelt's instrumental leadership in developing the Universal Declaration of Human Rights, see Mary Ann Glendon, *A World Made New: Eleanor Roosevelt and the Universal Declaration of Human Rights* (New York: Random House 2001).

7   "Statement on the Atomic Bomb," August 9, 1945. NCC Papers, RG 18, Box 24, Folder 16; PHS.

8   Cavert to Truman, August 9, 1945, and Truman to Cavert, August 11, 1945. Truman Papers, Official File Box 803, Folder 213; Harry S. Truman Presidential Library, Independence, MO (hereinafter HST). Curiously, two days earlier Truman had responded in a strikingly different tone to Sen. Richard Russell's call for even more aggressive measures against Japan. Truman replied that "I know that Japan is a terribly cruel and uncivilized nation in warfare but I can't bring myself to believe that, because they are beasts, we should ourselves act in the same manner." Cited in David McCullough, *Truman* (New York: Simon and Schuster 1992), 458. Note also that Mark Silk seems to misinterpret the FCC statements and Truman's response. Silk inaccurately presents the Oxnam and Dulles statement as an unequivocal condemnation of the atomic bombing of Japan, and describes Truman's letter as a response to Oxnam and Dulles, when in fact Truman was responding to Cavert's letter. See Silk, *Spiritual Politics: Religion and America Since World War II* (New York: Simon and Schuster 1988), 23–24.

Truman possessed his own fervent streak of Protestant idealism, of course, and it would influence strongly his approach to the Cold War. But he held no brief for the pious platitudes of naïve clerics.

In late December, another FCC Commission convened to address the atomic age. Consistent with mainline Protestantism's affinity for grandiose and almost interminable titles, the Commission on the Relation of the Church to the War in the Light of the Christian Faith set out its task with an urgency that its cumbersome name belied. The Calhoun Commission, taking its short-hand name from its chair, Yale's Robert Calhoun, had initially met in 1944 to evaluate America's military conduct in moral terms. The Commission assembled a remarkable collection of American theological luminaries, including Reinhold and H. Richard Niebuhr, Roland Bainton, John Bennett, and Henry Van Dusen. Its 1944 report reflected the Commission's own internal divisions and ambivalence, its distress over the Allied attacks on civilian populations together with its recognition of the extreme measures necessary to defeat the Axis evil.[9] Despite the sharp divisions between pacifists and just war propo-nents, the Commission arrived at an early consensus that the use of the bombs against Japan was a "wanton outrage" and indefensible for reasons including the direct targeting of non-combatants, the failure to warn the Japanese of the impending attack, and bombing Nagasaki before the Japanese government had time to respond diplomatically to the Hiroshima explosion. Looking to the future, the Commission agreed at its next meeting that America should renounce any further initial use of atomic weapons. Yet on this point, a sharp disagreement emerged. The discussion singled out Russia as a potential threat. Calhoun spoke vigorously on behalf of those commissioners – generally the pacifists – who wanted a pledge never to use the atomic bomb in any cir-cumstances. Reinhold Niebuhr argued just as forcefully for the opposing side. Asserting that the American culture and political system would prevent any aggressive use of the bomb, he maintained that the United States needed the option of atomic weapons for defensive or retaliatory purposes. And so this meeting saw America's Protestant leaders anticipate – perhaps prophetically, perhaps unwittingly – both the coming conflict with the Soviet Union and the emergence of nuclear deterrence as the cornerstone of Cold War strategy.[10]

The Commission released its report, "Atomic Warfare and the Chris-tian Faith," on March 6, 1946. True to their calling as theologians, the

---

[9] See Paul Boyer, *By the Bomb's Early Light: American Thought and Culture at the Dawn of the Atomic Age* (Chapel Hill, NC: University of North Carolina Press 1994), 213–214.

[10] "Report of the Meeting of the Commission on the Church and the War," December 28–29, 1945 and "Minutes of the Meeting," February 1–2, 1946; NCC Papers, RG 18, Box 25, Folder 7; PHS.

commissioners began with a searching discussion of the existential import of the new era. "The atomic bomb gives new and fearful meaning to the age-old plight of man," they declared. "The new weapon has destroyed at one blow the familiar conceptions of national security, changed the scale of destructive conflict among peoples, and opened before us all the prospect of swift ruin for civilization and even the possibility of a speedy end to man's life on earth." Not until one-third of the way into the report did they announce their verdict: "As American Christians, we are deeply penitent . . . the surprise bombings of Hiroshima and Nagasaki are morally indefensible. They repeated in a ghastly form the indiscriminate slaughter of non-combatants that has become familiar during World War II . . . we have sinned grievously against the laws of God and against the people of Japan." The commission went on to describe its fear that the deadly new combination of destructive weaponry and unlimited war would make the world's next conflict its last. The only practical hope lay in preventing future wars and in international control of the new technology. Yet even here the commission was skeptical. "Exclusive trust in a political structure of any sort to solve the problems posed by atomic warfare would be a dangerous illusion."[11]

Reinhold Niebuhr loomed large over American Protestantism. More than any other Protestant thinker at mid-century, he communicated the insights of theological reflection to the broader intellectual and policy communities and to the pressing issues of the day. Although a close participant in several of the mainline church organization's signature initiatives, his influence extended far beyond the church pews to the halls of academia, the newsrooms of major media outlets, and even the corridors of power in Washington. Always hesitant to identify himself too closely with any one organization or ideology, Niebuhr strove continually to maintain a prophetic, critical voice, warning any and all listeners – including himself – of the perils of self-interest and the folly of human pretensions. Niebuhr himself did not always take consistent positions, or fully appreciate the constraints that bedeviled policy-makers. But both within Protestantism and to the broader intellectual and policy communities, Niebuhr stood as the most influential theological voice of the day on matters of public life.[12]

---

[11] "Atomic Warfare and the Christian Faith: Report of the Commission on the Relation of the Church to the War in the Light of the Christian Faith to the Federal Council of the Churches of Christ in America," March 6, 1946; NCC Papers, RG 18, Box 24, Folder 16; PHS. For more on the Calhoun Commission, see Boyer, *By the Bomb's Early Light*, 202–203, 226–228.

[12] Perhaps the most authoritative biography of Niebuhr is Richard Wightman Fox's impressive *Reinhold Niebuhr: A Biography* (San Francisco: Harper and Row 1985). In many ways equally important is Charles C. Brown, *Niebuhr and His Age: Reinhold Niebuhr's Prophetic Role and*

Not surprisingly, almost as soon as the Calhoun Commission released its report, Niebuhr began distancing himself from some of its sterner conclusions. A week after its release, he shared with Calhoun his fear that the report might be "subject to misunderstanding" in its condemnation of the bombing of Japan. "We objected to the use of the bomb without warning, but could not have said that it should in no case have been used." This distinction, Niebuhr believed, "certainly existed in the minds of the Committee." When queried by Harvard President and prominent defense policy-maker James Conant, Niebuhr again sought to clarify his position. The report failed to make clear that "the eventual use of the bomb for the shortening of the war would have been justified. I myself consistently took the position that failing in achieving a Japanese surrender, the bomb would have had to be used to save the lives of thousands of American soldiers who would otherwise have perished on the beaches of Japan."[13] Here again is a poignant illustration of the vexing new world facing the churchmen, and indeed every American. Even a figure as steeped in the Christian just war tradition as Niebuhr showed a willingness to shirk the prohibition against direct targeting of civilians, if such was necessary to defeat the monstrous evil of the Axis powers. This moral and spiritual turbulence would only increase as the postwar world began to take ominous shape.

Poised as they were between despair over the atomic age and optimism at the prospect of creating a new and better world, America's Protestant leadership resolved to press ahead. John Foster Dulles continued to play a leading role in these efforts. If Niebuhr was the most prominent Protestant theologian in America, Dulles was perhaps the most prominent Protestant layman. He had attracted acclaim for his longstanding chairmanship of the FCC's "Commission on a Just and Durable Peace," among his other church activities. Though Dulles remained active as an international trade lawyer and foreign policy advisor to the Republican Party, his clerical allies believed the church commanded his highest allegiance. At the end of World War II, Cavert had informed Reinhold Niebuhr that "I personally have no shadow of

Legacy (Harrisburg, PA: Trinity Press International 2002). Though lacking Fox's narrative flow, Brown treats Niebuhr more seriously and more sympathetically as a theologian and as a Christian. Brown also avoids Fox's sometimes gratuitous criticisms of Niebuhr's anti-communism. For more on Niebuhr, particularly regarding international relations, see also Warren, *Theologians of a New World Order*, Ronald H. Stone, *Reinhold Niebuhr: Prophet to Politicians* (Nashville, TN: Abingdon Press 1972), and Paul Merkley, *Reinhold Niebuhr: A Political Account* (Montreal: McGill-Queen's University Press 1975).

[13] Niebuhr to Calhoun, March 13, 1946; Reinhold Niebuhr Papers (hereinafter RN Papers), Box 5, Folder: Federal Council of Churches 1944–48; Library of Congress (hereinafter LOC). Niebuhr to Conant quoted in Fox, 224–225.

doubt that Mr. Dulles is far more deeply committed to his Christian position than to a Republican position."[14] And although he was active in GOP circles, Dulles often served as the Protestant emissary to Truman, meeting with the President to deliver FCC recommendations and discuss foreign policy issues.[15]

Dulles also attracted a wider audience among the American public. In June 1946 he wrote two lengthy articles for *Life* magazine on "Thoughts on Soviet Foreign Policy and What to Do About It." Dulles feared an impending conflict between the United States and the Soviet Union, and warned in the first article that "the most urgent task" facing American foreign policy was to avert that clash. He pinpointed Russian ideology as the source of the problem. Soviet communism had global pretensions, claiming a universal vision for the nature of history, human relations, and the right ordering of society. This model conflicted at all points with America's own ideology of Judeo–Christian democratic capitalism. Dulles saw these two visions as fundamentally irreconcilable, since "the personal freedoms which [the Soviets] would take away constitute our most cherished political and religious heritage."

Dulles disavowed the possibility of a peace based on "any genuine reconciliation of our faith with that now held by the Soviet leadership." Yet while their convictions were inimical, conflict was not inevitable. If America could hold with passion and tenacity to its own ideals, the Soviet leaders, whom he described as "shrewd and realistic politicians," would abandon as futile any efforts to conquer the United States. Dulles then resurrected a persistent theme in American religious history: the Puritan admonition against "declension" and exhortation to righteousness for the sake of the common good. Alongside a picture of an American church and a caption bemoaning that only "a quarter of adult Americans attend church services," Dulles declared that the "most significant demonstration" that Americans could make of their resolve against the Soviets "is at the religious level." Confronted with such spiritual fortitude, the Kremlin would soon see the futility of conflict "against a people who believe that their freedoms flow from their Creator and who also use those freedoms with the restraint which is enjoined by divine commandment." Dulles also called for more tangible measures such as bolstering American military strength and increasing foreign aid. As one of the architects of the UN, he urged support for the world body, though he conceded that the

---

[14] Cavert to Niebuhr, April 16, 1945; RN Papers, Box 5, Folder: FCC; LOC. For more on Dulles, see chapters six and seven of this book.

[15] See, for example, letter from Truman to Oxnam reporting on Truman's meeting with Dulles, March 18, 1946; HST Papers, Official File Box 803, Folder 213; HST.

UN had some "severe limitations." Ideally, Dulles believed, the United States and USSR would each cultivate its own garden and present their respective societies as models to the world. "We would each hope that our example would be so good that men everywhere would follow it."

While hoping for peaceful coexistence and competition by example, Dulles believed more concrete and confrontational measures might be necessary. "So long as Soviet policy seeks its own security by achieving a *Pax Sovietica*, the United States will be disposed to resist all expansive manifestations of Soviet policy."[16] The policy Dulles advocated bore a striking similarity to the "containment" doctrine developed by George Kennan in his "Long Telegram" just a few months earlier. It is unclear if Dulles had read Kennan's essay at this point, but regardless he came to similar conclusions. Dulles and Kennan both diagnosed the fundamental conflicts between Soviet and American ideology, the universalist aspirations of Soviet communism, the importance of maintaining American ideals at home, and the need to prevent further Soviet expansion while avoiding all-out war with the USSR.

Dulles' role as chairman of an ecumenical commission illustrates an important institutional shift then taking place in the Protestant churches. By the 1940s, individual churches and denominational bodies had grown increasingly frustrated at what they perceived to be their limited cultural and political influence. America may have been predominantly Protestant – especially its leadership – but numeric superiority did not seem to be translating into cultural hegemony. At least not to the extent the Protestant clergy hoped. Many of these leading pastors made a deliberate decision to "develop more direct and structured forms of action that gave their social programs greater visibility and broader national scope." William McGuire King describes the creation of these commissions, task forces, and interdenominational organizations as the "reform establishment." No longer would Protestantism, by its very nature diffuse in body and diverse in voice, squander its public cultural capital with scattershot pronouncements from a multitude of pulpits. The crisis of history demanded an organized, unified response, both at home and abroad. Out of this conviction came the countless inter-denominational commissions, councils, and conferences of postwar American Protestantism. The reform establishment had two principal goals. It sought to influence and shape American government policy at the highest levels. And it sought

---

[16] Dulles, "Thoughts on Soviet Foreign Policy and What to Do About It," *Life*, 3 June 1946, 112–126, and 10 June 1946, 118–130. Italics original. In one of many Cold War ironies, Dulles eventually became at bitter odds with Kennan and later criticized containment as immoral, advocating instead "rollback" of communist regimes and "liberation" of captive peoples.

to create a "unified Protestantism" to "resist the secularization of American culture."[17] For a time, it looked as if the reform establishment might succeed.

II

Because international relations remained a singular concern, it only made sense to involve the international Protestant community as much as possible. Yet however arduously the Protestant leaders labored to create an international movement, the commissions and activities remained dominated by Americans. Dulles and Walter Van Kirk convened the first major conference of the post-war era at Cambridge University from August 4 to 7, 1946. This gathering, which drew Protestant leaders from all over the United States and Europe, sought nothing less than to "interpret the Will of God in relation to the tangled problems of world politics and economics," and established an organization to deal with such issues in a more systematic manner. Thus was born the Commission of the Churches on International Affairs (CCIA). Comparing its task with the "great missionary movements of the eighteenth and nineteenth centuries," the CCIA charter called for mobilizing "a new sense of concern" among Christians for foreign policy.[18]

Vague though the CCIA charter was, a companion essay by Henry Smith Leiper on "The Meaning of the Cambridge Conference," appended to the official conference report, offered more detail. For example, although it gave much consideration to "the importance of cooperation between the non-Roman Churches and the Roman Communion," the conference decided to take no formal steps towards rapprochement with Rome. This was largely "because of the danger that some might think the non-Roman Churches ready to join the Roman crusade against Russia and to support its hostile attitude towards the Orthodox Communion." Within Christendom at the time, only the Catholic Church saw Soviet communism as a mortal threat to faith and freedom. At the same time, the Vatican also regarded the Orthodox Church as hopelessly defiant against Rome's authority. And the Protestant leadership held no brief for Rome's posture in either dispute.

---

[17] William McGuire King, "The Reform Establishment and the Ambiguities of Influence," in William R. Hutchinson, ed., *Between the Times: The Travail of the Protestant Establishment in America, 1900–1960* (New York: Cambridge University Press 1989). Quotes from pp. 122, 125. For more on the intellectual development of Protestant liberalism and tensions with neo-orthodoxy within the mainline churches, see Hutchison, *The Modernist Impulse in American Protestantism* (Cambridge, MA: Harvard University Press 1976).

[18] Report of "Conference of Church Leaders on International Affairs at Cambridge," August 4–7, 1946; WCC Papers, RG 162, Box 20, Folder 141; YDSA.

Members of the CCIA soon found policy recommendations more of a contentious enterprise than they had imagined. The Commission's first report, covering the period 1946–1947, somberly observed "in only one field – human rights and, more particularly, religious freedom – has there been sufficient evidence of a common mind." In this regard the CCIA had urged successfully that the UN Declaration of Human Rights include a robust affirmation of religious liberty.[19] "On many other subjects," the report noted, "the Commission has been unable to take a stand." The report ascribed this paralysis to both an unformed Christian theological position and to the rapid pace of the international environment, to which churches were ill equipped to respond.[20] Squaring hopes with capabilities and taking clear stands were proving to be daunting challenges for the new commission.

Reinhold Niebuhr knew no such compunctions. For example, on October 21, 1946, Niebuhr published a landmark essay in *Life* magazine on "The Fight for Germany." The month before, Secretary of State James Byrnes had delivered a major address in Germany announcing America's commitment to bolstering the western zone and resisting Soviet encroachments. The United States government was undergoing a tremendous political and diplomatic shift as it recognized the burgeoning Soviet threat and prepared to respond. Dissenters such as Secretary of Commerce Henry Wallace, who saw the USSR as a benign partner, found themselves quite unwelcome in the Truman Administration – especially Wallace, whose outspoken views had resulted in his forced resignation from the Cabinet in late September.[21]

Niebuhr took Wallace's views as a point of departure for a stern call to arms. In Berlin at the time of the Commerce Secretary's notorious Madison Square Garden speech urging accommodation of the Soviet Union, Niebuhr described how Wallace's words had been embraced by Soviet propaganda while provoking "dismay" among "democratic forces" in Germany. "The confusion in American liberalism, of which the Wallace speech is the symbol," he continued, "must be regarded as catastrophic in the light of the European realities." Moreover, "the Wallace line of criticism is dangerous because it is based upon illusions similar to those held by the conservatives of another

---

[19] Though it should be noted that Glendon does not identify outside interest groups, including church organizations, as having played any significant role in forming the Declaration. This seems to be a weakness in her argument, focused as it is on the internal deliberations of the Human Rights Committee. On the other hand, the churches also may have exaggerated their own influence. See Glendon, *A World Made New.*

[20] Annual Report of the CCIA, 1946–1947; WCC Papers, RG 162, Box 6, Folder 32; YDSA.

[21] For more on this episode, see Alonzo Hamby, *Man of the People: A Life of Harry S. Truman* (New York: Oxford University Press 1995), 352–359.

decade in regard to Nazism. It involves us in the same fateful procedure: that of hastening war by a too desperate effort to avoid it." Niebuhr instead gave his firm endorsement to the developing position of the Truman Administration. Mere political firmness would not be sufficient, however. Niebuhr called for a more vigorous program of economic assistance to Germany as well, both to help the German people and to blunt Russian efforts to attribute Germany's economic misery to "capitalistic exploitation." Niebuhr concluded with a nod to the recent past: "it is a very tragic thing to wade through blood and spend the treasures of a generation in order to overcome one tyranny and then be faced with another."[22]

The next year Niebuhr continued his campaign on behalf of aid to Germany. Fearful that the United States was flagging in its responsibilities, he wrote an open letter to President Truman raising alarm at the "imminent danger of defeat" in the struggle for a democratic Germany. Niebuhr urged a more robust program of economic assistance, particularly trade credits to bolster Germany's export economy. Referring to the President's recent announcement of the "Truman Doctrine" and aid to Greece and Turkey, Niebuhr warned, "it will do little good to supply the Governments of Greece and Turkey with loans to assist them in resisting Communist infiltration if in our zone in Germany we create conditions which will lead to the growth of communism from within."[23] In this way Niebuhr urged Truman to implement containment more consistently. Soviet expansion posed just as much, if not more, of a threat to Germany as to the Mediterranean states. It would be met in Greece and Turkey with arms, and in Germany with dollars.

Niebuhr's colleagues in the FCC often differed with his more hawkish views. For example, on October 11, 1946 – shortly after the Wallace speech and just days before Niebuhr's *Life* article was published – the FCC issued a statement on "Soviet-American Relations" with a much different emphasis. Adopting a tone of moral equivalence, the FCC called on both sides to renounce the use of "intolerance" or force, urged the United States to "recognize that state socialism and free enterprise can learn from each other," and called on the American government to give more support to the UN and the cause of peace.[24] The FCC agreed with Niebuhr on the importance of American

---

[22] Reinhold Niebuhr, "The Fight for Germany" in *Life*, 21 October 1946, 65–72. Besides the extensive circulation of *Life*, Niebuhr's article gained further exposure when reprinted in *Reader's Digest*. See Fox, 229.

[23] "U.S. Is Seen Losing Contest in Germany; Truman Urged to Allow Production There," *New York Times*, 16 June 1947, A2.

[24] FCC statement quoted by Ernest Warren Lefever, "Protestants and United States Foreign Policy, 1925–1954," (Ph.D. diss., Yale University, 1956), 118. Curiously, Lefever's dissertation advisor was H. Richard Niebuhr.

economic assistance abroad, though not necessarily for the same reasons. The FCC issued a statement on January 13, 1948, offering its strong support for the European Recovery Program, more popularly known as the Marshall Plan, which became one of the Truman Administration's most notable Cold War initiatives in providing massive economic assistance for the reconstruction of western Europe. Ascribing the loftiest of ideals to the Marshall Plan, the FCC prophesied that it "can be one of history's most momentous affirmations of faith in the curative power of freedom and in the creative capacity of free men." But American interests threatened to taint this benevolence. The churches repeatedly admonished the United States not to impose conditions that "would seem to threaten the political independence of the nations of Europe, or their right to choose their own way of life." Moreover, the FCC naively sought to disentangle the Marshall Plan from any Cold War dynamics. Engaging in what the FCC intended to be even-handedness – but what reads in retrospect as moral obtuseness – the statement warned that some European nations "are fearful of the possibility that the United States may seek to make Europe over in its political and economic image, just as they are fearful in the knowledge that Soviet Russia is seeking to make Europe over in its image."[25] Individual members of the Protestant leadership at times were willing to make bolder judgments such as those by Niebuhr. But the FCC's consensus statements needed to encompass a broader range of views, and so more often amounted to less.

Even as American Protestants struggled to find their own voice, they led the way in dramatically amplifying the voices speaking for world Christianity. The year 1948 witnessed the most ambitious ecumenical project in modern church history. After decades of planning, representatives of hundreds of churches were to gather in Amsterdam for the founding conference of the World Council of Churches (WCC). Throughout 1948, as the August gathering in Amsterdam approached, the various preparatory commissions of the WCC made clear that their concerns would be as much social, economic, and political as they were theological. At its most audacious, the WCC aspired to be for churches what the United Nations aspired to be for nations – a united body where differences and self-interest could be subsumed by a common vision and common action.

The WCC adopted an agenda that was as much thought as action. Among other things, it undertook a massive intellectual project – forming a series of study commissions before the Amsterdam gathering to analyze the world situation under the rubric of "Man's Disorder and God's Design." Could fractious Protestantism unite not only organizationally but ideologically as

---

[25] FCC brochure, *The Churches and the European Recovery Program*, quoted by Lefever, 157.

well? Commission III on "The Church and the Disorder of Society," chaired
by Reinhold Niebuhr, concluded that the past decade had brought "the almost
universal recognition of the responsibility of Christians for the institutions of
society." Given this apparent consensus, ideological unity was not just possible
but imperative. No longer, Commission III asserted, could Protestants indulge
either in their historic tendency for schism along infinitely shifting lines, or in
their quietistic withdrawal and pietistic individualism. The welfare of world
institutions depended on a robust and coherent response.[26]

Niebuhr contributed his own essay to Commission III's deliberations, in
which he saw a bipolar pair of threats to the world: fascism and communism.
They were the "two forms of political religion which have aggravated the
social confusion in our day in their very effort to arrest it." And while the
two ideologies differed in content, Niebuhr found them only too similar in
practice. "The self-righteous fury of a consistent Marxism may be as dangerous
to the establishment of a community as the cynicism of a consistent fascism."
Fascism had essentially been buried two years before, but communism loomed
as ever more the menace. Not that Niebuhr was a partisan apologist for the
Christian West, which was plagued by its own pride, insecurities, and self-
interest. He admonished the commission against utopian solutions here on
earth: "the conflict between order and freedom is perfectly resolved only in
the Kingdom of God." Nevertheless, the church needed to put its own earthly
house in order, to be a prophetic voice in those lands where it was free.
"The possibility of avoiding another international conflict depends to a large
degree upon the measure of health which can be achieved in that part of
the world which is not under the dominion of communist totalitarianism."
Niebuhr held that "there is a divine judgment upon our sins in this travail
of the nations, in this fall of nations and empires, in this shaking of historic
stabilities and traditions."[27]

The WCC wanted to address international issues specifically, and asked the
CCIA to form Commission IV, tasked with examining the "Churches and
International Affairs." Commission IV embraced its agenda with gusto, as
several commissioners joined in October, 1947, to produce a massive prelim-
inary document titled "Antagonisms and Alignments in a Changing World."
Eschewing the simple-minded moralism that denounced "power politics,"
the study described power as a basic reality of international relations, neither

---

[26] WCC Preparatory Program "Man's Disorder and God's Design," May 17, 1947; WCC Papers
RG 162, Box 4, Folder 19; YDSA.

[27] Niebuhr, "God's Order and the Present Disorder of Civilisation," October 1947; WCC Papers,
RG 162, Box 3, Folder 15; YDSA.

intrinsically good nor bad. Meanwhile, the church needed to acknowledge its own decline and strengthen what remained, proclaiming its message to an increasingly troubled and indifferent world. The study did not hesitate to single out the source of these troubles. "The cause of the difficulties" afflicting international relations "is chiefly the Soviet Union." While acknowledging that all great powers seek to expand, the report noted that Soviet expansion often went hand-in-hand with "terrorism and oppression" of its subject peoples. In this spirit of realism, Commission IV also sought to dispel any illusions about the United Nations. The good works of UN humanitarian bodies "merit Christian support, but their activities must not be confused with the Gospel itself." Likewise, expectations of the UN should be tempered – it would not usher in a new moral order, but is only "recognized as a necessity on grounds of self-interest, and is chiefly aimed at the prevention of mutual destruction by war." Finally, while still calling for the global advance of aspirations such as the rule of law, social justice, education, and human rights, the study contained a vital Niebuhrian qualification. "It is important to emphasize that in fact order must *precede* justice."[28] The CCIA, formed just over one year before, already found itself grappling with the wide and widening gap between its ideals and the actual state of affairs it faced.

Perhaps the most eminent member of Commission IV was John Foster Dulles, who contributed his own essay to the Commission's preparatory work. In "Continuing Christian Responsibility in a Changing World," Dulles outlined his evolving thought on the emerging Soviet threat – and lit the flame under a conflict that would erupt the next year at the Amsterdam conference. Dulles began by highlighting one of his perennial themes: the constancy of "change" in the world. The challenge for Christians was to see change not as a threat but as an "opportunity to make the world more nearly one in which God's will is done on earth as it is in heaven." Thus Christians must observe thoughtfully the international scene and seek to channel the forces of change in constructive directions. Dulles then offered his own observations of the state of the world. He saw nations governed by either of two systems, "free societies" or dictatorships. And while the "free societies" were in no way perfect – Dulles mentioned in particular the depredations of colonialism, racism, and "mob psychology" – he believed that on balance, anchored by a virtuous Christian citizenry, the democratic system offered the best model.

[28] "Antagonisms and Alignments in a Changing World," October 1947; WCC Papers, RG 162, Box 3, Folder 17; YDSA. Emphasis in original. For an elaboration of Niebuhr's views on the relation between order and justice in international relations, see chapter 5 on "The World Community" in Reinhold Niebuhr, *The Children of Light and the Children of Darkness: A Vindication of Democracy and a Critique of its Traditional Defense* (New York: Scribners 1944).

As such, Dulles called the essential goal "to create in the world, as rapidly as possible, more areas of freedom."

Freedom had its enemy, however. Dulles singled out the Soviet Union as a mortal threat to his program of advancing liberty. He engaged in a lengthy analysis of communist doctrine, based on Lenin, Stalin, and Molotov's writings and on Soviet practice. His conclusions were not optimistic. "The Soviet programme is not only atheistic in the substance of its doctrine, but its methods are repugnant to Christian practice." It "seeks violent change in preference to peaceful change," it "does not recognize any equality of individuals," and it demands "absolute power." Dulles concluded that the "outstanding political issue in the world today" is "whether methods of violence, coercion, fraud and deceit are to continue to stamp out human liberty. On that issue the overwhelming mass of the human race is against the Soviet programme."

Yet instead of issuing a militant call to arms, Dulles suggested a more modest policy for the "free societies" of the world, in the same vein as his *Life* articles of the year before. These nations should defend their freedom, maintain their virtue, and model to a watching world a better way to live. He saw "two great assets with which to work": the moral law and the United Nations. The moral law stood as a universal code of right and wrong, transcending all governments and governing all peoples. Though communism denied it and free peoples frequently defied it, the moral law – if it would be acknowledged – still held great potential for restraining evil and cultivating peace. And the United Nations, flawed and limited though it was, offered a forum to "call every nation's international acts to the bar of public opinion." His highest hope was for Christians to "with our eyes on God and not on Russia, act with Christian purpose. Then we are the instruments of a force that will surely prevail."[29]

Dulles' essay attracted a favorable response from at least one influential reader. Reinhold Niebuhr described it as an "excellent paper" and expressed his complete agreement, except for a slight difference over Dulles' identification of "progress" with the "moral law."[30] Other commissioners were more hesitant to single out communism for condemnation. The minutes of Commission IV's meeting the next month indicate much concern with presenting a "balanced" assessment of communism, affirming its strengths and not just criticizing

[29] Dulles, "Continuing Christian Responsibility in a Changing World," October 1947; WCC Papers, RG 162, Box 3, Folder 17; YDSA.

[30] Niebuhr, undated memo; Henry Van Dusen Papers, Box AA, Folder: WCC-International Disorder; Union Theological Seminary Archives, New York, NY (hereinafter UTS).

its errors. European commissioners in particular did not want to be too harsh on the Soviet Union.[31] This reluctance provoked frustration among some Americans. O. Frederick Nolde, the Director of Commission IV and hardly a militant anticommunist, on January 30, 1948, wrote a private memo titled "The European Christian Mind on World Affairs." He complained that the European delegates refused "to specify the evils in the U.S.S.R. without delineating in great detail the evils in the U.S.," and speculated that this stemmed both from European geography and "their knowledge that criticism of the U.S. is less dangerous than criticism of Russia!" Nolde concluded rather smugly that the Europeans were not so much immoral as they were lazy and naïve. "I incline to the view that in face of the complexities in the above picture, our continental colleagues look to us to pull them through. I doubt whether they would admit this."[32] In a further irony, while some of the American churchmen faced domestic criticism in the United States for not being sufficiently anticommunist, these same churchmen found their European counterparts to be a bit "soft" on communism.

European Protestants may have been "soft" towards communism, but they were anything but that towards Catholicism. In this they shared the American churchmen's fervent antipathy towards the Roman Church. As the WCC's inaugural meeting approached, tensions escalated. The WCC leadership had long refused to invite official Catholic delegates, and Pope Pius XII similarly had rejected opportunities to extend an olive branch.[33] On August 22, the Sunday just before the Amsterdam convocation, the Catholic Archbishop and all other bishops of the Netherlands issued a pastoral letter read at all Catholic masses in the country. The letter announced that the Catholic Church was "compelled to stand aloof" from the WCC and that there could "be no question of the Holy Catholic Church taking part in the congress at Amsterdam." While the bishops' letter lauded the desire for Christian unity, such unity must occur on the terms of the Roman Catholic Church, the "only holy catholic and apostolic Church." Continuing, they declared that "the divisions between the Christians can only be put an end to in one way: by a return to Her."[34] Though the letter contained nothing new on the Catholic position, its timing and wide

---

[31] Minutes of Study Commission IV meeting, November 7–8, 1947, Sussex, England; Van Dusen Papers, Box AA, Folder: WCC-International Disorder; UTS.

[32] Nolde, "The European Christian Mind on World Affairs," January 30, 1948; Van Dusen Papers, Box AA, Folder: WCC-International Disorder; UTS.

[33] For more on this, particularly Ambassador Myron Taylor's campaign to persuade the WCC to invite the Catholics, see chapter three of this book.

[34] July 31, 1948 letter issued by Catholic Bishops (read in churches August 22, 1948); WCC Papers, RG 162, Box 6, Folder 132; YDSA.

distribution painfully reminded WCC participants and the watching world of the significant divisions that remained.

Another obstacle to unity loomed to the East. The Russian Orthodox Church announced that it would not attend the Amsterdam conference. In sharp contrast to the WCC's decidedly unwelcoming attitude towards Rome, the WCC leadership had courted fervently the Moscow patriarchate in the hope of including Russian delegates. Nothing doing, the Russian Orthodox Church declared, dismissing the WCC as more focused on political and social issues than on true Christian unity. Dr. Willem Adolf Visser t'Hooft, the Dutch general secretary of the WCC, disavowed any political agenda and lamented that the Russian Orthodox absence was based on a "complete mis-understanding of the true nature of our movement." He promised to "keep the door open," should the Russian Church change its mind.[35] Here was yet another irony: while many theological conservatives in the United States regarded the WCC as a front for liberal political causes, the Soviets seem to have feared the opposite, that anticommunist forces would use the WCC to push their agenda.

Both camps soon found much evidence to confirm their respective suspicions. In a tense face-off reported widely in the world press, John Foster Dulles and Czechoslovak theologian Josef Hromadka spent the conference's third session alternately denouncing and affirming the spread of communism. Dulles criticized communism for its rejection of moral law and human rights. Yet he also warned that armed force alone could not forestall communist advances. Christian democracies instead needed to promote a positive model of human freedom and equality. In sharp contrast to Dulles, Hromadka contended that Western supremacy in the world had ended, and that the countries of Eastern Europe did not believe the West possessed "the political skill, wisdom, and strength of conviction to rule our countries." Communism, on the other hand, although atheistic, represents "much of the social impetus of the living church." And while admitting the Soviets had at times used aggressive tactics, they should not be judged too harshly. "What appears a ruthless imperialism may be – at least in a measure – a precaution and self-defense against efforts to deprive the Soviet people of the fruits of victory and bring the great socialistic experiment to its fall."[36] These two positions, impassioned and irreconcilable,

---

[35] August 24, 1948 WCC press release no. 5; WCC Papers, RG 162, Box 6, Folder 36; YDSA. See also George Dugan, "Churches Create a World Council," *New York Times*, 24 August 1948. Clipping of article in Myron Taylor Papers, Box 1; HST (hereinafter MT Papers).

[36] August 24, 1948 WCC press release no. 10; WCC Papers, RG 162, Box 6, Folder 36; WCC brochure *We Intend to Stay Together: Highlights of the First Assembly of the World Council of Churches*; WCC Papers, RG 162, Box 6, Folder 39; YDSA. Also George Dugan, "Dulles

distilled an emerging dilemma that continued to plague the WCC. On the one hand it sought to include as many voices and as many positions as possible, yet on the other hand it desired to take clear, bold stands on contemporary issues. Each goal held a possible peril, of either retreating to vague generalities and insipid platitudes, or of provoking painful divisions and alienating core constituencies. As international tensions grew and the Cold War heated up, the WCC would find such vexing choices inescapable.

As if Dulles and Hromadka's public dispute was not enough, two other theological luminaries provided Amsterdam with further fireworks. Karl Barth of Switzerland, widely regarded as the greatest Protestant theologian of the century, delivered a keynote address that called delegates to a more spiritual understanding of their calling. "We ought to give up ... every thought that the care of the Church, the care of the world, is our care." Barth dismissed as merely a "Christian Marshall Plan" the efforts of many delegates to remake the international order. Christians ought to place their absolute trust in God alone, rather than in themselves and their own efforts.[37] This aroused the ire of Niebuhr, Barth's sometime nemesis, who regarded Barth's version of neo-orthodoxy as a quietistic betrayal of the gospel's social imperatives. Yet Niebuhr had also been appalled at Hromadka's communist apologetic. With his taste for dialectical arguments, Niebuhr denounced both models as unfaithful extremes, and instead charted a *via media*. In his keynote conference address several days later, he responded directly first to Hromadka. While acknowledging the faults of the West, Niebuhr emphatically rejected Hromadka's proposed solution. "When [Hromadka] speaks comparatively and presents the Soviet system as a possible alternative, we must insist that he has not dealt with the real tragedy of our age. That consists in the horrible evils generated by the Communist alternative to our civilization. Hell knows no fury like that of a prophet of a secular religion, become the priest-king of a Utopian State." And to Barth's skepticism of social involvement, Niebuhr responded in the simple language of Scripture. "From us [God] demands that we work while it is day, since the night cometh when no man can work." Niebuhr expanded this indictment of Barth and his acolytes in an article following the conference. "Yesterday, [Barthians] discovered that the church may be an ark in which to survive a flood. Today they seem so enamored of

Tells Churchmen Force Won't Check Reds," in *New York Times*, August 25, 1948; clipping in MT Papers, Box 1. In response to a query about Soviet repression, Hromadka declared his intention to resist if the Communists began to violate human rights. Eight years later during the Soviet invasion of Hungary he would adopt a different position, much to the dismay of his Western supporters. For more, see chapter two of this book.

[37] August 23, 1948 WCC Press Release no. 6; WCC Papers, RG 162, Box 6, Folder 36; YDSA.

this special function of the church that they have decided to turn the ark into a home on Mount Ararat and live in it perpetually."[38]

From Dulles' confidence in Western Christian civilization, to Neibuhr's Christian realism, to Barth's neo-orthodox eschewal of political involvement, to Hromadka's union of Christianity and communism, the Amsterdam conference presented a bewildering array of competing Christian visions of international relations – and those were only from the Protestant tradition, given the absence of the Catholic and Orthodox Churches. Were Amsterdam merely an academic symposium, the diverse viewpoints offered would mark it a stimulating success. The WCC aspired to a much different purpose, however, and found itself instead with a recurring problem: how to accommodate such a wide range of conviction while still speaking with a unified voice on a coherent plan of action.

In the near term, the WCC opted for a compromise, issuing resolutions on lowest-common-denominator agreements and reports couched in the even-handed diction of consensus and moral equivalency. For example, at the conclusion of the Amsterdam conference Commission III on the "Church and the Disorder of Society" presented its report calling on Christians to "reject the ideologies of both Communism and Laissez-Faire Capitalism." Commission III noted several "points" of conflict in turn between Christianity and communism, and between Christianity and capitalism. While commission co-chairman John Bennett tried to explain at a press conference that "the condemnation of communism is on a different level than the condemnation of capitalism," to many outraged American observers and even in the language of the WCC's own press release, it appeared that the Amsterdam delegates regarded both systems as equally problematic.[39]

Regardless, the WCC leadership regarded Amsterdam as a success and the organization as established on a solid foundation. Yet significant questions

---

[38] August 30, 1948 WCC Press Release nos. 38, 41; WCC Papers, RG 162, Box 6, Folder 37; YDSA. Quoted by Fox, 235. See also George Dugan, "Communism Held 'Christian Heresy', "*New York Times*, 29 August 1948, clipping in MT Papers, Box 1. For more on Niebuhr's complex relationship/rivalry with Barth, see Fox, 164–165, 231, 234–235, and 243–244.

[39] Report of Assembly Section III; WCC Papers, RG 162, Box 6, Folder 41; September 2, 1948 WCC Press Release nos. 52, 53; WCC Papers, RG 162, Box 6, Folder 38; YDSA. Curiously, even though Niebuhr chaired Commission III and concurred in its final report, the report's language does not seem to have fully comprehended his opposition to communism. This, and his seeming absence from the press conference announcing the report, raises questions about just how much ownership he claimed on the final document. For more on this, see Fox, 236–237. According to the WCC's own *We Intend to Stay Together* brochure, of all conference developments it was the report's criticism of capitalism that attracted the most editorial comment back in the United States, almost all of it negative. In WCC Papers, RG 162, Box 6, Folder 39; YDSA.

loomed, from the ongoing alienation from Rome to the difficulty of taking bold stands to the dominance of American influence on a "world" council. Much as the WCC's reports and resolutions may have tried to gloss them over, Amsterdam revealed sharp divisions and growing tensions in the world – between East and West, communism and capitalism, and the ideals of peace and the realities of conflict. The WCC had not, however, demonstrated itself capable of offering any tangible or realistic solutions to the emerging international crisis. That task would be taken up by church leaders in particular nations, especially the United States.

III

Americans who left the religious politics of Amsterdam returned home to the presidential politics of a dramatic election season. A few days after Harry Truman's shocking upset victory over Thomas Dewey, Niebuhr confided to his friend Will Scarlett that he had "voted for Truman without any enthusiasm." Niebuhr complained, "I am really quite afraid of his ineptness in foreign policy. It's frightening to have so little a man at the head of so great a nation."[40] Though skeptical of what he regarded as Truman's unilateralism, simplicity, and idealism, Niebuhr had not found the presidential alternatives at all attractive, or even palatable. He could not fathom voting for a Republican, and dismissed Wallace's Progressive candidacy with the opinion that "poor Henry really is a prisoner of the Commies."[41] And while unrelenting in his opposition to communism, Niebuhr was anything but an American triumphalist in the mold of Henry Luce. Shortly after the election, Luce rejected an article submitted by Niebuhr to *Fortune* magazine, complaining that whereas Niebuhr criticized America as overconfident and self-righteous, Luce feared instead his country was "actually very uncertain of itself, very divided and confused in its 'soul'," and needed to assert itself more robustly. Nevertheless, the publisher concluded in tribute, "please do not take my name off the list of your disciples."[42]

As 1949 unfolded, interest in Niebuhr's thought and demands on his time continued to grow. George Kennan invited him to meet with the State Department's influential Policy Planning Staff for three days in June. Niebuhr joined

---

[40] November 8, 1948 letter to William Scarlett; RN Papers, Box 27, Folder: Niebuhr-William Scarlett correspondence, 1938–1948; LOC. Niebuhr eventually came to a much more favorable assessment of Truman, later commenting that "in retrospect, I would say that Truman was one of the great presidents." Quoted in Brown, 153.

[41] Quoted in Fox, 236.

[42] January 8, 1949 letter from Luce to Niebuhr; RN Papers, Box 8, Folder: Henry Luce; LOC.

a few select luminaries such as J. Robert Oppenheimer, General Walter Bedell Smith, John McCloy, and Hans Morgenthau in Kennan's brainstorming sessions on American foreign policy and the question of Europe. Although it is doubtful that in this context Niebuhr directly shaped a particular American policy, more probably his "Christian realism" contributed to the worldview forming in the minds of many American decision-makers.[43] To them, he was a singular figure: a Christian theologian conversant in the realities of power and international affairs.

His growing prominence did not mean that Niebuhr had abandoned his church colleagues, of course. Along with Scarlett, Dulles, G. Bromley Oxnam, and Nolde, he played a major role at the FCC's "National Study Conference on the Churches and World Order" held in Cleveland in March 1949. In his plenary address, Niebuhr warned that despite the Soviet threat, a preemptive war waged by the United States would be not only immoral but also "an impious effort to usurp the place of God."[44] He also served as the primary author of the conference statement on "Moral Responsibility and United States Power." Here again, Niebuhr successfully persuaded his co-religionists to endorse his call for America to use its preponderance of power for a purpose higher than mere self-interest. He urged more economic development assistance to impoverished nations, the protection of human rights and freedoms, and American leadership in regional pacts and the United Nations. After all, "power is a trust for which we are accountable to God."[45]

The FCC conference was not without its lofty idealism. Rather than criticize the Soviets, the Methodist Bishop Oxnam in a plenary address called for a delegation of American business, academic, agricultural, and religious leaders to visit Russia and "become acquainted" with Russian life. Another panel called for peace negotiations with the Chinese Communists rather than military assistance to the Nationalists, while yet another urged churches to adapt to the "new mood" under communism in Eastern Europe. And after senior State Department official Charles Bohlen spent two hours explaining the proposed NATO alliance, the conference voted "neither to endorse nor oppose." Dulles delivered the keynote address, encouraging the delegates with examples of how Christian faith had shaped American foreign policy in recent years. He credited "our Christian people" with "developing public opinion" in support of the United Nations, promoting the Marshall Plan

---

[43] Wilson D. Miscamble, *George F. Kennan and the Making of American Foreign Policy, 1947–1950* (Princeton, NJ: Princeton University Press 1992), 283. Also Fox, 238–239.
[44] "Churches Speak for Peace," *The Messenger*, 29 March 1949, 3.
[45] Message and Findings of Third National Study Conference on the Churches and World Order, March 8–11, 1949; NCC Papers, RG 18, Box 37, Folder 20; PHS.

and other economic assistance, resisting calls for disarmament, and dealing firmly yet responsibly with the Soviets. This religious influence remained vital because "nothing would be more dangerous and destructive than to have the present great material power of the United States rattling around in the world detached from the guiding direction of a righteous faith."[46]

Crisis upon crisis seemed to buffet the world over the next fourteen months. The year 1949 saw the Soviets detonate their first atomic bomb and China fall to Mao Zedong's communists. The next year Truman announced that the United States intended to develop the hydrogen bomb, and war erupted in Korea. How were the churchmen to respond? Many Protestant leaders remained hesitant to denounce the Soviets definitively. Some cautiously endorsed aspects of communism, others rejected it, and others were simply confused. One illustration of this ambivalence came in the pages of the *Messenger*, a Protestant journal that published regular columns by Niebuhr disparaging communism, yet also ran a glowing profile of Hromadka in June 1949. Acknowledging the Czechoslovakian theologian's sympathies with communism, the magazine lauded his "deep theology" as "so clear and relevant for present life situations."[47] Such articles only gave more ammunition to broadsides by conservative and fundamentalist Protestants against the FCC for giving aid and comfort to America's foes. Early in 1950, Roswell Barnes of the FCC complained to Liston Pope, dean of Yale Divinity School, of the "current widespread campaign" attacking the FCC as "a socialistic and near-communistic agency." Barnes requested that Pope assemble a file of information on their opponents, "on their interrelationships and on their source of income and support." Barnes stressed that while FCC members would defend themselves, they would not apologize for their efforts "in the interest of justice and liberal economic policy."[48]

Meanwhile, in the wake of Truman's announcement, Nolde's CCIA endorsed and circulated a statement by the WCC that condemned the

---

[46] March 8, 1949 FCC Press Releases, 10:30 a.m. and 7:00 p.m.; March 9, 1949 FCC Press Release; NCC Papers, RG 18, Box 37, Folder 22; PHS. Also see Dulles, "American Power and the World," *The Messenger*, 12 April 1949, 8–13.

[47] Paul Bock, "Joseph L. Hromadka – Churchman Behind the Iron Curtain," *The Messenger*, 21 June 1949, 16–18. See also *The Messenger*'s favorable article on the award given to Oxnam in 1949 by the *Churchman*, another liberal magazine. The article criticized "what appeared to be an organized Roman Catholic attempt in the name of anti-Communism" to disparage Oxnam and the *Churchman*. American Catholics, presumably annoyed by the anti-Catholicism of Oxnam and other leading Protestants, apparently responded with their own charges. "Protestants Protest Attack on Magazine," *The Messenger*, 15 March 1949.

[48] January 23, 1950 letter from Barnes to Pope; Liston Pope Papers, RG 49, Box 11, Folder 173; YDSA.

hydrogen bomb. The WCC urged the United States and USSR "to enter into negotiations once again." This "tragic impasse" between them, moreover, "can be broken most readily if the intermediate and smaller powers press strongly for action."[49] Notably the WCC did not draw any moral distinction between the two "hostile camps," treating both sides as equally legitimate and equally culpable. This may have been in part due to the WCC's need to incorporate the opinions of European church leaders, who, as a frustrated Nolde had earlier complained, often were reluctant to criticize the USSR.

The FCC shared much of the WCC's idealism while having its own array of opinions to balance. Issuing its own statement on the hydrogen bomb, the FCC noted that its leaders were divided on some basic moral questions, rendering the FCC unable either to endorse or condemn the bomb. The statement settled for complaining about the secrecy surrounding the bomb's development and called for more public information. The FCC, unlike the WCC, did not disregard the fundamental ideological difference at the heart of the conflict, and singled out Soviet communism as an unambiguous threat. "Between the belief in the dignity and worth of man and the beliefs of international communism stand moral issues which can be neither evaded nor settled by compromise of basic convictions." Nevertheless, the FCC did not give up its hope for "a fresh start in the search for adequate and acceptable methods of international control of atomic energy."[50]

The *Christian Century* magazine, a venerable voice of liberal Protestant opinion, likewise raised an alarm at the escalating world crisis. It denounced Truman's hydrogen bomb announcement for "starting a new and infinitely more deadly phase of the world armament race."[51] America's "main task," *CC* editorialized a few months later, is not building up its military or protecting its sphere of influence but is "organiz[ing] a world missionary movement on behalf of democracy."[52] And though the United States needed to take the lead in spreading the democratic gospel, the United Nations offered the best vessel for such an effort. In a May 17, 1950 editorial, *CC* echoed the WCC's call for a more assertive world community, particularly smaller nations, to put the proverbial brakes on the emerging power blocs. "We hope that at the next assembly of the United Nations those countries which are being driven by our policy and Russia's between two lines of fire will seize that platform" to

49   March 22, 1950 statement from CCIA; WCC Papers, RG 162, Box 20, Folder 141A; YDSA.
50   "The Churches and the Hydrogen Bomb," March 21, 1950 statement from FCC; NCC Papers, RG 18, Box 25, Folder 11; PHS.
51   "President Truman Steps Up Arms Race," *Christian Century*, 15 February 1950, 198–199.
52   "Marshall Plan of Ideas," *Christian Century*, 19 April 1950, 486–487.

assert their independence.[53] The outbreak of war the next month in Korea only increased *CC*'s faith in the UN. A *CC* editorial urged that "the total problem of peace in Asia be turned over to the United Nations." Declaring the beginnings of a "revolution in foreign policy," the editorial called for America to submit its actions and devote substantially more of its resources to the UN, and for the admission of all nations to UN membership. After all, the UN "offers the one ray of political hope in a world of darkness."[54]

Whether the UN could fulfill such messianic aspirations remained to be seen. Niebuhr, for one, was skeptical. After attending a UN-sponsored conference late in 1949, he reported "from a Christian standpoint, I find such an organization ideologically weak because it believes too simply that information and knowledge will inevitably make for peace. Many of the illusions of modern secularism are in it."[55] Nevertheless, he commended the UN ideals and urged its support – as long as Christians did not attach to it their own eschatological hopes. His views on Korea reflected a similar realism. "We did right in defending Korea," Niebuhr wrote to Will Scarlett, though he groused that if Korea "had not been written off" by the Truman Administration in the first place, "it would not have cost so much to defend." In an eerily prescient insight, Niebuhr then predicted the coming course of conflict. The Russians would avoid starting a world war they could not win, "but intend to harass us with political and military ventures all over the world, some of which they will win, particularly in Asia. I think we must dismiss our fears of an atomic war but become concerned about the possibility of carrying on this sort of things for decades to come."[56]

Niebuhr continued to consult with senior policy-makers. A front-page *New York Times* article early in 1951 described him as one of twelve "leaders of American thought" invited by the State Department to confer for two days on strengthening the "ideological offensive against international communism." Along with the likes of Henry Steele Commager, Arthur Schlesinger, Jr., and labor leader James B. Carey, Niebuhr assisted the State Department in analyzing the program and appeal of communism as well as considering ways to oppose it more effectively.[57] Meanwhile, as international tensions and the magnitude of atomic weapons both escalated, the FCC in late 1949

---

[53] "The Lippman Thesis," *Christian Century*, 17 May 1950, 605–607.
[54] "Revolution in Foreign Policy," *CC*, 9 August 1950, 941–943.
[55] Niebuhr, "The Nation and the International Community," *The Messenger*, 11 October 1949.
[56] Undated letter in 1950 from Niebuhr to Will and Leah Scarlett; RN Papers, Box 27, Folder:Niebuhr-William Scarlett correspondence, undated; LOC.
[57] Walter H. Waggoner, "U.S. Calls in Civic Leaders to Help Fight Red Ideology," *New York Times*, 14 January 1951, A1.

decided to convene again a group of theologians to revisit "The Christian
Conscience and Weapons of Mass Destruction." In addition to Niebuhr,
the rest of the new commission's membership overlapped quite a bit with
the Calhoun Commission of 1946, with the important additions of laymen
such as physicist Arthur Compton and William Waymack from the Atomic
Energy Commission. Perhaps of equal significance were two other changes.
H. Richard Niebuhr of Yale, equal to his older brother in brilliance and yet
more pessimistic about the church's plight in the present age, declined to
serve on the commission, believing its very inquiry to be futile in light of the
dramatic divide between Christian fidelity and the horrors of modern war.
And former chairman Robert Calhoun of Yale, while agreeing to serve on the
commission, deferred to Episcopal Bishop Angus Dun of Washington, DC, as
the new chairman.[58]

The commission deliberated throughout 1950 and released its report at
the end of the year. While sharing many of its predecessor's qualms about
the barbarism of modern conflict, attacks on civilians, and "preventive war,"
the new commission made a significant departure. It identified "two great
dangers threaten[ing] mankind – the danger that totalitarian tyranny may
be extended over the world and the danger of global war." Now that the
commission believed totalitarianism had become a threat of equal gravity as
worldwide war, the calculus of permissible or even obligatory actions had
changed.

> For the United States to abandon its atomic weapons, or to give the impres-
> sion that they would not be used, would leave the non-Communist world
> with totally inadequate defense. For Christians to advocate such a policy
> would be for them to share responsibility for the worldwide tyranny that
> might result. We believe that American military strength, which must include
> atomic weapons as long as any other nation may possess them, is an essential
> factor in the possibility of preventing both world war and tyranny. If atomic
> weapons or other weapons of parallel destructiveness are used against us or
> our friends in Europe or Asia, we believe that it could be justifiable for our
> government to use them in retaliation with all possible restraint.[59]

Only two of the commission's nineteen members dissented from this conclusion. Robert Calhoun, grieved to see how far things had moved from
his chairmanship of just five years earlier, and Georgia Harkness of Garrett

---

[58] December 6, 1949 FCC "Resolution on Commission of Christian Scholars"; May 4, 1950 letter
from Richard Fagley to Liston Pope; Pope Papers, RG 49, Box 11, Folder 173; YDSA.

[59] "The Christian Conscience and Weapons of Mass Destruction," *Christian Century*, 13 December 1950, 1489–1491. For more on Niebuhr's influence on this report, see Fox 240–241.

Biblical Institute both refused to embrace such an endorsement of the bomb. Historian Paul Boyer argues that the report "provides a benchmark for the cultural and political changes between 1946 and 1950," in which the use of atomic weapons for deterrence and even the possibility of nuclear war became more accepted. "In the 1946 Calhoun Commission report, the 'pro-bomb' position had been relegated to an uneasy footnote. In the FCC's 1950 report it was far more explicitly and vigorously articulated, with the two lonely dissenters consigned to a footnote."[60]

Issuing the report was one of the FCC's very last official acts, for the end of 1950 also witnessed the FCC become re-born as the National Council of Churches (NCC). Upon its inauguration the new organization declared that "without making national interest our chief end, but shaping our own policies in the light of the aims of the United Nations . . . let us live and, if need be, die as loyal members of the world community."[61] Convened almost simultaneously with the release of the commission's report, the NCC leaders gave considerable attention to nuclear concerns. Their statements reflect the palpable shift that had occurred. In response to Secretary of State Dean Acheson's address to the NCC conference on the Korean conflict, a panel of NCC leaders – including new NCC president and Episcopal Bishop Henry Knox Sherrill, Oxnam, Nolde, and Dr. Edward Pruden, president of the American Baptist Convention and sometime pastor to President Truman – all stated their willingness to support even the first use of atomic weapons if future military or moral circumstances demanded so. They added the marginally reassuring caveat that they did not think the present crisis in Korea yet warranted nuclear attack.[62]

The NCC also sought to insulate itself from the familiar charges of communist sympathies leveled by its fundamentalist critics. Sponsored by the politically conservative oil tycoon and philanthropist J. Howard Pew of Philadelphia, the NCC agreed to maintain a "committee of 80 prominent laymen of wealth and prestige" in order to "offset any 'left-wing' charges." The lay committee, which along with business leaders included Stassen and prominent anticommunist Congressman Walter Judd, would advise the clerical and staff leadership of the NCC on policies and publications.[63]

---

[60] Boyer, 346–347.
[61] George Dugan, "Church Group asks 'Courage in Peril'," *New York Times*, 2 December 1950. Also "The National Council and the World Crisis," *National Council Outlook*, January 1951, 20.
[62] Max Gilstrap, "Council Hails Acheson Talk," *Christian Science Monitor*, 30 November 1950, 11.
[63] Max Gilstrap, "Protestants Told to Trust in Lawgiver," *Christian Science Monitor*, 2 December 1950, A1.

Criticism of the NCC did not just come from the right. Though generally favorable towards the formation of the new organization, and though many of its contributors were also active in the NCC, the *Christian Century* found the new religious attitudes towards the atomic bomb profoundly disconcerting. In a December 13, 1950, editorial immediately following the NCC's formation and the release of the FCC report, *CC* expressed its horror at the combination of changing attitudes and growing threats. Acheson's address to the NCC conference had denounced the "increasing boldness of the international communist movement" and called for "vigorous and united support for the measures we must take to meet this danger." At a press conference the next day, President Truman had rather blithely indicated his consideration of using nuclear weapons in the Korean conflict. Is this one of the "measures" Acheson had called on the NCC to support? the editorial wondered. And did this "pressure" of possessing the bomb account for the FCC commission's shocking endorsement of retaliatory use? The *CC* editorial dismissed the FCC commission's call for "all possible restraint" as a "pathetic addendum" to its capitulation. The only viable solution, the *CC* believed, was "immediately turning over to the United Nations every atom bomb which we possess."[64] As the first half of this troubled century drew to a close, the world seemed suddenly even more dangerous, and American Christendom's efforts at unity showed growing strains.

                                     IV

While mainline Protestant leaders wrestled with the vexing questions of peace, war, international order, and America's role in the world, a new set of Christian voices began to join the clamor. Neo-evangelicalism emerged immediately after World War II as a burgeoning movement. Rooting their theological lineage broadly in historic Protestantism and more directly in fundamentalism, neo-evangelicals nevertheless rejected fundamentalism's separatist and anti-intellectual impulses, advocating instead a broader engagement with culture, politics, and the life of the mind. Yet if the neo-evangelicals regarded fundamentalism as just an embarrassing eccentric uncle, they saw mainline Protestantism as a veritable wicked stepmother. While distancing themselves from fundamentalist excesses, evangelicals maintained militant opposition to what they saw as the theological and political liberalism of mainline Protestantism and its suspicious offspring, the neo-orthodoxy of figures such as Niebuhr and Barth. Led intellectually by the likes of theologians Carl F. H.

[64] "This Nation Under God," *Christian Century*, 13 December 1950, 1478–1479.

Henry, E. J. Carnell, and Harold John Ockenga, and represented popularly by evangelists Charles Fuller and especially Billy Graham, neo-evangelicalism soon attained a prominent place in the pantheon of American religion.

Evangelicals also took notice of foreign policy, but they did not begin with a mature or even coherent theology of international relations. Rather, evangelicals began with a desire to be heard, and to provide an alternative Christian voice to mainline Protestantism. L. Nelson Bell, former medical missionary to China, father-in-law to Billy Graham, and an early evangelical leader, complained in a 1947 letter to the Associated Press that "I am one of a number of Christian laymen who are thoroughly fed-up with the political meddling of the Federal Council, in the name of the Church."[65] As it turned out, Bell was not so much opposed to church leaders getting involved in politics as he was to their support for liberal political causes. His own theological community soon gained recognition. Founded in 1943, the National Association of Evangelicals (NAE) breathlessly reported to its supporters just five years later that the State Department's Division of Public Relations had invited an NAE representative to join a liaison committee between the State Department and American churches. An exhilarated NAE now had a seat at the table long monopolized by the mainline.[66]

The NAE did not share any of the American mainline's enthusiasm for the UN. Commenting on a proposed Congressional resolution in support of expanding the UN, a confidential NAE notice voiced skepticism that people in communist countries felt any "moral responsibility" to obey universal law. The NAE suggested instead that Congress "pass a resolution making it the long-range policy of the United States to support and strengthen missionary endeavors throughout the world" in order to "raise the moral responsibility of all citizens to the point where they will obey world law."[67] At its annual convention in 1950, NAE delegates displayed their muscular conservatism with a series of resolutions enthusiastically endorsing "free enterprise," "private property," and "moral integrity." Moreover, the NAE denounced "vague proposals for world federation and world government" (presumably coming from the FCC and WCC) as "invitations to disaster for our national sovereignty" and openings for "world socialism and world dictatorship." Even the Universal

---

[65] March 13, 1947 letter from Bell to AP; L. Nelson Bell Papers, Box 39, Folder 3; Billy Graham Center Archives, Wheaton, IL (hereinafter BGCA).

[66] March 4, 1948 NAE "Flash Sheet" newsletter; Evangelical Foreign Missions Association Papers (hereinafter EFMA Papers), Box 1, Folder 49; BGCA.

[67] October 15, 1949 NAE Confidential News Service; Herbert J. Taylor Papers (hereinafter Taylor Papers), Box 67, Folder 2; BGCA. The report seemed to realize the futility of this proposal, and only offered it to show the practical ineffectiveness of the UN.

Declaration of Human Rights came under attack. While they favored "basic freedoms for all mankind," the evangelical delegates urged that the Declaration be revised because it represented human rights "as man's due reward for his goodness, whereas we consider them bounties from God to His creatures."[68] Ever eager to be taken more seriously in the corridors of power, the NAE excitedly informed supporters that some of these resolutions had been inserted into the Congressional Record. Moreover, a few unnamed senators had told an NAE official that the Marshall Plan needed to meet not only the physical needs of Europeans but also "their spiritual need," and had apparently suggested "giving publicity to the spiritual work that our missionary organizations are doing."[69]

In seeking to distinguish themselves from their mainline Protestant rivals, evangelicals stressed their unambiguous anticommunism, their unapologetic patriotism, and the priority they gave to "spiritual" needs over "physical" needs. After all, evangelicals persistently complained that liberal Protestant theology had abandoned faith in the supernatural for an emphasis on ethics and the "social Gospel." Hence they were suspicious of initiatives like the Marshall Plan or the United Nations, which they regarded as attempts to reform the social order without changing the human heart. They likewise accused liberal Protestant missionary efforts of focusing on education and humanitarian work instead of saving souls.[70] Yet while critiquing the mainline, evangelicals struggled to develop a distinctive or even coherent political theology of their own. Their foreign policy pronouncements in their early years dealt either with general themes like anticommunism and suspicion of the UN, or with more parochial concerns like religious liberty for missionaries and other overseas Protestants.[71]

These squabbling Protestants did agree on one issue: anti-Catholicism. Despite their own profound theological differences, mainline and evangelical Protestants united in antipathy towards the Church of Rome. Their

---

[68] Resolutions adopted by 8th Annual NAE Convention, April 21, 1950; Taylor Papers, Box 67, Folder 9; BGCA. The NAE's resolution on the Human Rights Declaration, it should be noted, perhaps unwittingly touched on what had also been a significant point of contention among the Declaration's drafters over the foundation of human rights. See Glendon, 66–69.

[69] May 23, 1950 NAE letter; Taylor Papers, Box 67, Folder 2; BGCA.

[70] This description of changes in Protestant missionary strategy was generally accurate, as partisans on both sides would agree. For more on the evolution of the Protestant missionary movement in America, see William R. Hutchison, *Errand to the World: American Protestant Thought and Foreign Missions* (Chicago: University of Chicago Press 1987).

[71] See, for example, the August 1, 1950 NAE Confidential News Release; EFMA Papers, Box 2, Folder 37, and October 11–12, 1951 NAE Secretary of Affairs Report; EFMA Papers, Box 2, Folder 56; BGCA.

reasons varied somewhat. The mainline saw the Catholic Church as a totalitarian threat to political and religious liberty, while evangelicals also dismissed Catholicism as superstitious and heretical. Neither camp welcomed
Catholic influence in the United States. Both wanted American foreign policy
to curb Catholic influence abroad.

For example, the venerable Henry Sloane Coffin of Union Theological
Seminary wrote to John Mott to advocate "combating the specious teaching of the [Roman Catholic] propagandists seeking to win converts." The
Christian Century published an ominous editorial in 1950 warning against
America allying too closely with the Vatican against communism in a "holy
war" of the Vatican's design. "The Roman church always has its own purposes... [and] these always involve its own eventual aggrandizement," *CC*
warned. "It is also out to extend its own spiritual authority and ecclesiastical
power over all the earth."[72] Clyde Taylor, a leading NAE official, sounded a
similar alarm in a speech that same year. Warning against the United States
allying with the Vatican, he compared Catholicism with communism and
said the Catholic Church "confidently believes the day will come when it will
rule the world in a Church-State."[73] Likewise, the mainline and evangelicals
strenuously opposed Truman's attempts to confer diplomatic recognition on
the Vatican.[74] And both communities consistently pressured the U.S. government to intervene on behalf of Protestants being harassed or persecuted
by Catholic authorities in nations such as Colombia, Spain, and Italy. Evangelicals were especially mobilized in this regard, and complicated the White
House's efforts to assist Catholic anticommunist governments. They complained to the Truman Administration about its support for Italian Catholics,
passed a resolution against assisting or even recognizing General Francisco
Franco's Spain, and wrote Secretary of State Acheson urging investigations of
Catholic attacks on Protestants in Colombia.[75] NAE Secretary of Affairs Clyde
Taylor aptly summarized the prevailing Protestant sentiment. Describing

[72] March 30, 1946 letter from Coffin to Mott; Mott Papers, RG 45, Box 15, Folder 289; YDSA. "Is
the Cold War a Holy War?" *Christian Century*, 11 January 1950, 39–41.

[73] Taylor, "The Persecution of Protestants in South America," August 13, 1950 speech; EFMA
Papers, Box 84, Folder 20; BGCA.

[74] See, for example, the official NCC statement on October 31, 1951, "Church Council's Statement
Opposing a U.S. Envoy to Vatican," *New York Times*, 1 November 1951, and NAE Confidential
News Releases of January 15, 1951 and March 1, 1951; Taylor Papers, Box 67, Folder 9; BGCA.
For more on the FCC and NCC's opposition to the Vatican appointment, see chapter three
of this book.

[75] See, for example, the CCIA's July 24, 1952 "Resolution on the Colombian Situation"; WCC
Papers, RG 162, Box 20, Folder 142; YDSA; April 12, 1948 and April 26, 1948 NAE Confidential
News Services; EFMA Papers, Box 1, Folder 49; May 1, 1952 NAE News Release "Protest to
State Department Re Italy"; Taylor Papers, Box 67, Folder 17; January 20, 1950 letter from

the cooperation of evangelicals and mainline Protestants in organizing Protestants and Other Americans United for Separation of Church and State (POAU) – formed largely to oppose Catholicism – he declared in 1951 that "never have we been better prepared to combat the interest of the Roman Catholic Hierarchy and Communism as well as we are now."[76]

Niebuhr in this case refused to toe the Protestant party line. In a 1952 article in his journal *Christianity and Crisis*, he accused many Americans of holding a monolithic and "very inaccurate concept of Roman Catholic political thought and life." Niebuhr made clear that he had his own differences with Catholicism – particularly some of its religious–political unions, its identification of the "historic Church with the Kingdom of God," and the rigidity of its "natural law" moral tradition. Protestants erred, however, in judging Catholicism only by its worst excesses and corruptions. In some important ways it improved on Protestant social ethics. Niebuhr pointed out that Catholicism often promoted a more robust vision of economic justice than Protestantism, both in the United States and abroad. And Catholic teaching on foreign policy was more subtle and sophisticated than the Protestant caricature. Catholicism, he concluded, "has many moral and spiritual resources which can act creatively in a free and responsible society."[77] Niebuhr's relatively straightforward Protestant appreciation for the diversity of Catholicism and the virtues of Catholic social thought may seem on its face unremarkable, but in the context of the pervasive anti-Catholicism of his day, his own perspective was quite exceptional.

And so American Protestants found themselves in 1952 more divided than united. Mainliners and evangelicals had severe differences over matters of

NAE to Acheson; EFMA Papers, Box 2, Folder 3; December 29, 1951 letter from Clyde Taylor to Acheson; EFMA Papers, Box 84, Folder 21; BGCA.

[76] October 11–12, 1951 Report of the Secretary of Affairs; EFMA Papers, Box 2, Folder 59; BGCA.

[77] Niebuhr, "Catholics and Politics: Some Misconceptions," *Christianity and Crisis*, 23 June 1952, 83–85. Not surprisingly, Niebuhr also did not object to Truman's attempt to appoint a Vatican ambassador. While viewing it as unnecessary, Niebuhr believed it posed no church-state problems. See Lefever, 234. For background on *Christianity and Crisis*, the most comprehensive study is Mark Hulsether's *Building a Protestant Left: Christianity and Crisis Magazine, 1941–1993* (Knoxville, TN: University of Tennessee Press 1999). Hulsether's voluminously researched book traces the entire course of *C & C*'s history and makes a persuasive case for *C & C*'s disproportionate political, intellectual, and theological influence relative to its persistently small circulation. This work suffers considerably, however, from its own manifestly partisan agenda – to promote "unity between moderate liberals and radicals of various stripes...against the greater enemy of neoconservatism." It becomes difficult, at times, to take seriously an argument that dismisses *C & C* for being written "almost exclusively from a white male Protestant standpoint" and accuses *C & C* of complicity in perpetuating "unjust power relationships between white male Protestants and various others." (quotes from pp. viii, 49).

both theology and politics. Leaders within the mainline, while sharing more common ground theologically, often found themselves at odds over matters of American foreign policy, international organizations, even peace and war. Ernest Lefever, whose long career included significant involvement as both participant in and observer of the activities of mainline Protestantism, argued as early as 1956 that mainline Protestantism had split into two camps, the majority of whom were "utopians" and the minority (led by Niebuhr) who were "realists." Lefever describes the ambiguity and inconsistency that plagued many of the FCC and NCC's statements during these years, yet his analysis tries to categorize the confusion too neatly into the "majority" and "minority" positions of the liberals and the realists.[78] The reality seems to have been messier. Some of the leading mainline officials did not fit easily into either camp, but rather vacillated between emphasizing more liberal positions and more realist positions. Even Niebuhr himself was institutionally ambivalent, serving sometimes as a chief architect of the churchmen's statements and other times as an outside critic. And he was not unaware of the confusion this potentially wrought. In 1950 he denounced much of the advice offered by Protestant organizations as "either so irrelevant or so dangerous that a wise statesman will do well to ignore most of it," and noted that the often conflicting "Christian" positions enabled policy-makers to pick and choose advice so as "to make this indifference politically expedient."[79]

American Protestants certainly did not want for effort, or concern. One of the few generalizations warranted during the years 1945–1952 is that American Protestant leaders cared intensely about their nation's role in the world, and expended significant energy trying to form coherent – and influential – foreign policy positions. Though they often failed to find consensus among themselves, and they wielded little influence over the decision-making of the Truman Administration, their efforts should not be dismissed too easily. Both mainline and evangelical leaders succeeded in focusing the attention of many of their religious followers on American foreign policy. They also provided American Protestants with a sense that the conflict between the United States and USSR had a strong spiritual dimension, and with a set of vocabularies for discussing the crisis. Finally, their persistent attempts to influence the Truman Administration and the Congress regularly reminded American political leaders that many of their constituents saw the Cold War in spiritual terms,

---

[78] Lefever, "Protestants and American Foreign Policy, 1925–1954." Before completing his dissertation, Lefever had served as Associate Secretary of the NCC's Department of International Justice and Goodwill from 1952–1954. He had also contributed several articles to *Christianity and Crisis* and the *Christian Century*.

[79] Quoted in Lefever, 237.

and sought at least in part a spiritual solution. In this regard, as subsequent chapters will demonstrate, American Protestants shared with many of their political leaders a common conviction that the Cold War was a religious conflict. And in yet another of the Cold War's many ironies, it would fall to American political leaders to formulate a more coherent diplomatic theology than American religious leaders had been able to do.

In 1952, however, American Protestants had only begun to fight. Late that year the American people elected a new president who promised new values and new directions in their nation's foreign policy. America's Protestant leaders – mainline and evangelical, liberal and realist – in turn renewed their efforts to bring divine insight into America's role in the world.

2

ॐ

Unity Dissolved: Protestants and Foreign Policy, 1953–1960

I

The year 1953 witnessed a growing paradox in the knotty relationship between religion and politics. On the one hand, America inaugurated a new president who presided over perhaps the greatest flowering of civil religion in the nation's history. Protestant, Catholic, and Jew were all urged to unite under the banner of "God and country," as President Dwight Eisenhower and his Administration sought to create a new ecumenism that did not just transcend but actually erased old sectarian boundaries. On the other hand, many of America's religious leaders, particularly within Protestantism, grew more divided than ever on fundamental matters of faith and practice. While the political leadership sought to create religious and political unity, the religious leadership only deepened its religious and political discord. For the Protestant combatants fighting in the theological trenches, the pacific and prosperous 1950s were anything but.

Robert Wuthnow has described the religious convulsions of the postwar years as the "restructuring" of American religion. Traditional denominational distinctions – Methodist, Baptist, Presbyterian, Episcopalian – became less and less meaningful, as religion in America fractured not along denominational lines, but across them.[1] Theological conservatives of several denominational flavors began to ally together in neo-evangelicalism and in reform movements within their various communions. Along the way, they often discovered that they shared conservative political convictions as well, coupled with an aversion to the political liberalism of their denominational hierarchies. On the other side, theological liberals continued to make common cause as they solidified their control of the National Council of Churches

[1] Robert Wuthnow, *The Restructuring of American Religion.*

(NCC) and World Council of Churches (WCC) – and began to pursue a more overtly liberal political agenda. Meanwhile, Reinhold Niebuhr and his fellow "Christian realists" faced an uncertain future as they sought to chart their course amidst an increasingly frayed Protestant culture.

Niebuhr entered 1953 with little energy and even less hope. Slowly recovering from a severe stroke, he viewed the incoming Eisenhower Administration with a wary eye, and yet also saw global communism as more menacing than ever. After American citizens Julius and Ethel Rosenberg received death sentences for passing atomic secrets to the Soviets – a case that captivated the nation – Niebuhr wrote an approving editorial in *Christianity and Crisis*. "Traitors are never ordinary criminals and the Rosenbergs are quite obviously fiercely loyal Communists. While the death penalty may be unprecedented, it is also obvious that the cold war in which we stand is an unprecedented form of peace and stealing atomic secrets is an unprecedented crime."[2] Nor did Niebuhr spare the American intelligentsia from his ire. He submitted an article to the *Atlantic Monthly* that accused intellectuals of succumbing too readily to the seductions of Marxism. In eschewing the often crude and unpalatable anticommunism of the political right, American intellectuals failed to "admit the universality of the influence of the Marxist dogma over their own minds." While conservatism suffered from many errors, it at least preserved "a multiplicity of centers of power in society." In contrast, Niebuhr identified Marxism's "single greatest error: it creates unintended disproportions and a monopoly of power."[3] He feared that his comrades in the thinking class risked undermining the Cold War cause by uncritically importing Marxist assumptions while failing to appreciate the virtues of American pluralism, socially and politically.

Niebuhr's anticommunism hardly translated into support for Republicans, however. He penned the bleak lead editorial "We Stand Alone" in the September 21, 1953, issue of *Christianity and Crisis*. He did not intend the title as a compliment. Just eight months into Eisenhower's presidency, Niebuhr found little to laud and much to lament in the new administration's foreign policy. "We are more completely isolated than at any time since we assumed the

<hr/>

[2] Niebuhr, editorial note, *Christianity and Crisis*, 16 March 1953, 26. It should be noted that Niebuhr eventually came to regret his support of the death penalty for the Rosenbergs, deciding instead that life imprisonment would have been more appropriate and less politically contentious. See Richard Fox, *Reinhold Niebuhr: A Biography*, 254. For more on Niebuhr's skepticism of Eisenhower, see Fox, 249–256.

[3] Niebuhr, May 28, 1953 manuscript; Reinhold Niebuhr Papers, Box 16, Folder: "The Intellectuals, the Administration, and the Marxist Heresy"; Library of Congress, Washington DC (hereinafter LOC).

precarious role of world leadership," he bemoaned. And the fault was almost all American. U.S. obstinacy in refusing even to discuss the status of Communist China in the United Nations had severely harmed relations with a host of important allies over a range of other issues. Seeing only pride and fear instead of humility and courage, he drew a characteristically ironic conclusion. "We have become weak in the hour of our greatest strength, because our strength tempted us to a nationalistic arrogance to stand alone and defy our friends as well as our foes on issues which are important only to our self-esteem."[4]

Just three months later, however, Niebuhr found reason for hope. Eisenhower delivered his landmark "Atoms for Peace" address to the United Nations on December 8, 1953, proposing that the world's nuclear powers (the United States, United Kingdom, and USSR) voluntarily donate their fissionable materials to an international agency for peaceful energy purposes. If Republicans could change their policies, Niebuhr could change his mind – at least in part. Eisenhower's proposal "could turn out to be a master stroke," Niebuhr wrote, as a gesture to the world demonstrating America's commitment to international cooperation. "It will certainly do much to convince our allies that we are not bent on war; and it will help to change the caricature of ourselves which McCarthyism has made so plausible." Nevertheless, Niebuhr remained convinced, with some justification, that Eisenhower was doing too little to restrain McCarthy. Niebuhr concluded his editorial on an acerbic note. "The picture of an amiable and politically inept president, wanting to do the right things but remaining nevertheless a prisoner of the right wing of his party despite his superior strength in the country, remains unrelieved or untouched. It is a rather pathetic spectacle."[5]

The Eisenhower years also saw mainline Protestantism continue to propound its views on foreign policy through its beloved commissions and conferences with letterhead-consuming titles. Thus, in Cleveland October 27–30, 1953, the Department of International Justice and Goodwill of the National Council of Churches of Christ held its Fourth National Study Conference on the Churches and World Order. The conference report reflected some of the ongoing dynamics perplexing the churchmen as they struggled to formulate a coherent vision of international order: the tension between realism and idealism (or between what is and what ought to be), the need for both general principles and specific applications, and the burden of maintaining consensus without succumbing to insipid platitudes.

---

[4] Niebuhr, "We Stand Alone," *Christianity and Crisis*, 21 September 1953, 113–114.
[5] Niebuhr, "Editorial Notes," *Christianity and Crisis*, 28 December 1953, 170.

Bishop William Martin, president of the NCC, introduced the report by
noting America's new position of world leadership and expressing his concern
that "many [Americans] believe that the price of world leadership is too high."
He singled out "increasingly frequent and unjustified attacks upon the United
Nations" and "opposition to all forms of economic and technical assistance
abroad" – both presumably coming from political conservatives – as evidence
of the "moral isolationism" that the NCC stood squarely against. The report's
most significant section was its "Message to the Churches," issued by the entire
conference and directed to the pews and pulpits of NCC member churches. It
devoted the vast majority of its attention to the "conflict between the Soviet
world and the free world." While claiming that American policy needed to
center on two goals – resisting "the extension of Communist totalitarianism"
and avoiding "a third world war" – the message offered little in the way of
specific proposals. And though it admitted the UN's limitations, highlighted
by the Soviet Union's persistent use of its Security Council veto, the report
still urged the United States to "press for the largest practicable degree of
disarmament through the UN, as we seek the goal of universal enforceable
disarmament."[6] The NCC also presented copies of the report to its former
colleague-turned-cabinet member, Secretary of State John Foster Dulles, as
well as to UN Ambassador Henry Cabot Lodge, with the assurance that "the
overwhelming majority of the people of our churches" support the UN.[7]

Eight years into its existence, the Commission of the Churches on International Affairs (CCIA), a partner organization of the NCC and WCC, was
still trying to define and justify its existence. A 1954 CCIA brochure described
its principal goal as pursuing peace. The global Cold War and the recent
regional "hot war" in Korea had tempered the CCIA's initial lofty hopes at
its inception for a new world order. But its leaders, especially its American
director O. Frederick Nolde, continued to believe passionately in the CCIA's
relevance. They had learned some lessons, of course. Admitting that "periodic conferences" were not as effective as "day-to-day" operations, and that
"resolutions and statements by churches have political effect only when they
are directed to the time and place where international decisions are made,"
the CCIA had begun to realize the limits of its effectiveness. Nevertheless, it
still hoped to "educate" and "enlighten" its followers in the church pews, and

---

[6] NCC Report of Fourth World Study Order Conference, "Christian Faith and International
Responsibility"; NCC Papers, Record Group 6, Box 27, Folder 17, Presbyterian Historical
Society, Philadelphia, PA (hereinafter PHS).

[7] December 4, 1953 letter from Walter Van Kirk to Liston Pope; Liston Pope Papers (hereinafter
Pope Papers), RG 49, Box 19, Folder 328; Yale Divinity School Archives, New Haven, CT
(hereinafter YDSA).

"to bring the convictions of Christian people about peace to bear just where and when they can produce changes in policy."[8] The organization's agenda was as notable for what it did not include. The CCIA avoided grappling with the hard questions of just how peace could be achieved, or how force might be necessary to restrain evil and restore order. Unless and until it could offer credible insights on such vexing matters, the CCIA would find elusive the policy relevance it so desperately sought.

Perhaps because of his willingness to immerse himself in the messiness of specific international problems, Niebuhr was both more interesting and more influential than organizations like the CCIA. For example, he enthusiastically backed the North Atlantic Treaty Organization. At the request of the National Business Committee for NATO, a group of American corporate leaders formed to mobilize support for the alliance, Niebuhr agreed to write an article on the "spiritual significance of NATO" five years after its formation. He observed that the "Atlantic community" was bound not necessarily by a "unified culture," but rather by "a way of making diversity tolerable under conditions of freedom." Such tolerance and freedom were rooted in Europe's various versions of "Biblical faith," Jewish and Christian, all of which affirmed both the intrinsic dignity of the human person and the supremacy of divine authority over all human collectives. Threatening this diverse, complex community loomed the "tyranny" of a "simple utopian creed" that seeks "to unify the whole of human society upon the basis of a new and pretentious secular religion." Ever the realist, Niebuhr defended NATO's division of Europe and inclusion of the North American nations on the grounds that "the spiritual facts correspond to the strategic necessities." In other words, the East European countries "have been separated from this spiritual community" by both "the power of Russian arms" and their own lack of "the political and cultural prerequisites for the open society."[9]

Yet Niebuhr also had to confront the embarrassing fact of the Atlantic alliance's divisions. His 1954 essay "Why They Dislike America" probed the "well-nigh universal anti-American sentiment throughout Europe and Asia." He began by distinguishing between the inevitable and the contingent factors. Regarding the former, he admitted that the disproportionate wealth and power wielded by America would be enough to provoke international resentment when held by any country. Such is the nature of humans, and of nations.

---

[8] CCIA, 1954 brochure; WCC Papers, RG 162, Box 20, Folder 143; YDSA.

[9] May 5, 1954 letter from David Martin to Niebuhr; Essay by Niebuhr on "The Moral and Spiritual Content of the Atlantic Community"; both in RN Papers, Box 16, Folder: "Moral and Spiritual Content of the Atlantic Community," LOC.

However, the United States still bore some blame for its own actions. Niebuhr singled out Truman's 1950 decision to allow German rearmament without thoroughly consulting Britain or France. More recently, he believed that the Eisenhower and Dulles policies of "liberation" and the "new look" had frightened Europeans as too truculent, and that McCarthyism on the domestic front had only confirmed European suspicions that American anticommunism was inherently hysterical. The final factor Niebuhr identified "is the feeling that we are inflexible and unrealistic in our attitude toward Communist China." In this essay and elsewhere, Niebuhr then called for admitting the People's Republic of China to the United Nations. He saw no good purpose in keeping China out, a stance that to him smacked of self-righteousness and needlessly antagonized the rest of the world.[10]

II

The leadership of the World Council of Churches, meanwhile, prepared for the organization's second world assembly, six years after its formation in Amsterdam, to be held in Evanston, Illinois, in August, 1954. Its founding optimism diminished, the WCC began with more questions than answers. It seemed to be following world events more than leading them, reacting more than shaping. And it still remained incapable of rendering any decisive moral judgments beyond anguished hand-wringing and saccharine paeans to "peace" and "justice" and "reconciliation."

In this spirit, and in the tradition of its rejection in 1948 of "both Communism and Laissez-Faire Capitalism," a WCC preparatory committee for the Evanston conference issued a rebuke to both communism and democracy. The latter, the report contended, permits "inequality, discrimination, injustice, reliance on naked power, exploitation and aggression." Communism did not fare much better. Admitting that communism was "alive with hope" for many of its followers, the report still scored Marxism for its atheism and its frequently totalitarian behavior. Nevertheless, and not surprisingly, it was the committee's targeting of democracy that attracted the most comment, and the greatest concern.[11] Here the WCC committee displayed a remarkable lack

---

[10] Niebuhr, "Why They Dislike America," *The New Leader*, 12 April 1954, 3–5. See also Niebuhr letter to the Editor, New York Times, 19 July 1954, 18, and "Editorial Notes," *Christianity and Crisis*, 26 July 1954, 98–99.

[11] "Churches Assail Democracy Flaws," *New York Times*, 15 June 1954. It should be noted that this report provoked considerable division at the conference itself, and the full WCC assembly did not accept the report without extensive discussion and revision. See Henry P. Van Dusen, "Evanston in Retrospect," *Christianity and Crisis*, 18 October 1954, 131–134.

of political sense for tone and timing. While the world remained gripped in a mortal and ideological conflict between two competing worldviews, with potentially cataclysmic stakes, the WCC insisted on an almost absurd attempt at balance. Placing "democracy" alongside "communism," both seriously flawed and both in need of reform, seemed to obscure rather than to clarify the nature of the conflict. Nor did it bode well for the WCC's hopes for relevance and respect. Meanwhile, Niebuhr, though scheduled to speak, viewed the conference's ambitions with skepticism. Suffering from exhaustion and depression, he wrote a friend on August 25, 1954, that "today is the day I was supposed to go to Evanston, and I am glad I am not going."[12]

Though Niebuhr's infirmities kept him from attending, his friend, Episcopal Bishop Angus Dun, read Niebuhr's prepared remarks to the plenary session. The speech condensed many of Niebuhr's perennial themes. He called for looking "at the whole drama of life in the wisdom borrowed from the Cross" where "divine goodness was in conflict, not chiefly with obvious human evil but with human goodness. It was Roman justice, the best justice of its day, and Hebraic religion, the highest religion of its day, which were implicated in the Crucifixion." The lessons were clear: human idealism and zeal for the good, when unrestrained by self-awareness and unchastened by humility, could produce tremendous injustices. Niebuhr singled out communism as the incarnation of this problem, for it "changed the righteousness of the poor into the cruelty of the powerful because it did not understand the ambiguity of all human virtue and the foolishness of all human wisdom." But lest his fellow Christians battling communism become too self-assured, Niebuhr quickly warned against making "the Christian cause to appear to be a contest between the God-fearing believers and the unrighteous unbelievers." After all, "it is not only those who deny God but those who profess Him but claim Him too simply as an ally of their purposes . . . who bring evil into the world." Nor should Christians "make too uncritical application of the rediscovered Biblical fact that all men are sinners" – "neutralism" was an evasion rather than a solution. Niebuhr dismissed in fact, if not in name, the moralism of figures like Dulles, as well as the moral equivalency of the WCC.[13]

The WCC also faced the uncomfortable fact of Cold War divisions within its own membership. Determining parameters for membership in the WCC posed both a theoretical and a practical problem. Those participating in the

---

[12] August 25, 1954 letter from Niebuhr to June Bingham; RN Papers, Box 26, Folder: August 1954–April 1955; LOC.
[13] Niebuhr, "Our Dependence Is Upon God," August 29, 1954 plenary address to WCC Second Assembly, Evanston, Illinois; WCC Papers, RG 162, Box 9, Folder 57; YDSA. See also Fox, 259.

WCC presumably had some measure of its approval, and their words and actions would carry the WCC's imprimatur. And so the WCC's invitation to clergy from Soviet bloc countries such as Hungary and Czechoslovakia showed that the organization itself did not regard communism and Christianity as fundamentally incompatible.

However, these clerics needed to be "invited" not only by the WCC but also by the U.S. Government, or at least issued visas to attend the Evanston conference. After some internal debate and entreaties from WCC officials, Secretary of State Dulles agreed to approve the visas. The State Department did not miss this opportunity to press its own agenda, however, and put the WCC on notice. The Department's press release announcing the visa decision condemned the Soviet bloc's "campaign of intimidation and persecution against all forms of religion" and noted skeptically that in Eastern Europe some clergy had reconciled "their faith with public support of Communism." Nevertheless, averred State, the American creed would hold true. "The spiritual foundation on which this nation rests is too strong to be adversely affected by any pro-Communist activities in which this small group of delegates from communist-dominated areas might attempt to engage." Americans and other WCC members could "judge by the conduct of these delegates whether they come here as churchmen or as propagandists of an aggressive and materialistic philosophy fundamentally hostile to religious faith." Moreover, exposure to the "spiritual life of America could have a beneficial effect" on the Iron Curtain clerics, and perhaps lead to "a spiritual strengthening of the churches in Czechoslovakia and Hungary in the face of the constant and ruthless pressure to which they are subjected."[14]

The conference had another notable visitor. Consistent with his State Department's hopes that the Evanston conference would display America's "spiritual foundation," President Eisenhower accepted an invitation to deliver a plenary address at the conference. Besides the customary platitudes paying tribute to faith, morality, and peace, the president's speech contained two intriguing elements. First, Eisenhower claimed that America was becoming more devout. The percentage of Americans belonging to churches "steadily increases," he noted, having tripled over the last century. Bible distribution also continued to climb. These signs indicated that "our interest in religion is serious and genuine" and a source of national strength. They also served as a warning to the Soviets and an assurance to the West that Eisenhower presided over a robust, faithful nation.

---

[14] July 17, 1954 State Department Press Release, no. 390; Dwight D. Eisenhower Papers, Official File Box 858, Folder: OF 172; Eisenhower Library, Abilene, Kansas (hereinafter DDE Papers).

Second, the president made a rather dramatic and unusual proposal. Speaking not as Chief Executive but only "as a private citizen" and member of a WCC constituent church, he urged "every single person, in every single country in the world, who believes in the power of a Supreme Being, to join in a mighty, simultaneous, intense act of faith." Specifically, Eisenhower called for "a personal prayer, delivered simultaneously and fervently, by hundreds of millions . . . to work unceasingly for a just and lasting peace."[15] Only the most fervent communist–atheist could object to a "prayer for peace," of course, so in one fell homiletical swoop Eisenhower attempted to isolate the Kremlin and bring the "spiritual" peoples of the world into the American camp. The president's proposal received much favorable media coverage. Henry Luce published a glowing endorsement in a *Life* editorial that concluded with a sentiment Eisenhower no doubt shared but could not have said in Evanston: he "must seek the world's prayers, time and again, in the hope that enough faith *can* move even the Soviet mountain."[16]

The Soviet peril aside, the president's edict faced the almost equally formidable task of moving the mountain of church bureaucracy. A somewhat sheepish Samuel McCrea Cavert, WCC Executive Secretary, wrote Eisenhower that while he quite appreciated the president's suggestion, "we face a difficult problem just because of the many days of prayer which are already in the church calendar." After describing three different upcoming prayer periods, Cavert confessed "it seems doubtful whether the new proposal at this time could get the response which its importance demands."[17] The WCC appears to have taken no further action on Eisenhower's prayer plan.

A similar reticence pervaded the WCC's foreign policy. The CCIA at Evanston maintained its status as the WCC's foremost voice on international relations. Its leadership had changed somewhat since the Amsterdam conference in 1948. Niebuhr was no longer on the commission, leaving more influence to liberal American figures such as Nolde, Richard Fagley, and Walter Van Kirk, not to mention Joseph Hromadka, the Czechoslovak theologian who had defended communism so vocally at Amsterdam. Perhaps it should be no surprise that the final report, addressed to all WCC member churches, strenuously avoided even mentioning "communism," or singling out any countries by name. It was a model of analytical passivity. "Opposing

---

[15] Eisenhower, August 19, 1954 "Address at the Second Assembly of the World Council of Churches, Evanston, Illinois," *Public Papers of the Presidents: Dwight D. Eisenhower, 1954* (Washington: United States Government Printing Office 1960), 734–740.

[16] "A Path to Peace Through Prayer," *Life* editorial, printed as full-page advertisement in *New York Times*, 29 September 1954. Emphasis original.

[17] October 27, 1954 letter from Cavert to Eisenhower; OF Box 738, Folder: OF 144H; DDE Papers.

ideologies compete for the minds and souls of men. Rival power blocs imperil the peace of nations large and small." It condemned equally "totalitarian tyranny and aggression" as well as "the exploitation of any people by economic monopoly or political imperialism" – thinly-veiled references to the Soviet and American spheres, respectively. The report called for a strengthening of the United Nations, the elimination of weapons of mass destruction, and the development of a new "international ethos."[18] The CCIA report also marked the beginning of a turning point, as the influence of Niebuhr and his "Christian realism" on mainline organizations such as the CCIA and the NCC began to wane.

The divisions evident at Evanston appeared as well in several evaluations following the conference. Henry Van Dusen of Union Seminary admitted that the WCC had been "sharply divided on a number of issues," but he optimistically viewed these rifts as signs of diversity and strength, not as paralysis or weakness.[19] Ernest W. Lefever, on the other hand – erstwhile NCC staff member and Yale doctoral student under H. Richard Niebuhr – wrote a withering critique of the CCIA report for *Christianity and Crisis*. Lefever found the report thoroughly flawed. Among other things, the WCC had rather insouciantly urged the United States and the USSR to turn their disagreements over to an "impartial international organization" and abide by its decisions, an idea that Lefever found ludicrous and "no less than a demand for world government now." He concluded that the report offered nothing but "peripheral, irrelevant and ineffective recommendations for improving the world situation."

Walter Van Kirk – a leading NCC official and architect of the WCC report, who had also served as Lefever's supervisor at the NCC until Lefever's resignation just two months earlier – took great umbrage at his former employee's criticism. In a letter to the editor, Van Kirk denounced "Lefever's blunderbuss attack" as "pathetically inadequate." He defended the report as merely "another stage on a long ecumenical journey" that did not pretend to solve all global problems, and should be lauded instead of lambasted.[20] But the beleaguered WCC came under attack from the Kremlin as well. Soviet radio propagandists, seizing especially on Eisenhower's address, denounced the conference as a religious ploy "organized" by the United States "solely for

---

[18] CCIA, "Christians in the Struggle for World Community," Report to WCC Second Assembly, August, 1954; WCC Papers, RG 162, Box 9, Folder 62; YDSA.
[19] Van Dusen, "Evanston in Retrospect," *Christianity and Crisis*, 18 October 1954, 131–134.
[20] Ernest W. Lefever, "Evanston on International Affairs: A Critique of the Report from Section IV," *Christianity and Crisis*, 29 November 1954. Walter Van Kirk, letter to editor, *Christianity and Crisis*, 27 December 1954, 173, 176.

the purpose of making political capital."[21] Criticized from without and from within, from the left and from the right, the WCC coupled a confused identity with an uncertain future.

III

American evangelicals, meanwhile, entered the Eisenhower era with unbridled optimism. What they still lacked in institutional and intellectual credibility, they tried to compensate for with organization and energy. But evangelical foreign policy concerns remained distinctly parochial. Bulletins and press releases from the National Association of Evangelicals (NAE) still centered on Catholic persecution of evangelicals in Latin America, Spain, and Italy, and on the needs of missionaries.[22] Clyde Taylor, the NAE Executive Secretary, traveled in 1953 to Spain for meetings with Spanish evangelicals, missionaries, and diplomats at the American Embassy, the latter of whom admitted to Taylor their own frustrations with Franco's Catholic theocratic proclivities. Taylor and other evangelical leaders continued to pressure Congress and the Eisenhower Administration to terminate financial assistance to Franco's regime, which the United States had offered in exchange for strategic air bases in Spain.[23] Much as evangelicals loathed communism, they would not support what they regarded as compromising alliances with Catholic powers in the Cold War cause.

Evangelical leaders likewise obsessed over keeping at bay any possible Catholic influences on the new Eisenhower Administration, an agenda that at times took rather bizarre turns. For example, a confidential memo written

---

[21] "Russians Told U.S. Sponsored Evanston Assembly," *Christianity and Crisis*, 18 October 1954, 130.

[22] See, for example, January 1, 1953 NAE News Release; Herbert J. Taylor Papers (hereinafter Taylor Papers), Box 67, Folder 26; Billy Graham Center Archives, Wheaton, Illinois (hereinafter BGCA).

[23] June 22, 1953 letter from Taylor to Miss Nona McClure; Taylor, August 17, 1953 "Confidential Report on Spain"; Taylor, September 15, 1953 Memorandum on Spain; September 30, 1953 letter from Taylor to Rev. Samuel Vila; EFMA Papers, Box 88, Folder 6; BGCA. See also June 3, 1954 letter from Taylor to Ernest H. Trenchard and Rev. Charles W. Whitten; EFMA Papers, Box 88, Folder 7; BGCA. For evangelical concerns that the marriage procedures for American military personnel based in Spain not be governed by Catholic law, see December 28, 1954 letter from NAE President Henry Savage to Secretary of Defense Charles Wilson, and the January 20, 1955 letter of reply; EFMA Papers, Box 88, Folder 8; BGCA. Finally, note that liberal Protestant leaders were also concerned over religious liberty in Spain. See, for example, the April 13, 1954 telegram from NCC leaders, including Harry Emerson Fosdick, to President Eisenhower, saying they are "shocked by report of continued persecutions in Spain . . . of Protestants who exercise liberty of conscience"; Central File, General File Box 831, Folder 122 Spain; DDE Papers.

early in 1954 by an NAE leader and sent to a small group of evangelical leaders, including Billy Graham and Fuller Seminary President Harold Ockenga,
warned that "the only way to head off the Roman Catholic menace to our
nation is by using the same legal tactics they do, and that is 'legal infiltration'
of the various branches of our government." The memo then detailed system-
atically the numbers and names of Catholics appointed to high positions in
the Eisenhower Administration. Turning to the State Department, the memo
lamented that five out of Dulles's top six aides were Catholic. More ominous still was an ironic by-product of McCarthyism. "The direct or indirect
result of Senator McCarthy's investigations is a disproportionate discharging
of Protestants and hiring of Roman Catholics under the false belief that this
would protect the security of our nation."[24] McCarthyism has been criticized for many things, then and now, but surely the concern of conservative
Protestants that it might benefit Catholics was a novel objection. As fervent
as they could be in their hatred of communism, evangelicals blanched at
the notion that the agitations of America's most prominent anticommunist
were benefiting their Catholic nemeses. To their mind, this made it all the
more vital to place their own people in positions of power. None others could
be trusted.

Not that evangelicals had ceased combating their other perennial enemies –
communists and liberal Protestants – especially when the two appeared to
make common cause. For example, L. Nelson Bell wrote to his friend and
congressional ally Walter Judd requesting a copy of the report by the House
Committee on Un-American Activities on the "Communist sympathies" of
Dr. John Mackay, president of Princeton Theological Seminary. Bell regarded
Mackay as particularly threatening for two reasons. Not only was he a prominent voice for theological liberalism in the Presbyterian denomination, but
Mackay also advocated the "recognition of Red China" and "at the same time
urges our Government to sit down at the conference table with the Com-
munists." To a conservative Presbyterian and former China missionary like
Bell, this was apostasy twice over. Judd sent the requested information to
Bell. The report indicated that Mackay had long been affiliated with left-wing

---

[24] February 15, 1954 Confidential Memo "The Washington Picture"; Evangelical Foreign Mission
Association Papers (hereinafter EFMA Papers), Box 88, Folder 7; BGCA. Fundamentalists
seemed to share this concern that McCarthy's anticommunist crusade not provide cover
for Catholic advances in public life. See, for example, the November 13, 1954 "Resolution
on Investigating Committees" adopted by the American Council of Christian Churches,
which resolved "Protestants must be on constant guard against being drawn into the orbit of
Roman Catholicism as a professed major enemy of Communism"; Central File, General File,
Box 1301, Folder: 201 1954; DDE Papers.

organizations and causes, some of which might also have been communist front groups or included communist members. While this no doubt furthered Bell's suspicions of Mackay, it did not indicate that Mackay himself was a party member.[25]

Though not nearly as strident or alarmist as Bell, Niebuhr continued to harbor concerns over the political liberalism of his Protestant colleagues. The beginning of 1955 witnessed the 15th anniversary of *Christianity and Crisis*, and occasioned a reflective editorial from Niebuhr on his journal's purposes, past and present. The previous decade and a half had seen three major developments, he argued: the dramatic emergence of American power, the "growth and consolidation" of the worldwide communist movement, and the advent of nuclear weapons and the concomitant arms race. The world remained in "crisis," Niebuhr contended, albeit a crisis much different from that of 1940. Yet too many Christians still held to a simplistic solution, that nations should just "disavow the use of nuclear weapons." Doing so might well "increase the danger of war, and since war cannot be avoided without running the risk of it, it is not the business of the church to offer statesmen solutions which they must instinctively regard as irrelevant." The "Christian counsel to this nation should be primarily religious, rather than purely moral," he declared, such as reminding "the nation in its majesty of a divine majesty before which even great nations are as 'a drop in the bucket.'"[26]

In disparaging "irrelevant solutions" from church leaders, Niebuhr probably had in mind letters like the one sent just two months later from NCC leader Ernest Gross to Harold Stassen, a former NCC official who had been appointed a Special Assistant to President Eisenhower for nuclear weaponry issues. Gross reminded Stassen of "how long and steadfastly the churches have sought to bring the armament race to an end" and hoped "a solution to the disarmament problem can be found," especially if Stassen would help "strengthen and reinforce the operations of the UN" in pushing for disarmament.[27] Though heartened that another one of their own now occupied a senior policy position, the NCC found discouraging that their policies were not as well received.

The year 1955 witnessed a new Cold War flare-up, as the PRC escalated its pressure on the offshore islands of Quemoy and Matsu, held by the Chinese Nationalists on Taiwan. Niebuhr took this as yet another opportunity

[25] December 10, 1954 letter from Bell to Judd; December 14, 1954 "Information from the Files of the Committee on Un-American Activities" memo; L. Nelson Bell Papers (hereinafter Bell Papers), Box 31, Folder 4; BGCA.

[26] Niebuhr, "Our Fifteenth Birthday," *Christianity and Crisis*, 7 February 1955, 1–3.

[27] April 22, 1955 letter from Gross to Stassen; NCC Papers, RG 6, Box 19, Folder 20; PHS.

to tweak liberal churchmen. "The whole crisis reveals the irrelevance" of a major recommendation in the CCIA's Evanston report, which had called for refraining from the use of force "beyond existing bloc frontiers," he wrote. Niebuhr sardonically noted that most Cold War conflicts developed precisely in those places lacking "sharply defined 'bloc frontiers'" such as Korea, Germany, and the Taiwan Strait. He affirmed the Eisenhower Administration's commitment to include Taiwan itself within the American defensive sphere, but he was sharply critical of the Administration on the larger course of the conflict. Niebuhr described to a friend how many senior American military leaders "are outraged by us getting into the ridiculous position of defining our defense perimeter a few miles from hostile shores. They think that we are in this condition because of Dulles' stupidity and Eisenhower's indecision."[28]

As tensions mounted through March, the NCC leadership of Gross, Van Kirk, and President Eugene Carson Blake wrote Eisenhower urging "negotiation" as the solution to the conflict, and rejecting "unilateral action" or "force."[29] Two days later, a collection of 14 Protestant clergy led by John Mackay and Guy Shipler, editor of the liberal journal *The Churchman*, sent a widely publicized letter to the President demanding in rather alarmist tones that he reject the "irresponsible policy," the "folly," indeed the "crime of the first magnitude" of even threatening to use nuclear weapons to defend Taiwan. The "only way to find a solution . . . is by negotiation," these clergy concluded.[30] Not surprisingly, such appeals drew the ire of Bell. Three days later he fired off a letter to Eisenhower and Dulles (themselves both Presbyterians) asserting that "there are many Christians and many Presbyterians who most heartily disagree" with the foreign policy agenda pushed by the NCC and by certain Presbyterian leaders. "There are thousands of us who believe that our policy with reference to Communism cannot further be compromised, either by negotiation with the Communists, or by permitting them to take the off-shore Islands opposite Formosa." Perhaps unaware of the irony that he, a prominent Christian leader, was advocating his own political views, Bell closed by repeating a frequent complaint. "Many of us resent the intrusion of Ecclesiastical leaders into the realm of International politics. We do not feel that they are qualified in such matters and furthermore, we sincerely distrust

[28]   Niebuhr, "Editorial Notes," *Christianity and Crisis*, 7 March 1955, 18; April 6, 1955 letter from Niebuhr to June Bingham; RN Papers, Box 26, Folder: Aug. 1954– Apr. 1955; LOC.

[29]   March 30, 1955 letter from Blake, Gross, and Van Kirk to Eisenhower; NCC Papers, RG 6, Box 19, Folder 20; PHS.

[30]   April 1, 1955 letter from Mackay, Shipler, et al. to Eisenhower; Official File Box 856, Folder: 168-B-1; DDE Papers. See also "President Asked to Stop War Drift," *New York Times*, 3 April 1955.

their judgment when they are willing to negotiate with Communism."[31] Had Bell been more candid with himself, he might have admitted that his real objection was not the fact that religious leaders were taking political positions *per se*, but that they took *liberal* political positions.

Bell did not stand alone in his criticism. In direct response to the Mackay–Shipler letter, a group of 14 religious leaders (Protestant, Catholic, Orthodox, and Jewish) led by Rev. Daniel Poling, editor of the *Christian Herald* magazine, wrote to the President declaring their unequivocal support for his assertive stance in the Far East. The communist nations sought "the subjugation of free men to an atheistic tyranny," and must be resisted by "the strength and unity of the free world." The letter rejected the views of "certain influential fellow Americans" that "appeasement and further withdrawal" would produce peace, and came out firmly in defense of Taiwan and against recognizing the PRC or admitting it to the UN. Finally, on the contested matter of public opinion, the writers claimed that their views were "held by the vast majority of our fellow religionists, both clerical and lay."[32] While welcoming this support, Eisenhower's advisors faced the ticklish problem of how to respond without seeming to take sides in an internecine religious dispute. They considered sending a letter of appreciation to Poling from the President himself, but decided instead to have Special Assistant Nelson Rockefeller write the response, as he had done with much less enthusiasm for the Mackay–Shipler letter.[33]

Internal divisions aside, the 1950s certainly saw the flourishing of religious observance. The NCC issued a press release in 1956 trumpeting the fact that American church membership had exceeded 100 million for the first time in history, indicating that 60.9% of Americans belonged to churches – also a record high, up from 57% in 1950 and 49% in 1940. This did not include people who might attend worship services but not formally join, so the number of "church-goers" could well have been higher. Of all Americans, 35.5% were Protestant and 20.3% were Roman Catholic. Moreover, the NCC noted, "Protestantism is far from as divided as it may seem," since more than 85% of the nation's Protestants belonged to one of just nine denominational families.[34] But this assertion of unity glossed over the very real divisions within

---

[31]   April 4, 1955 letter from Bell to Eisenhower and Dulles; Bell Papers, Box 23, Folder 20; BGCA.

[32]   May 30, 1955 letter from Poling, et al. to Eisenhower; OF Box 856, Folder: OF 168-B-1(2); DDE Papers.

[33]   See April 8, 1955 letter from Rockefeller to Shipler; OF Box 856, Folder: 168-B-1; June 3, 1955 memo from Don Irwin to Rockefeller; June 6, 1955 letter from Rockefeller to Poling; OF Box 856, Folder OF 168-B-1(2); DDE Papers.

[34]   September 10, 1956 NCC Press Release; Pope Papers; RG 49, Box 19, Folder 331; YDSA.

each Protestant denomination, as theological conservatives and liberals, evangelical and mainline, idealists and realists, all battled for control.

Early in 1956, the NCC decided to send a delegation of church leaders on a trip to the Soviet Union. This immediately drew the attention of the White House. National Security Council official Edward P. Lilly, who focused on religion and American propaganda, urged a minister friend to see "that these gentlemen obtain detailed briefings as to recent Soviet lines regarding religion, as well as . . . techniques which the Russians have developed for handling visitors to the advantage of USSR." Lilly admitted the impropriety of having the U.S. government itself contact the NCC clergy, but hoped that his intermediary might appraise the delegation of Soviet duplicity. Lilly also hinted that the Eisenhower Administration had "some special interests which might be exploitable after the visit has been completed," but would need the NCC's cooperation. The government's propaganda hopes notwithstanding, nothing seems to have come of this suggestion.[35]

The visit itself was less remarkable than might have been expected. The nine NCC representatives, including President Blake, General Secretary Roswell Barnes, Van Kirk, and former President Henry Knox Sherrill, generally refrained from either stern criticism of the USSR, or from making the pleas for "peace" and "co-existence" that invariably provoked the wrath of their conservative critics. Engaging in lengthy discussions with the leadership of the Russian Orthodox Church, the NCC delegation concluded that while the Russian Church maintained some degree of spiritual autonomy and vitality, its activities were monitored closely and severely constrained by the Kremlin. Moreover, the NCC lamented that "in return for freedom of worship the leaders of the churches have apparently inclined to go along with Soviet communist leadership in important areas," particularly "peace propaganda."[36]

Though never hesitant to criticize his clerical colleagues, Niebuhr gave the visit a surprisingly positive review. "Nothing but good can be said" about the NCC trip, he wrote, noting that the delegation avoided liberal follies and realistically assessed the true nature of church and state in the Soviet Union. Moreover, such visits could give hope to the Russian Christians, and lay the

---

[35] February 2, 1956 letter from Edward P. Lilly to Rev. Ronald Bridges; White House Office File, NSC Staff, OCB Central File, Box 2, Folder: OCB 000.3 File #1 (3); DDE Papers.

[36] "A Beginning Has Been Made: An Appraisal of the Visit to Russia," *National Council Outlook*, April 1956, 3–7, 25–28. See also coverage in *U.S. News and World Report*, 6 April 1956, 137–142, and the NCC brochure on the trip; Henry Knox Sherrill Papers, RG 67, Box 27, Folder 558; YDSA.

groundwork for avenues "by which Russia might gradually be brought into the community of nations after long isolation."[37]

Shifting his focus from the USSR, Niebuhr began to sound alarms about emerging Cold War trends in the developing world. He worried about declining American influence and ascendant Arab nationalism in the Middle East, particularly under Egypt's Gamal Nasser, whose military was "still smarting over the defeat by Israel and spoiling for revenge. The situation was made to order for the Russians, who are arming the Arab states." Niebuhr warned of an impending "catastrophe in the Middle East, in which the very existence of Israel may be at stake . . . [and] the alienation of the Arab world from the West is an almost inevitable consequence." Turning to the rest of Asia and Africa, he chastised the "idealists" who thought democracy could be exported easily to the Third World, as well as the "realists" who too blithely made common cause with Third World nationalist dictators and ignored social and economic needs. Communism, meanwhile, appeared to be taking root in revolutionary societies around the globe.[38]

Niebuhr's near-term prophecy of conflagration in the Middle East proved all too true. The eruption of hostilities between Egypt and Israel, Britain, and France in late October, 1956, occurred almost simultaneously with the brutal Soviet invasion of Hungary. These crises also furthered the rift between Niebuhr and the mainline Protestant leadership, and between Niebuhr and the Eisenhower Administration. For once the NCC found itself in accord with Eisenhower and Dulles, declaring its "strong support" for their policy of acting through the UN against the military actions of Britain, France, and Israel.[39] Niebuhr, on the other hand, bitterly despaired. Not since the 1930s "has our prestige been so low and world prospects so ominous." He chastised the Eisenhower Administration for disregarding European oil needs, ignoring Soviet designs on the Arab world, and dismissing Israel's desperate plight, all of which led to the "shattering of the Western alliance" as the Anglo–French forces joined with Israel in a regrettable, but understandable, attack on Egypt.

Niebuhr reserved his greatest contempt for the "absolute pacifism" that he ascribed to the Eisenhower–Dulles team. Just as American pacifists two decades before had ignored the Nazi peril, so now did the Administration's aversion to war threaten to "allow Nasser to succeed in his sworn intention

[37] Niebuhr, "The National Council Delegation to the Russian Church," *Christianity and Crisis*, 30 April 1956, 49–50.

[38] Niebuhr, "The Second Geneva," *The New Leader*, 28 November 1955, 7–8, and "A Qualified Faith," *The New Republic*, 13 February 1956, 14–15.

[39] December 6, 1956 telegram from NCC to Eisenhower; OF Box 823, Folder: 154 N; DDE Papers.

to annihilate Israel." All of this rendered the United Nations worse than impotent, for not only had it failed to guarantee Israel's security, but Soviet and American cooperation in the UN perversely had helped to ensure Nasser's survival, as he continued his "Nazi measures" and developed "qualities of both imperialism and totalitarianism."[40] The next month found Niebuhr slightly more sanguine. He noted with grudging approval that through economic assistance and military alertness, Eisenhower had "taken action to fill the dangerous power vacuum in the Middle East and to prevent the Russians from exploiting the situation." Nevertheless, "Russian influence and prestige" had been enhanced in the Arab world, a development that boded ill for the future.[41]

While frustrated with his government's passivity in the Middle East, Niebuhr was realistic enough to agree that the United States could do little to aid the Hungarian people fighting desperately for their freedom. Horrified and repulsed by the brutality of the Russian invasion, he also found that it further eroded the UN's already diminished credibility. "One of the saddest aspects . . . was the sight of the United Nations passing impotent resolutions demanding that its Secretary General be admitted to Hungary, while no action was taken to challenge the credentials of the representative of the puppet government of Hungary."[42] The UN may have been feckless as an organization, but such a fault paled alongside the moral bankruptcy of some Protestant leaders. Niebuhr singled out his old rival Karl Barth for particular scorn after Barth, who had encouraged Hungarian church leaders to cooperate with the communist government, remained silent in the face of Soviet depredations. No doubt writing with Barth in mind, Niebuhr noted the bitter irony that Russian credibility had collapsed everywhere in Europe, "except of course in certain neutralist Protestant theological circles, which seem to lack the moral sensitivity of secular European fellow-travellers." If even secular communist sympathizers had awoken to the Soviet evil, why had not Barth? Niebuhr felt it especially important to expose and denounce what he saw as, in Richard Fox's words, Barth's "cult of eschatological irresponsibility" that had such seductive appeal to many American seminarians and church leaders.[43]

Less prominent but no less outrageous was the Czech theologian Josef Hromadka, whom Niebuhr had first battled in Amsterdam in 1948. In the

---

[40] Niebuhr, "Seven Great Errors of U.S. Foreign Policy," *The New Leader*, 24–31 December 1956, 3–5.

[41] Niebuhr, "Filling the Middle East Vacuum," *Christianity and Crisis*, 21 January 1957, 189–190.

[42] Niebuhr, "Seven Great Errors of U.S. Foreign Policy," *The New Leader*, 24–31 December 1956, 3–5.

[43] Niebuhr, "Filling the Middle East Vacuum," *Christianity and Crisis*, 21 January 1957, 189–190. Also Fox, 265.

intervening years, Hromadka had maintained his appeal and his influence in Western Protestant circles, serving on WCC committees and writing for theological journals. He had always kept an uneasy relationship with the Soviet bloc authorities. In the wake of the Budapest horror, however, Hromadka issued a statement criticizing the Hungarian revolt and defending the Soviet invasion. This was too much. John Bennett, Niebuhr's close friend and colleague at *Christianity and Crisis*, issued a stinging rebuke, saying Hromadka's attitude "reveals either extraordinary blindness to realities or it is the final exposure of a deliberate intention to rationalize every Russian move... it is hard to see how his many friends in the West... can again take seriously what he says."[44]

IV

Meanwhile, a new theological journal was watching closely these world crises and the religious divisions they provoked. *Christianity Today (CT)*, whose inaugural issue came out just two weeks before the eruptions in Egypt and Hungary, saw an opportunity to provide a thoughtful, sophisticated evangelical voice where none had been before. *CT* believed the Suez conflict "dramatizes the breakdown of international political morality." No actor stood untainted. While supporting Israel's right to exist, the editorial criticized Israel for being "ruthless and aggressive" towards Palestinian refugees. It dismissed the "Anglo-French approach" as merely "the power politics of the past." And while, unlike Niebuhr, *CT* applauded Eisenhower's pressure on the British and French through the UN, the editorial also worried that the Administration was too reluctant to use military force, and placed "an excessive trust in the power of colossal human organization, in the United Nations as the potent resolver of all major world disputes."[45] *CT* responded to Hungary with much more vigor. "A slap on the wrist is not the answer to what Russia has done in Hungary. Expulsion from the United Nations, with its accompanying disintegrating effect on world Communism, is the least Christians should demand."[46]

Just what was this audacious new journal, and from where did it come? Born out of a quintessentially American amalgam of conservative theology and free-market economics, of denominational fissures and evangelical unity, and of the theological genius of Carl Henry, the organizational energy of L. Nelson

44 John C. Bennett, "A Matter for Regret," *Christianity and Crisis*, 21 January 1957, 190.
45 "International Crisis on the Sandy Wastes of Sinai," *Christianity Today*, 12 November 1956.
46 "Christian Responsibility and Communist Brutality," *Christianity Today*, 26 November 1956.

Bell, the burgeoning celebrity of Billy Graham, and the limitless checkbook of J. Howard Pew, *Christianity Today* could not be ignored. Yet even its founders seemed to differ on its purposes. In an initial letter to Pew appealing for financial support, Bell declared that "the greatest single need in Protestantism is a voice which speaks with authority...based on God's inspired Word." Bell immodestly hoped that "this magazine could become the greatest single influence for changing the entire course of Protestant Christianity."[47] Graham shared his father-in-law's focus on theological orthodoxy as the magazine's raison d'être. Writing to Pew from Scotland during a series of evangelistic crusades, Graham lamented the European origins of much of American theological liberalism, and declared his core mission for the magazine: "we must get the clergy changed." However, no doubt casting an eye towards Pew's own proclivities, Graham also lamented the trend of American universities that had been founded on Protestant orthodoxy to "degenerate into secular, pagan, and socialistic institutions, due to the fact that the founding fathers lost control."

Determined that this fate would not befall his journal, Graham pledged his abiding commitment "to see that this vision that I believe is from God carried out and properly controlled." To that end he suggested an "inner board of directors" consisting of himself and a select few, including Pew, Bell, and Ockenga, to be "a silent, non-published group of men who actually control the magazine."[48] Graham and Bell also shared their vision with Rev. Edward Elson of National Presbyterian Church, whose friends and parishioners included Eisenhower and Dulles. Elson promised his enthusiastic support for the magazine, since "we genuinely need an intelligent antidote to one or two other journals."[49] *CT*'s founders of course agreed with Elson's thinly-veiled aversion to the *Christian Century* and its ilk, and they prized the endorsement of the President's pastor.

Aside from their occasional digs against "socialism," Bell and Graham primarily conceived of *CT* as a theological journal for pastors, presenting a winsome, erudite template of conservative Protestantism. But Pew had a much different focus. Fed up with the economic liberalism of mainline magazines and organizations such as the NCC, the Sun Oil Company chairman pledged

---

[47]   January 14, 1955 letter from Bell to Pew; Bell Papers, Box 41, Folder 17; BGCA.
[48]   April 13, 1955 letter from Graham to Pew; Bell Papers, Box 41, Folder 17; BGCA.
[49]   May 10, 1955 letter from Elson to Bell; Bell Papers, Box 24, Folder 11; BGCA. Elson later claimed that he lost the 1956 election for moderator (equivalent to president) of the General Assembly of the Presbyterian Church because of suspicions and resentments among many Presbyterians over Elson's ties to *CT* and Pew. See Elson, *Wide Was His Parish* (Wheaton, IL: Tyndale House 1986), 128–129. For more on Elson, see chapters six and seven of this book.

$150,000 per year to *CT* in the hope that it would enthusiastically promote Christianity and free enterprise. Pew had previously chaired an NCC laymen's committee designed to restrain that organization's political liberalism. With the committee now disbanded and the NCC still hopelessly left-wing, he believed he had found in *CT* a new and potentially more effective platform. In appealing to a fellow industrialist to help fund the magazine, Pew lamented that while only 30% of American Protestant clergy were either "ideological Communists . . . Socialists, [or] . . . various shades of pink," this minority controlled "the machinery of our denominations" and the NCC. A new voice was needed to sound the political views of the "majority" of clergy and laity, and Pew believed *CT* was the answer.[50]

Pew feared, and perhaps for good reason, that Carl F.H. Henry, the editor selected by Graham and Bell to steer the new magazine, did not share his agenda. Brilliant, ambitious, polemical, and unflagging in his zeal for the evangelical cause, Henry brought to his new post two earned doctorates in philosophy and theology and several years of experience as a professor at the movement's flagship school, Fuller Theological Seminary in California. Henry had first come to prominence in 1947 with the publication of *The Uneasy Conscience of Modern Fundamentalism*, in which he chastised fundamentalism for neglecting the social imperatives of the Christian message. While in full accord with Graham and Bell's theological convictions, Henry also saw *CT* as a vehicle "to apply the Biblical revelation vigorously to the contemporary social crisis, by presenting the implications of the total Gospel message in every area of life."[51]

Such sentiments only stirred Pew's suspicions. Bell sought to assuage their patron's concerns, writing to Pew on the eve of the inaugural issue that "it is most unfortunate that a question should have injected into your mind with reference to Dr. Henry, for he does *not* have socialistic tendencies."[52] This did not seem to appease Pew. He then suggested that board members, including

[50] April 17, 1956 letter from Pew to Bell; June 25, 1956 letter from Pew to L. E. Faulkner of Mississippi Central Railroad Company; Bell Papers, Box 41, Folder 17; BGCA. For more on Pew, see Michael S. Hamilton and Johanna G. Yngvason, "Patrons of the Evangelical Mind," *Christianity Today*, 8 July 2002.

[51] "Christianity Today: Statement of Policy and Purpose," 1956 brochure; *Christianity Today* Papers (hereinafter CT Papers); Box 15, Folder 11; BGCA. Carl F. H. Henry, *The Uneasy Conscience of Modern Fundamentalism* (Grand Rapids, MI: Eerdmans 1947). For more on Henry, see George Marsden, *Reforming Fundamentalism: Fuller Seminary and the New Evangelicalism* (Grand Rapids, MI: Eerdmans 1987) and Carl F. H. Henry, *Confessions of a Theologian: An Autobiography* (Waco, TX: Word Books 1986).

[52] September 4, 1956 letter from Bell to Pew; CT Papers, Box 1, Folder 57; BGCA. Emphasis original.

himself, have the right to review each issue before publication. Now it was Graham's turn at pacification. "I do not think that our three editors are going to allow anything to appear in the magazine that will conflict with our views on economics and socialism," he assured Pew. "However, I do not believe we can expect them to submit . . . each issue before it goes to print. It would be like a minister submitting his manuscript to his elders before preaching it."[53]

Had it been public, this dispute would only have confirmed the presumptions of Niebuhr and Bennett, who had viewed with ambivalence the new journal's birth. Niebuhr did not disguise his distaste for Graham. On learning in early 1956 of the evangelist's plans to hold a series of crusades in New York, Niebuhr noted smugly that "we dread the prospect." He lambasted Graham for combining "demagogic gifts with a rather obscurantist version of the Christian faith."[54] After reading a CT prospectus, Bennett was hardly more welcoming. He dismissed Bell as "one of the most intransigently conservative leaders" of the Presbyterian Church, and declared that while Pew may be "sincere," the tycoon "wrongly identifies Christianity with his own version of economic individualism." Bennett praised Henry, however, for his "sophisticated and irenic theological conservatism" and his concern with Christianity's social dimension. Hence the problem. Bennett cautioned that Henry's differences in emphasis and temperament from Pew and Bell could "cause the enterprise to fall apart."[55] Even Niebuhr preferred Graham when compared with Pew and Bell, commenting to a friend that "I honestly believe that [Graham] is better than his backers."[56]

The neo-evangelicals relished this attention, even if critical, and saw a chance to contend on the gridiron of respectability against their opponents in the ranks of Christian realism. In response to Niebuhr's complaints and in anticipation of Graham's upcoming evangelistic campaign in New York City, theologian and Fuller Seminary President E. J. Carnell issued a challenge in the pages of CT titled "Can Billy Graham Slay the Giant?" The "giant," of course, was Niebuhr, New York's most towering Protestant figure. And Carnell was no mere benighted critic. The author of a scholarly book and articles on Niebuhr's theology, Carnell "cheerfully acknowledge[d] a personal

---

53 September 27, 1956 letter from Graham to Pew; Bell Papers, Box 41, Folder 17; BGCA.
54 Niebuhr, "Editorial Notes," *Christianity and Crisis*, 5 March 1956, 18–19.
55 Bennett, "The Resourceful Mr. Pew," *C & C*, 11 June 1956, 75. Bennett's concerns proved prophetic, as twelve years later in 1968 Henry would be forced to resign as editor-in-chief, in large part at Pew's behest. For more on this, see Henry, *Confessions of a Theologian.*
56 June 20, 1956 letter from Niebuhr to Theodore McGill; RN Papers, Box 16, Folder: "A Proposal for Billy Graham"; LOC. For more on the tensions between Niebuhr and Graham, et al., see Mark Silk, *Spiritual Politics: Religion and America Since World War II* (New York: Touchstone 1988), 101–107.

indebtedness" to Niebuhr, whose writings revealed to Carnell "the power and pretense of sin in my own life." However, Carnell saw a crucial difference between Graham's orthodoxy and Niebuhr's realism. "Orthodoxy mediates problems of man and history from the perspective of Scripture, while realism mediates problems of Scripture from the perspective of man and history." To Carnell, this was not just academic trifling. "When it comes to the acid test" of personal faith, "realism is not very realistic after all. A concrete view of sin converts to an abstract view of salvation." Niebuhr might speak of Christ's cross and resurrection as "symbols" instead of literal realities, "but of what value are these symbols to an anxious New York cabby?" In the final analysis, Carnell suggested ironically, evangelical orthodoxy was more "realistic" than Christian realism.[57]

The new magazine sought to distinguish itself not just on matters of theology but on foreign policy as well. Henry's lead editorial in the inaugural issue addressed "The Fragility of Freedom in the West." In a searching inquiry into the nature of order, liberty, and human civilization, he tapped the roots of the Cold War conflict and found the West wanting. Communist totalitarianism was diabolical, of course, and must be defeated. But what of the alternative? "The West's concept of liberty is indefinite and fuzzy," and too often consists only of individual license. Absent a more robust, transcendent political vision, "freedom deteriorates until democracy becomes a struggle for factional advantage, free enterprise becomes animal competition, capitalism become economic imperialism." This was just the sort of language that Pew had feared. Moreover, "without personal freedom over the enslaving power of immorality in individual life, national and social freedoms still leave the soul a vacuum, and . . . provide an invitation to the Soviet orbit of ideas." The only solution Henry saw was for a recovery of religious truth in public life. "The vindication of a supernatural order of truth and goodness is therefore prerequisite to the vindication of the enduring value of democracy and human freedom." Henry shared with Niebuhr an affinity for ordered liberty as the only basis for full human flourishing and the common good. Yet he added a twist, connecting the traditional evangelical concern for individual salvation with the corporate crisis threatening the West. "The solution to the national problem of freedom is no different from the solution of the individual problem of freedom. Human freedom is a divine gift: Jesus Christ can restore it to a shackled generation."[58]

---

[57] Carnell, "Can Billy Graham Slay the Giant?" *CT*, 13 May 1957, 3–5. Carnell succeeded Ockenga as Fuller's President in 1954.

[58] Henry, "The Fragility of Freedom in the West," *CT*, 15 October 1956, 8–18.

Having, he hoped, established his and his journal's intellectual and theological credibility, Henry returned again and again to the Cold War. Almost every single issue of *CT* during its first year carried an editorial or feature article on foreign policy. The United Nations became a favored target of criticism. Whereas the NCC still regarded strengthening the UN as an antidote to much that ailed the world – and for all of his criticism of its pretensions and illusions, Niebuhr still considered the organization worthy of support – Henry and his cohorts found in it little redeeming value. He wrote a lengthy criticism of the UN's Universal Declaration of Human Rights because it "incorporates no references to a supernatural Creator, nor does it anywhere assert that God endows mankind with specific rights" and it consequently "neglects the equally important subject of human duties."[59] He noted with disdain the emergence under India's leadership of the "neutralist" African–Asian bloc of voting nations, with the result that the UN considered "sanctions against Israel while declining to employ them against Russia." This bloc, coupled with the USSR's promiscuous use of its veto power, meant that control of the UN "now rests in the hands of nations totally lacking in the moral and spiritual concepts basic in the Judeo-Christian heritage."[60] The next month found Henry even more despondent. After detailing a litany of perceived problems in the UN, from vitriolic debates to gridlocked initiatives to the widespread acceptance of communist propaganda to "the lack of moral basis," Henry concluded bitterly that the UN "has been a tragedy in which the world, by the passion of limitations of its diplomats, is being brought to the brink of catastrophe."[61]

In addition to their aversion to the UN, Henry and many evangelicals were also skeptical of foreign aid. This was not a reflexive isolationism, however. While supporting American involvement abroad, Henry feared that U.S. aid dollars had not been effective because the programs were "largely shaped in the absence of Christian principles" and were detached "from an overarching philosophy of individual and international well-being." Too often, he worried, American money was dispensed with a secular–liberal presumption that human needs could be met by material assistance alone. Moreover, he criticized the United States Information Agency (USIA) and Voice of America (VOA) for "esteeming religion for sheer purposes of propaganda." While lauding Elton Trueblood's leadership in incorporating religion into

---

[59] Henry, "Human Rights in an Age of Tyranny," *CT*, 4 February 1957, 20–22.
[60] Henry, "Spiritual-Moral Unity Wanes in United Nations," *CT*, 4 March 1957, 21–22.
[61] Henry, "UN: Town Meeting? Or Tragedy?", *CT*, 1 April 1957, 20–22.

USIA programs, Henry was appalled at a recent bulletin that had effectively affirmed Mohammed as a true prophet and Islam as an admirable faith. "Non-Christian religion is flattered and encouraged, and the tax-supported policy of the American government casts weight against the Christian witness of American foreign missionaries." To Henry, this smacked of reducing religion to "what is diplomatically serviceable" rather than truly respecting "spiritual priorities."[62] The Cold War did shift Henry's thinking towards other faiths in one important area, in which he also seemed to depart from his more strident colleagues at the NAE. He informed *CT*'s board that he did not consider Catholicism to be as much of a threat as communism, "for despite Rome's religious totalitarianism, it stands on the side of an objective moral order and is anti-communist."[63]

A *CT* survey of Protestant ministers on the eve of the 1956 election reinforced the new journal's interest in foreign affairs. Noting that the pastors responding favored Eisenhower over Adlai Stevenson by a margin of eight to one (though *CT*'s readership, more conservative theologically and politically, should hardly be taken as a representative sample of clerical opinion), the editorial speculated that Eisenhower's popularity "sprang from his identification with an attitude of faith in God and in objective moral norms more than sheer party considerations." When asked about policy concerns, almost every category of clergy focused on "an improved foreign policy" as "the greatest imperative." Pastors divided sharply over whether to increase or decrease involvement in the UN, and while most favored reducing foreign aid, a noticeable minority favored increasing it. More generally, pastors overwhelmingly advocated a more "aggressive spiritual-moral international policy," though again, aside from discontent with mere *realpolitik* and power-balancing, there was little agreement on just what form this more idealistic foreign policy would take. In a none too subtle dig at the mainline denominational hierarchies, the editorial concluded that the poll "dramatizes the risk of attempting to express 'the position' of a denomination ... on political and economic issues."[64] And if any officials in the Eisenhower Administration were paying attention, they probably concluded that they needed to bolster their efforts to frame American foreign policy in spiritual terms. American churchgoers were listening.

---

[62] Henry, "The Spirit of Foreign Policy," *CT*, 29 April, 20–22. For more on Trueblood, see chapter seven of this book.

[63] Henry, May 28, 1957 Report to the Board; CT Papers, Box 1, Folder 3; BGCA. At the time most Protestants regarded Catholicism as another "faith" entirely.

[64] Editorial, "Where Do We Go From Here?" *CT*, 12 November 1956.

V

The American government's geopolitical strategy may have been most focused on the Soviet Union, but American Christians showed disproportionate concern for China. Not that they disregarded the USSR; indeed, most American Christians would likely have agreed that Soviet communism posed the gravest threat to their nation and to the world. Yet China retained a curious, enchanting fixation in the hearts of many Americans to a degree that outweighed its strategic importance – at least its importance in the minds of most policy-makers. The long history of American missionaries active in China, its exotic status as a distant, mysterious civilization, and the revolutionary ferment of China's recent past all combined to make this Eastern land endlessly fascinating. Shared passion did not imply shared agreement, however. The U.S.–China relationship engendered some of the most heated debates and bitter divisions within American Protestantism. These only served to make China all the more problematic for policy-makers, who dreaded touching this proverbial "third rail," knowing full well that whatever position they took, they risked incurring the spiritual indignation of some sector of Christendom.

Evangelicals in general fiercely opposed the Chinese communist government, maintaining unswerving loyalty to Chiang Kai-shek and the Kuomintang (KMT). The Chiangs' profession of Christian faith no doubt accounted for much of their appeal. Bell, a former medical missionary to China, wrote to Madame Chiang in 1956 describing himself and Billy Graham as some of "General Chiang's most ardent admirers here in America. . . . You and the General are constantly in our prayers and thoughts, and we thank God for your clear Christian testimony and for your unswerving stand for righteousness."[65]

Chiang was not the only Nationalist leader who identified himself as a Christian. Bell and Henry cultivated a relationship with Hollington K. Tong, the KMT Ambassador to the United States, and published several articles by Tong in CT. After one meeting with Tong, Bell wrote appreciatively, "I found in you a true Christian brother, a fellowship which bridges all else."[66] Tong for his part seems to have realized that these evangelicals formed a vital base of support for the KMT government. In one article for CT on "Christianity in China," Tong declared that "most of the important government leaders"

---

[65] September 4, 1956 letter from Bell to Madame Chiang Kai-shek; Bell Papers, Box 18, Folder 15; BGCA.

[66] June 7, 1956 letter from Bell to Tong; Bell Papers, Box 52, Folder 17; BGCA.

on Taiwan "are professing Christians." Tong compared this with the brutal and systematic persecution suffered by Christians under Mao Zedong. He concluded with a promise sure to tantalize his American Christian readers. The Nationalists would eventually return to govern the mainland, and "once we are back, we shall give Christianity the first place in our religious activities." While the KMT would guarantee freedom for all faiths, "those who will direct the affairs of state will be largely Christians."[67] Tong repeated a similar message to the Presidential Prayer Breakfast gathering in Washington, in a speech titled "How Communism Wars on Christianity."[68] While Tong no doubt had some political motives for his dramatic contrasts between the PRC's communism and the KMT's Christianity, he also appears to have had a sincere Christian commitment. Following his diplomatic career, he and his wife returned to Taiwan to work as full-time missionaries.[69]

    CT proved a reliable critic of the PRC and supporter of the Nationalists. Among many such articles published was one by Senate Republican Leader William F. Knowland (not known as an evangelical) arguing against giving diplomatic recognition to the PRC or admitting it to the UN, followed by a stern CT editorial along the same lines. The editorial, likely written by Bell, hyperbolically described the recognition question as "the greatest political and moral problem" in American foreign policy. Detailing a litany of communist atrocities in contrast with the high standards necessary for diplomatic recognition, the editorial apocalyptically warned that "recognition would mean the triumph of cruel and cunning men who are plotting the destruction of human liberties everywhere."[70] CT determined to hold American foreign policy to a high standard of idealism and morality, pragmatic considerations notwithstanding.

    China also provided the evangelicals an opportunity to tweak their mainline adversaries – and perhaps show the U.S. government that liberal Protestantism was not to be trusted. One dispute began in early January 1957, when Clyde Taylor of the NAE wrote to Dulles complaining of the NCC's alleged plans to pressure the State Department to allow American churchmen to visit the PRC and meet with Chinese clergy in Beijing's government-controlled Protestant organization. This was the religious equivalent of granting diplomatic recognition. Moreover, Taylor accused these Chinese clergy of collaborating

---

[67] Tong, "Christianity in China," CT, 21 January 1957, 10–13.
[68] Tong, "How Communism Wars on Christianity," February 7, 1957 speech to International Christian Leadership, Washington DC; CT Papers, Box 16, Folder 23; BGCA.
[69] May 28, 1961 letter from Tong to Henry; CT Papers, Box 16, Folder 23; BGCA.
[70] "Red China and World Morality," CT, 10 December 1956, 20–22.

with the regime and betraying other Chinese Christians.[71] *CT* echoed these concerns in a stern editorial two weeks later. "Is it judicious for American churchmen to go abroad and confer recognition and dignity upon foreign churchmen standing in cordial relations with a regime that has martyred and imprisoned hosts of believers?" The editorial then paralleled the theological and political convictions of Chinese Christians, concluding "the evangelical spirit in China has gone to prison and martyrdom, whereas the liberal spirit is the moving force in the pro-Communist ecclesiastical thrust."[72] These purported connections between liberal theology and liberal politics, at home and abroad, only fueled evangelical hostility.

Foggy Bottom seemed to agree. State Department official Walter McConaughy replied on behalf of Dulles to Taylor's letter. McConaughy thanked Taylor for his "very helpful letter," and reiterated State's "efforts to discourage travel by American citizens" to the PRC. Moreover, McConaughy lauded the NAE for seeing through "the Chinese Communists' motive in encouraging the travel of certain American citizens to Communist China." But the question remains of whether the NCC really wanted to send a delegation to China or not. An NCC spokesman denied that any "official action" had been taken for such a visit, saying that only a small study committee had recommended it.[73] Wallace Merwin, chairman of the NCC's China Executive Committee, sent indignant letters to Taylor and to the editorial board at *CT* asserting the same, that the NCC had not given official approval for a China trip, and that while it was frequently discussed, the missionary community did "not feel that the American churches should propose such a visit at this time."[74]

Though technically accurate, Merwin's letters were not fully forthcoming. Just two days before replying to Taylor, Merwin had sent a confidential memo to NCC General Secretary Roy G. Ross detailing the China Committee's ongoing planning for "interchange of visits" with Chinese leaders.[75] John Mackay, Bell's nemesis on all things related to China, also wrote urging the NCC to send a delegation to the PRC. Ross put off any decision, uncomfortable with how charged the issue had become.[76] His colleague Roswell Barnes tried

---

[71]   Religion News Service (RNS) wire story, "State Dept. Opposes Visit of Clergymen to China," 2 February 1957. Also January 30, 1957 letter from McConaughy to Taylor; NCC Papers, RG 4, Box 17, Folder 18; PHS.

[72]   "Conversations with Chinese Christians," *CT*, 21 January 1957, 20–23.

[73]   RNS wire story.

[74]   February 20, 1957 letter from Merwin to Taylor; February 26, 1957 letter from Merwin to Editors of *CT*; NCC Papers, RG 4, Box 17, Folder 18; PHS.

[75]   February 18, 1957 memo from Merwin to Ross; NCC Papers, RG 4, Box 17, Folder 18; PHS.

[76]   February 23, 1957 letter from Mackay to Ross; March 4, 1957 letter from Ross to Mackay; NCC Papers, RG 4, Box 17, Folder 18; PHS.

damage control, complaining to the State Department that McConaughy's letter had only inflamed the issue, even though no NCC committee had yet made an official resolution favoring a China trip.[77] Two months later the China Executive Committee did just that, urging "private approaches to the State Department at the highest level" to secure permission for an NCC delegation to visit China.[78] Though quite annoyed with its evangelical rivals, the NCC determined to press ahead with its own foreign policy vision. The evangelicals, meanwhile, reveled in their newfound agreement with the State Department. And this squabble among church groups over China policy foreshadowed the eruption that was soon to come.

1957 also witnessed a sharpening Protestant debate over American nuclear policy. Mainline Protestants initiated the discussions with a series of pronouncements issued jointly by the WCC and the CCIA. Meeting in July and August of 1957 at Yale Divinity School, the WCC/CCIA committees urged all nations to halt "the testing of nuclear weapons and . . . the production of nuclear weapons." Lest its recommendations be dismissed as naïve idealism, the report also called for an effective verification system, and conceded that "partial disarmament" measures would be acceptable steps towards the ultimate goal, as the WCC put it, of "the abolition of war itself."[79] A delegation including CCIA Executive Director Nolde and NCC official Roswell Barnes met with Dulles the next month to present him with the statement. Nolde reported with some disappointment that while Dulles expressed agreement with the statement's broad goals, he had emphasized that the U.S. Government and its allies believed further testing was still needed.[80]

The WCC/CCIA report caught the attention of Carl Henry as well. *Christianity Today* for its first year had generally refrained from extensive comment on nuclear matters, but no longer. His metaphysical fancy seized, Henry began a lead editorial with the grandiose premise that "to preserve the universe from capitulating to pagan views of origin and existence, each generation must delineate and declare the relationship between Christ and the atom." The twentieth-century mind was held captive by the philosophies of naturalism and materialism, which denied the divine origins of life and left only

[77] March 12, 1957 letter from Barnes to McConaughy; NCC Papers, RG 4, Box 17, Folder 18; PHS.
[78] Confidential Supplement to Minutes of China Executive Committee Meeting, June 10, 1957; NCC Papers, RG 4, Box 21, Folder 15; PHS.
[79] "Atomic Tests and Disarmament" Statement of CCIA Executive Committee and WCC Central Committee, 24 July 1957 and 5 August 1957; WCC Papers, RG 162, Box 20, Folder 145; See also "Disarmament and Nuclear Tests," a compendium of CCIA and WCC statements from 1954 to 1960; WCC Papers, RG 162, Box 20, Folder 145; YDSA.
[80] Nolde, August 13, 1958 report on actions taken on "Atomic Tests and Disarmament" Statements; WCC Papers, RG 162, Box 20, Folder 145; YDSA.

sinister uses for scientific discoveries such as atomic energy. But Henry called for thinking "beyond . . . nuclear energy to the higher principle of the spiritual purposes of the universe." On how precisely to integrate the bomb with these "spiritual purposes," however, Henry was unclear. He quickly turned instead to the WCC/CCIA report, complaining that once again, in attempting to speak for "the Church," these organizations had ascribed "to multitudes of parishioners opinions which they as individuals do not in fact entertain," and consequently had gone "beyond the scope of the Church's legitimate function." Even worse, in calling for an end to testing, the report "actually supported present Soviet Russian policy" and supplied "a tremendous asset to the Russians in their present jockeying for world sympathy." Defending the right and even divine responsibility of the U.S. Government to maintain order and restrain evil through an effective military deterrent, Henry reminded "modern man" that the only hope for "peaceful existence in these dark decades lies in the recognition of the lordship of Christ . . . and in the dedication of the atom and the atom bomb to the service of righteousness and love."[81] Henry was most clear and most effective in his political and theological critique of the mainline Protestant hierarchy. When attempting to sacralize nuclear energy, however, he left his readers confused, and his authority diminished.

Niebuhr also took notice of this debate, in discussions both within Protestantism and between the American and Soviet governments. Dispensing with the theoretical musings and lofty rhetoric that abounded on all sides, he simply noted that the prevailing disarmament proposals and negotiations "are bound to fail." This was true for the "*a priori* reason" that "international tensions are not mitigated by disarmament, but disarmament is made possible by the relaxation of tensions."[82] Niebuhr was no apologist for nuclear weapons, however, which horrified him with their apocalyptic power. "There is obviously no security in the armaments which our realists so insistently commend, nor in the disarmament proposals which intrigue the idealists." The bomb served as protector and peril, an ironic burden that promised the only effective defense against Soviet malfeasance – if it did not first destroy the planet. The United States, Niebuhr argued, needed to bear this burden humbly and responsibly, while demonstrating to the watching world the relative wisdom of the American way.[83]

[81] Henry, "Christ and the Atom Bomb," *CT*, 2 September 1957, 20–22.
[82] Niebuhr, "The Dismal Prospects for Disarmament," *Christianity and Crisis*, 16 September 1957, 113–114.
[83] Niebuhr, "The Moral Insecurity of Our Security," *C&C*, 6 January 1958, 177–178.

American Protestantism had now frayed into three distinctive strands on foreign policy. All three traditions contested the right to speak authoritatively *to* Protestants on questions of public policy, and to speak *for* Protestants in the public square. Two of these factions came from within the mainline ranks: the liberal idealism of the NCC and WCC hierarchies, and the realism of Niebuhr and his allies. This split developed in part from Niebuhr's diminished involvement with the mainline organizations. His active leadership on these commissions in the 1940s and early 1950s had formed significantly the more "realistic," anticommunist posture they had sometimes embraced but by now had abandoned. Increasingly outnumbered by those who did not share his views, and further debilitated by ongoing health maladies and periodic bouts with depression, Niebuhr gradually withdrew as a presence in the mainline hierarchy. Meanwhile, the rise of evangelicalism now gave Protestantism a third voice.

The mainline organizations embraced a liberal platform that downplayed the Soviet threat, praised the United Nations, and focused on peace, negotiations, and disarmament. They rather consistently criticized the Eisenhower Administration. Niebuhr and his small cohort of "Christian realists" counseled vigilance against Soviet communism and the need for military strength, but also called for more assistance to the developing world and cooperation with the United Nations. Niebuhr kept a critical distance from Eisenhower and Dulles, frequently castigating their rhetoric and specific policies while coming to a grudging admiration of their efforts to maintain order in a dangerous world. And while Niebuhr did not preside over the vast organizational or denominational networks of the mainline and the evangelicals, his public prominence gave him a disproportionate influence as a distinctive voice. The evangelicals had emerged as ardent conservatives, advocating a strong defense, militant opposition to global communism, and promotion of "Judeo-Christian values." They generally supported Eisenhower and his foreign policy. All camps agreed on the need for a "Christian" foreign policy; none agreed on what that would mean.

VI

These Protestants illustrated their different approaches in another series of foreign policy crises in the Middle and Far East in 1958. Seeking to avert the destabilizing spread of Nasser's pan-Arab nationalism, Eisenhower deployed American troops in Lebanon to deter any efforts to topple the pro-Western Lebanese government. The British did likewise in Jordan, while both the United States and UK looked on in dismay as a coup in Iraq brought a more

Arabist – and thus less savory – regime to power. Mao, meanwhile, took American preoccupations in the Middle East as an opportunity to ratchet up pressure on Taiwan, and PRC artillery began once again re-arranging the landscapes of its perennial targets, Quemoy and Matsu. Eisenhower and Dulles responded with a series of warnings backed up by the conspicuous presence of the Seventh Fleet.

True to form, the CCIA issued a resolution on the Middle East that did little more than call on the governments involved to work out their differences through the UN.[84] Likewise with the China crisis; NCC President Edwin Dahlberg wrote to Eisenhower urging "negotiations" instead of "military might" in dealing with the PRC. Not surprisingly, this approach irked the evangelicals. *CT* disparaged Dahlberg's letter with the skeptical question, "Churchmanship or Effrontery?" and then sketched out a different approach based on the perceived linkage of events. Dismissing the fact that Quemoy was so much closer to the mainland than to Taiwan, the editorial asserted, "the basic consideration is not geography but principle. The attack on Quemoy was decided two days after the United States landed troops in Lebanon. The maneuver is part of a pattern of aggression. . . . Standing for Quemoy could *prevent* a war, not start one."[85] For his part, Niebuhr found much to lament and almost nothing to praise. He described "this whole series of events" in the Middle East as a "major disaster for United States' foreign policy." Niebuhr focused on the larger dynamics at play. America needed to "contain" Nasser and his imperialistic "pan-Arab supranationalism," as well as checking the increase of Soviet influence in the Arab world. This could not be done through mere negotiations or military power, but only through a wholesale strategic overhaul of the Western presence in the Middle East.[86] Concerning Asia, Niebuhr's colleague and former China missionary M. Searle Bates penned a lead editorial for *C&C*. He defended Eisenhower and Dulles against liberal church critics who discounted the communist threat and demanded that only the United States make concessions. Yet Bates also chastened the Administration for what he saw as its inconsistent policies and its failure to understand the strategic perspective of the PRC. Bates admitted that the crisis held no simple solutions, but he and his fellow Christian realists thought the United States could be much more consistent and sophisticated

[84] CCIA "Resolution on the Middle East," August 15–19, 1958; WCC Papers, RG 162, Box 20, Folder 145; YDSA.
[85] September 9, 1958 letter from Dahlberg to Eisenhower; Bell Papers, Box 39, Folder 3; BGCA. "Don't Let the Geography Confuse You," *CT*, 27 October 1958, 21. Emphasis original.
[86] Niebuhr, "Disaster in United States Foreign Policy," *C&C*, 15 September 1958, 117–118.

in countering the communist threat without supporting Chiang in gratuitous provocations.[87]

Cleveland may seem an unlikely locale for heated ecclesial controversy – especially when compared with the historic church debates symbolized by cities such as Rome, Constantinople, Wittenberg, and Geneva – but it was this unassuming Ohio city that witnessed yet another eruption of Protestant acrimony in November 1958. The occasion was the NCC's fifth "World Order Study Conference." The gathering began auspiciously enough with a keynote address by Dulles, who gave a vigorous defense of U.S. policy and critique of communism.[88] Conference delegates then immersed themselves in four days of panels, discussions, and meetings, after which they produced a consensus report that departed markedly from prevailing American foreign policy. This "Message to the Churches" called not only for a suspension of nuclear testing but for "universal disarmament," for the abolition of the military draft, and for respecting "neutral" countries rather than pressuring them to align with the Western bloc. On communism, the delegates called for finding "ways of living with the communist nations," combining "competition between ways of life with cooperation for limited objectives." In a pointed rebuke to Eisenhower and especially Dulles, the report declared "we should avoid the posture of general hostility to [communist nations] and cease the practice of continual moral lectures to them by our leaders."

To conservatives, these resolutions alone would have been enough to declare the NCC apostate, but it was the very next paragraph in the Message that ignited the subsequent firestorm. Not surprisingly, the topic was China. "Christians should urge reconsideration by our government of its policy in regard to the People's Republic of China . . . steps should be taken towards the inclusion of the [PRC] in the United Nations and for its recognition by our government." The delegates may have hastened to add that "such recognition does not imply approval," but the agenda was clear, and the deed was done.[89] The NCC seemed aware of its significance; the first page of the NCC's own press release described its "calls for major changes in current United States foreign policy" and specified the China recommendation as one of particular import.[90]

Swift, and furious, came the evangelical reaction. As soon as he learned of the NCC Message, Herbert Mekeel, president of the NAE, sent a statement to

---

[87] Bates, "Straits that are Desperate," *C&C*, 13 October 1958, 137–138.

[88] NCC Press Release, November 26, 1958; CT Papers, Box 4, Folder 3; BGCA.

[89] "Christian Responsibility on a Changing Planet," Message to the Churches adopted by the Fifth World Order Study Conference, 1958; NCC Papers, RG 6, Box 27, Folder 23; PHS.

[90] NCC Press Release, November 26, 1958; CT Papers, Box 4, Folder 3; BGCA.

Dulles that he also released to the press. Denouncing the Cleveland report's "left wing clichés" and "typical Communist 'soft' approach," Mekeel catalogued "Red China's" record of malfeasance, domestic and international, and warned that any assistance to the PRC would render America "morally and spiritually bankrupt." He also reassured Dulles, and any other readers, of a perennial theme: the NCC statement "does not represent the true sentiment of masses of members of American churches" either within or outside of the NCC.[91] *CT* took this one step further, publishing an editorial blasting the NCC's "misleading and spurious statement," and dismissing the contention that "recognition and admission into the family of nations has a reformatory effect," noting that the American recognition of the USSR in 1933 had yet to produce any improvement in Soviet behavior.[92] L. Nelson Bell was apoplectic. He wrote a series of indignant letters to the likes of Henry Luce, Walter Judd, Pew, Van Dusen, and evangelical missionary leaders, denouncing the NCC and urging action. Referring to his twenty-five years in China, Bell warned that recognition "could have the gravest possible consequences for the Church and for the free world." Judd shared Bell's outrage, both at the NCC's position and at the impression it gave of speaking for all American Protestants. He warned Bell that the NCC had been "infiltrated" by communists, making it all the more important for churches to speak out on their own, and not through NCC channels. Judd had already joined prominent clergy such as Norman Vincent Peale and Daniel Poling in sending a letter to 50,000 Protestant clergy denouncing the NCC and warning against recognizing the PRC. Bell likewise, and with great satisfaction, informed Pew that respondents to a *CT* poll had by eight to one rejected the NCC positions on China.[93]

Unlike some earlier such controversies, this one did not abate quickly. Three months after Cleveland, the NCC General Board met in Hartford, Connecticut and issued its "Hartford Appeal" to all American churches (not just NCC member churches). Bemoaning the fierce response to its Cleveland message, the NCC complained that it had "repeatedly been charged by enemies and criticized by worried friends as being soft towards communism." Somewhat defensively, the NCC upheld its "right and duty" to speak out on issues of

---

91   NAE Press Release, November 24, 1958; CT Papers, Box 4, Folder 3; BGCA.
92   "NCC World Order Policy Softens on Red China," *CT*, 22 December 1958, 22.
93   November 25, 1958 letter from Bell to Van Dusen; Bell Papers, Box 53, Folder 3; December 16, 1958 letter from Bell to Dr. C. Darby Fulton (Board of World Missions); Bell Papers, Box 39, Folder 3; December 20, 1958 letter from Bell to Luce; Bell Papers, Box 33, Folder 38; December 20, 1958 letter from Bell to Judd; December 23, 1958 letter from Judd to Bell; Bell Papers, Box 31, Folder 4; January 8, 1959 letter from Bell to Pew; CT Papers, Box 1, Folder 57; BGCA.

the day, and defined the central issue as the right of citizens to "express judgments, without exposure to attacks upon motive or integrity."[94] *CT* took great umbrage at the Hartford Appeal, accusing the NCC of shirking responsibility for its actions and of "following the example of left-wing organizations who raise the question of freedom of speech whenever the content of their pronouncements is questioned or criticized."[95]

On an official visit to Taiwan sponsored by the U.S. government the next year, NCC official Edwin Dahlberg faced a hostile gathering of American Protestant missionaries still steamed over the Cleveland report. Dahlberg's defense of it drew numerous protests from the missionaries, who charged that Dahlberg had "embarrassed" the missionary community and had abused his diplomatic immunity in advocating for the PRC while on "Free China soil."[96] A few months later, *CT* published an article by the renowned Swiss theologian Emil Brunner expressing his "utter alarm" at the Cleveland report and its disregard of the mortal threat posed by the "devilish system" of "world bolshevism."[97] Brunner's essay was notable not only for the timing of its publication (demonstrating that almost a year and half after its release, the Message was still under attack), but also because, as his *CT* byline noted, he was a "neo-orthodox" theologian similar to Karl Barth. Evangelicals at the time customarily regarded neo-orthodoxy as theologically errant and even dangerous; that they would welcome such a theologian into the pages of their flagship journal shows just how exercised they remained over Cleveland.

Niebuhr and "Christian realism" were largely absent from this debate. At the time of the Cleveland conference, he was on leave in Princeton, ostensibly working on a book but also severely debilitated by his continuing depression.[98] While he had for several years advocated the PRC's admission to the UN and been skeptical of U.S. support for the Nationalists, his views had never sparked much outrage. This was in part because he spoke only as an individual, and in part because his anticommunism was well known and likely insulated him from attack. Just as two decades later only a dedicated anticommunist such as Richard Nixon could "go to China," in the 1950s only Niebuhr could "recognize China." *C&C* did run an editorial by another editor, Wayne Cowan, which disparaged "reactionary Protestants" and the "primitive anti-Communist" feelings stirred up by Cleveland, and effectively endorsed

---

[94] "The Hartford Appeal," February 25, 1959; NCC Papers, RG 4, Box 25, Folder 19; PHS.
[95] "NCC Sidesteps Action on Cleveland Report," *CT*, 16 March 1959, 25–26.
[96] "NCC Head Pleads Red China's Case in Formosa," *CT*, 1 February 1960, 27.
[97] Brunner, "A Fresh Appraisal: The Cleveland Report on Red China," *CT*, 25 April 1960, 3–6.
[98] Fox, 267–269.

the Message.[99] Niebuhr's longtime *C&C* colleague, John Bennett, had actually been one of the leading architects of the Cleveland report, symbolizing Bennett's ongoing move away from a firm anticommunism to a more liberal outlook. But it would be only a small exaggeration to say that on matters of foreign policy, by 1959 a deep chasm had emerged separating Protestant evangelicalism from Protestant liberalism – and Christian realism was slipping into a void.

Cleveland further inflamed the debate over who spoke for American Protestantism. For fifteen years, evangelicals had been protesting that the mainline was not mainstream; that the NCC hierarchy was theologically and politically alienated from the average Protestant, both clergy and lay. As Niebuhr's moderating influence waned, a less restrained Protestant liberalism began to veer further left. The mainline leadership, while developing a grudging admiration for evangelical vitality and its occasional moments of sophistication, still suspected evangelicals of reactionary conservatism and anticommunist hysteria.

Henry's editorial broadside in the aftermath of Cleveland – "Why is NCC Prestige Sagging?" – did nothing to encourage any semblance of détente. Detailing the barrage of criticism leveled at the Cleveland conference from, variously, the U.S. Government (specifically, Dulles), Catholic leaders, other Protestant groups, Protestant journalists, laity, and even some of the NCC's own member communions (specifically, the Greek Orthodox Church), Henry concluded that "disregard of scriptural authority" accounted for the NCC's root problem. Not only did this neglect lead to "theological license," but it meant losing "the controlling principles of revealed ethics as well." Henry then suggested a more sinister factor behind the NCC's liberalism: "Communist infiltration of the churches is no idle dream; it is an announced Communist objective." This, along with Henry's reckless citation of a charge that "at least 105 of the 237 clergy registered for Cleveland have Communist affiliations," drew a sharp rebuke from Robert McAfee Brown in an editorial for *C&C*.[100] Accusing *CT* of employing "the old McCarthy technique" of imputing communist influences to its opponents, Brown dismissed the editorial as both unfair and dishonest.[101]

Besides differences over political matters, Protestants were divided over the more fundamental question of the church's role in public life. To the

---

[99] Cowan, "The Red China Discussion," *C&C*, 6 July 1959, 98–99.
[100] Henry, "Why is NCC Prestige Sagging?" *CT*, 2 February 1959, 5–8. See also February 16, 1959 letter from Bell to Pew; CT Papers, Box 1, Folder 57; BGCA.
[101] Brown, "Difference of Opinion vs. Distortion of Fact," *C&C*, 2 March 1959, 18–19.

evangelical mind, not only were the NCC's positions on specific issues incorrect, but the organization's propensity to speak out at all was ill-advised. Harold John Ockenga – longtime evangelical pastor of Boston's historic Park Street Congregational Church, founding president of Fuller Seminary, and *CT* board member – reminded his *CT* colleagues of the need to "differentiate between the corporate voice of the Church (for which the NCC has no mandate to speak), and the voice of *Christianity Today* or of a minister in his pulpit."[102] Bell tried repeatedly – though with little success – to make this point to Pew, who continued to fire barrages against the mainline for "destroying our American freedoms" and "planting the seeds of Socialism and Communism in the minds of many of the American people."[103] Before Pew was to meet with NCC leader Eugene Carson Blake, Bell coached the industrialist to "distinguish between those moral issues on which the Bible takes a clear stand, and on which the Church therefore can and should take a stand, and those fringe issues on which men of equal piety disagree." For example, said Bell, singling out some of Pew's favorite issues, "'right to work,' political policy, economic measures which mean inflation . . . come outside the duty and understanding of the Church as a corporate body. Here the Church should stick to *spiritual principles* and let the individual Christian take his stand at the ballot box."[104]

Nor did Bell think red-baiting was either right or helpful. Responding to an especially agitated NCC critic, Bell warned, "to say that the NCC is dominated by Communists is simply *untrue*. It is statements such as this which hurt our cause for the truth . . . the trouble is with the philosophy of the Church" held by the NCC.[105] Bell's greater concern was to distinguish the role of the church *qua* church from that of individual Christians – or individual magazines. Hence he criticized the NCC on both political and theological grounds, whereas he generally restricted his complaints about outlets such as the *Christian Century*

---

[102] Minutes of the Meeting of the Board of Directors of *Christianity Today*, January 6, 1959; CT Papers, Box 1, Folder 9; BGCA.

[103] May 15, 1959 letter from Pew to Bell (and copy of Pew's remarks for speech in Boston); CT Papers, Box 1, Folder 57; BGCA. This accusation of communist influence on the NCC was not just made by Pew. In a widely publicized controversy, the NCC protested vigorously upon learning in 1960 that a United States Air Force training manual contained a section describing the NCC as a Communist organization. Secretary of Defense Thomas Gates quickly apologized and had the manual recalled. For documents and correspondence on this episode, see NCC Papers, RG 4, Box 25, Folder 20; PHS.

[104] April 20, 1959 letter from Bell to Pew; CT Papers, Box 1, Folder 58; BGCA. Emphasis original.

[105] April 15, 1960 letter from Bell to J. H. Patterson; Bell Papers, Box 39, Folder 3; BGCA. Bell does not seem to have been as candid or direct in rebuking Pew's accusations of communist infiltration of the NCC. This may have been in part because of the sensitivities involved in Pew's funding of *CT*, which Bell did not want to jeopardize.

to its political views, since as a journal the *CC* was not subject to the same restraints as the church. This also enabled Bell (and Henry, and many other evangelicals) to justify their own political activism, or *CT*'s political stances, as being conducted in their own names, rather than in the name of the church. They did not always apply this standard equally, however, and sometimes conveniently failed to protest when the NAE issued its own resolutions on political matters.

Criticism of the NCC for failing in its task did not just come from the right. In November 1959, three leaders of the Episcopal Church, who sympathized with the theology and the politics of the NCC, sent a blistering letter to NCC President Dahlberg. The irked Episcopalians had attended the NCC's recent "Nationwide Program for Peace" conference in Washington. They had gathered with about 100 other denominational leaders and NCC officials for a day of meetings and presentations, including an audience with President Eisenhower. Describing themselves as "deeply disturbed," the Episcopalians questioned "whether it was a wise use of time (and money!) to bring a hundred people together to promote a study program." The NCC had focused too much on self-promotion and not enough on preparation, with the result that Eisenhower's remarks "showed little awareness of the announced purpose of our visit, beyond his rather typical endorsement of religion in the cause of Western foreign policy." The NCC's program and efforts, far from having any substance or influence, were "pathetic." Most pointedly, referring to Eisenhower's description of his recent conversation with the prominent Catholic leader Francis Cardinal Spellman of New York, the Episcopalians complained that "Cardinal Spellman unquestionably accomplished more by a 'long talk on the phone' than one hundred people in a captive audience." They concluded on a bitter note: "we deeply need to . . . stop congratulating ourselves on how 'successful' our programs are," and instead reconsider the entire approach of how to influence U.S. policy.[106]

Just what had Eisenhower said to this group? In extemporaneous remarks that were subsequently transcribed and released to the press, the President had warned the churchmen that America's great enemy was "a godless atheism . . . denying all human rights, any kind of human dignity." The United States, in contrast, needed to remember that its government, like "every type of free government, is a political expression of some form of religious belief." This provides the "strongest link that we have among all the countries of the West. Indeed I think this even includes the Mohammadens, the Buddhists and

---

[106] November 5, 1959 letter from Warren H. Turner, Jr., Frederick John Warnecke, and Arthur E. Walmsley to Edwin T. Dahlberg; NCC Papers, RG 4, Box 25, Folder 7; PHS.

the rest; because they, too, strongly believe that they achieve a right to human dignity because of their relationship to the Supreme Being." Eisenhower concluded by exhorting his clerical audience to help him in "uniting the free world through this common respect for religion." And in an afterthought that surely needled some if not most of his Protestant listeners, the President told them of his recent "long talk" with Cardinal Spellman on the phone, and assured them that "our Catholic brothers are joining you in these hours of prayer for peace."[107]

VII

The churchmen had tried fervently for fifteen years to construct a religious vision and template for America's role in the world – indeed, for the shape of the world itself. They had even seen one from their own ranks become Secretary of State. Yet by 1960 they beheld a world more divided and more dangerous than ever, and within their own camp they saw only enmity, confusion, and diminished relevance. Dulles had died a few months after Cleveland, having grown further alienated from his erstwhile allies in the mainline Protestant hierarchy. Niebuhr had become more distanced from his churchmen friends on questions of policy, and more distant from public life because of his own physical and emotional fragility. Christian realism could less and less restrain or moderate the liberal impulses in mainline Protestantism. Amidst all this, a new challenge had emerged, seemingly from the religious hinterlands. Evangelicalism initially had clamored just for recognition as *a* legitimate Protestant voice in the public square, but through the decade its aspirations grew to supplant the NCC coterie as *the* voice of Protestantism. In this it did not succeed entirely, but its critique of liberal Protestant excesses further diminished the mainline's cultural authority, and evangelicalism came to represent a growing sector of the populace. Conservative politicians still did not fully understand the religious identity of these "born agains." But many political leaders – Republicans especially – enjoyed the amiable embrace of evangelicalism's most visible leader, Billy Graham. They welcomed the undiluted anticommunism of evangelicals, and coveted evangelical votes. The inescapable fact remained, however, that Protestant leaders had failed to exercise a significant or determinative influence on the actual formation of American foreign policy.

Not that religion had no place in the matter. Despite their manifest divisions, Protestant leaders of all persuasions had succeeded in placing Cold

---

[107] September 9, 1959 White House Press Release; NCC Papers, RG 4, Box 25, Folder 7; PHS.

War concerns in the forefront of American pews and pulpits. They helped to develop a public vocabulary that spoke of America's world role in spiritual terms. In this they were not alone. As Eisenhower's remarks indicated, many American political leaders also saw the Cold War in a religious context. Indeed, a diplomatic theology of containment strongly influenced the development of American foreign policy during these crucial years. It was a theology, however, that had been constructed not in the churches, but in the White House itself.

PART TWO

3

∾

The "Real" Truman Doctrine: Harry Truman's Theology of Containment

I

Prophets, and presidents, are often unlikely people from unexpected places. Out of a humble Midwestern town, educated only through high school, emerged the Baptist president who defined God's purpose for America in the post-war world. Harry S. Truman, the unassuming Missourian who found himself thrust suddenly into the White House and onto the stage of history, took office just as his nation emerged from one world crisis only to face another. Yet Dean Acheson's "captain with a mighty heart" willingly embraced the monumental task he believed God and history had ordained for him.

Truman's accession to the presidency may have been more by accident than by design, but he believed nothing of the sort about America. He proclaimed in a 1948 speech the conviction he often echoed during his public life. "We are faced now with what Almighty God intended us to be faced with in 1920. We are faced with the leadership of the free peoples of the world. We must assume that leadership, if we expect our children not to have to go through the same situation that we had to go through with during the last five or six years. Get these things in your mind, and use your influence to do what God Almighty intended us to do: to get the right sort of peace in the world."[1]

[1] Truman, speech by HST to American Society of Newspaper Editors, April 17, 1948; Charles Murphy File, Presidential Speech File, Box 1; Truman Papers, Truman Library, Independence, Missouri (hereinafter HST Papers). For other examples of Truman expressing this conviction, see his June 11, 1949 remarks at the dedication at the World War II Memorial Park in Little Rock, AR (Murphy file, Box 5), his July 19, 1949 speech to the Shriners Diamond Jubilee Banquet in Chicago (Murphy file, Box 4), or his February 7, 1951 remarks to a group of Methodist ministers ("In 1920 I think the Almighty intended us to take leadership in the world to meet the very situation with which we are faced now. We didn't accept that invitation, and the Second World War was the result"). From *Public Papers of the Presidents: Harry S. Truman, 1951* (Washington: United States Government Printing Office 1965), 141. See also Frank McNaughton and Walter Hehmeyer, *This Man Truman* (New York: McGraw-Hill

In sentiments that Woodrow Wilson would have appreciated, Truman firmly believed that in the wake of the First World War, America had shirked its divine calling to assert vigorous leadership in a broken and chaotic world. He lamented America's indulgent isolationism of the 1920s, when the Senate's rejection of the League of Nations had precipitated a broader retreat from international affairs. Out of this leadership vacuum had spun worldwide economic depression, followed by the twin evils of European fascism and Japanese imperialism, while the United States had remained mired in its own domestic concerns.

World War II changed all this, thrusting a reluctant America into a role at once unfamiliar and yet altogether fitting – to lead the Allies in a global campaign to defeat the Axis powers. The end of the war raised as many new questions as it answered old ones. Foremost among them was whether the United States' recently acquired international eminence represented a momentary aberration from the normal isolation to which America would soon repair, or whether it revealed a new paradigm of American leadership in the world. Truman firmly believed the latter. God had graciously given America a second chance to fulfill its calling, he maintained, and the American people had an obligation to respond with good works. Truman determined that, insofar as he was able, they would not again fail to fulfill their divine obligation.[2]

Under Truman, the containment doctrine first articulated by George Kennan emerged as the dominant paradigm governing the United States' role in the world. Containment would define America's international priorities, determine America's international relationships, and dictate America's international actions. The most prominent features of Truman's containment policy – the Marshall Plan, aid to Turkey and Greece, intervention in Korea, massive military spending – were not inconsistent with Truman's religious agenda, but rather complemented it. Exploring the role of religion may seem a departure from conventional interpretations of Truman's foreign policy, but Truman himself would not have found it strange, for his faith helps to explain why he opposed communism so relentlessly, why he involved the

1945), 179. Note as well the comments by Truman speechwriter George Elsey that, regarding Truman's expressions of a divinely ordained role for American foreign policy, "this was very much a part of President Truman's own belief and feeling. Many of these phrases and sentences were added by him in longhand very near the final draft of a speech." Oral history interview, George Elsey, March 9, 1965, pp. 94–95, Truman Library.

[2] This notion of a "second chance" at international involvement was not confined to Truman, of course. For more on the internationalist movement, see Robert A. Divine, *Second Chance: The Triumph of Internationalism in America During World War II* (New York: Atheneum 1967).

United States in the world so eagerly, and how he sought to undermine the appeal and authority of communism so tenaciously.

Containment under Truman had a strong religious dimension, which operated in two ways. First, it helped to define the lines of conflict – to determine which nations would do the "containing," and which would be "contained." As Truman tirelessly proclaimed, the fundamental conflict in the world was between those nations who believed in God and morality, and those who did not. The United States needed to lead the world's religious forces in opposing the forces of atheism and irreligion controlled by the Soviet Union. Second, religion provided a valuable instrument to be used in containing the Soviet communists. Predicated on the assumption that an all-out military conflict between the United States and the USSR would be catastrophically destructive, not to mention unwinnable, containment sought instead to prevent further communist expansion while encouraging the internal collapse of the Soviet Union. Truman saw religion as a potent tool to undermine faith in the Soviet system, and to bring about its eventual demise.

Truman's Cold War convictions reflected his own lifelong religious faith. Though not trained in theology and not always familiar with the particular doctrines that defined different Christian traditions, Truman nonetheless possessed a basic set of theological beliefs about God, morality, peace, freedom, and America's purpose in the world. Unlike Eisenhower, whose religious practice would not develop fully until he took office, Truman remained true to the faith he had known since childhood. Reared as a devout Baptist, he had been steeped in the text of the Bible that he read several times as a boy and continued to read throughout his life.[3] While skeptical of public displays of piety, and not always a regular churchgoer, Truman nonetheless retained an intimate knowledge of the biblical narrative and a deep faith in God's guidance and purposes. "I am a Baptist by education and by the belief that John the Baptist recognized and baptized the Savior of the world, Jesus," he affirmed.[4] Moreover, he declared on several occasions "my political philosophy is based on the Sermon on the Mount."[5]

---

[3] For a more extensive discussion of Truman's religious faith, see Michael T. Benson, *Harry S. Truman and the Founding of Israel* (Westport, CT: Prager 1997), 30–37 and Elizabeth Edwards Spalding, *The First Cold Warrior: Harry Truman, Containment, and the Remaking of Liberal Internationalism* (Lexington, KY: University Press of Kentucky 2006), 199–222. Aside from Benson and Spalding, Truman's religious identity has received remarkably little scholarly attention.

[4] Harry S. Truman, *Mr. Citizen* (New York: Bernard Geis Associates 1960), 139–140.

[5] Truman, address in Kansas City, MO, September 29, 1949. *Public Papers of the Presidents: Harry S. Truman, 1949* (Washington: United States Government Printing Office 1964), 494. See also p. 510, transcript of Truman press conference.

This emphasis on Christianity's ethics, rather than its doctrines of salvation or church, influenced Truman's attitudes towards other religions. At one point he commented that "a man cannot have character unless he lives within a fundamental system of morals that creates character . . . the moral code of the Christian religion is about as good as there is. The Mohammedans have a code based closely on the Christian precepts, and the Buddhists have a moral code that is excellent, as do the Confucians."[6] And just weeks after becoming president, Truman wrote a diary memo to himself which, in typically blunt and colorful terms, laid out the wrong and right way to live:

> I've no faith in any totalitarian state, be it Russian, German, Spanish, Argentinian, Dago, or Japanese. They all start with a wrong premise – that lies are justified and that the old, disproven Jesuit formula, the end justifies the means, is right and necessary to maintain the power of government. I don't agree, nor do I believe that either formula can help humanity to the long hoped for millennium. Honest Communism, as set out in the "Acts of the Apostles," would work. But Russian Godless Pervert Systems won't work.
>
> ANYWAY, the human animal can't be trusted for anything *good* except en masse. The combined thought and action of the whole people of any race, creed, or nationality will always point in the Right Direction – "As ye would others should do unto you do ye also unto them." Confucius, Buddha, Christ, and all moralists come to the same conclusion.[7]

This captures the essence of Truman's faith. Copious biblical allusions and quotations, an emphasis on morality, a sympathy for other religions, an eschatological eagerness for a new world under God (the "long hoped for millennium"), and a contempt for communism because of its atheism, were all themes to which Truman would repeatedly return. The memo also reveals the continuity between his personal convictions and his public theology. Though written as a candid, private "note to self" and not intended for any public use, it anticipates many of Truman's public speeches as well as a significant diplomatic initiative he would undertake. In a major speech on American foreign policy just a few months later, Truman proclaimed that "we shall not relent in our efforts to bring the Golden Rule into the international affairs of the world."[8] In virtually equating "religion" with "morality" – a widespread belief among many mainline Protestants of the day – and in downplaying

---

[6] Truman, *Mr. Citizen*, 131.
[7] Quoted in Alonzo L. Hamby, *Man of the People: A Life of Harry S. Truman* (New York: Oxford University Press 1995), 314–315.
[8] Quoted in Henry Kissinger, *Diplomacy* (New York: Touchstone 1994), 437.

doctrinal distinctions between different faiths, Truman foreshadowed his campaign to create a religious alliance against communism.

Within the first year of his presidency, Harry Truman laid out the religious creed from which he hoped to govern and shape American public life. Neither sectarian nor dogmatic, but nevertheless pervasively spiritual, Truman's political theology set the course for America's role in the emerging world. At times shallow and manipulative, at other times stirring and robust, his public spirituality served several functions. It illuminated some of the motivations for America's engagement in the Cold War, drew crucial distinctions between the United States and the communist nations, helped maintain popular domestic support for American foreign policy, enlisted certain domestic and international religious leaders in the Cold War cause, and appealed to people of faith around the world on behalf of America and the fight against communism.

The day after accompanying Winston Churchill to Fulton, Missouri where Churchill had delivered his ominous "Iron Curtain" speech warning of growing Soviet control in Central and Eastern Europe, Truman gave his own less-noticed but also notable speech to the Federal Council of Churches. He sounded many of the spiritual themes that would resonate throughout his presidency. "This conference... represents no particular sect or creed, but rather... represents the spirit of the worship of God.... We are all bound together in a single unity – the unity of individual freedom in a democracy. We have just come through a decade in which forces of evil in various parts of the world have been lined up in a bitter fight to banish from the face of the earth both these ideals – religion and democracy." Having married faith and freedom, Truman argued that they shared both a common foundation and a common enemy. "Both religion and democracy are founded on one basic principle, the worth and dignity of the individual man and woman. Dictatorship, on the other hand, has always rejected that principle" and "is founded on the doctrine that the individual amounts to nothing; that the State is the only thing that counts."[9] Though lacking Churchill's eloquence, in his own way Truman was beginning to lay the theological foundation for opposing the Soviets.

He continued his speech with an apocalyptic turn. "If the civilized world as we know it today is to survive, the gigantic power which man has acquired through atomic energy must be matched by spiritual strength of greater magnitude. All mankind now stands in the doorway to destruction – or upon the

---

[9] Truman, speech to Federal Council of Churches, March 6, 1946. *Public Papers of the Presidents: Harry S. Truman, 1946* (Washington: United States Government Printing Office 1962), 141.

threshold of the greatest age in history." The problems may have been complex, but Truman offered a relatively simple solution. "If men and nations would but live by the precepts of the ancient prophets and the teachings of the Sermon on the Mount, problems which now seem so difficult would soon disappear." America's religious leaders, in turn, had a vital role to play. "This is the supreme opportunity for the Church to continue to fulfill its mission on earth. The Protestant Church, the Catholic Church, and the Jewish Synagogue – bound together in the American unity of brotherhood – must provide the shock forces to accomplish this moral and spiritual awakening. No other agency can do it. Unless it is done we are headed for the disaster we would deserve."[10] Eschewing the customary platitudes of civil religion, Truman urgently warned that America, and the world, faced a peril of unparalleled magnitude. In turn, however, a renewed commitment to religious faith could prepare the nation to face such a threat – and perhaps forestall the potential apocalypse.

The next month Truman elaborated on some of these themes in a letter to the General Assembly of the Presbyterian Church. "Religion and democracy in this country . . . have mutually strengthened each other. . . . Here, as perhaps nowhere else in the world, the fundamental unity of Christianity and freedom has been demonstrated." Besides providing the foundation for American civic life, Truman believed that religion offered the human race its only hope. "Religion alone has the answer for humanity's twentieth century cry of despair, 'What must I do to be saved?' In this time of grave anxiety the voice of science unites with the voice of religion to affirm that the words of Jesus, 'Do good to them that hate you,' are not only the words of Christian idealism but also the command of democratic realism."[11] Concepts previously considered at odds with each other, such as science and religion, or idealism and realism, were now united, Truman declared, in affirming a common hope. Humanity faced a new era, in which old disputes had been resolved and unprecedented challenges awaited.

Curiously, Truman initially pointed not to competing ideologies but to the nuclear age itself as the harbinger of change. "The atomic bomb destroyed selfish nationalism and the last defense of isolationism more completely than it razed an enemy city. It ended one age and began another: the new and unpredictable age of the soul."[12] He ascribed an almost eschatological

[10] *Public Papers*, 142.
[11] Truman to Reverend William P. Lampe, April 29, 1946; White House Central File (WHCF): President's Personal File (PPF) 449, folder 260; HST Papers.
[12] *Ibid.*

significance to nuclear weaponry. It had not merely revolutionized diplomacy and warfare; it had ushered in a new spiritual reality. The American people now needed to look clearly at the world, and peer into their own soul, and resolve how they would live. Parochial withdrawal from international affairs was not an option, Truman insisted, nor was callow sentimentality. The new reality demanded an America that would eschew its insecurities and confront its challenges.

The state of this new world soon began to take shape, and it was grim to behold. Truman's cautious concern in 1946 gave way to a firm resolve in 1947 to counter the emerging communist threat. The Soviet Union appeared to Truman as an expansionist menace, threatening not only countries on its borders or even the security of the United States, but also the very notion of freedom and the existence of those who cherished it. In response came his announcement on March 12, 1947 of what became known as the Truman Doctrine: "to support free peoples who are resisting attempted subjugation by armed minorities or by outside pressures."[13] Although in this speech he ostensibly asked only for financial assistance to Greece and Turkey to stave off communist insurgencies, the president's language globalized the conflict. Threats to freedom anywhere now became threats to freedom everywhere.

The new conflict demanded not just a new foreign policy but a new theology as well. Eschewing the customary hostility to Catholicism of many of his fellow Protestants, Truman sought to make common cause with the Vatican. In 1948 he wrote to Pope Pius XII two extraordinary letters describing the spiritual nature of the Cold War struggle. Lamenting the renewal of global tensions so soon after World War II, the president admitted that "our hopes for an enduring peace have been deferred. But we do not despair." Instead, "this Nation desires to march forward in amity with all men who unite their efforts to bring the Kingdom of God home to this fair Earth. We shall strive, therefore . . . to fulfill the prophecy of unity of world peoples under God." Whether self-consciously or not, here Truman aligned himself with the optimistic tradition of post-millenialism, the belief that Christians should not wait passively for Christ's return to Earth, but should instead prepare the way for their Lord's second coming by constructing a divine order on earth. Truman desired to enlist as many as possible in this effort. "It has been the paramount purpose of the people and government of the United States . . . to seek the establishment of a moral world order." Human freedom would form

---

[13] Truman, Special Message to the Congress on Greece and Turkey: The Truman Doctrine, March 12, 1947. *Public Papers of the Presidents: Harry S. Truman, 1947* (Washington: United States Government Printing Office 1963), 177–178.

the foundation of this new order, and all who affirmed freedom were invited, even urged, to join the struggle. While casting about broadly for potential allies, Truman still believed the United States to be anchored in a particular tradition. "This nation, as a Christian nation, prays that all moral forces of the world will unite."[14] Truman's syncretism, in other words, only went so far. Much as he affirmed the social utility of all religious faiths against a common communist enemy, his saw his own nation as indisputably Christian.

Truman's next letter to Pius XII adopted a more militant tone. Even allowing for a degree of rhetorical license, his language bespeaks a profound spiritual conflict. "I share your apprehension over the threat to Christian civilization. All who cherish Christian and democratic institutions should unite against the common enemy. That enemy is the Soviet Union which would substitute the Marxian doctrine of atheistic communism for Revelation." The battle lines could not be drawn more clearly. On one side stood those nations that affirmed the supremacy of God and the liberty of man. In relentless, irreconcilable opposition lurked the communist bloc, which denied not merely God's supremacy, but his very existence. Truman then defined American foreign policy by these ideals. "The peaceful prosperity of democratic Europe . . . is a goal to be gained for its own sake, not as a means of restraining the power of modern Russia." Accordingly, he described the Marshall Plan in missionary terms. "The primary purpose of the Marshall plan was and is to bind up the wounds of war, to feed the hungry, to give shelter to the homeless. Through labor and industry, with the blessing of God, these sorely stricken nations shall again become masters of their own destiny."[15]

Truman did not confine his religious rhetoric to speeches before church groups or letters to spiritual leaders. His State of the Union Address in 1948, for example, resonates with some of these same themes. After detailing America's economic and political strengths, Truman asserted that "the basic source of our strength is spiritual. For we are a people with a faith. We believe in the dignity of man. We believe that he was created in the image of the Father of us all." He then drew a contrast with the basic anthropology of communism. "We do not believe that men exist merely to strengthen the state or to be cogs in the economic machine. We do believe that governments are created to serve the people and that economic systems exist to minister to their wants."[16]

---

[14] Truman to Pope Pius XII, March 26, 1948; Myron Taylor Papers, Box 1; HST Papers.

[15] Truman to Pope Pius XII, August 11, 1948; Myron Taylor Papers, Box 1; HST Papers.

[16] Truman, Message to the Congress on the State of the Union, January 7, 1948. *Public Papers of the Presidents: Harry S. Truman, 1948* (Washington: United States Government Printing Office 1964), 7–10. It seems likely that David Lilienthal, Chairman of the Atomic Energy Commission, persuaded Truman to include the theme of America's spiritual strength in

In drawing this distinction, Truman also made the connection between his theology and his foreign policy. In turn, he appealed to the American people to understand the nature of their own society and the dimensions of their conflict with the Soviet Union – and to respond accordingly.

Truman's idealism was not naïve utopianism. Much as he professed a desire to reshape the world by more divine standards, he harbored no delusions and little patience towards the Soviets. And he expressed similar repugnance towards those in America who thought otherwise. In 1948 the Federal Council of Churches' Department of International Justice and Goodwill submitted to Truman a copy of its "Positive Program for Peace," which recommended reduced military power, increased spending on social welfare programs and international aid, and renewed dialogue with the USSR. In one of those rare and deliciously revealing moments of unguarded candor, Truman scribbled a note on the cover of the proposal to his chief personal aide: "This is a perfectly asinine document – as full of sophistry as a communist manifesto. Let's analyze it for what it is."[17] While he may have cherished lofty hopes for a just world order and a durable peace, Truman determined that the path towards these goals demanded realism, strength, and the willingness to suffer entanglement in a fallen world.

And Providence, though it may shine most abundantly on America, did not intend for the United States to hoard its blessings. Truman believed that American ideals were universal ideals, to be adopted, embraced, and enjoyed by all peoples. While he disavowed colonialism – "The United States Government has no ambitions as a colonial power or as an exploiter of people or other races" – he sought to re-shape the world in America's image. He remarked in 1951 to a group of Methodist ministers that "our only ambition is to see that the people in the world have the things that are necessary to make life worthwhile, and that they have and live by the moral code in which we believe. That is the fundamental principle of the foreign policy of the United

---

the speech. See Charles Murphy File, Box 1, folder: State of Union 1948, HST Papers. For similar statements from Truman on the notion that America's most fundamental strength is spiritual, see his October 29, 1949 radio address to the "Religion in American Life" program, his October 26, 1950 letter to the National Laymen's Committee on Religion in American Life, and his May 12, 1952 statement to the 164th General Assembly of the Presbyterian Church, all found in WHCF: PPF 449, folder 260; HST Papers. See also the numerous letters from the National Security Council, in response to requests from American women's groups for "a statement of what constitutes our nation's primary security." The NSC form letter in response cited many of President Truman's public statements asserting America's spiritual strength. From Staff Member and Office Files (SMOF): National Security Council Files: Chronological File 8, folder 1949 (October–November); HST Papers.

17 Truman to William Hassett; Official File (OF) 803, folder 213; HST Papers.

States."[18] Even stated so simply, the ramifications of Truman's principle for America's national ideals and interests were profound. Moreover, to translate such a principle into practice would create difficult choices, painful trade-offs, and complex questions, both strategic and tactical.

In a 1951 address at Washington's famed New York Avenue Presbyterian Church, Truman preached a virtual sermon on America's role in the world. He elaborated on the vexing relationship between the divine will, armed strength, American goodness, and communist evil. "We are under divine orders – not only to refrain from doing evil, but also to do good and to make this world a better place in which to live." This mandate carried with it a mission. "At the present time our nation is engaged in a great effort to maintain justice and peace in the world. An essential feature of this effort is our program to build up the defenses of our country. There has never been a greater cause. . . . We are defending the religious principles upon which our Nation and our whole way of life are founded." *Contra* the leadership of the Federal Council of Churches and their plan for peace through reduced armaments and negotiations, Truman proclaimed the doctrine of "peace through strength." He feared that an apocalyptic fate awaited the nation should it quail in the face of the threat. "The international Communist movement is based on a fierce and terrible fanaticism. It denies the existence of God and, wherever it can, it stamps out the worship of God. . . . Our faith shows us the way to create a society where man can find his greatest happiness under God. Surely we can follow that faith with the same devotion and determination that Communists give to their godless creed." The Cold War, in other words, had erupted not merely between two nations with contrary economic and political systems, but between two different religions. This made communism all the more pernicious, for not only did Marxism oppose Truman's universal moral law, it also possessed its own universalist pretensions. The battle lines stood stark and clear. Two ideologies and two systems asserted their rival claims to reality, neither one willing – or even able, if they would be true to themselves – to shrink from their confessions of truth.

Truman concluded his speech on a note of cautious hope. "I have the feeling that God has created us and brought us to our present position of power and strength for some great purpose. And up to now we have been shirking it. Now we are assuming it, and now we must carry it through."[19] Providence

[18]   Truman, remarks to Methodist Ministers, February 7, 1951. *Public Papers of the Presidents: Harry S. Truman, 1951* (Washington: United States Government Printing Office 1965), 141.
[19]   Truman, address at New York Avenue Presbyterian Church, April 3, 1951. *Public Papers of the Presidents: Harry S. Truman, 1951* (Washington: United States Government Printing Office 1965), 210–213.

was having its way with a previously unwilling people. At last America had accepted the divine mandate thrust upon it, and Truman resolved to bear the cross of leadership.

Truman stood squarely in a long line of American leaders who believed that the United States enjoyed a distinctive covenant bond with God. Just as God had entered into a special, privileged relationship with Old Testament Israel, so now he had selected out America from among the nations. Covenants, of course, carry obligations as well as privileges, the threat of divine curse along with the promise of divine blessing. It followed that the American people had a particular responsibility to live up to the highest of standards. Appearing in 1951 before a group of church leaders, Truman warned, "The people of Israel... did not, because of their covenant with God, have an easier time than other nations. Their standards were higher than those of other nations and the judgment upon them and their shortcomings was more terrible. A religious heritage such as ours is not a comfortable thing to live with.... [It] imposes great responsibilities upon us as we face the problems of today."[20] For too long, the president worried, Americans had borne insouciantly their covenant responsibilities. As the Puritan ministers of colonial America had sternly warned their congregations against the dangers of spiritual decline and covenant neglect, so Truman now resurrected that tradition of public exhortation.

Truman then offered a notable series of warnings. Perhaps mindful of the potential volatility of invoking a divine mandate for the Cold War struggle, he sought to restrain the possible excesses that could arise if spiritual resolve spun out of control, employing the America-as-Israel theme to fashion a compelling warning. "Our religious heritage also means that we must struggle to maintain our civil liberties," he declared. "No nation which hopes to live by the law of God can afford to suppress dissent and criticism. You may remember that Israel persecuted the prophets.... But the prophets were right, and Israel was punished as the prophets had said it would be." Likewise, Truman cautioned against the hubris of unwarranted certainty. "We must always keep the way open for self-criticism." God may be guiding the nation, but human sin and frailty too often tainted America. Only an awareness of these limits, and a willingness to heed them, could guard the United States against further error. Finally, "we must not be led astray by self-righteousness."[21]

[20] Truman, address to the Washington Pilgrimage of American Churchmen, September 28, 1951. *Public Papers of the Presidents: Harry S. Truman, 1951* (Washington: United States Government Printing Office 1965), 547–550.

[21] Truman, September 28, 1951 address.

Self-righteousness, in many ways the mirror image of self-criticism, bespoke a nation too confident in itself and too ignorant of the Almighty.

The welfare of the world lay in the balance. Truman concluded with a stirring portrait of a civilization in crisis. "Today, our problem is not just to preserve our own religious heritage in our own lives and our own country. . . . It is to preserve a world civilization in which man's belief in God can survive. . . . Today, the whole human enterprise is in danger – and serious danger." Such a cataclysmic threat could not be met by mere military power, of course, and Truman harbored no delusions to the contrary. "In this crisis of human affairs, all men who profess to believe in God should unite in asking His help and His guidance. We should lay aside our differences and come together now – for never have our differences seemed so petty and so insignificant as they do in the face of the peril we confront today."[22] A common threat has a way of rendering old divisions trivial, and forging new alliances.

While Truman's speeches radiate with spiritual language, the question arises whether he was simply employing religious rhetoric for political gain. After all, what better way to enlist the support of a politically skeptical but spiritually sensitive public than by baptizing Cold War policies in sacred imagery and appealing to the will of God? Perhaps Truman's religious exhortations amounted to nothing more than a spiritual version of Senator Vandenberg's legendary assertion of the need to "scare the hell out of the country."[23] To be sure, the desire to maintain domestic political support at least partly motivated him. But as Truman's personal correspondence and covert activities reveal, the president seems to have held these convictions about the spiritual stakes of the Cold War as strongly in private as he did in public. Moreover, Truman paid a steep political price for some of his "religious diplomacy." The opposition of American Protestants, both lay and clerical, to the appointment of a presidential representative to the Vatican was widespread, virulent, and relentless. Truman seems to have calculated that the diplomatic benefits of attempting to forge a religious anticommunist alliance overseas outweighed the domestic political costs of maintaining this mission.

Truman's conception of the Cold War as a grand spiritual drama received tangible expression in certain policy initiatives. For one, during this time the U.S. government began developing an elaborate psychological warfare and

---

[22] *Ibid.*
[23] Vandenberg's quote may be "legendary" in both senses of the term, as it is not certain that he actually made this comment, which seems subsequently to have been attributed to him by Loy Henderson. See James Chace, *Acheson: The Secretary of State Who Created the American World* (New York: Simon and Schuster 1998), 166.

propaganda operation, in hopes of gaining ground in the worldwide ideological conflict. The Psychological Strategy Board (PSB), created by Truman's
secret directive of April 4, 1951, attempted to coordinate and implement the
array of measures – some innovative, some effective, some feckless, and some
merely bizarre – designed to persuade peoples around the world of the vice
of communism and the virtue of the United States.[24] Religion soon emerged
as a potential weapon in the propaganda effort.

Even Foggy Bottom caught the religious spirit. The State Department
devised an advisory panel of Protestant, Catholic, and Jewish religious leaders
to evaluate policies and offer guidance on how to incorporate spiritual factors
into the United States Information Exchange (USIE) programs. In 1951 this
panel and a few other religious luminaries – Francis Cardinal Spellman and
Truman's own pastor Rev. Edward Pruden of First Baptist Church, among
them – helped the Assistant Secretary of State for Public Affairs to draft a
Special Policy Guidance on "Moral and Religious Factors in the USIE Program." A remarkable manifesto, the Policy Guidance articulated the spiritual
dimensions of the Cold War, diagnosed particular areas of vulnerability and
concern, and established the religious ideology that would inform U.S. propaganda efforts. Surveying the landscape in America and the world, the Policy
Guidance offered an assessment similar to Truman's, calling for "the arousing
of men everywhere, who cherish moral and spiritual freedom, to the need of
defending that freedom against totalitarian aggression."[25]

In candor remarkable for a propaganda treatise, the Policy Guidance admitted certain shortcomings in America, including materialism, arrogance, and
self-righteousness. "The unsavory aspects of American life should not be
denied or covered. To do either would be both dishonest and poor propaganda." Rather, an effective information program "can place the uncompli-
mentary aspects [of American life] in perspective, it can help to correct those
attitudes which are based on misunderstanding, and it can contribute to a
fuller understanding of the moral and spiritual values in our life and institutions." Likewise, America needed to "make clear that religious forces in the
U.S. are not under the control of the government, and to explain how religion

---

[24] For background on the PSB, see Edward P. Lilly, "The Psychological Strategy Board and
Its Predecessors: Foreign Policy Coordination, 1938–1953" in Gaetano L. Vincitorio, ed.,
Studies in Modern History (New York: St. John's University Press 1968), 337–382, and Scott
Lucas, *Freedom's War: The American Crusade Against the Soviet Union* (New York: New York
University Press 1999), 128–162 and 175–177.

[25] Department of State Information Program Guidance on "Moral and Religious Factors in the
USIE Program," June 22, 1951 and Memorandum from Gordon Gray to Joseph B. Phillips,
August 23, 1951; SMOF: Psychological Strategy Board Files 1, folder 000.3; HST Papers.

is a potent element in all aspects of American life as a leavening and influencing force." The authors singled out as a particular example that "much
of our foreign policy cannot be explained, or understood, apart from moral
and religious considerations." American foreign assistance projects, and especially American policy towards China, were cited as evidence of the influence
of faith on foreign affairs.[26] Whether suspected of infidelity by the religious
nations of the world, or accused of superstition and religious manipulation by
the communist bloc, the United States first needed to explain its own unique
balance of the sacred and the secular, and the faith that inspired its role in the
world.

Only then might America "unite all people threatened by Communism in a
great moral and spiritual offensive." This was easier said than done, however,
and the Policy Guidance did not gloss over religious differences. While "the
Christian and Jewish faiths offer a broad base on which to build for a united
effort," other faiths such as Islam, Buddhism, Hinduism, and Confucianism
"offer much more limited opportunities." The authors of the Policy Guidance, unlike President Truman, did not ascribe uniform moral teachings to
all religions, regardless of doctrine. However, "a common denominator of
all religions is not necessary. It is not our purpose to develop a universal
eclecticism."[27] Instead, alliances for co-belligerency could be built on values
shared among the distinctive religious faiths. To the eyes of those engulfed in
the Cold War, religions that once appeared dramatically different now looked
to share much more in light of the threat of atheistic communism.

Harnessing this power would not be simple. Having explained the intellectual basis for employing religion as an instrument in propaganda efforts,
the Psychological Strategy Board needed now to instruct the relevant agencies
on implementation. In January 1952, the PSB issued a classified memo to
the Central Intelligence Agency, the National Security Council, the Defense
Department, and the State Department describing the resources available for
psychological operations. One section addressed religion, asserting that "the
potentialities of religion as an instrumentality for combating Communism are
universally tremendous . . . our over-all objective in seeking the use of religion
as a cold war instrument should be the furtherance of world spiritual health;
for the Communist threat could not exist in a spiritually healthy world."
Furthermore, "current information from the Iron Curtain countries testifies
to the effectiveness of even sporadic and unorganized religious opposition to
the Communist regimes." The memo recommended that the USIE and Voice

---

[26] *Ibid.*
[27] *Ibid.*

of America publicize at every opportunity the threat communism posed to religious belief, that religious leaders continue to provide policy guidance to the State Department in this area, and that the State Department "encourage churches, their leaders, and their members to oppose Communist doctrine and practices."[28] And so the last year of the Truman Administration saw the beginnings of a systematic effort by the U.S. government to employ religion as an ideological weapon in the effort to contain Soviet communism.

II

Most likely unbeknownst to the officials at the Psychological Strategy Board, President Truman had several years earlier initiated his own covert effort to win the religious campaign of the Cold War. Truman's chosen agent was Myron Taylor, one of the more quixotic, controversial, and elusive figures in the annals of American diplomacy. Taylor's dour square-jawed visage, diminutive stature, and Yankee reserve cloaked a passion for intrigue and a boiling idealism. Neither a traditional diplomat nor a clergyman, he carried a commission to serve as President Truman's personal representative to Pope Pius XII. In one of the more peculiar ecumenical alliances that only international politics can breed, the low-church Baptist politician appointed a patrician Episcopalian industrialist as envoy to the supreme pontiff of the Roman Catholic Church.[29]

Taylor's religious faith shared much with Truman's, in its emphasis on morality and good works and its diminution of doctrine. Behind "my heritage as an Episcopalian is a strong infusion of the benign teaching of the Society

---

[28] January 5, 1952 PSB "Inventory of Resources Presently Available for Psychological Operations Planning." SMOF: PSB 34, folder 385; HST Papers.

[29] Taylor's activities have received very little scholarly attention. Owen Chadwick's *Britain and the Vatican During the Second World War* (Cambridge, UK: Cambridge University Press 1986) gives passing mention of Taylor, 100–103. J. Bruce Nichols notes Taylor's work with European refugees during World War II in *The Uneasy Alliance: Religion, Refugee Work, and U.S. Foreign Policy* (New York: Oxford University Press 1988). Robert Moats Miller, in his biography of Bishop Oxnam, gives a cursory description of Taylor's activities, but pays most attention to the Protestant leadership's campaign against representation at the Vatican. See Miller, *Bishop G. Bromley Oxnam: Paladin of Liberal Protestantism* (Nashville: Abingdon Press 1990), 411–429. Spalding briefly addresses Taylor's missions in her chapter on Truman's faith and foreign policy. Hamby, in his biography of Truman, only makes a brief mention of Taylor's mission to the Vatican and the recognition controversy. And while Hamby devotes two paragraphs to Truman's attempt to build a religious coalition, he errs in saying that it "never surfaced publicly" and also fails to connect Taylor with it. See Hamby, 572–573. McCullough does not mention Taylor at all. For a cursory overview of Taylor's activities written by then-U.S. Ambassador to the Vatican Jim Nicholson, see *The United States and the Holy See: The Long Road* (Rome, Italy: 30 Days Books 2002).

of Friends," Taylor commented at one point. "My own religious predilections
have been to the liberal side," giving primacy to "practical Christianity which
means good works."[30] A man of means, Taylor had attained both a fortune and
great acclaim after becoming the chief executive of the United States Steel Cor-
poration in 1932. Six years later he retired, announcing his rather immodest
hope to spend "a sabbatical year of philosophic meditation on the problems of
modern civilization." Modern civilization's problems soon rudely interrupted
on their own terms, however, as President Roosevelt requested that his old
friend Taylor coordinate aid for refugees suffering under Europe's growing
troubles. In what became a recurring pattern, Taylor's refugee assistance post
apparently served as a cover for a more sensitive operation: helping supervise
the smuggling of some of Germany's best nuclear scientists to the United
States.[31] The next year Roosevelt appointed Taylor as his personal representative with the rank of Ambassador to Pope Pius XII. In a 1940 handwritten letter
to the Pope, Roosevelt described the purpose of Taylor's mission as one of
ensuring "that our parallel endeavors for peace and the alleviation of suffering
might be assisted."[32] Again, this honorific masked a more important mission,
for Roosevelt saw the Vatican, with its unique network of clerical sources
throughout the land, as an invaluable source of intelligence on developments
in Europe, particularly in Mussolini's Italy. Roosevelt also tasked Taylor with
an array of other duties, from initial (and ultimately futile) diplomatic efforts
to work with the Vatican in keeping Mussolini's Italy from entering the war,
to (also ultimately futile) political efforts to persuade the Vatican to restrict
American radio personality and Roosevelt critic Father Charles Coughlin or
to elevate to Cardinal a favored American Bishop.[33] While Roosevelt did not
take the politically volatile step of extending official diplomatic recognition
to the Vatican, he went as far as possible in forging an alliance with the Pope.
And Taylor, no stranger to mediating vexing labor disputes during his days in
business, now found himself with a new title of "Ambassador" and a new set
of challenges to negotiate.

During World War II Taylor engaged in a myriad of activities, including
consultations with leaders such as Churchill in England and Franco in Spain.
Taylor also served as an official advisor to Secretary of State Cordell Hull on

---

[30]   Taylor to Archbishop of Canterbury, October 25, 1951; Myron Taylor Papers 2; HST Papers.
[31]   "Behind the Headlines: Myron Taylor – Secret Agent" in *London News Review*, February 9,
       1950.
[32]   Roosevelt to Pope Pius XII, February 14, 1940; President Dwight D. Eisenhower Papers; Ann
       Whitman File; Name Series 32, folder: Taylor; Dwight D. Eisenhower Library, Abilene, Kansas
       (henceforth DDE Papers).
[33]   Nicholson, 31.

the question of the post-war world order, and in 1944 and 1945 coordinated American relief efforts to a defeated Italy ravaged by war.[34] President Truman inherited Taylor and his mission from President Roosevelt after the latter's death. Though some of the original purposes of Taylor's mission – including refugee assistance and relief efforts – soon became obsolete, Truman determined that the crafty Taylor and his network of European contacts still held significant value for the United States in its conflict with its newest enemy.

Even as Truman worked to define the murky postwar world and relations between the United States and the Soviet Union, Taylor came to his own firm conclusion about the nature of the nascent conflict. On June 11, 1946, Taylor shared with Truman his own impressions of the world situation from his vantage point at the Vatican. "The cause of Communism versus Christianity and Democracy transcends minor differences in Christian creeds. It is the *Great Issue* of the future and thus of today." Moreover, the United States, should it rise to the challenge, had a powerful and eager ally in the Catholic Church. "The Pope has openly challenged Communism from the beginning. He and the Catholic Church are the great bulwark of democracy in continental Europe today." Theologically, politically, and even geographically, the Vatican stood poised on a vital precipice. "This peninsula may well become the Mediterranean bulwark separating the Democratic West from what is fast becoming Communist Eastern Europe."[35] The acute sensitivity of the Mediterranean region certainly informed Truman's momentous decision the next year to support anticommunist forces in Greece and Turkey. Because of its strategic location in Italy, its tremendous cultural influence the world over, and its leadership in developing Christendom's anticommunism, the Vatican held great appeal for Taylor, and soon enough for Truman, as a Cold War ally. Truman followed up Taylor's observations by making his own direct appeal to the Pope. In a November 21, 1946, letter to Pius XII, Truman asserted that "this nation, as a Christian nation, prays that all moral forces of the world will unite their strength and will create . . . the conditions of life and the enduring world peace to which mankind will find well-being, peace, security, and freedom in an enduring world order."[36] Even allowing for the excesses of lofty rhetoric,

---

[34] Taylor to President Eisenhower, March 31, 1953; Eisenhower Papers; WHCF: Confidential Subject Series 83, folder: Taylor; DDE Papers. For more on Taylor's activities during World War II, see Franklin D. Roosevelt, *Wartime Correspondence Between President Roosevelt and Pope Pius XII* (New York: The Macmillan Company 1947), including the introduction written by Taylor.

[35] Taylor to Truman, June 11, 1946; WHCF; State Department File, Myron C. Taylor 44; HST Papers. Emphasis original.

[36] Truman to Pope Pius XII, November 21, 1946; Official File (OF) 76-B; HST Papers.

Truman's words are revealing. In one fell linguistic swoop he recast the world landscape, aligning all of the devout and pious in a single united block. He also hinted at his next assignment for Taylor – to marry word and deed.

Truman's faith informed not just his rhetoric, but some of his policy decisions as well – most notably, the grandiose, secretive plan concocted by Truman and Taylor to unite the leaders of the various factions of Christendom in a pan-religious alliance against communism. Almost 2000 years of conflict, corruption, and doctrinal disputes had rent Christianity into a dizzying array of communions, denominations, and sects. Truman and Taylor aimed for nothing less than reversing this process and bringing the Christian churches back together – not around a shared confession but against a shared opponent.

The basis for this religious unity was to be moral and political, not theological. Truman viewed religious faith as a powerful antidote to communist totalitarianism. Because it taught codes of universal morality based on humanity's creation in the image of God, religion offered a compelling alternative to Marxist social engineering. And because it demanded mankind's highest allegiance above even the dictates of the state, religious faith challenged vigorously the totalitarian state's pretensions to absolute control. Characteristically impatient with what he considered petty theological divisions, Truman appealed instead to what he perceived as the commonalities of religion, and the common threat against religious faith. In this he found a willing ally in Pope Pius XII, but only up to a point. For neither the Pope nor the several Protestant leaders that Truman and Taylor sought to enlist would ever be persuaded to eschew completely their theological distinctives.

President Truman and the Pope exchanged letters in 1947 in which both articulated their respective hopes for mobilizing the faithful. Truman declared his intentions to "do everything in my power to support and to contribute to a concert of all the forces striving for a moral world," and he defined these "forces" as all persons who sought to abide by the Golden Rule. "As a Christian nation our earnest desire is to work with men of good will everywhere to banish war and the causes of war from the world. . . . I believe that the greatest need of the world today, fundamental to all else, is a renewal of faith. I seek to encourage renewed faith in the dignity and worth of the human person in all lands." Though Truman subsequently would focus his efforts exclusively on mobilizing Christian leaders behind his plan, he still sought to cast his rhetorical net as wide as possible, making clear his purpose to create a new order on earth, not in heaven. This new order knew certain limits, however. "I believe," concluded Truman, "that those who do not recognize their responsibility to Almighty God cannot meet their full duty toward their fellow men."[37] Atheists, and implicitly communists as well, could not be good citizens.

The Pope responded enthusiastically to Truman's missive, and offered a discourse on Catholic social thought. He first affirmed that the foundations of world peace "can be secure only if they rest on bedrock faith in the One, True God, the Creator of all men. It was He who of necessity assigned man's purpose in life; it is from Him, with consequent necessity, that man derives personal imprescriptible rights to pursue that purpose and to be unhindered in the attainment of it." Because God had established the world and ordained the rights that inhered in all people, a robust peace could only be built on such a basis. Communities and governments likewise must recognize their divine source.

> CIVIL Society is also of divine origin and indicated by nature itself; but it is subsequent to man and meant to be a means to defend him and to help him in the legitimate exercise of his God-given rights. Once the State, to the exclusion of God, makes itself the source of the rights of the human person, man is forthwith reduced to the condition of a slave, of a mere civic commodity to be exploited for the selfish aims of a group that happens to have power. The order of God is overturned; and history surely makes it clear to those who wish to read, that the inevitable result is the subversion of order between peoples, is war.[38]

The Soviet system stood indicted. In claiming to be the ultimate source of its citizens' rights and duties, the Kremlin idolatrously had presumed the role of God. Such a metaphysical violation could not stand. If tolerated, Pius XII believed, only war would follow.

The Pope then offered a veritable manifesto on the Catholic Church's primacy and resolve. He reaffirmed the Vatican's alliance with the United States, while asserting that Catholic prerogatives would not be compromised.

> Certainly Your Excellency and all defenders of the rights of the human person will find wholehearted cooperation from God's Church. Faithful custodian of eternal truth and loving mother of all, from her foundation almost two thousand years ago, she has championed the individual against despotic rule, the labouring man against oppression, religion against persecution. Her Divinely-given mission often brings her into conflict with the powers of evil. . . . But the Church is unafraid. She cannot compromise with an avowed

---

[37] Truman to Pope Pius XII, August 6, 1947; WHCF; State Department, Myron Taylor 45; HST Papers.

[38] Pope Pius XII to Truman, August 26, 1947; WHCF; State Department, Myron Taylor 44; HST Papers.

enemy of God. . . . In striving with all the resources at her power to bring
man and nations to a clear realization of their duty to God, the Church will
go on, as she has always done, to offer the most effective contribution to the
world's peace and man's eternal salvation.[39]

The Bishop of Rome made clear his implacable opposition to the communist system, which was nothing less than an "avowed enemy of God." He
seemed almost as eager, however, to guard the Catholic prerogative as "God's
Church." Such assertions, while nothing new at the Vatican, would soon
enough confound Truman and Taylor's ambitions for a religious alliance.

Taylor, meanwhile, plunged into his expanded assignment with characteristic vigor. Besides serving as Truman's liaison to the Pope, the President
had also tasked Taylor with mobilizing other European Christian leaders who
might support the religious effort against communism.[40] Taylor would bypass
the State Department and report directly to Truman, and many of Taylor's
letters and reports to Truman would be shrouded in a secret code.[41] Taylor
embarked on several weeks of spiritual shuttle diplomacy during August and
September, 1947, meeting with, among others, the Archbishop of Canterbury,
the Lutheran Bishop of Berlin, the Catholic Bishop of London, the Papal
Nuncio in Paris, and of course the Pope in Rome. He offered a general sketch
of his emerging plan, "that if people of all religious faiths would, in the
present world crisis, unite upon a universal two-point declaration embody-
ing the spirit of belief in God and belief in human liberty, to which mankind
would dedicate itself, it might help temporarily and be effective permanently
in bringing people to a better basis of understanding in the interest of world
peace." Taylor reported to Truman that, at least in initial discussions, these
church leaders sounded receptive to the proposal. But he soon encountered
the intricacies of religious politics, as he gingerly explored the possibility of
meeting with the Eastern Orthodox Patriarch in Istanbul. Both the Anglicans and the Catholics informed him that the Church of England enjoyed
closer relations with the Orthodox Church than did the Church of Rome,
so any possible approach should be mediated by Canterbury rather than the
Vatican.[42]

---

[39] *Ibid.*
[40] Truman to Taylor, August 7, 1947; WHCF; State Department, Myron Taylor 45; HST Papers.
[41] Memorandum from Taylor to Truman, August 26, 1949 reads in part: "From almost the
beginning, State Department has been hostile to the Personal Representative and resents
private reporting to the President." Myron Taylor Papers 2; HST Papers. Also Miller gives an
account of Taylor revealing the existence of the "secret code" to a small group of Protestant
clergy. See Miller, 425.
[42] Taylor to Truman, September 25, 1947; Myron Taylor Papers 1; HST Papers.

Not all of Taylor's efforts remained veiled in secrecy. During his meeting with General Lucius D. Clay, commander of the Allied Occupation Forces in Germany, the Ambassador shared copies of some of the correspondence between President Truman and the Pope, which was about to be made public in the United States. Clay realized the considerable public relations value offered by the warming relations between Truman and Pius XII. He informed Taylor that "we are arranging to distribute the exchange of letters between the Pope and the President. The distribution will help us in raising our resistance to communism to a high level."[43] No doubt the warm words and common purposes shared by Truman and the Pope would demonstrate to Germany's Catholics whose side they should take. The Soviets took notice of Taylor's meetings as well, though not with favor. The Soviet-sponsored newspaper *SED*, published in Berlin, ran an article sternly warning that "evidently the German Princes of the Church are to play a special part in a dark Jesuit intrigue." The newspaper elsewhere painted a picture of an elaborate conspiracy involving Taylor, Germany's Catholic leadership, and the Pope as evidence why "Dr. Adenauer, the political confidant of the Archbishop of Cologne, cannot bring himself to breathe the freer air of the Eastern zone even in the narrow circle of his party friends."[44] The Soviets refused to sit passively by as religion was mobilized against them.

While Truman and Taylor often described their project's purposes in the lofty prose of "peace," "brotherhood," and "unity," at other times they revealed a more pointed agenda. Taylor described to Lord Halifax his intention to "arouse religious unity among all denominations in an effort to combat the propaganda and accomplishments of communism, particularly as related to Russia."[45] In a similar vein, Taylor wrote to the Archbishop of Canterbury of his desire to create "a beneficent influence to offset the growing propaganda and accomplishments of the Soviet which are contrary to our faith and imperil human liberties."[46] This rhetorical ambiguity was perhaps a shrewd tactic designed to maintain the moral high ground of idealism while stirring up fears of communism.

One church official, at least, soon emerged as a valuable ally. Bishop Otto Dibelius, the Lutheran Bishop of Berlin and the leader of the German

[43] Lucius D. Clay to Taylor, September 15, 1947; Taylor Papers 1; HST Papers.
[44] Translations of articles included with letter from Taylor to Pius XII, October 8, 1947; Taylor Papers 1; HST Papers.
[45] Taylor to Lord Halifax, October 8, 1947; WHCF: State Department Papers, Myron Taylor 45; HST Papers.
[46] Taylor to Archbishop Geoffrey Fisher, October 8, 1947; WHCF: State Department Papers, Myron Taylor 45; HST Papers.

Protestant churches, was known both for his vocal opposition to the Nazis, which landed him a lengthy stay in prison during the war, and for his equally fervent anticommunism. During their meeting in Berlin, Dibelius had warned Taylor that perhaps 50,000 German children in the Russian zone had been abducted by the Soviets and taken away for communist indoctrination. Shocked at this news, and impressed by the bishop's resolve, Taylor became an advocate for Dibelius, ensuring that the Allied authorities granted him sufficient paper for his sermons to be printed and distributed, and arranging for Dibelius to meet with General Clay.[47] Taylor also arranged for a White House meeting with Truman during Dibelius' visit to the United States in late October, 1947. Truman's correspondence secretary and trusted aide William Hassett gave a glowing report on the meeting, describing Truman as "captivated" by Dibelius. Hassett noted in particular the bishop's comment to Truman that "now is the first time in recorded history that the victor nations are seeking to help the vanquished to get back on their feet."[48]

In the midst of trying to mobilize Christian leaders in Europe, Truman and Taylor found themselves fending off fervent criticism from many Protestant clerics in America. The American tradition of religious disestablishment made many Protestants quite wary of any steps towards granting official recognition to the Vatican, which they perceived as violating the boundaries between church and state. Even Taylor's lesser status as the President's "personal" representative to the Vatican – as opposed to an official ambassador heading an Embassy – caused many American Protestant churchmen profound apprehension. As a result, Taylor attracted heated criticism from American Protestants throughout his tenure, but most especially under Truman. Truman firmly rejected this criticism, complaining to Taylor at one point of the "earnest but narrow zealots who are continually protesting your presence in

---

[47] Taylor to Truman, September 25, 1947; Myron Taylor Papers 1; HST Papers. Taylor also passed on to the White House a similar request from Berlin's Catholic Cardinal von Preysing for more printing paper from the Allied authorities for the diocesan newspaper. Cardinal von Preysing stated that "the battle in and for Germany is fundamentally a battle between belief in God and Atheism . . . if the people do not remain firm in their Christian faith, the struggle for the ideals of democracy, freedom and the dignity of man, is doomed to failure." He thanked the Allies for assisting him in establishing a publishing office and appealed for a greater paper supply so he could reach German Catholics in the Soviet zone of Berlin, since "if a generous contribution could be made toward the obtaining and distribution of paper, much could be done in a religious way, and the Christians, strengthened in their religious principles, would be less likely to succumb to pernicious ideas." Statement by Cardinal von Preysing, April 18, 1948; WHCF: State Department Papers, Myron Taylor 46; HST Papers.

[48] Hassett to Taylor, November 7, 1947; WHCF: State Department Papers, Myron Taylor 46; HST Papers.

Rome."[49] Hassett echoed this sentiment, suggesting in 1947 that Truman send a note of encouragement to Taylor "since all he gets for his work is a fusillade of brickbats and dead cats."[50]

Angry missives and feline cadavers notwithstanding, Taylor decided to confront directly his clerical critics. On October 20, 1947, he met in New York with several Protestant leaders concerned about his mission and activities. Those present were a veritable "who's who" of the Protestant establishment, including Samuel McCrea Cavert of the Federal Council of Churches, G. Bromley Oxnam of the Methodist Church, Edwin Dahlberg of the Northern Baptist Convention, and William Pugh of the Presbyterian Church. Taylor began the meeting by giving a detailed narrative of his activities as President Roosevelt's representative to the Pope during World War II, and then describing the considerable number of nations that maintained formal diplomatic relations with the Vatican. He also related his own longstanding relationship with Pius XII. They had met in New York in 1936, he told them, during the Pope's pre-papal days as Cardinal Secretary of State, when he had warned Taylor that "the time is coming, and it is not far off, when all religious people regardless of denomination will have to stand together to fight communism and atheism." Taylor then attempted to impress upon the Protestant leaders the geopolitical dimensions of a potential religious alliance against communism. He handed them copies of a map displaying the distribution of Protestants, Catholics, and Orthodox in Europe, asserting that the Catholic Church exerted the strongest religious influence, particularly in European nations coming under Soviet control. In view of Europe's Christian identity, and the looming crisis, Taylor urged the others to support his ecumenical efforts, as he claimed the Pope, the Archbishop of Canterbury, and the Lutheran Bishop Dibelius seemed inclined to do. "Without going into denominational discussions or affairs, can we not organize all believers in God, to try to save this world of ours? Because it's slipping very fast, and it's slipping in an anti-God fashion."[51]

---

[49] Truman to Taylor, June 15, 1946; WHCF: State Department Papers, Myron Taylor 44; HST Papers.

[50] Hassett to Truman, October 16, 1947; WHCF: State Department Papers, Myron Taylor 45; HST Papers.

[51] Transcript, Meeting of Protestant Clergymen with Myron C. Taylor at Union Club, New York, October 20, 1947; Myron Taylor Papers 1; HST Papers. Louie Newton, the President of the Southern Baptist Convention, had refused even to attend the meeting, citing his concern that acceptance of the invitation would "imply at least tacit acknowledgement that Mr. Taylor's mission to the Vatican was thus approved." Newton to Cavert, October 10, 1947; WHCF: State Department Papers, Myron Taylor 45; HST Papers.

The Protestant leaders were not impressed with this appeal. They continued to focus on Taylor's – and by extension on Truman's – disturbingly close ties to the Pope. Bishop Oxnam complained of restrictions on Protestantism's religious liberty by Catholic authorities around the world, and worried aloud that Truman and Taylor's relationship with the Pope implicitly condoned these violations. Taylor evaded this charge, and instead reiterated his efforts to bring Christian leaders of various communions together against the communist threat. Rev. Dahlberg took exception to Taylor's entire agenda. He expressed his fear that an American alliance with the Vatican might precipitate war with Russia. "The deadly antagonisms in Europe are between Catholicism and communism," he averred. "The more we are related to these ecclesiastical entanglements, the more we are going to be sunk in the maelstrom. . . . I would hate to see us in any kind of diplomatic relationship that seems to unite Protestantism with Catholicism in a common war against Russia. I am willing to oppose communism but I would hate to see the Protestant churches pulling Catholicism out of the fire." A somewhat incredulous Taylor then asked if Dahlberg thought the United States could avoid conflict with atheistic communism. Dahlberg's reply was emphatic: "I would as much hate to be thrown into opposition to Russia by supporting what I call ecclesiastical totalitarianism as I would be against communism."[52] To any who doubted the intensity of Protestant hostility to Catholicism, here was stark evidence. Catholicism and communism, in the mind of at least one prominent Protestant leader, were equally repressive, equally threatening, and therefore equally reprehensible. President Truman's conviction that all religious believers, and certainly all Christians, together stood imperiled by communism did not resonate with some Protestant leaders. The president, and Taylor as his lieutenant, faced a formidable task. They needed to persuade the American Protestant establishment that Catholicism was not so malignant a threat – nor was communism so benign an alternative.

A final side discussion in the meeting hinted at what would become a point of major contention. Taylor related that in his meetings in Europe the previous month, the Archbishop of Canterbury had agreed that Taylor should ask the Pope to send observers to the organizational meetings for the World Council of Churches the following year in Amsterdam. Taylor, however, revealed that he and Truman knew little about the proposed WCC. Cavert pronounced Taylor's unfamiliarity "rather appalling" and complained that "the President completely ignores" the ecumenical movement. If Truman and Taylor knew more about current Protestant ecumenism, Cavert suggested, they would not

52 *Ibid.*

be so insistent on their own agenda for a religious alliance. "The unity that the President wants he can secure, I am confident, if he proceeds in terms of American principles."[53] Just what those American principles entailed was another matter.

The next month a similar delegation of American Protestant leaders, headed by Bishop Oxnam, met with Truman at the White House. Oxnam repeated to the President an idea he had earlier suggested to Taylor, that Taylor be "appointed as personal representative of the President to the religious leaders of the world." Oxnam believed this arrangement would resolve the thorny church–state issues that continued to nettle American Protestants fearful of Vatican influences.[54] Truman, in turn, inquired whether the WCC would represent only world Protestantism. The churchmen replied that the WCC hoped to represent not just Protestantism, but other Christian communions as well. In so answering they unwittingly opened themselves to Truman's subsequent campaign to persuade the WCC to include the Catholic Church. Hassett reported to Taylor on the meeting, dismissing Oxnam's suggestion because "it does not make much sense."[55]

The organizers of the World Council of Churches conceived of their mission as distinctively, and exclusively, spiritual. They hoped to establish an unprecedented Christian unity among all of the world's non-Catholic churches. President Truman and Ambassador Taylor believed their mission to be spiritual also, but only in addition to its political, diplomatic, moral, and social components. Every dimension of human existence needed to be marshaled against the apocalyptic threat to world civilization posed by Soviet communism. It only made sense to Truman and Taylor to enlist the World Council of Churches in this cause. And it only made sense to the WCC to resist.

In early 1948 Truman and Taylor began a campaign to bring the formation of the World Council into line with America's Cold War agenda. They focused on two objectives – keeping the Russian Orthodox Church out, and getting the Roman Catholic Church in. Additionally, Truman hoped to send Taylor as the President's representative to the World Council's organizational meeting.[56] Taylor soon embarked on a delicate campaign of clerical shuttle diplomacy, attempting to navigate a religious landscape rife with almost 2,000 years of ecclesiastical controversy. He soon learned that old animosities, disputes, and

[53] *Ibid.*
[54] Oxnam to Truman, November 15, 1947; WHCF: State Department Papers, Myron Taylor 46; HST Papers.
[55] Hassett to Taylor, November 20, 1947; WHCF: State Department Papers, Myron Taylor 46; HST Papers.
[56] Hassett to Taylor, March 19, 1948; Myron Taylor Papers 1; HST Papers.

misunderstandings die hard, even – or perhaps especially – among religious groups.

Taylor conducted several initiatives at once, and while each may have seemed discrete, they all merged under the grand strategy of forging a religious alliance against communism. On the WCC front, Taylor contacted the Archbishop of Canterbury to begin gathering support. "I assume that you would like to have me renew the suggestion which I made to His Holiness the Pope last Autumn when I was in Rome, to send observers to the assembly of the World Council of Churches in Amsterdam. I believe I reported to you that His Holiness looked upon the proposal with favor at that time."[57] Having encouraged the Pope to send representatives to the WCC, Taylor now needed to persuade the WCC to invite the Catholic delegation. Meanwhile, Taylor also began researching his suspicions concerning the Russian Orthodox Church. He discussed these issues at length with Monsignor Domenico Tardini, the Vatican Secretary of State, in an April 26, 1948, meeting in Rome. Tardini detailed the Vatican's grim assessment of the Orthodox Church:

> In every country outside the area of Russian control the Orthodox Church is an instrument for propagandising elements in sympathy with Orthodoxy and preparing their reconciliation with the Soviet regime. Again, in every country where a philo-Soviet government is established the local Orthodox Church is using its influence to bolster support of the Communist controlled government and the parties supporting these regimes.... In sum, evidence from every hand adds up to the conclusion that the Russian Orthodox Church under Patriarch Alexius of Moscow is the vehicle of Soviet political activity and an arm of Soviet imperialism.

Finally, the Vatican believed that the Soviets sought to extend this control, warning of an upcoming conference of Orthodox bishops in which Patriarch Alexius "may seek to divorce the bishops from their allegiance in matters liturgical and doctrinal to the Patriarch of Istanbul and to transfer this allegiance to the Patriarch of Moscow."[58] The Vatican's analysis painted a bleak picture that only reinforced Taylor's worst fears. A powerful and prominent communion such as the Orthodox Church, controlled by the Soviet Union, would pose a formidable challenge to Truman and Taylor's united front of religious anticommunism.

The next day Taylor flew from Rome to Geneva, the geographic distance eclipsed by the theological distance between the seat of Catholicism and the

---

[57] Taylor to Archbishop Geoffrey Fisher, March 26, 1948; Myron Taylor Papers 1; HST Papers.
[58] Memorandum of Taylor's Conversation with Monsignor Domenico Tardini, April 26, 1948; Myron Taylor Papers 1; HST Papers.

nativity ground of Calvinism. His journey brought him to the disorganized headquarters of the World Council of Churches and its Dutch Secretary General, Dr. Willem Adolf Visser t'Hooft. At the outset Taylor explained his mission as Truman's emissary and his hopes to address several issues, including the Ambassador's attendance at the WCC on behalf of the U.S. Government, the question of Catholic participation at the upcoming Amsterdam conference, and the status of relations between the WCC and the Russian Orthodox Church.[59]

On each of these three points Taylor and Visser t'Hooft clashed. Visser t'Hooft emphatically rejected the participation of any government representatives in the WCC, Taylor included, and stressed that the WCC was an exclusively "spiritual" union that affirmed separation of church and state. Taylor met with similar rejection on the matter of the Catholic Church. Visser t'Hooft "stressed most emphatically that neither representatives nor 'official observers' of the 'Church of Rome' would be invited to attend the Congress at Amsterdam, although ten Catholic individuals might 'observe' the proceedings without taking part in them but only as individuals." Visser t'Hooft further insisted that the WCC would not even consider inviting mere individual, unaffiliated Catholics unless the Vatican first made a formal request for such invitations. This caused Taylor no small degree of consternation, as he had understood from the Archbishop of Canterbury that Catholic representatives would be welcome, and therefore had informed the Pope of the same.[60]

Even more distressing to Taylor was Visser t'Hooft's attitude towards the Russian Orthodox Church. The Dutchman "emphasized most vigorously that the World Council did not draw the line at the Iron Curtain," hoped to strengthen ties with Orthodox churches, and regarded Patriarch Alexius as a sincere Christian who would be welcomed enthusiastically in Amsterdam. Taylor, for his part, found this position "a contradiction between Dr. t'Hooft's [sic] emphasis upon the separation of Church and State and his vigorous defense of Russian membership in the Council. . . . The Patriarchate, it is increasingly clear, is to every practical intent and purpose an arm of the Soviet State, an agency of Soviet propaganda and an instrument of Soviet imperialism." Moreover, Taylor warned Visser t'Hooft "that the presence of a Russian delegation at the Congress of Amsterdam would open Pandora's box of sabotage and obstructionism similar to the Russian tactics at the United

---

[59] Memorandum of Conversation with W.A. Visser t'Hooft in Geneva, April 27, 1948; Myron Taylor Papers 1; HST Papers.

[60] *Ibid.*

Nations." To these objections Visser t'Hooft only reiterated his belief that
the WCC could cooperate with and encourage the Russian Church and its
leadership, and he did not want political concerns to interfere.[61]

With considerable disappointment Taylor reported back to Truman. The
Ambassador described a "deep fissure within the Christian world" over the
Russian Orthodox Church, with the Catholics regarding it as a mere tool of the
Kremlin while the WCC considered the Orthodox a faithful religious body.[62]
The enmity between Rome and Geneva, coupled with the apparent warmth
between Moscow and Geneva, loomed as formidable obstacles to Truman's
grand designs. Religion was not as simple an instrument of containment as
Truman may have hoped. Meanwhile, Taylor resolved to continue his nego-
tiations with European church leaders in efforts to forge an anticommunist
alliance. He also began to focus even more attention on the Eastern Orthodox
Church.

For some time Taylor had harbored hopes of meeting with the Patriarch
of the Greek Orthodox Church in Istanbul, Turkey, the historic seat of the
Church. He had several purposes, including bolstering the anticommunist
resolve of the Greek and Turkish peoples, driving a deeper wedge between the
Greek Orthodox and the Russian Orthodox churches, and possibly enlisting
the Eastern church in Truman's pan-religious coalition. The situation of the
Greek church assumed further urgency in early 1948 when health problems
prompted the Ecumenical Patriarch Maximos to step down. Many powers
both political and ecclesial had an acute interest in his successor, who would
be the ostensible head of the entire Orthodox communion.[63] Taylor requested
a report from Edwin Wilson, the American Ambassador to Turkey. Wilson
described the succession issue as "a continuing series of Byzantine intrigues in
their most intricate form." While several church leaders maneuvered for the
position, it appeared that an American citizen, Athenagoras, had emerged as
the leading candidate, favored by Truman, Taylor, and Wilson, and enjoying
the support of both the Greek and Turkish governments, in their own rare
display of agreement. Wilson warned, however, "of the efforts being made by
Patriarch Alexei of Moscow to increase his own authority and influence at the
expense of that of the Oecumenical Patriarch." Furthermore, Athenagoras'

---

[61] *Ibid.*
[62] Taylor to Truman, April 29, 1948; Myron Taylor Papers 1; HST Papers.
[63] The relationship between the Ecumenical Patriarch and the Patriarchs of the other branches
of the Orthodox Church, particularly the Russian Church, is not easily delineated. The
Ecumenical Patriarch is traditionally described as "First among equals," in a linguistically
paradoxical effort to affirm both his primacy and the relative autonomy of each Orthodox
communion.

candidacy posed its own complications. "The fact that an American citizen known to be anticommunist is the leading candidate for the position is naturally excellent grist for the propaganda mill of the Soviet Union. . . . We must of course expect that any visit made by you to the Phanar will be used by the Soviet Union and its satellites to charge that the United States is now intervening at the Patriarchate."[64] Wilson did recommend that as soon as the new Patriarch had been seated, Taylor should visit the Phanar on behalf of Truman.[65] Not immune from their own Byzantine intrigues, Taylor and Wilson needed to strike the elusive balance between seeing their favored candidate become Patriarch and not leaving any diplomatic fingerprints open to Kremlin exploitation.

Taylor wrote to the Pope and informed him of America's position. "Archbishop Athenagoras conferred with me in New York on several occasions before I left America and has been for a long time in close contact with President Truman as he previously was with President Roosevelt. He urged me to visit Istanbul and Athens. Should he be chosen for the high post under consideration we believe that it would be a most desirable solution."[66] Taylor also consulted with Monsignor Angelo Roncalli, the Papal Nuncio in Paris and an expert on the Orthodox Church. The Nuncio echoed the counsel cautioning Taylor against a visit to Istanbul. While the Nuncio believed the Russian church to be just a tool of the Kremlin, he did not want to allow further grist for Russian accusations of "American imperialism" in Christendom. Instead, the United States should "proceed with caution to strengthen the American position with the Holy Synod and the Greek Bishops and to seat Bishop Athenagoras in the Patriarchate of Istanbul with as little fanfare as possible." The Nuncio also encouraged Taylor to utilize the warm relations between the Anglican Church and the Eastern Orthodox.[67] Overall, prospects seemed encouraging for continued resistance to communism by the Eastern Church, and Taylor's hopes for a visit were not dashed, but only deferred.

Taylor continued to push his agenda for the World Council of Churches, and continued to meet with frustration. On April 30, 1948, he met in London

---

[64] Wilson to Taylor, April 23, 1948; WHCF: State Department Papers, Myron Taylor 46. See also Taylor to Wilson, May 25, 1948; Myron Taylor 1; HST Papers. Note that "Oecumenical" is an alternative spelling. "Phanar" refers to the Greek section of Constantinople, as Istanbul had previously been known.

[65] Wilson to Taylor, June 26, 1948; WHCF: State Department Papers, Myron Taylor 46; HST Papers.

[66] Taylor to Pope Pius XII, May 22, 1948; Myron Taylor Papers 1; HST Papers.

[67] Memorandum of Conversation, Taylor and Monsignor Roncalli, May 6, 1948; Myron Taylor Papers 1; HST Papers. Note also that Roncalli was eventually elected Pope, and as John XXIII would convene the Second Vatican Council.

with British Prime Minister Clement Attlee, the Archbishop of Canterbury, and Lewis Douglas, the American Ambassador to the Court of St. James. The Archbishop responded with some skepticism to Taylor's plan to unite religious leaders against communism, saying that while he supported bringing all the Christian churches together, he did not think the "Mohammedans nor the Buddhists" should be included, since they did not worship the Christian God and did not respect the rights of the individual. On the question of the WCC and the Russian Orthodox, the Archbishop and Attlee parted ways, with the Archbishop supporting the inclusion of the Russian Orthodox in the WCC since he believed it to be a genuine Christian church, and Attlee sharing Taylor's suspicions that the Kremlin controlled the church. Finally, the Archbishop admitted that he and Visser t'Hooft disagreed on the Catholic problem. The Archbishop favored inviting the Pope to send official observers to Amsterdam and was trying to persuade Visser t'Hooft to do so.[68]

Further complications arose in France. Taylor met with Rev. Marc Boegner, one of five co-presidents of the WCC and leader of the French Protestants, in Paris on May 4. Boegner shared Taylor's concerns about Soviet communism but believed "the threat should be met not negatively, that is by an align-ment against Russia, but positively, through evangelization and Christian approaches to the Russians, using every means still available to maintain and re-establish bridges to them." But Boegner's positive inclinations only went so far. He, like the Archbishop of Canterbury, expressed skepticism towards cooperating with other religions, believing that merely bringing Christians together was a more realistic goal. Regarding the WCC, Boegner hoped very much that a Russian Orthodox delegation would attend but emphatically rejected representation of any governments, including Taylor on behalf of the United States. And while Boegner personally did not object to official Catholic observers, he stressed that as Chairman of the WCC he needed to mind the views of all participants. Ironically, given Truman and Taylor's stren-uous advocacy on behalf of the Catholics, Boegner intimated that the fiercest opposition to a Catholic presence arose in Truman and Taylor's own back-yard, from the American Protestant churches. The objections of American Protestant leaders notwithstanding, Boegner offered to mediate between the Vatican and the WCC. An excited Taylor reported back to Truman that French negotiation might yet provide a solution.[69]

---

[68] Taylor to Truman, May 4, 1948; WHCF: State Department Papers, Myron Taylor 46; HST Papers. Details come from a summary of the meeting enclosed with Taylor's letter to Truman.

[69] Taylor to Truman, May 5, 1948; Myron Taylor Papers 1; HST Papers. Attached to Taylor's letter was a memorandum of Taylor's meeting with Boegner.

Boegner's subsequent efforts were not encouraging. Backpedaling from his earlier openness to Catholic representation, Boegner informed Taylor a few days later that of the other four co-presidents of the WCC, only the Archbishop of Canterbury would even consider official Catholic participation. Boegner himself now sided with missionary leader John Mott of the United States, Archbishop Eidem of Sweden, and Archbishop Germanos of the Greek Orthodox Church in opposing Catholic representation. Boegner gave Taylor a letter clarifying the WCC's position: the WCC welcomed up to ten individual Catholics to observe the assembly as *private* citizens; if the Pope desired a more official status, he could request that the WCC invite him to designate two *official* observers instead of the ten private attendees. Should the Pope make this appeal, the WCC co-presidents would agree, at least, to consider it.[70] Such contention over linguistic subtleties like the question of "official" or "private," "observer" or "representative," and which party needed to initiate the negotiations, hearkened to the most recondite of theological or diplomatic disputes. Even Taylor, who relished the finer nuances of diplomacy, grew exasperated, writing to Truman that both of them needed to avoid being "drawn into the center of this religious controversy."[71] Taylor only generated further contention when he leaked a report to the *New York Times* describing his efforts on behalf of Truman to "make the Amsterdam meeting inclusive of all Christianity and turn the influence of all Christian sentiment in the world toward the preservation of peace."[72] Not surprisingly, this public attempt to pressure the WCC backfired. It prompted an angry response from Associate General Secretary Henry Smith Leiper, who protested the "very erroneous impressions" created by the article, and asserted that, contrary to Taylor's portrayal, the WCC was already both inclusive of Christian denominations and dedicated to world peace.[73]

Truman continued to support his Ambassador while growing more and more frustrated with the WCC. He wrote to Taylor sympathizing with "the embarrassing position in which you find yourself as a result of the intransigence of the religious leaders" organizing the WCC. While Truman acknowledged the right of religious bodies to determine their own membership standards, he believed "it is deplorable that all sorts and conditions of professing Christians... cannot unite in common cause against those twin blights –

---

[70] Memorandum of Conversation between Taylor and Boegner, May 7, 1948. Letter from Boegner to Taylor, May 7, 1948; Myron Taylor Papers 1; HST Papers.
[71] Taylor to Truman, May 10, 1948; Myron Taylor Papers 1; HST Papers.
[72] Transcript of article "Taylor to End Tour on Christian Unity" in *The New York Times*, May 11, 1948; Myron Taylor Papers 1; HST Papers.
[73] Leiper to Editor of *New York Times*, May 20, 1948; Myron Taylor Papers 1; HST Papers.

atheism and communism." Truman simply could not fathom the divisions
that continued to plague Christendom:

> If our earnest appeal in behalf of Christian brotherhood fails we must be
> content to leave to the judgment of Christians everywhere and to the verdict
> of history the merits of our effort. It is rather ironical that an organization
> which has established itself as the World Council of Churches... should
> exclude from its assembly observers from the oldest and most numerous
> body of Christians in the world while accepting prelates from out of the
> darkness beyond the Iron Curtain. Meanwhile, who shall quench the flames
> of anger, hatred, envy and malice which threaten to consume Christian
> civilization?[74]

The incessant negotiations and internecine religious squabbles that mired
Taylor's diplomacy should not obscure the essential drama of his efforts.
Truman had dispatched Taylor on a radical mission: to re-shape the internal
organization, membership, and agenda of a religious community. In doing so
Truman and Taylor acted out of their own religious convictions in determining
the essentials of religious faith, the identity of "true believers," and the proper
mission of the church. Political leaders have often tried to influence the
political agendas of religious organizations. But attempting to change the
religious agendas of religious organizations, as Truman and Taylor tried to do
with the WCC, was another matter entirely.

Their effort was not only unusual but also unsuccessful. In a letter to Boegner that Taylor drafted in consultation with the Pope and with Truman's support, the Ambassador ended the campaign in surrender. Taylor complained
that Boegner's proposal for the Pope to request permission from the WCC
to send Catholic observers would have placed the Pope in the embarrassing
position of petitioning the Protestants only to face almost certain rejection.
With great regret Taylor lamented "that only a section of Christendom will
be assembled at Amsterdam in August with the inference that there is a rift
in the Western religious world." He still held that "both Church and State,
in the face of the menace which today threatens Christendom, have a common obligation to man the parapets of our civilization and watch so that the
destructive forces of atheism and materialism will not overrun and utterly
destroy it."[75] Truman echoed Taylor's frustration and affirmed the decision
to give up on the WCC.[76] Having failed in their attempt to bring Catholics

---

[74] Truman to Taylor, May 19, 1948; Myron Taylor Papers 1; HST Papers.
[75] Taylor to Boegner, May 25, 1948; Myron Taylor Papers 1; HST Papers.
[76] Truman to Taylor, June 18, 1948; Myron Taylor Papers 1; HST Papers.

into the WCC in a common front against communism, Truman and Taylor resolved to press on with their campaign in other promising directions.

III

American assistance to the Vatican was not limited to diplomatic encouragement. Shortly after the Italian elections of 1948, in which the Vatican expended tremendous sums of money and effort to ensure that the Italian Communist Party did not gain power, Secretary of State George Marshall met with Cardinal Spellman in New York. Marshall informed Spellman that, in response to the Cardinal's appeals at the behest of Pius XII, the U.S. government covertly would reimburse the Vatican for the millions of dollars it had spent on the elections.[77] The Pope, appreciative of the American government's vigorous advocacy and assistance, offered some of his own reflections on America's role in the present crisis. July, 1948 found Taylor returning to Washington bearing a letter to Truman from the Vatican. No doubt reinforcing Truman's own belief in a providential role for America, the Pope declaimed that "on the foreign policy of the United States of America chiefly hinges the issue of the fateful struggle between what remains of a free world and God-less totalitarianism." The Pope singled out the Marshall Plan as a particularly notable, and noble, initiative. To succeed, however, it must follow certain principles. European recovery must be seen as an end in its own right and not just a crass tool used to contain the Soviets. The American people must support their government and embrace European recovery as a worthy goal. Finally, it would not be sufficient to focus on just one European country. All of Europe must be revived, and a spirit of cooperation and independence must be established and "guaranteed by some international authority." Fearful of resurgent German hegemony as well as Soviet designs on the continent, the Pope threw his firm support behind a European mutual security regime. Political and economic reform alone would not do. "Any program of assistance will fail of its purpose unless it takes into account the imperative need for men to return to God."[78] This succinctly reinforced Truman's own agenda to integrate the religious forces of the world into the effort to contain the Soviet Union.

The next year found Taylor resuming one of his most dreaded activities, trying to mollify his persistent critics among the mainline Protestant leadership.

---

[77] John Cooney, *The American Pope: The Life and Times of Francis Cardinal Spellman* (New York: Times Books 1984), 157–168.

[78] Pope Pius XII to Truman, July 19, 1948; Myron Taylor Papers 1; HST Papers.

On May 3, 1949, Taylor met again in New York with several clergymen, including four from the previous group: Cavert, Dahlberg, Oxnam, and Pugh. The group spent a good portion of the meeting haggling over who was to blame for the absence of Roman Catholic representatives from the WCC meeting in Amsterdam. The churchmen, particularly Cavert and Oxnam, insisted that the Vatican bore responsibility for its own exclusion. They pointed to the more than twenty-year history of conferences laying the foundation for the WCC such as Lausanne in 1927 and Oxford and Edinburgh in 1937, and claimed that the Roman Catholic Church had flatly rejected any and all invitations to participate in the conferences or even dialogue from afar. Only against this backdrop could the Catholic absence from Amsterdam in 1948 be understood. Taylor, to the contrary, offered detailed accounts of his negotiations with WCC leaders over the last two years, and concluded that while Pius XII had been willing and eager to send official observers, Protestant intransigence had torpedoed any possible rapprochement.[79]

Taylor also made his now customary pitch for "harmony among the religious groups – and particularly the Protestants, the Catholics and the Jews" in light of the "great peril" facing the world. Perhaps surprising to Taylor, some in his audience took umbrage at this entire notion. Dr. Eppling Reinartz, leader of the United Lutheran Church, complained that Truman and Taylor's "whole operation is based on a very naïve view of the relationship of the churches and the world religions." Protestants held firmly to a set of doctrines that distinguished them from other faiths, and these doctrines should not be cast easily aside. The WCC "is not an association to stop communism, nor an effort to block atheism as such. . . . I wish our President could be disabused of the idea that there is some moral unity in Mohammedanism, in Judaism and Christianity that could be associated structurally or in an informal way to estop the on-rush of communism or of atheism."[80]

Here was a direct and fundamental challenge to the very foundation of Truman and Taylor's campaign. They had based their agenda on the premise that all religions possessed more or less similar social utility. The dogmatic beliefs of the respective faiths mattered little; much more important was that they produced good citizens loyal to a supreme being – and resistant to a totalitarian state. Dr. Reinartz, echoed by at least some of his clerical colleagues, insisted on preserving the distinctives of their faith. The nature of God, the person of Jesus Christ, the truth or falsehood of the Bible, the

[79] Transcript of Meeting of Protestant Clergymen with Myron C. Taylor, May 3, 1949; Myron Taylor Papers 2; HST Papers.
[80] *Ibid.*

leadership structures of the church, all held immense importance in separating religions from each other. Besides accusing Truman and Taylor of naiveté, Reinartz regarded their campaign as condescending as well. Pugh elaborated on this point when he warned Taylor against the "clericalism that is as great a problem as is communism." Describing Catholic violations of Protestant religious liberty in Europe, Pugh intoned ominously that "communism is a child of that problem."[81] The very office of the Pope inspired intense fear and loathing in these Protestants, who meant no hyperbole in equating the Vatican with the Kremlin. From such a vantage point Taylor's mission appeared profoundly threatening.

The Protestants continued to emphasize what they believed to be the religious, as opposed to the political, agenda of the WCC and the Amsterdam conference. Pugh insisted that their primary interest "was not necessarily world peace or the fight of the religions against communism" but rather the ecumenical movement. Part of this separation of the "political" from the "religious" seems to have come from their rather benign assessment of the communist threat. "In the Protestant communities in Europe the infiltration of communism has not been serious," Oxnam claimed. Catholicism, on the other hand, was doubly pernicious because of its own authoritarianism and its apparent susceptibility to communism. The Protestant leaders concluded their time with Taylor by entreating him several times to arrange for them to meet with Truman and clarify the purposes of the WCC.[82]

The Protestant leaders were not fully candid in describing the purposes and agenda of the WCC, which of course involved itself quite extensively in questions of international politics, peace, and conflict at Amsterdam and in the years following. Perhaps realizing that he shared little common ground with the churchmen and that further dialogue would not be fruitful, Taylor prepared to return to Europe. Truman urged him to resume his consultations with leaders of the various Christian communions.[83]

Truman revealed his strategy in a colorful letter to his beloved wife Bess. After one particular meeting with Taylor at the White House, Truman wrote:

> Looks as if [Taylor] and I may get the morals of the world on our side. We are talking to the Archbishop of Canterbury, the bishop at the head of the Lutheran Church, the Metropolitan of the Greek Church at Istanbul, and the Pope. I may send him to see the top Buddhist and the Grand Lama of Tibet. If I can mobilize the people who believe in a moral world against

---

[81] *Ibid.*
[82] *Ibid.*
[83] Truman to Taylor, May 4, 1949; Myron Taylor Papers 2; HST Papers.

the Bolshevik materialists who believe as Henry Wallace does – "that the end justifies the means" – we can win this fight. Treaties, agreements, or the moral code mean nothing to Communists. So we've got to organize the people who believe in honor and the Golden Rule to win the world back to peace and Christianity. Ain't it hell![84]

This letter is vintage Truman – blunt, fervent, idealistic, at once pious and profane. It encapsulates his motives and means in fighting the Cold War. It also vividly illustrates his own conviction that morality is the most important product of religion, and while all faiths teach a similar moral code, the most preferred faith is Christianity.

Taylor soon returned to his customary intrigues, immersing himself back into the diplomatic delicacies of European religion and politics. He reported back to Truman, with a mixture of excitement and apprehension, that the Greek Orthodox Archbishop Damaskinos of Athens had suddenly died. "The appointment of his successor is of vital importance – both political and religious." No doubt the Russian Orthodox Church would push for an Archbishop sympathetic to communism and the Soviet bloc. At the urging of Vatican authorities, who viewed developments in the Orthodox Church with great interest despite Rome's own estrangement from Constantinople, Taylor began to look for ways to influence the selection in a manner favorable to the West. He decided to send a letter to Patriarch Athenagoras, an ally of the United States who would be overseeing the appointment process, and inquire about making a secret visit to Istanbul and Athens. Taylor also expressed to Truman his hopes for exerting American leverage on the situation. Alluding to the history of Greek–American relations and ongoing American support for Greece's struggle against communist insurrection, Taylor commented, "I assume the Greeks are under heavy obligation to our Government. This can be handled discreetly. . . . Publicity would be harmful. But action is imperative."[85] Soon after Taylor met again with the Pope, who offered to transmit his letter to Athenagoras directly through the Vatican's secret back channels with the Orthodox Church. Taylor reported back to Truman that the Pope remained a resolute ally in the fight against communism, a struggle which the Pope regarded "as a duty to mankind and to God which he cannot shirk regardless of consequences."[86]

---

[84] Quoted in Miller, 428.
[85] Taylor to Truman, May 1949 (exact day unspecified); WHCF: State Department Papers, Myron Taylor 44; HST Papers.
[86] Taylor to Truman, May 1949 (exact date unspecified); Myron Taylor Papers 2; HST Papers.

The events of the next two weeks remain obscured. At some point during that time Archbishop Spyridion received the appointment to succeed Damaskinos as Patriarch of the Orthodox Church in Athens. Truman and Taylor believed Spyridion to be a favorable choice, and welcomed him as a new ally in their spiritual campaign against communism. To what extent Truman, Taylor, or other American officials directly influenced this appointment is unclear, or at least not revealed by currently available documents. On June 12 Taylor wrote Truman that the Pope's communication channels had been successful, and Taylor had arranged to visit Athenagoras in Istanbul and the newly-installed Spyridion in Athens.[87] Truman wrote back on June 17, applauding Taylor for his resourcefulness and expressing excitement at Taylor's upcoming meetings. Truman singled out Patriarch Athenagoras for special praise: "It is well that the forces of Christianity and democracy have such a staunch advocate and defender as he. He is indeed in a position to exercise great influence in his exalted station in Istanbul." Truman even encouraged Taylor to consider extending his trip "to pierce the iron curtain to negotiate with the Patriarch of Moscow along the lines we discussed before you departed for Europe."[88]

Taylor's visits to Istanbul and Athens the next week seemed to bear fruit. In a lengthy letter to Truman reporting on his meetings, Taylor described Patriarch Athenagoras's endorsement of their campaign. Truman and Taylor's efforts had thus far almost entirely focused on enlisting Protestant and Catholic leaders in their hoped-for alliance. Now it seemed that the third leg of Christendom, the Orthodox Church, would join. The next day Taylor journeyed to Athens to meet with the new Archbishop Spyridion. While the Archbishop voiced continuing frustration over what he perceived as the indifference of the Catholic Church towards the Orthodox, he seemed willing to place such feelings aside in the face of the present crisis. As Taylor described it, "the Patriarch was so emphatic about the moral decline of the world and especially of Europe that he indicated that if His Holiness would be willing to nominate two observers or, still better, two representatives, to a meeting of the World Council of Churches, it should be called at once."[89]

This was no small development. Though enmity between the Eastern and Western Churches had been codified by their formal split in 1054, it traced back even further to the earliest centuries of the Christian faith. Differences over matters of doctrine, worship, culture, and especially church authority

---

[87] Taylor to Truman, June 12, 1949; Myron Taylor Papers 2; HST Papers.
[88] Truman to Taylor, June 17, 1949; Myron Taylor Papers 2; HST Papers.
[89] Taylor to Truman, June 24, 1949; Myron Taylor Papers 2; HST Papers.

had deepened the chasm separating the two communions. Now both faced what they regarded as an apocalyptic threat: Bolshevism lurked dangerously close in the immediate backyards of the Catholic and Orthodox Churches, in Italy and Greece and Turkey, to say nothing of communism's apparent designs on the rest of the world. Though the real differences and grievances separating Rome from Constantinople did not disappear, they paled in the glare of the communist peril.

The Eastern Church had its own embarrassing conundrum, and to that Taylor and Spyridion next turned. The theological tradition of the Eastern Orthodox had always endorsed the closest of relations between church and state, between the faith and the nation. In the case of countries such as Greece aligned with the political West, this relationship placed the Greek Orthodox Church firmly against communism. A system that was an advantage in Greece became a disadvantage in Russia, however. The Soviet state controlled the tightly interwoven Russian nation and Orthodox Church. Spyridion confirmed Taylor's suspicions, that the Russian church "was an arm of the state and could not be looked upon as an independent religious body." He did not regard the Russian church as completely apostate, however, and cautiously endorsed Truman's idea of a covert mission by Taylor to the Russian Patriarch Alexis. Spyridion "believed that in a religious sense the heart of the Russian Patriarch was good, that political necessity compelled him to bow to the Stalin regime, that the people were very religious." Moreover, Taylor informed Truman, "His Beatitude was definite that in due course if the flame of religion is kept alive it will be the only influence, short of military force from the outside, that will arouse the people to overthrow the present regime."[90] Containment held the premise that if the United States maintained external pressure at strategic points against Kremlin expansion, the Soviet state would eventually collapse under the weight of its own internal contradictions. Truman and Taylor shared the Archbishop's belief that the vital and independent religious faith of the Russian people, if sustained, might well kindle the fire that would engulf the USSR from within.

Truman remained impressed and encouraged by Taylor's efforts. In a July 8, 1949 letter, Truman described Athenagoras and Spyridion as "two more avenues through which you can work for peace in parallel efforts with His Holiness in Rome and with the other religious leaders with whom you have been in consultation." In what Truman regarded as an unfortunate irony, at the same time as Taylor succeeded in enlarging the ecumenical coalition

[90] *Ibid.* Also Taylor's Memorandum of Conversation, June 24, 1949; Myron Taylor Papers 2; HST Papers.

abroad, American Protestant leaders increased their own protests against Truman's unofficial recognition of the Vatican.

> One can earnestly hope... that the intense and unremitting opposition to your mission engendered in the hearts and minds of some of our American religious leaders may be dispelled. There is work for us all if we could but unite against the forces of atheistic communism which beset us on all fronts. These reflections emphasize sad and tragic divisions among Christian forces... one finds only anger, enmity, and ill will where Christian men should be working together to bring the Kingdom of God nearer to this world.[91]

Here again Truman's postmillennialism reasserted itself. Though not theologically sophisticated, the President had a basic set of religious convictions about God, humanity, and history. He believed that the various Christian groups needed to set aside what he regarded as their petty doctrinal squabbles, and come together around the common task of defeating communism and building a new Kingdom of God here on earth.

The next week Taylor reluctantly notified Truman that he would not be journeying to Russia. After his trip to Greece and Turkey Taylor had traveled to Germany to seek the counsel of Commissioner John McCloy, Ambassador Robert Murphy, and Cardinal Count von Preysing of Berlin. All three unanimously advised against a secret visit by Taylor to Patriarch Alexis in Moscow. Several concerns emerged, among them the fears that the close surveillance of the Patriarch would render candid conversation impossible, that the Soviets might distort Taylor's visit for their own propaganda purposes, and that the presence of someone so closely tied to the Vatican might bring increased persecution on the Catholic Church in Russia.[92] The religious alliance against communism would not include the Russian Orthodox Church, after all.

Yet that same week brought encouraging news as well. The Pope issued an edict announcing that the Catholic Church would "most warmly welcome collaboration with Protestants in the common fight of religious persons against the communist atheist" [sic]. A Vatican official described the edict as a "great turning point" in Catholic–Protestant relations, on the same scale as the 1520 papal bull denouncing the Protestant reformers, with the crucial difference that this new edict sought unity instead of division. Taylor excitedly related this news to Truman, averring that this was "the first open offer of

---

[91] Truman to Taylor, July 8, 1949; Myron Taylor Papers 2; HST Papers.
[92] Taylor to Truman, July 15, 1949; Myron Taylor Papers 2; HST Papers.

collaboration" by the Pope to the Protestants.[93] The Vatican also announced the excommunication of communists and those who aid and abet communism.[94] Monsignor Roncalli described to Taylor the purposes behind the excommunication. While the Pope acknowledged the appeal communism held to some who earnestly desired to improve the social and economic lot of mankind, communism conflicted too fundamentally with Christianity. Moreover, the Vatican expressed alarm at the recent collaboration of "progressive Christian groups" with communists. This could only lead to communist infiltration of free societies and the subsequent extinguishing of all religious faith.[95] The Vatican acted accordingly, in the same week removing any last vestige of fellowship with communists while extending the hand of cooperation to Protestants.

President Truman in turn urged Taylor to redouble his efforts. On November 3, 1949, shortly after meeting with Taylor to discuss the next stage of his mission, Truman wrote Taylor a lengthy, and revealing, letter. Truman began by lamenting the continuing tensions in the world, but did not succumb to despair. Citing a passage in the book of Acts that anticipated a unified human family living peacefully in the world, he resolved that "ours is the duty to contribute our utmost to the realization of that prophecy in our own day and generation." He then added a new item to Taylor's agenda. As he returned to Europe, Taylor should "sound out sentiment regarding the plan you and I have discussed to convene here in Washington an assembly representative of the religious and, therefore, the moral forces of both hemispheres."[96] No longer would Taylor just shuttle from European cleric to European cleric attempting to cobble together some sort of vague anticommunist agreement. Now he would try to gather Christian leaders in Washington, where Truman and Taylor could oversee a vigorous statement in favor of world peace – and in firm opposition to communist totalitarianism.

Holding the assembly in the United States would carry great symbolic importance. Truman believed that America represented the ideals and

---

[93] Taylor to Truman, July 15, 1949; Myron Taylor Papers 2; HST Papers. Letter contains excerpt of Pope's statement and Vatican official's commentary.

[94] The year before, the Pope had excommunicated certain communists in Italy who had been working for a communist victory in the Italian elections. This decree, in July 1949, marked a categorical and universal condemnation of communism and its proponents. A CIA analysis of the Pope's decree described it as "a very powerful factor in the East-West struggle" and noted that now "the two most powerful organizations for moving men to act on behalf of a doctrine [Catholicism and Communism] are brought into open and basic conflict." Quoted in Cooney, *The American Pope*, pp. 157–168.

[95] Memorandum by Taylor, July 19, 1949; Myron Taylor Papers 2; HST Papers.

[96] Truman to Taylor, November 3, 1949; Myron Taylor Papers 2; HST Papers.

aspirations of the entire world. "Our own Nation, drawn from men of all bloods and every religious allegiance, is, therefore, a cross section of the whole world.... What we have here achieved among all races, colors, and faiths points the way and offers encouragement to all other nations." Truman drew inspiration and hope not only from American ideals but also from recent history. World War II, he believed, had witnessed a similar unity of purpose among world religions.

> My prayer will ever be that we may again achieve in the quest for a true peace something of the spirit of tolerance, understanding, and good will which enabled Catholics, Protestants, Jews and men and women of all faiths whether Mohammedans, Buddhists or Hindus to submerge their religious differences during the fighting war ... against the totalitarian enemies whom we together faced in that challenging ordeal. I think we should aim to enlist the active interest and support of all nations in a new quest for peace, based on unity of moral values and on common belief in one God who is Lord of Lords, and King of Kings.[97]

As the spiritual division of the world hardened, Truman began to reveal his campaign to the public. In a November 11, 1949, address to the National Conference of Christians and Jews, Truman clarified the conflict. The repressive communist regimes "threaten to undo the slow and hard-won achievements of civilization. They represent a new barbarism, more terrible than that of ancient times. These are the acts of men who conceive of other men as slaves, and not as brethren." America and the rest of the Western world, on the other hand, cherished a freedom based on unity and diversity. "We have achieved our unity in this country, not by eliminating our differences in religion ... but by holding to a concept which rises above them all, the concept of the brotherhood of man." Religious distinctives were not inconsequential, but Truman believed they paled in comparison to the "only sure bedrock of human brotherhood," which is "the knowledge that God is the Father of mankind." Truman then revealed his agenda: "I am doing everything of which I am capable to organize the moral forces of the world to meet this situation." Such people needed to "organize themselves," because "it is only the people of religious faith throughout the world who have the power to overcome the force of tyranny."[98] Though Truman did not disclose any of the details of Taylor's mission, he made clear that the Cold War was being fought

---

[97] *Ibid.*
[98] Truman, Address to the National Conference of Christians and Jews, November 11, 1949. *Public Papers of the Presidents: Harry S. Truman, 1949* (Washington: United States Government Printing Office 1964), 561–563.

not merely with economic, diplomatic, and military means, but with religion as well.

Yet the Protestant leadership posed continuing difficulties. The Archbishop of Canterbury, in response to the invitation to the proposed conference in Washington, wrote Taylor of his misgivings. While acknowledging that "a proposal of this sort, coming from the President of the United States, commands one's most earnest consideration," the Archbishop described himself and his colleague the Archbishop of York as "disturbed and anxious" as to the wisdom of the assembly. He expressed particular concern over the participants and agenda of the conference. Leaders from different religions grappling with a broad mandate would ultimately be "meaningless, since each group would have its own ideas of God, and there are wide differences in those ideas in relation to human freedoms and, for instance, to religious liberty." On the other hand, the two Archbishops believed that if the conference were only confined to Christian leaders it would be a futile redundancy, since each Christian communion already had its own offices or leaders to make pronouncements on the world situation. Finally, the Archbishops feared that, given world tensions, the conference would be perceived widely as "having a political slant," and this they could not endorse.[99] Of course a "political slant" was precisely what Truman and Taylor envisioned, though they regarded it as a moral and even religious imperative. But rather than directly responding to the concerns of the Archbishops, Taylor just urged them to attend the meeting and be open to further discussions.[100]

Taylor, meanwhile, had reached a critical decision in his own life. His health faltering, and faced with unrelenting Protestant criticism of his "unofficial" mission to the Vatican, he decided to resign his position as the President's representative to the Pope. In a letter informing Pius XII of his decision, Taylor also shared with the Pope Truman's "intention . . . to recommend to the Congress of the United States at an early date" the appointment of an official Ambassador to the Vatican.[101] More immediately, Taylor assured the Pope of his intentions to continue the effort to forge a coalition of Christian leaders against communism. Taylor described Truman's plan to "invite representatives of the Catholic Church and other churches to convene in a meeting in Washington at an early practicable date."[102]

---

[99] Archbishop of Canterbury Geoffrey Cantuar to Taylor, November 30, 1949; Myron Taylor Papers 2; HST Papers.
[100] Taylor to Cantuar, December 7, 1949; Myron Taylor Papers 2; HST Papers.
[101] Taylor to Pius XII, December 13, 1949; WHCF: State Department Papers, Myron Taylor 46; HST Papers.
[102] *Ibid.*

IV

Even without Taylor's mission to the Pope as a point of contention, the divide between Protestants and Catholics remained a thorny hindrance. The dawn of the new year found Taylor in Paris meeting again with Marc Boegner. Boegner agreed "fully that all religions should work together against the scourge of Communism" but voiced his skepticism yet again about the feasibility of such a united front, because of the doctrinal differences and historic animosities between the different groups. Boegner even responded favorably when Taylor described Truman's idea of convening a meeting in Washington "for the purpose of consolidating the Christian forces of the world in their fight against Communist atheism." In a related vein, Boegner suggested that the Pope "invite theologians of all sects to meet together to discuss doctrines and dogmas, with a view to establishing the fundamentals which were common to all Christian sects." But as to the French Protestant Church ever reuniting with Rome, in Boegner's view that was an "impossibility."[103] Boegner believed that shared doctrine must precede shared political action.

On further reflection, Boegner's skepticism increased. Three weeks later he sent a letter to Taylor, which Taylor shared with Truman, warning of the "grave misunderstandings which might result" from Truman's proposed convocation of Christian leaders in Washington. Boegner described a dilemma to Taylor and Truman: on the one hand, a comprehensive meeting would have to include the Catholic Church, but on the other hand, the presence of Catholics would provoke "very vivid reactions" from the other church leaders. Furthermore, such a meeting would inevitably be seen as political and would undermine the mandate of the churches to "remain within their own real territory – the territory of the preaching of the Gospel."[104] Boegner's cold feet greatly dispirited the White House. Truman's aide William Hassett suspected Bishop Oxnam's nefarious influence. The nettlesome Methodist, he wrote, "has it in his power to torpedo the conference if he so wills and he has never been slow to assert his nuisance value."[105] Boegner commanded wide respect among American and European churchmen, and without his active participation, the conference's prospects looked dim. Truman grew increasingly exasperated at the inability, or refusal, of the various church groups to come together against

---

[103] Memorandum of Conversation between Taylor and Boegner, January 3, 1950; Myron Taylor Papers 2; HST Papers.

[104] Boegner to Taylor, January 23, 1950. Also, Taylor to Truman, February 3, 1950; Myron Taylor Papers 2; HST Papers.

[105] Memorandum from Hassett to Truman, February 8, 1950; WHCF: State Department Papers, Myron Taylor 50; HST Papers.

communism, complaining to his pastor Edward Pruden that "we have one common enemy to fight at the present time and we shouldn't do so much fighting amongst ourselves."[106]

Truman and Taylor, though discouraged, did not give up. Truman invited Boegner to a private meeting at the White House in June, and informed Boegner that he had found the difficulties in bringing the Christian groups together against communism "disappointing." Furthermore, he had no agenda for the proposed conference other than a focus on peace (which would no doubt negatively implicate communism). Truman believed he had made some progress in alleviating Boegner's concerns, and was hopeful of future cooperation from the French pastor. Given Boegner's leading position with the WCC as well as his status as head of the French Protestant churches, Truman realized that Boegner carried great sway with Protestants around the world. Determined to see his plan succeed, he was willing to engage in some old-fashioned arm-twisting with stubborn clerics. After meeting with Boegner, Truman was "delighted" to learn that Bishop Dibelius would be in the United States the next month, as he desired to meet with the German as well.[107]

A couple of weeks later Taylor accompanied Dibelius to the White House for another meeting with Truman. Dibelius had continued to impress Taylor and Truman with his steadfast opposition to communism, most recently defying Soviet threats and issuing a pastoral letter from his church in East Berlin to all 19,000 Lutheran clergy throughout Germany that sternly criticized communism. Taylor informed Truman of Dibelius' request for $50,000 for establishing educational programs in the western zones of Germany to counteract Soviet propaganda and to attract Germans, particularly German children, living in the Soviet zone. Truman quickly agreed to this request and instructed the Economic Cooperation Administration (ECA) and Commissioner McCloy in Germany to look into providing the funds. Dibelius also expressed ready agreement with Truman's plan for a united front of Christian leaders, and proclaimed his willingness to cooperate in any way.[108]

---

[106]   Truman to Pruden, May 4, 1950; President's Personal File (PPF) 490, folder 627; HST Papers.
[107]   Hassett to Taylor, June 29, 1950; WHCF: State Department Papers, Myron Taylor 44; HST Papers.
[108]   Memorandum from Taylor to Truman, July 7, 1950; WHCF: State Department Papers, Myron Taylor 47. Also telegram from McCloy to William Forster, July 17, 1950; WHCF: State Department Papers, Myron Taylor 48; letter from Taylor to Truman, July 18, 1950; Myron Taylor Papers 2; letter from Truman to Taylor, July 21, 1950: President's Secretary's Files (PSF): Chronological File 295: folder: Myron Taylor; HST Papers. In a dizzying series of bureaucratic twists and turns, it took several more months before Dibelius received the money. The ECA initially raised concerns about ensuring that the money would be expended in a non-sectarian manner. When those had been allayed, some of the American

Even though Taylor had resigned his post as Truman's representative to the Pope, both Taylor and Truman moved ahead with their plan. On July 15, 1950, Truman sent Taylor a letter asking him to return to Europe to work on arranging the long-hoped for meeting of religious leaders in Washington. The President made clear his conviction that a serious and persistent obstacle to peace remained, namely "the machinations of one wicked man who is spokesman for a cabal of evil associates," resulting in "whole populations held in slavery under totalitarian tyranny."[109] This particular letter of Truman's, drafted by Hassett and approved by Truman, contains unusually florid language, especially for the famously plainspoken President. Given that Taylor would be returning to Europe without his customary diplomatic commission, Truman and Taylor intended this letter to be shown to the European religious and political leaders Taylor would be meeting with, to demonstrate his bona fides.[110]

The documentary record for the next several months remains frustratingly thin. It appears that Truman's desired convocation of religious leaders in Washington did not occur that year, because of the all too familiar divisions between the different communions. Truman reviewed his efforts and vented his frustrations in a February 15, 1951, letter to Lewis Strauss.

> I have been trying my best to organize the moral forces of the world, which included the desire to send a representative to the Vatican. I have had special representatives call on the Patriarch of Istanbul, who is a friend of ours, and I myself have talked to the Chief Rabbi of Israel, as well as a great many of the religious leaders of all sects and opinions here in this country. I have also seen the Chief Bishop of the Lutheran Church in Germany, who has

Embassy staff in Germany expressed reservations that Dibelius might not be sufficiently anticommunist. Finally, on March 23, 1951, Secretary of State Acheson sent a memo to Truman noting that the $50,000 had been disbursed to Dibelius "to help this man in his fight against the communists." The relationship between the United States and Dibelius continued, with the CIA under Walter Bedell Smith and then Allen Dulles continuing to provide him smaller amounts of funding. Dibelius eventually received wide renown when *Time* magazine profiled him in an April 6, 1953 cover story titled "It is Not Easy to Live as a Christian." See Dibelius to Taylor, February 1, 1951 and February 24, 1951; Myron Taylor Papers 2; Memorandum from Acheson to Truman, March 23, 1951; PSF: General File, Myron C. Taylor 44; Henry Byroade (State Department Director of German Affairs) to Taylor, March 23, 1951; Myron Taylor Papers 2; Dibelius to Taylor, December 18, 1952; Myron Taylor Papers 2; Taylor to Truman, December 23, 1952; Myron Taylor Papers 2; Taylor to Allen Dulles, January 9, 1953; Myron Taylor Papers 2; Dulles to Taylor, January 17, 1953; Myron Taylor Papers 2; HST Papers.

[109] Truman to Taylor, July 15, 1950; Myron Taylor Papers 2; HST Papers.

[110] See, for example, Taylor's letter to Truman of July 5, 1951, where Taylor describes the reading of Truman's letter at a meeting of Anglican and Episcopal church leaders. Myron Taylor Papers 2; HST Papers.

called on me twice. I've talked to four of the Cardinals in this country on the subject and have had personal correspondence with the Pope on the same subject.

Truman placed the blame for his initiative's failure squarely on one group. "Some of our Protestant leaders in this country are much more interested in a controversy with the Catholic Church here at home" than in uniting in a common religious front against communism. "As soon as I can overcome that attitude I think we will accomplish something."[111]

As always, he turned again to Taylor. Designating Taylor as "Personal Representative of the President of the United States with the rank of Ambassador," Truman sent him back to Europe for further efforts at persuading European church leaders to attend the proposed conference in Washington. Truman also encouraged Taylor to solicit support from Bishop Henry Knox Sherrill, leader of the American Episcopal Church and President of the newly formed NCC.[112] In a departure from the customary resistance of other American Protestant leaders, Sherrill demonstrated a genuine interest in the project. He and Taylor had discussed having several world Christian leaders issue a statement on the world situation. Sherrill informed Taylor that he was "not thinking of it so much as a denunciation of communism, per se . . . but I am thinking of it as a positive declaration of the moral and spiritual foundations which are essential to civilization and freedom." Even such a broad statement would be useful in the current conflict, Sherrill hoped, suggesting that it "could be broadcast over the Voice of America . . . and could make a profound impression upon the people behind the Iron Curtain." Most shocking was Sherrill's opinion that "the participation of the Roman Catholic Church is an essential feature" for the declaration to have any impact. While not denying the very real theological differences separating Protestants and Catholics, Sherrill believed it appropriate and even necessary for a united Christian voice to speak to the world's troubles. "I believe that if a statement could be agreed upon, to be signed by say the Archbishop of Canterbury, Pastor Boegner, the Archbishop of Sweden, Athenagoras, and myself, with His Holiness, it would make a great impression upon the entire world."[113]

Taylor met again with the Pope on June 6, 1951. Following their meeting, Taylor reported back to Truman that the Pope had been very receptive to the

[111] Truman to Strauss, February 15, 1951; PSF: Chronological File 294, folder: Strauss, Lewis; HST Papers.
[112] Truman to Taylor, April 26, 1951; WHCF: State Department Papers; Myron Taylor Papers 47; HST Papers.
[113] Sherrill to Taylor, Myron Taylor Papers 2; HST Papers.

plan for a joint declaration. Taylor had even suggested that Pius XII write the first draft of the statement, an idea the Pope seemed to favor, or at least he agreed to "give it very careful consideration."[114] Truman felt encouraged at these developments, thanking Taylor for helping to cultivate "enthusiasm for a united gathering of representatives of the various religious bodies under the leadership of the President.... I agree with you that we are sowing seeds which will eventually produce a rich harvest."[115]

Surprisingly, the next significant problem came from the Pope himself. The previous year, Pius XII, speaking infallibly from the Chair of Peter, had proclaimed the Assumption of the Virgin Mary to be a dogmatic article of faith. Protestant groups, many already hostile to Rome and suspicious of claims to papal authority, had been infuriated. The Anglican Church issued a statement complaining that the Catholic Church "has chosen by this act to increase dogmatic differences in Christendom and has thereby gravely injured the growth of understanding between Christians."[116] Protestants' worst fears about Catholic totalitarianism had seemingly been confirmed, despite Truman and Taylor's strenuous efforts to persuade them otherwise. And the Pope did not forget or forgive the Protestant response. Two weeks after his meeting with Taylor on June 6, 1951, the Pope gave Taylor a statement announcing that "it seems difficult, not to say impossible, to arrive at a formula of a common declaration, to which ... the Holy Father could adhere." The Pope complained that "authoritative protestant personages have manifested a hostile attitude towards the Catholic Church," particularly singling out "the bitter manner with which the Holy See was criticized on the occasion of the proclamation of the Dogma of the Assumption."[117] This had clearly been too much for the Pope, who now saw little reason for and little fruit from cooperating with the Protestants.

Taylor was shocked, and deeply disappointed. He had spent 12 years cultivating a close and sympathetic relationship with the Pope and could not fathom this apparent reversal. As a non-dogmatic Episcopalian more concerned with the ethics of religion than with its doctrines, Taylor still could not comprehend those who took their theological distinctives so seriously. He wrote a long letter to the Pope the next day, trying to persuade the Catholic leader to reconsider. Taylor began by reminding him of their first meeting in 1936, before either had assumed their current positions, when the Pope had

---

[114] Taylor to Truman, June 6, 1951; Myron Taylor Papers 2; HST Papers.
[115] Truman to Taylor, June 7, 1951; Myron Taylor Papers 2; HST Papers.
[116] Quoted in "Anglicans Assail New Dogma," *The New York Times*, August 18, 1950. Copy of Article in Myron Taylor Papers 2; HST Papers.
[117] Statement of Pope Pius XII, June 19, 1951; Myron Taylor Papers 2; HST Papers.

predicted that "the time will come when all men and women of all religions will have to stand together to resist the evil tendencies of Communism." Taylor then traced the subsequent years of war and economic travail, and concluded that in the present crisis only the "last great resource" of spiritual unity held out any hope for the free world. Concerning the Pope's reluctance to cooperate in a common declaration, Taylor gently indicated that Pius XII himself bore some responsibility for provoking Protestant resistance because of his "recent dogma which might have a tendency to preclude a concert of action at this time."[118] Here again was a potent illustration of the curious dynamics of religion and politics wrought by the Cold War. An American Ambassador, representing the President of the United States, criticized the pontiff of the Roman Catholic Church on a point of doctrinal conviction. Just as Taylor and Truman had sought to influence the internal religious composition of the World Council of Churches, they did not hesitate to push the Catholic Church on matters of theological confession either.

Nothing if not persistent, Taylor made one final effort in the summer of 1951. He met with Bishop Dibelius, who as always pledged his unequivocal commitment to the plan, and with leaders of the Anglican Church at Lambeth Palace including Bishop Sherrill, the Archbishop of Canterbury, and the Archbishop of York. The Archbishop of Canterbury voiced enthusiasm for a joint declaration and even offered to preside over the drafting of possible statements. Two months later, however, in the now familiar pattern of a clergyman's profession of support turning into a confession of reluctance, the Archbishop of Canterbury wrote Taylor that he and his colleagues thought the prospect of persuading Protestant, Catholic, and Orthodox leaders to sign any statement "is so remote that the attempt ought to be abandoned." He included a recent pronouncement by the WCC discouraging such efforts at inter-communion cooperation and offered his sincere apologies to Taylor. Perhaps to demonstrate that he had not given up without an effort, the Archbishop included drafts of two possible statements that he and his colleagues had written. The statements were distinguished only by their copious platitudes and bland inoffensiveness. Unable or unwilling to join in the simplest of affirmations, the world's churches remained profoundly divided, leaving Truman and Taylor bitterly disappointed.[119]

The president now lost his last measure of tolerance for these church disputes. For four years he and his deputy Taylor had labored – diligently,

---

118 Taylor to Pope Pius XII, June 20, 1951; Myron Taylor Papers 2; HST Papers.
119 Taylor to Truman, July 5, 1951; Myron Taylor Papers 2. Archbishop of Canterbury to Taylor, September 6, 1951; Myron Taylor Papers 2; HST Papers.

patiently, faithfully – to bring Christian leaders together in a simple campaign against a common threat. Their persistent inability to get along baffled and angered him. He decided to vent his frustrations publicly. Appearing before a large meeting of Washington clergymen on September 29, 1951, Truman preached a virtual sermon on the spiritual foundations of America's greatness, America's divinely ordained role in the world, and the malicious threat posed by Soviet communism to "a world civilization in which man's belief in God can survive." Truman's speech, which received wide media coverage, concluded with remarkable candor. He described his efforts to bring "the religious leaders of the world together in a common affirmation," but regretted that he could report little fruit.

> I am sorry to say that it has not yet been possible to bring the religious faiths together for the purpose of bearing witness in one united affirmation that God is the way of truth and peace. Even the Christian churches have not yet found themselves able to say, with one voice, that Christ is their Master and Redeemer and the source of their strength against the hosts of irreligion and danger to the world and that will be the cause of world catastrophe. They haven't been able to agree on as simple a statement as that. I have been working at it for years.[120]

Expressing his palpable frustration, Truman also revealed once again his own theological agenda. In order to bring the churches together against the threat of communism, he first had tried to convince them that they shared a common Christian identity. In both attempts he had failed.

Edward Pruden, Truman's pastor at First Baptist Church, responded with alarm to Truman's address. Pruden was close friends with many mainline Protestant leaders and hoped to heal the rift between his clerical colleagues and his most eminent parishioner. Proclaiming his support for the idea of a united religious front, Pruden explained to Truman that some of the opposition had resulted from misunderstandings between the WCC and other churches. Furthermore, while not personally acquainted with Taylor, Pruden had heard from other churchmen that Taylor "is by no means capable of achieving the goal which you have in mind." Some believed that Taylor "has very little grasp of church life, and is woefully uninformed," while others complained that Taylor's advanced age hindered his diplomatic interactions.

---

[120] Truman, address to the Washington Pilgrimage of American Churchmen, September 28, 1951. *Public Papers of the Presidents: Harry S. Truman, 1951* (Washington: United States Government Printing Office 1965), 547–550. See also *New York Times* and *New York Herald-Tribune* articles of September 29, 1951, clippings in WHCF: State Department Papers; Myron Taylor Papers 50; HST Papers.

Nevertheless, Pruden encouraged Truman not to abandon the effort. The President responded with his usual bluntness. His agenda had not been "to interfere with church government or to put the Church into politics, but to let people who believe in honor and morals be lined up on one side and let the people who do not believe in honor and morals be lined up on the other."[121] Truman still could not fathom why the churchmen had not seen it that way.

Old convictions die hard, however, and sometimes do not die at all. Taylor shared Truman's regret at the failure of their project, and remained convinced that it was both a good and right endeavor. Its noble goals notwithstanding, he lamented to the Archbishop of Canterbury, "it has ended in seeming failure." The Archbishop echoed Taylor's sorrow, yet felt compelled to remind him of the real culprit "Part of the trouble in all this conflict against Communism is that we cannot whole-heartedly claim the Roman Church as a champion of freedom against Communist tyranny when . . . the Roman system is itself a spiritual absolutism, which is really foreign to Christian doctrine."[122]

That same month, Truman raised Protestant hackles even more when he followed through on his earlier pledge to the Pope. Declaring that official recognition of the Vatican would "assist in coordinating the effort to combat the Communist menace," on October 21, 1951 Truman submitted to the Senate the nomination of General Mark Clark to be Ambassador to the Holy See. The next two months witnessed a furious protest by Protestant groups across the theological spectrum. The White House received over 100,000 letters opposing the Clark nomination. Yet at least one notable Protestant leader did not object publicly. Billy Graham, trying to persuade Truman that attending Graham's upcoming evangelistic crusade in Washington might help his frayed relations with Protestants, wrote the President that "I have refused to make any comment on the Vatican appointment because I didn't want to be put in a position of opposing you." Truman, who had distrusted Graham since their first meeting had ended with Graham posing for newspaper photos in front of the White House, doubted Graham's sincerity and turned down the invitation.[123] The effort to recognize the Vatican meanwhile floundered, and in January, 1952, Clark with Truman's consent withdrew as the nominee, and Truman did not pursue the matter further.[124] The enmity between

---

[121]   Pruden to Truman, October 5, 1951; Truman to Pruden, October 9, 1951; PPF 490, folder 627; HST Papers.

[122]   Taylor to Archbishop of Canterbury, October 25, 1951; Archbishop to Taylor, October 30, 1951; Myron Taylor Papers 2; HST Papers.

[123]   Cited in Nancy Gibbs and Michael Duffy, *The Preacher and the Presidents: Billy Graham in the White House* (New York: Center Street 2007), 26.

[124]   For more on this, see A. Roger Davis, *Harry Truman and Vatican Relations, 1945–1952* (unpublished M.A. thesis, March 1988, Southwest Missouri State University).

Protestantism and Catholicism, grounded both in historic prejudices and substantive theological differences, proved too intractable even for the concerted diplomacy of Truman and Taylor and the crisis of the Cold War.

With a resigned spirit and a heavy heart, Truman shuttered his campaign. He exchanged final letters with the Pope, in which both lamented how the fury of Protestant opposition had derailed formal diplomatic relations between the United States and the Vatican.[125] In two letters to Taylor thanking him for his service, Truman informed his Ambassador that "no man could have had a more effective representative than you have been for the policies which I have been trying to implement." The President regretted that because of religious divisions "our efforts fell short of success." Looking wistfully towards the future, Truman expressed his "hope for the coming of peace on earth and my abiding trust that my successor, whoever he may be, in the office of the Presidency of this Christian Nation, will labor earnestly toward this honorable goal."[126]

V

Truman's campaign reveals a side of him comparatively unknown and under appreciated: the spiritual idealist. This aspect of the President co-existed, sometimes uneasily, with the pragmatic necessities of national security. And whatever sort of world Truman may have dreamed of at night, during his waking hours he generally pursued a realistic policy of military strength and muscular diplomacy. Yet pervading his lofty language and idealistic hopes lay a calculated truth: military and economic might alone would not defeat the Soviet Union. The conflict would be fought, and won, in the hearts and minds of people the world over. Despite casting his ideological and spiritual net as wide as possible, Truman's vision of world unity clearly excluded both the Soviet bloc and the newly established People's Republic of China. The communist world did not share a "unity of moral values" or a "common belief in one God." Peace was not possible in such a

[125] Truman to Pope Pius XII, May 14, 1952; Pope Pius XII to Truman, July 10, 1952; Myron Taylor Papers 2; HST Papers.

[126] Truman to Taylor, January 19, 1953; PSF: Chronological File 295, folder: Myron Taylor; Truman to Taylor, May 12, 1952; Myron Taylor Papers 2; HST Papers. Truman and Taylor also could not resist some final parting shots at their old nemesis Bishop Oxnam. Noting that Oxnam had recently taken up residence in Washington, Taylor pointed out one upside of Truman's leaving office: "I am glad, for at least one reason, that you will not be near at hand for him to lay down the law. You will be spared that!" Truman agreed, describing Oxnam as just like Bishop Cannon "who brought about prohibition in this country." Taylor to Truman, January 2, 1953; Myron Taylor Papers 2; Truman to Taylor, January 9, 1953; PSF: General File, Myron Taylor 44; HST Papers.

divided world. The lines of containment were drawn, boldly and unequivocally

If we take him at his words, the roots of Truman's anticommunism are
not hard to perceive. The President feared and loathed communism because
it stood implacably opposed to the religious faith so vital to him and to his
country. It was an enemy not just because of its totalitarianism, its aggression,
its command economy, and its political restrictions, but most fundamentally
because it held atheism and materialism as cardinal tenets, and declared
religion to be anathema. Truman was realistic enough to see that the Soviet
Union could not be defeated immediately, but neither could it be ignored.
He determined to contain it. To do so, he needed to persuade the American
people to support him in this unprecedented challenge, to shine the heat and
light of religious faith on the Iron Curtain.

The very potency of religion, which Truman found so attractive, also proved
ultimately to undermine his plan. He believed that the distinctions in religious
belief and practice that defined different denominations and even religions
were less genuine disagreements over the true nature and worship of the divine
than they were unfortunate causes of unnecessary disunity. Many Christian
leaders thought differently, and their dedication to their own theological
convictions finally precluded meaningful cooperation with others. But the
failure of Truman's plan did not finally spell the failure of his vision.

Truman successfully defined the Cold War as a spiritual conflict. And
while his labors on behalf of a united religious front never came to fruition,
he established the religious blueprint that his White House successor largely
would follow, as Truman had hoped. In that sense, the Truman Administration
birthed and bequeathed a grander legacy than has been appreciated. He
developed containment not just as a strategic doctrine, but also as an article
of faith.

4

∾

To Save China: Protestant Missionaries and
Sino–American Relations

I

Adopting containment as the strategic doctrine of the United States raised almost as many new questions as it answered old ones. For instance, how were the lines of containment to be drawn? Would the United States try to contain only the Soviet Union, or all of global communism? And how did containment apply to the turmoil in China? This last matter caused policymakers particular consternation. Perhaps no other nation aroused as much passion and contention among the American people. This mysterious land in the Orient had long enchanted the American imagination. In the early twentieth century, explorers, sailors, traders, and missionaries – especially missionaries – returning to the United States from their China sojourns brought tales of an ancient civilization, innovative inventions, unusual cuisine, and a people allegedly in desperate need of Western culture and the Christian faith. Public figures such as *Time-Life* media baron Henry Luce and author Pearl Buck, who had spent their childhoods in China as missionary children, kept China in the headlines and in the forefront of many American minds.

Chinese President Chiang Kai-shek's apparent Christian faith only added to this allure.[1] Following Sun Yat-sen as the second president of the Republic of China, Chiang also adopted his predecessor's religion, as did a number of his Nationalist colleagues. Chiang's conversion and baptism in 1928, widely publicized in American church circles, further endeared him to many Christians in the United States. For his part, Chiang did not hesitate to advertise his faith before eager American audiences, missionary and stateside. Nor did he hesitate to draw from it his own political implications, especially with the

---

[1] For clarity and in deference to prevailing usage, this book will generally use the Wade–Giles system of romanization for Chinese personal names, with just a few exceptions such as "Mao Zedong" reflecting current Pinyin usage. For place names, Pinyin will generally be used.

growing threat his government faced from Mao Zedong's communist forces. In a 1938 Easter radio broadcast in China (subsequently translated into English and reprinted in the *Christian Century*), Chiang connected his faith with "the work of revolution," and encouraged his listeners to follow "Jesus' revolutionary spirit." Chiang also appealed to Sun Yat-sen's legacy. He identified himself as "Sun's successor," and praised Sun for "cherishing love for God and man, suffused with the revolutionary spirit of Jesus." Remarkably, Chiang closed by urging the people of China to adopt Christianity – or at least Chiang's particular version of it. "I firmly believe that in seeking to bring national recovery and social progress, we must advocate Jesus' spirit of universal love and of sacrifice."[2] Chiang's motives remain a puzzle. Certainly he was seeking to balance several tensions – his desire for his country to modernize and forge closer ties with the West, the need to co-opt the growing appeal of communist revolution, his personal ambition, and his ambiguous spiritual convictions. Chiang added his particular emphasis to the message brought by American missionaries, and then used it for his own purposes.

Not all missionaries shared this unbridled enthusiasm for merging Christian ethics with the agenda of political revolution. Shortly after Chiang's baptism, an evangelical missionary with the China Inland Mission (CIM) wrote to his board back in the United States. "With such leading men in the National Government [becoming Christians], sincerity of purpose demands an effort to bring their policy into alignment with the principles of the Gospel. . . . [We must] pray that they may not merely embrace the ethics of Scripture, while by their actions they ignore or minimize the spiritual content."[3] Some evangelicals feared that instead of being adopted into the Christian faith, Chiang might seek to adopt Jesus only for the Nationalists' own "revolutionary" cause. Yet other missionaries proudly trumpeted the Chiangs' piety. William Richard Johnson wrote a glowing article for an American Christian periodical describing General and Madame Chiang's faithful practice of their "morning watch" devotional time of prayer and Bible reading.[4] The National Association of Evangelicals (NAE) later invited Chiang to speak at their national convention, and in a news release touted the testimony of Chiang's former secretary that

---

[2]   Chiang Kai-shek, "Why I Believe in Jesus," *Christian Century*, 8 June 1938. See also "The Faith of Generalissimo Chiang Kai-shek," copy of March 26, 1937 address from Chiang to Methodist Episcopal Church conference in Nanking, China. John Mott Papers, RG 45, Box 15, Folder: 270; Yale Divinity School Archives (hereinafter YDSA).

[3]   October 27, 1930 letter from W.H. Warren to CIM Board; CIM Papers, Box 2, Folder 21; Billy Graham Center Archives, Wheaton, IL (hereinafter BGCA).

[4]   William R. Johnson, "An Inspiring Example for China: Marshal and Madame Chiang Kai-shek Keep the Morning Watch," *Zion's Herald*, 22 January 1941, 82.

"the Generalissimo was one of the truest Christians he had ever known . . . in prayer daily, reading the Scriptures and in every way comporting himself as a follower of Christ."[5] Such apparent spiritual fervor smoothed over the doubts many evangelicals might have had about Chiang's "revolutionary" theology.

The end of World War II brought the renewal of combat in China's long-standing civil war, between Mao Zedong's Chinese Communist Party (CCP) and Chiang's Nationalists, or Kuomintang (KMT). Emboldened by support from their Soviet ally, Mao's forces began to emerge from the hinterlands and advance once again. Meanwhile, Joseph Stalin's tightening control in Eastern Europe, coupled with communist insurrections in Greece and Turkey, had prompted President Truman to take decisive measures to contain any further Soviet expansion in Europe. To many Americans, this raised an obvious question: if the United States would oppose communism in Europe, why not in Asia as well? And to many of the Americans most familiar with China – current and former missionaries – the renewed crisis in China prompted their own agonizing question: what would it mean to save China? Both questions emerged from a general uncertainty over how containment applied to China, whether as a political doctrine or as a theology. Many American missionaries thought they knew the answer, but they differed as to what it was.

II

Questions of America's relationship with China were nothing new to the missionary community. Soon after Woodrow Wilson's election as president in 1912, many missionaries had contacted him to urge diplomatic recognition for the newly formed Republic of China. Wilson agreed, and selected John Mott, then a prominent YMCA official and perhaps America's most influential missionary leader, to serve as the United States Ambassador to China. Citing the "serious obligations" of his missionary work, however, Mott respectfully declined Wilson's nomination.[6] Thirty-three years later another missionary found himself facing a similar decision yet came to a different answer. President Harry Truman in 1946 nominated lifelong missionary J. Leighton Stuart to represent the United States in China. Stuart agreed to serve as Ambassador in the belief that "if I could help at all to bring peace to [China] it would be the best use of my time."[7]

[5] May 15, 1951 NAE News Release; Herbert John Taylor Papers, Box 67, Folder 9; BGCA
[6] C. Howard Hopkins, *John R. Mott, 1865–1955* (Grand Rapids, MI: Eerdmans 1979), 398.
[7] John Leighton Stuart, *Fifty Years in China* (New York: Random House 1954), 166.

Stuart's role as a missionary involved in U.S.–China relations was not unusual. From 1945 to 1950, Protestant missionaries participated intensely in the debate over what America's policy should be towards a China buffeted by civil war between the Nationalists and the Communists. More remarkably, in the midst of the debate two missionaries themselves came to occupy prominent foreign policy-making positions within the United States Government.[8] Stuart, a lifelong Presbyterian missionary in China, served as the American Ambassador to China from 1946 to 1953. Walter Judd, following ten years as a medical missionary in China, was elected to Congress in 1943. As a member of the House Foreign Affairs Committee, he soon emerged as one of Congress' most impassioned, articulate voices on China policy. A third missionary, William Richard Johnson, retired in 1945 after forty years of service in China only to embark immediately on a virtual second career as a full-time anticommunist activist and lobbyist. While Stuart, Judd, and Johnson were perhaps the most visible former missionaries in the debate over U.S.–China relations, they were not alone. Functioning as both inside operators and outside agitators, many American missionaries sought to direct the relationship between the United States and China during the critical years between 1945 and 1950. Yet there was not a unanimous "missionary position"; while all agreed that spiritual imperatives should guide American policy, they disagreed in which direction it should go.

Dr. J. Leighton Stuart was born and reared in China as the son of missionary parents. He then served himself as a missionary and educator in China for more than 40 years. By 1945, Stuart knew the Chinese language, people, and culture as well as any Westerner could. A dignified, reserved figure, in another time he would likely have been comfortable in the patrician life of a Southern gentleman. Although Stuart generally preferred to avoid religious and political conflict, he seemed most sympathetic to both the theological liberalism in vogue in his day and the international idealism exemplified by his fellow Southern Presbyterian, Woodrow Wilson.[9] After returning to China as a young man with an early missions focus on evangelism, Stuart had spent decades as a professor of theology at Nanking Seminary and then as the first president of Yenching University in Beijing.

When the end of World War II renewed hostilities in China between the Nationalists and the Communists, it also brought a new role for the old "China

---

[8] While it has not been standard for missionary organizations to get involved with political issues, individual missionaries and missionary children have frequently gone on to serve in the State Department and other foreign policy divisions of the United States Government.

[9] Yu-Ming Shaw, *An American Missionary in China: John Leighton Stuart and Chinese-American Relations* (Cambridge, MA: Harvard University Press 1992), 35–37.

hand," who made an almost effortless transition from missionary to diplomat. Stuart had known Chiang Kai-shek since the late 1920s, and had been following the development of Mao Zedong and the Communists for almost as long. Initially attracted to Chiang's charisma and profession of Christian faith, Stuart had developed a close friendship with him. This eventually grew strained amidst Stuart's disillusionment with what he perceived to be Chiang's arrogance and corruption. Meanwhile, Stuart's visceral aversion to communism had given way to a grudging yet wary respect for Mao and the CCP.

In 1946, Truman sent General George Marshall to China to attempt to broker a peace between the warring parties. At Chiang Kai-shek's recommendation, Marshall sought to tap into Stuart's wealth of knowledge about virtually all things Chinese and requested that Stuart serve him as an informal advisor. While the "Marshall mission," as it came to be known, ended without any peace agreement, Stuart's expert performance prompted Marshall to urge President Truman to select Stuart as the new Ambassador to China. Given his unconventional background, Stuart proved to be a surprisingly conventional diplomat. He performed as a capable yet undistinguished representative, gamely shuttling between the KMT and the CCP in vain attempts to broker some sort of peace agreement or power-sharing arrangement, while on occasion trying in futility to secure more American aid for the Nationalists. More of a pragmatist than an ideologue, Stuart preferred the Nationalists to the Communists and regarded the latter as generally incompatible with Christianity. Yet he over time grew resigned to the fact of Mao's impending triumph in China. Stuart's overarching concern during these years seems to have been maintaining an open door for continued American involvement in China, no matter what the ruling regime. In this sense, he never abandoned his missionary calling nor his fervent love for China, for he hoped until the end that China would remain open to the twin benefits of democracy and Christian morality.

Intense where Stuart was reserved, and ideological where Stuart was pragmatic, Dr. Walter Judd emerged as a leading voice in the American Congress on U.S.–China relations in the 1940s and 50s.[10] Judd possessed a rare depth of insight about China, having spent a total of ten years there during the 1920s and 30s as a medical missionary serving with the venerable American Board of Commissioners for Foreign Missions (ABCFM). He had experienced

---

[10] Scholarly literature on Judd is very limited. For a more popular biography that is largely hagiographic, see Lee Edwards, *Missionary for Freedom: The Life and Times of Walter Judd* (New York: Paragon House 1990). See also Tony Ladd, "Mission to Capitol Hill: A Study of the Impact of Missionary Idealism on the Congressional Career of Walter H. Judd," in Neils, ed., *United States Attitudes and Policies Toward China: The Impact of American Missionaries.*

firsthand many of the conflicts consuming China at the time. Besides numerous encounters with both Nationalist and Communist troops, Judd's hospital
had been bombed by the Japanese invaders, eventually forcing him and his
family to flee China to escape the Japanese onslaught. Judd had been horrified to observe the Japanese military using American-made armaments to
make war on China, and upon returning to the United States he immediately
embarked on a crusade to bring an end to America's export of war materials
to Japan. A capable orator, he undertook a nationwide speaking tour from
1938 to 1940, warning in hundreds of speeches that the United States must
stop arming the Japanese forces.[11]

After settling in Minneapolis and opening a medical practice, in 1942 Judd
won election to Congress as a Republican representing Minnesota's Fifth Dis-
trict, and commenced twenty years of service in the House of Representatives.
Not easy to categorize, Judd generally came to be known as a moderate on
social and economic issues, and a hawkish internationalist on foreign policy. His admirers and detractors alike agreed that he displayed a mastery of
issues and maintained a strenuous work ethic. While a vigorous supporter
of Truman's Marshall Plan for European reconstruction as well as American
involvement in the nascent United Nations, Judd's abiding passion remained
China. He frequently argued that the United States needed to support Chiang
and the Nationalists in order to maintain "a strong friendly China as the bulwark to our own security in the Pacific."[12] Although retaining much affection
and admiration for China, Judd was no benighted sentimentalist. He regarded
the advance of communism in China as both a pernicious encroachment on
the liberties and welfare of the Chinese people and a potentially grave security
threat to the United States.

Although always an adamant supporter of Chiang Kai-shek and the KMT,
Judd never knew Chiang well and had met the Chinese leader only once before
being elected to Congress.[13] Unlike Ambassador Stuart, Judd's support for the
Nationalists was not contingent on a personal friendship with the notoriously
difficult Chiang. Rather, Judd regarded the Nationalists as the best among a
limited set of undesirable options, and counseled America to remain patient
as Chiang tried to lead his sprawling, fractured nation out of the ravages of
World War II and away from the threat of communist revolution. Judd's hostility to communism did grow out of his personal experiences. While serving
as a medical missionary in rural China he had repeated encounters with

---

[11] Copy of Judd speech, Walter H. Judd Collection (hereinafter WHJ), Box 33, Hoover Institution
       Archives (hereinafter HIA), Stanford, CA.
[12] Letter written by Walter Judd, November 16, 1945. WHJ Collection, Box 34, HIA.
[13] Judd, letter, November 23, 1945. WHJ Collection, Box 34, HIA.

Communist forces. He later referenced these in his congressional speeches, warning that "the Chinese Communists came into South China where I lived, and their program was to set up Russian Communism. It was utterly ruthless."[14]

William Richard Johnson, a Methodist missionary in China for almost forty years, like Judd arrived at his passionate anticommunism from personal experience. In a 1946 letter to the editor of the *New York Times*, Johnson repeated what became a familiar theme for the next several years. Referring to his years serving as a missionary educator in Communist-occupied territory in Jiangxi province, he wrote that "in areas controlled by [the Communists], population was reduced by firing squads and terrorism by 30 to 50 percent. . . . As an administrator of relief in areas from which Communists had been driven, I have seen the devastating effects of their occupation."[15] Ironically, it had not been the Chinese Communists but rather the Japanese who had forced Johnson to leave China in the first place. After their invasion of China, the Japanese army had detained Johnson in a prison camp along with other foreigners, and after several months he had been released and repatriated to the United States. During the waning months of the war in 1945, Johnson had appealed strenuously to the Methodist Foreign Mission Board to allow him to return to China. The Board rejected his request and virtually forced him to retire, citing his age (approaching 70) and his declining health.[16] Displaying a somewhat endearing, yet almost obsessive desire to go back to his adopted home, Johnson immediately sought other opportunities to work in China. He frenetically applied for numerous positions with agencies such as the Foreign Service Auxiliary, the United Nations Relief and Rehabilitation Administration, and private educational organizations, only to be rejected time and again for various reasons including his age and China's political instability.[17] Curiously, Johnson's overriding desire simply appears to have been returning to his beloved China. Judging from the broad array of organizations to which he applied and the diverse duties those positions would have entailed, he did not seem particularly concerned with resuming missionary work or even affiliating with an explicitly Christian organization. He regarded his responsibility as service in China through educational and humanitarian means, and did not display a purely religious sense of calling.

---

[14] Walter Judd, December 27, 1945 statement on "Town Hall Meeting of the Air." WHJ Collection, Box 35, HIA.

[15] Johnson, September 12, 1946 letter. William Richard Johnson Collection (hereinafter WRJ), Record Group 6 (hereinafter RG), Box 18, folder 297, YDSA.

[16] Letter to Johnson, August 13, 1945. WRJ Collection, RG 6, Box 17, folder 290, YDSA.

[17] Letters to Johnson. WRJ Collection, RG 6, Boxes 17, 18, folders 292, 294, YDSA.

Failing in his efforts to return to China, Johnson plunged full-time into domestic efforts to strengthen American support of Chiang Kai-shek and opposition to the communists. Johnson held Chiang in the highest regard. He once described Chiang as "a God-sent leader for these times" and harbored few if any doubts about the Nationalist President's capabilities and character.[18] Johnson and Chiang had known each other in China, although it is unclear how close their relationship was. Johnson later said that he and Chiang "knew each other quite well," but there is little evidence that they maintained direct contact after Johnson left China.[19] Meanwhile, Johnson became a tireless pamphleteer, churning out numerous tracts, articles, and letters directed to church leaders, government officials, and anyone else who would listen to his warnings about the dire threat facing China. Although based out of his home in Polo, Illinois, Johnson traveled regularly to New York, Washington, DC, and elsewhere, delivering speeches before civic groups, meeting with his allies in the anticommunist cause, and lobbying government officials to support the KMT. Following a lifetime of missionary work, Johnson was not a man of means. He found himself continually requesting funding for his travels and publications from any supporters sympathetic to his efforts. His most frequent and faithful patron was Alfred Kohlberg, the wealthy textile merchant who helped found the anticommunist American China Policy Association.[20]

The Presbyterian Stuart, the Congregationalist Judd, and the Methodist Johnson all shared theological convictions that placed them comfortably in the mainline of American Protestantism. None was a fundamentalist, nor even evangelical as the term was understood at the time. Furthermore, all three presumably shared the discomfort of the Protestant mainline towards vigorous theological disputes or rigorous doctrinal formulations. Missionary work, for them, consisted not so much in evangelism as it did in education, humanitarian relief, and promoting the virtues of Christian civilization, broadly construed. On matters concerning China, however, Stuart, Judd, and Johnson demonstrated passionate interest and, at times, different convictions over the correct United States policy towards the two sides.

III

Two successive, inter-related issues dominated the post–World War II debate about U.S.–China policy. First, the resumption of hostilities between the

---

[18] Johnson, letter, December 24, 1948. WRJ Collection, RG 6, Box 19, folder 314, YDSA.

[19] Johnson, letter to Alfred Kohlberg, August 3, 1949. WRJ Collection, RG 6, Box 19, folder 319, YDSA.

[20] Johnson's papers are replete with requests for and acknowledgments of financial gifts in support of his anticommunist activities.

KMT and CCP immediately after the war forced America to consider whether and how much it would support Nationalist President Chiang Kai-shek in his struggle to defeat the Communists. Second, once the CCP successfully conquered mainland China in 1949, the United States faced the question of whether it would recognize the new "People's Republic of China" as China's legitimate government, or whether it would continue to recognize Chiang Kai-shek's exiled government on Taiwan. On both of these questions, ex-missionaries working in government such as Stuart and Judd, as well as missionaries still active in the field, spoke out vociferously though not unan-imously on how they believed the United States should respond.[21]

Truman's nomination of Stuart to be Ambassador in 1946 revealed these emerging rifts. On learning of the nomination, Johnson attempted to send a memo to Henry Luce (who had grown up in China as the son of mis-sionaries) questioning Stuart's anticommunist credentials and urging that he be opposed.[22] Luce, apparently not receiving the memo in time, instead published a story in *Time* lauding Stuart as "the dean of [China's] U.S. mis-sionaries" and an "excellently inspired choice" for Ambassador. Meanwhile, Johnson traveled to Washington where he and Alfred Kohlberg met with Rep. Judd. According to Johnson's report on the meeting, Judd shared their fears that Stuart might not be an effective advocate for the Nationalists, but Judd resisted entreaties to work against Stuart's nomination. He reminded Johnson and Kohlberg of the presidential prerogative for ambassadorial nominations and also apparently expressed the concern that waging a public fight against Stuart might offend many Christian leaders.[23] In the months following Stu-art's appointment, Johnson continued to voice severe misgivings. He referred to Stuart's supporters in the State Department as "Commies," and described Stuart's appointment as one of several "measures of appeasement" towards the

---

[21] In many ways Stuart and Judd served as official sounding boards for the debate that emerged, while Johnson used his decades of China experience to agitate from retirement. Most mis-sionaries still in full-time missionary service did not get as involved on the political questions as those who made a virtual career of such matters like Stuart, Judd, and Johnson. This can partly be attributed to the logistical difficulties in communicating with policy-makers from the other side of the world, and partly to the reluctance of missionaries to poten-tially jeopardize their status by entering such a contentious political debate. But on many occasions missionaries still active in mission work did not hesitate to make their views known.

[22] An earlier candidate for Ambassador favored by the more staunchly pro-KMT cohort, General Albert Wedemeyer, had apparently been opposed by the influential General Marshall, who instead suggested Stuart.

[23] Letters from Johnson to James Crider, Geraldine Fitch, on August 2, 5, and 10, 1946. Letter from Crider to Johnson, August 6, 1946 (*Time* article enclosed). WRJ collection, RG 6, Box 18, folder 298, YDSA.

CCP.[24] Even after Judd told Johnson that the latter was "mistaken" in his negative assessment of Stuart and that Stuart was not responsible for the Truman Administration's weak support for the Nationalists, Johnson refused to concede. He continued to complain about Stuart that "Judd is too easy on him!"[25]

Perhaps contributing to Johnson's frustration was the fact that Stuart's positions towards the KMT and CCP were often difficult to ascertain. In many ways the consummate diplomat, Stuart seemed adept at remaining on amicable terms with many people of differing convictions, while concealing his own views. At times he did advocate a strong stance. In 1947, in separate meetings with Rep. Judd (who was visiting China) and General Marshall, Stuart disparaged the current American policy as too weak and advocated giving "aggressive military aid" to the Nationalists.[26] However, one year later Stuart had soured on Chiang's prospects for staving off Mao's armies. He cabled Marshall in October 1948 that "any direct aid to resistance group on theory that we are fighting communism all over the world around . . . [will] only delay their ultimate liquidation and would meanwhile arouse increased anti-American sentiment."[27] Abandoning his usual circumspection, Stuart confided to a friend the next month that "the series of military debacles this autumn has been worse even than could have been expected. The incompetence is unbelievable."[28] A few weeks later he singled out Chiang for criticism, describing to the same friend how the KMT "spins on to its inevitable doom by the willpower of one man."[29]

As 1948 progressed, Stuart came to find himself squeezed to the diplomatic margins, as he advocated positions at odds both with the American Embassy staff serving under him and with Secretary Marshall serving over him. Stuart's disillusionment with Chiang led the ambassador to advocate the formation of a coalition government that included the communists. The embassy staff disagreed, arguing instead for increasing aid to the Nationalists along with building specific autonomous regions to focus Nationalist strength. Marshall would have none of this, rejecting both negotiations with the communists

---

[24] Johnson, letters, October 7, November 9, 1946. WRJ Collection, RG 6, Box 18, folder 298, YDSA.

[25] Johnson, letters, August 26, 1947, February 4, 1948. WRJ Collection, RG 6, Box 18, folder 304, and Box 19, folder 309, YDSA.

[26] Stuart, 178–179. Also, Walter Judd's notes from October, 1947 meeting with Stuart. WHJ Collection, Box 200, HIA.

[27] Cited in Christensen, 78.

[28] Letter from Stuart, November 28, 1948. UBCHEA Collection, RG 11, Box 360, folder 5550, YDSA.

[29] Letter from Stuart, December 19, 1948. UBCHEA Collection, RG 11, Box 360, folder 5550, YDSA.

and further aid to the KMT. Early the next year Stuart continued his campaign for a new approach towards Mao's forces. He cabled Acting Secretary
of State Robert Lovett a long message suggesting that the United States consider "elements of progress and reform" in the CCP, and speculated that
involvement in a coalition government might enhance these tendencies while
ameliorating communism's harsher side. Moreover, drawing on his missionary past, he pointed out that further efforts by private American educational
and religious organizations could help smooth the transition and strengthen
a coalition government. Lovett apparently did not reply to Stuart's memo,
and Stuart's staff continued to disagree with him. Increasingly desperate and
despondent, he began to realize that he could do little to save the country he
had loved for fifty years.[30]

Around this same time Ambassador Stuart gave an address to a December
1948 Federal Council of Churches (FCC) conference that was reprinted the
next month in the religious periodical, *The Messenger*. Like Chiang, Stuart characterized Jesus in the vernacular of "revolution" that he naively
hoped would entice Chinese ears. Stuart declared confidently that "Christian faith . . . as a determined effort to realize the ideal social order which Jesus
described as the kingdom of heaven on earth, as the most dynamic revolutionary movement of all time, cannot fail in its appeal to the Oriental peoples."[31]
In other words, Stuart hoped that a derivation of Jesus' social ethics would
prevail in China over Maoist military insurgency. And because communism
appealed to the legitimate grievances of the oppressed and impoverished, "no
Asiatic government can hereafter hope to neutralize the Communist menace
unless it is able to concern itself with the welfare of the common people as has
never been done in the past."[32] Now that Asia's traditional religions seemed to
be waning and liberal Protestantism had accommodated itself to the "marvels
of modern science," Stuart believed that Christianity faced just one remaining challenge. "The struggle now is between godless materialism and belief
in spiritual realities" since "*the fundamental issues of our time are religious.*"
To Stuart, this conflict should be engaged more through social reform than
through military conflict, and as much by missionaries as by generals.[33] In

---

[30] Brewer and Rea, 236–241.

[31] Stuart, "What Asia Thinks of Jesus Christ," *The Messenger*, 18 January 1949, 12–14. Note
that his diplomatic duties in China prevented Stuart from delivering his address to the FCC
conference in person; Roswell Barnes read the address on Stuart's behalf.

[32] Stuart, "Asia's Aim – Free Men," *The Messenger*, 1 February 1949, 8–10. Note that this article
is part two of his article in the previous issue, both apparently drawn from his FCC address.
Emphasis original.

[33] *Ibid.* Italics original.

another essay, he conceded that while because of communist advances the present outlook for missionaries "seems rather bleak," nevertheless "in this environment missionaries have a superlative opportunity to bear witness to the meaning and value of an adventurously dynamic faith while also helping to demonstrate the spirit of Christian civilization."[34] Although Stuart presented communism as a competitor to Christianity, he hardly seemed to regard it as a monstrous evil. In another essay, he described communism as "a new and powerful incentive to intelligent action, an inspiration if you will, rather than something to be feared or hated in itself."[35] Sentiments of this type, which rendered communism merely a competing ideology to Christianity, rather than an apocalyptic threat, help explain his advocacy for a coalition government with the communists. This perspective also aroused the suspicion if not the animosity of individuals such as Judd and Johnson, even while it endeared him to missionaries less hostile to the CCP.

The immediate aftermath of Mao's victory changed Stuart's assessment. The communists' defiant imprisonment of U.S. Consul General Angus Ward, their violent denunciations of the United States, and their apparent affinity for the Soviets all combined to embitter Stuart.[36] In his memoir *50 Years in China*, written in 1954, Stuart presented a somewhat different picture of himself than the accommodationist of 1948–49. He described communism as an "evil monstrosity," "a system which begins with the denial of the existence of God . . . and which aspires to world domination." It "cannot be appeased" and "must be opposed."[37] Such strong language sounded more reminiscent of the rhetoric of Judd or Johnson than the once-conciliatory Stuart. But writing with the benefit of hindsight, Stuart portrayed himself as an unreconstructed Cold Warrior. He called unequivocally for the United States to maintain its program of assistance for the KMT outpost on Taiwan. The Nationalists are "aligned on the side of the free world in the fight against communism" and "it is very important to the security of the free world that the advance of communism in eastern Asia be halted."[38] Furthermore, "both for its own good and for the good of all mankind," the United States must not only refuse to recognize the PRC, but it must also oppose the PRC's admission to the United Nations and prohibit trade with the Communists.[39] The record of Stuart's

---

[34]   Stuart, "The Future of Christian Missions," undated essay (c. 1949–1950), 5–7. John Leighton Stuart Collection, Box 1, HIA.
[35]   John Leighton Stuart, "The Christian Responsibility in the Modern World," undated essay (c. 1949–1950), 8. John Leighton Stuart Collection, Box 1, HIA.
[36]   Brewer and Rea, 241.
[37]   Stuart, 303.
[38]   Stuart, 309.
[39]   Stuart, 310–311.

beliefs and actions during his tenure as Ambassador, however, obviously presents a more complex picture. To be fair, Stuart conceded at points in his memoirs that his judgment as Ambassador may have been wrong. He wrote that "in retrospect, with what we now know of the Communist intentions and methods," some of the negotiation proposals promoted by the United States may have been too favorable towards the Communists.[40]

IV

Stuart's position as Ambassador in China kept him away from much of the domestic debate over China policy led by Judd and Johnson. Yet as active as they were, Judd and Johnson never monopolized missionary involvement in the question over what policy the United States should develop towards China. From the years 1945 to 1948, a cacophony of missionary voices began to sound out on China, often discordantly. Some anticommunist missionaries joined Judd and Johnson to make themselves heard. Others began to voice serious criticism of the Nationalists.[41]

A few anticommunist missionaries sometimes formed coalitions with other like-minded citizens to press their concerns on China. Judd and Johnson, for example, joined several other former missionaries, along with more than 40 academics, business leaders, journalists, and retired military officers to form the American China Policy Association (ACPA). Bolstered by a broad constituency focused on a single interest, the ACPA issued statements and policy papers, and pressed the U.S. government to take a firmer stance in support of the KMT.[42]

Anticommunist missionaries often appealed their cause directly to the White House. Just after Truman assumed the presidency, and before Japan had even surrendered, Methodist Bishop Logan Roots sent Truman a lengthy memo alerting him to the precarious situation. Roots had served forty-two years in China, and during that time had befriended Chiang and come to know many communist leaders as well. He had also become active in Moral Re-Armament, and taught its principles of prayer and ideology to the Nationalist president.[43] Writing to Truman on May 30, 1945, Roots laid out many of the themes that would define the pro-Nationalist discourse for the next decade. First, he said, the CCP was in league with the Soviet Union. "Since 1934 the Chinese Communists to date have followed explicitly the 'line' from Moscow,"

[40] Stuart, 181.
[41] As will be discussed below, it would not be until 1949 with the defeat of the Nationalists imminent that numerous missionaries grew more vocal in their concerns about the KMT.
[42] ACPA statement, July 24, 1946. WRJ Collection, RG 6, Box 18, folder 295, YDSA.
[43] For more on Moral Re-Armament, see chapter five of this book.

their leadership had been trained in the USSR, and they remained committed to international communist ideology over loyalty to China. Second, Generalissimo and Madame Chiang were devoted Christians, and Chiang "actively seeks Divine Guidance for the affairs of State." Third, the KMT desperately depended on American assistance. "Either Chiang stays, with America's honest and full support, or he goes and a Marxist revolution grips China." And fourth, the stakes extended far beyond just China, to the rest of Asia and potentially the entire globe. If it supports the Nationalists, "America will be able to have a hand in shaping the policies and programs of a restored, potentially sound China," but if the United States pulled back, "an alien materialistic ideology will control not only Europe but all of Asia." Roots concluded on an eschatological note. "If we accurately discern the Signs of the Times we will act wisely, under God, before it is too late." Truman, no doubt preoccupied with the more pressing concerns of Germany's surrender settlement and finishing the war with Japan, had little time for such prophecies. The new president sent Roots a perfunctory acknowledgement.[44]

Evangelical and fundamentalist organizations frequently based their advocacy for the KMT on the need to keep China open to missionary work. In late October 1947, the Independent Board for Presbyterian Foreign Missions, a theologically conservative Presbyterian splinter group, cabled Truman with an urgent telegram. "To prevent Manchuria and North China from falling into the complete dominance of godless communist[s]," the United States needed "to help the Chinese Nationalist Government with money equipment and supplies in whatever ways possible to achieve the complete suppression of all armed communists in both countries in order to preserve the nation for freedom and open doors for the preaching of the Gospel of Jesus Christ." The fundamentalist American Council of Christian Churches (ACCC) sent Truman a similar resolution, urging as much American aid as possible to the Nationalists, because "if China is overcome by Communists there will be left no liberty throughout that great land for the preaching of the Gospel of Christ which is the best gift America has to give any land."[45] At least some missionary organizations, particularly the more doctrinally conservative, saw their work as an extension of American foreign policy – and saw American foreign policy as an extension of their work. For them, the United States needed to maintain

---

44 May 30, 1945 letter from Logan Roots to President Truman; June 8, 1945 letter from Truman to Roots; Truman Papers, OF 150, Box 758, Folder: Miscellaneous; HST Papers.

45 October 13, 1947 telegram from Independent Board for Presbyterian Foreign Missions to Truman; October 16, 1947 letter from ACCC to Truman; Truman Papers, OF 150, Box 759; HST Papers.

its assistance to the KMT not just as a strategic imperative, but as a spiritual duty.

In Congress, Walter Judd became the principal spokesman for anticommunist missionaries across the theological spectrum. In his literally thousands of speeches, essays, and letters on America's policy towards China during these years, Rep. Judd incessantly urged sending massive amounts of military assistance (although not U.S. troops themselves) to the Nationalists. He rarely couched his advocacy in terms of what would benefit the missionary endeavor in China, however. He eschewed making appeals on behalf of what might be construed as parochial missionary interests. Supporting the Nationalists, Judd declared, would encourage the growth of democracy and economic prosperity in China, and would help protect the American economic and security interests jeopardized by communism.

On occasion, however, Judd revealed his own personal concerns about how Chinese communism threatened missionary efforts. He wrote to a Catholic priest in 1945 of his fear that if communism "should come to dominate China [it] would mean the end of all of our missionary endeavors."[46] Judd sometimes served as a liaison between the missionary community and Congress, communicating the concerns of one to the other. He frequently attempted to persuade American Christians, particularly missionaries, that communism posed a grave threat to them and their activities. The Methodist foreign missions board distributed one of his speeches denouncing the CCP to all Methodist missionaries and mission executives.[47] Many missionaries, some of whom might otherwise have been reticent about political involvement, wrote Judd to express their concerns about the Communist advance in China. One former China missionary said he contacted Judd because "you are more in touch with things than others in Washington, and understand the missionary viewpoint."[48] Judd, in turn, occasionally circulated to his colleagues in Congress letters from missionaries describing firsthand their negative perceptions of communism in China.[49]

William Richard Johnson, meanwhile, became extremely active in attempting to influence Congress and the Truman Administration on China policy. He maintained a steady stream of correspondence, exhorting the White House, State Department, and congressional offices to support Chiang Kai-shek and

---

[46] Letter, May 19, 1945. WHJ Collection, Box 163, HIA.
[47] Letter to Judd from Foreign Missions Division of the Methodist Church, November 11, 1947. WHJ Collection, Box 158, HIA. As will be discussed further, this mailing was rather ironic in light of subsequent pronouncements by some Methodist officials on U.S.–China policy.
[48] Letter to Judd, May 21, 1946. WHJ Collection, Box 158, HIA.
[49] Letter from Judd, April 21, 1948. WHJ Collection, Box 163, HIA.

oppose the Communists. Johnson also frequently traveled to Washington for visits of anywhere from a few days to three months, where he would meet with White House and State Department staff as well as Members of Congress and their staff. On one such typical trip in December 1947, the indefatigable Johnson reported that over a period of ten days he met with about 60 Senators and Representatives, and more than 250 Congressional staffers. He distributed provocative essays and pamphlets he had written with colorful titles such as "The United States Sells China Down the Amur."[50] Many of these meetings were quite brief, of course, and while some Members appear to have shared Johnson's perspective and perhaps been influenced by his views, the extent of his effectiveness remains in doubt. Johnson himself later admitted that he had "often wondered just what tramping those corridors may have accomplished. About the only substantial evidence I have is the fact that I later discovered that some of the Congressmen actually had my earlier material in their files."[51] Whether genuinely influential or merely exasperating, Johnson continued to subject official Washington to a steady cavalcade of letters, tracts, and in-person exhortations. Like Judd, Johnson generally did not base his arguments against the CCP primarily on the threat they posed to missionary work, but more commonly raised alarms about communism's enmity towards peace and freedom in China and its menace to American security interests.

As the Chinese civil war began to escalate, more and more missionaries began to voice their opinions. For example, evangelical leader L. Nelson Bell, a former medical missionary in China, wrote in 1946 to Secretary of State Byrnes urging the United States to support strongly the KMT in the "elimination of the Communists."[52] A former Presbyterian missionary, Dr. Charles Scott, established the "China Emergency Committee" and circulated pamphlets demanding more American assistance to the Nationalists. Scott, whose daughter and son-in-law had also been China missionaries until they were killed by Communist troops in 1934, called for his readers to contact Congress and "request that they subpoena Dr. Charles E. Scott to appear before the Foreign Relations Committee so that they may know the whole

---

[50] Johnson, letters, August 16, 1945, November 6, 1947, January 6, 1948. WRJ Collection, RG 6, Boxes 17, 18, 19, folders 290, 303, 306, 308, YDSA.

[51] Letter to Alfred Kohlberg, August 3, 1949. WRJ Collection, RG 6, Box 19, folder 319, YDSA. As a former Congressional staff member with firsthand knowledge of Congressional filing habits, the author can attest that maintaining a file of such papers does not necessarily indicate significant influence. It does not disprove influence either, of course.

[52] Letter, April 21, 1946. WHJ Collection, Box 158, HIA. For more on Bell, see chapter two of this book.

truth about China."[53] Baptist missionary John Abernathy wrote from China to Judd that "unless the United States Government wakes up and goes all out to help China at an early date, with money and military aid, China will be sunk and all other countries in the far east will soon follow suit." During his 28 years in China, Abernathy had also been temporarily employed in diplomatic work by both the United States and the Chinese Government, and now he offered to travel to Washington to brief Congress on his experiences. Abernathy concluded his letter to Judd on a note that reveals much about the complexity of missionary allegiances: "We are both missionaries and have the best interests of two countries at heart."[54] Whereas many American Christians have at times struggled to reconcile their loyalty to both the United States and the "kingdom of God," American missionaries frequently felt this tension compounded by their fidelity both to God and to *two* nations.

Not all missionaries offered such unequivocal support for the Nationalists. Frank Cartwright, a senior Methodist missionary executive, in 1947 argued to William Richard Johnson that both the KMT and the CCP suffered equally from corruption and ineptitude.[55] A Methodist Bishop, stating his disagreement with Judd, reported that significant numbers of non-communist Chinese were opposed to Chiang's government.[56] Dr. Lucius Porter, a missionary professor at Stuart's old school, Yenching University, wrote to Judd in 1948 recommending that the United States withhold military support from the KMT and instead focus on economic development work in China.[57] Accusing Judd of being a "disseminator of false information," former missionary Spencer Kennard wrote an editorial reporting that his own experiences in China had turned him against the Nationalists and convinced him of the merits of the CCP.[58] Another Methodist missionary in a communist-controlled region in 1948 enthusiastically described communist governance as "a marvelous phenomenon to behold."[59] While some missionaries during the years 1945 to 1948 voiced similar support for the CCP, anti-Nationalist missionaries in this period generally focused their comments on criticizing the KMT, variously highlighting its corruption, ineptitude, or autocratic rule. Those who did cautiously venture forth actually to praise the CCP usually perceived in the

---

[53] Brochure for "China Emergency Committee," 1948. WRJ Collection, RG 6, Box 19, folder 314, YDSA.

[54] Letter, June 26, 1948. WHJ Collection, Box 158, HIA.

[55] Letter, April 30, 1947. WRJ Collection, RG 6, Box 18, folder 302, YDSA.

[56] Letter to Johnson, February 5, 1948. WRJ Collection, RG 6, Box 18, folder 309, YDSA.

[57] Letter from Dr. Lucius Porter, October 7, 1948. WHJ Collection, Box 163, HIA.

[58] J. Spencer Kennard, Jr., "Honesty in your Facts, Please, Congressman Judd," *The Protestant*, October 1945, 22–25.

[59] Letter to Johnson, May 20, 1948. WRJ Collection, RG 6, Box 19, folder 311, YDSA.

communists virtues such as egalitarianism, self-sacrifice, patriotism, and a commitment to "agrarian reforms."

Given the antipathy that activists such as Judd and Johnson felt towards communism, the fact that some of their missionary colleagues would find merit in the CCP struck them as ignorance at best, and perfidy at worst. At times Judd ascribed to such persons benevolent motives but lack of discernment. "The infiltration by the Communists in various good-hearted but soft-headed religious groups is too dangerous to allow it to be considered with tolerance," he wrote to a sympathetic journalist in 1948.[60] That same year he told the Evangelical Lutheran Church Mission Board of his unceasing efforts "to persuade the leaders of my own denomination and of the Foreign Mission Conference to recognize that if they did not wake up to the realities of Communism in China and deal with them effectively, there would not long be opportunity to carry on Missionary work at all."[61] In a letter to the editor of the *Christian Century*, Johnson accused some missionary organizations of suppressing reports of communist persecution of Christians, and warned that endorsing Mao's cause would only further undermine the missionary enterprise.[62] Some anticommunist missionaries believed that those Christians who differed with them were simply disregarding reality. Perry Hanson, a frustrated Methodist missionary in Jinan, China, wrote to Judd in early 1948 complaining that the Methodist church leadership in America seemed to be opposing Chiang Kai-shek and tacitly supporting the communists. Hanson challenged Methodist church executives to "talk with those coming up out of the great tribulation of life among the Reds, or, better yet just try a trip across Red territory [in China]," and went on to urge full support for the Nationalists.[63]

The missionary debate intensified as a Communist victory loomed ever larger in 1949. William Richard Johnson began the year, appropriately enough, with consecutive multi-week visits to Washington, where he engaged in his usual series of whirlwind meetings in Congressional, State Department, and White House offices.[64] Johnson excitedly reported to Judd that in his meeting with President Truman's assistant John Steelman, the White House aide had apparently promised to peruse carefully the copious literature Johnson gave him. Judd, not sharing Johnson's optimism, sensed that the end was near for the Nationalists. He replied to Johnson that "our main fight now is to

---

[60] Letter, April 9, 1948. WRJ Collection, RG 6, Box 19, folder 310, YDSA.
[61] Statement, November 30, 1948. WHJ Collection, Box 36, HIA.
[62] Letter, January 3, 1948. WRJ Collection, RG 6, Box 19, folder 308, YDSA.
[63] Letter from Perry O. Hanson, January 26, 1948. WHJ Collection, Box 176, HIA.
[64] Letters, WRJ Collection, RG 6, Box 19, folder 315, YDSA.

try and prevent the Administration from getting away with its desperate line that it did everything possible to try and help China put down the Communist rebellion."[65] Meanwhile, Earle Ballou, a leading executive with the ABCFM (Judd's old missionary agency), wrote Judd questioning the wisdom of continuing support for the KMT. While disclaiming any affinity for communism, Ballou said he "gave up hope several months ago that we can do anything at this late stage" and instead advocated only sending relief aid to the Chinese people.[66]

Meanwhile, mainline Protestant church organizations issued official pronouncements attempting to influence the debate and shape policy. The Federal Council of Churches (FCC) in March issued a report which held "hope and possibility for higher levels of life" following the conflict in China, and called on the United States to maintain positive relations with whomever emerged as the ruling regime. Judd, correctly sensing veiled sympathy for the Chinese Communists, scribbled a note in the margins of the report acerbically describing the FCC document as an example of "how muddle-headed many church people are." He later denounced it as "one of the most loaded misrepresentations I have ever seen – all the more diabolical and dangerous because so cleverly shaded."[67] But Judd's frustration with the FCC paled in comparison with his outrage at a letter issued two months later.

On May 5, 1949, a coalition calling itself the "China Committee of the Foreign Missions Conference of North America" released an open letter to the Senate Foreign Relations Committee and the House Foreign Affairs Committee that, in the words of their accompanying press release, "voiced vigorous opposition to any further military aid to China and urged support of the State Department's non-intervention policy in China." Authored by Frank Cartwright, a senior executive with the Methodist Foreign Missions Board (Johnson's agency), and Rowland Cross, an official with the ABCFM, it purported to speak on behalf of 26 major Protestant denominations and to represent the convictions of the majority of American Protestant missionaries active in China. National media attention, including an article in the *New York Times*, guaranteed their message would receive a wide audience.

In addition to calling for an immediate cessation of military assistance to the KMT, the letter made clear the China Committee's conviction that Chiang's government retained virtually no support among the Chinese people.

[65] Letters, April 21, 1949, May 10, 1949, WHJ Collection, Box 159, HIA.
[66] Letter, March 2, 1949. WHJ Collection, Box 159, HIA.
[67] "Message and Findings" of the Third National Study Conference on the Churches and World Order, issued by the Federal Council of Churches, March 8–11, 1949. WHJ Collection, Boxes 176, 37, HIA.

Further American attempts towards even a negotiated settlement were futile, they argued, leaving as the only options either a full-scale American military intervention or the complete abdication of involvement. The letter offered little in the way of predictions or prescriptions. "We believe that the form of government should be decided by the forces now at work within China," it said, avoiding the clear implication that such a government would be ruled by Mao Zedong. Regarding the United States, the China Committee recommended continued provision only of economic aid "through the present Kuomintang government or any other recognized government under such conditions as will safeguard the freedom of the people and promote genuine and adequate economic development." Above all else, the mission executives affirmed their "desire that the long-standing friendship between the United States and China may be maintained and strengthened."[68]

Remarkable as its recommendations were, the letter was perhaps even more notable for what it did not say. It made no judgments regarding which form of government would be preferable for China. It not only refrained from invoking theological principles or Christian distinctives; it only once even mentioned missionary work, and then only as an aside. The missionary officials who drafted it attempted to speak simply as interested American citizens with considerable insight on China.

Only not all missionaries themselves agreed on these "insights," and some differed quite virulently. Judd and Johnson, predictably, were apoplectic. As a member of the House Foreign Affairs Committee, Judd was an official recipient of the letter. He composed a four page, paragraph-by-paragraph rebuttal of the mission board statement, taking exception with the credibility of its authors, their analysis of China's problems, their policy recommendations, even their sincerity. He concluded with an impassioned series of rhetorical questions:

> Does "concern for people" ordinarily lead one to acquiesce in their enslavement?.... It is hardly short of self-righteous hypocrisy to pretend to be desirous of maintaining and strengthening the long-standing friendship by turning China over to the control of a godless, totally unmoral despotism that is openly and avowedly dedicated to wiping out every American influence in China and every bit of goodwill for America. I can understand why Communists should work to destroy the missionary enterprise; but why should missionary executives be encouraging and assisting them, either actively or passively?[69]

[68] Letter and press release, May 5–6, 1949. WRJ Collection, RG 6, Box 19, folder 317, YDSA.
[69] Judd, comments, May, 1949. WHJ Collection, Box 37, HIA.

Ironically, Judd had been invited to give a major speech the next week at a Madison Square Garden missionary rally sponsored by many of the same organizations who had commissioned the letter. Torn between not wanting to politicize an address on missions and yet not wanting seemingly to endorse the statement by failing to denounce it, Judd wrote to the rally organizers and offered to withdraw. It appears that a compromise was arranged allowing him to mention briefly "the difference of opinion on American policy" that existed among missionaries, in the process of delivering his prepared speech on "The World Mission of the Christian Church."[70]

William Richard Johnson, perhaps even more irate than Walter Judd, composed a six-page letter in response to the statement. While addressed to the leadership of the Methodist church, Johnson titled it an "open letter" and mailed 10,000 copies to clergy and mission executives around the country. In a rambling, kinetic discourse on the history of communist aggression, Johnson made the acid observation that the China Committee's policy suggestions closely resembled those recommended by the Communist Party of the United States. Besides identifying himself as a retired missionary, Johnson's letter made almost no mention of the potential ramifications of events in China for missionary work and the Christian faith. He dwelt instead on what he regarded as American policy errors in not supporting the KMT more actively, and on the general menace posed by communism to world peace and freedom.[71]

This particular exchange of letters and arguments by missionaries is remarkable for being almost completely devoid of theological issues. All the participants stood solidly in the tradition of mainline Protestantism. Because of this kinship, theological convictions do not seem to have determined any particular political positions. Rather than arguing over religious doctrine or missionary practices, these Christians carried on an extensive public debate about foreign policy. In the process of making their arguments in terms accessible to all Americans, the missionaries abandoned any distinctive appeal to revealed truths or the unique interests of missionary work. Their identities as "missionaries" came to connote not so much a religious vocation as it indicated a particular experience with and concern for another country – in this case, China.

The China Committee's letter opposing support for the Nationalists also revealed what had been a growing sentiment among some China missionaries: perhaps the Communists were not so bad. One of Ambassador Stuart's former

---

[70] Judd, letter, May 7, 1949. WHJ Collection, Box 37, HIA.
[71] Letters, May and June, 1949. WRJ Collection, RG 6, Boxes 19, 28, folders 32, 319, YDSA.

faculty colleagues at Yenching University wrote to him in May 1949 describing life in Beijng under the new Communist authorities. "The work they do is most inspiring," he proclaimed. "China never had a better government within the last 3,000 years."[72] A senior executive with Judd's old mission agency, the ABCFM, in July passed on to Judd a letter from an ABCFM missionary currently serving in Beijng. The missionary's letter chided Judd for his support for Chiang, and concluded that "we have to decide whether we hate communism so much that we'd rather give up China than be friends with communists, or whether we love China so much that we'll work with her even though it means being friends with communists."[73]

Some missionaries found it little problem to be friends with communists. Albert Smit, a Christian Reformed pastor working in the city of Xuzhou in Jiangsu province, wrote a glowing letter to his mission board in June 1949, shortly after communist forces occupied his city. He contemptuously related the oppression and looting by the Nationalist troops before the communists arrived, and described the new government as "a great improvement for the common people." Crime had decreased dramatically, order had been restored, the military obeyed its leaders, and "the present government is much closer to the common people than the former regime." As to his own work, Smit acknowledged an uncertain future. "Just what, if any, restrictions will be placed on the work of missionaries is not as yet clear. No doubt, much will depend upon America's attitude towards the new government." He remained optimistic, however, for himself and for China. "The mode of life of the people will not be affected much, but wealth will be more equally distributed . . . [and we] are hopeful that the work of our Mission can go on."[74]

Though subsequent developments in China would prove his predictions profoundly wrong, Smit did not stand alone in his optimism. Through the end of 1949, the *Messenger*, a liberal Protestant fortnightly, published a series of letters and articles from other China missionaries reporting favorably on life under the new communist control. One related that conditions were "normal and peaceful" and described Mao's forces – without any apparent irony – as "liberators." Another article by Lucius Porter, a professor at Stuart's old school, Yenching University, described the CCP's victories as "one more act in the great drama of revolution that has been enacted by the Chinese since the

---

[72] Letter to Amb. Stuart, May 31, 1949. John Leighton Stuart Collection, Box 1, HIA. Even though the CCP had not yet conquered all of the mainland and established the PRC, at this point they controlled significant portions of the country, including Beijing.

[73] Letter from Alice Mary Huggins, July 11, 1949. WHJ Collection, Box 159, HIA.

[74] June 14, 1949 letter from Albert Smit to Christian Reformed Board of Missions; EFMA Papers, Box 2, Folder 2; BGCA.

Boxer Movement of 1900," and happily reported that "Yenching has received especially favorable treatment from the new regime." Porter concluded with an anecdote about his school hosting simultaneously a church conference and a training session for CCP cadres. "That picture of Christian and Communistic training carried out on our campus seems to me a sign of the possibility of working together – which is what our experience has taught us."[75]

The ABCFM convened a seminar in Massachusetts in September 1949 on the topic "Christianity for this day in China." Held on the eve of Mao's establishment of the PRC, the seminar provided mission executives an opportunity to strategize on how they would carry out their work under the new regime in China. Lucius Porter participated, and described himself as "more or less" enthusiastic for the new government. He quoted Ambassador Stuart as recommending that missionaries needed to "work with these Communists, trying to dilute their extremism." Other mission executives speaking at the seminar had met with Ambassador Stuart recently, and while aware that Stuart did not favor the communists, the mission executives believed him to be quite sympathetic with their perspective. Seminar participants also discussed plans to provide further policy recommendations to political leaders in Washington. Finally, several participants, displaying their familiarity with Marxism's rhetorical appeal, expressed their hope that Christianity could become sufficiently "revolutionary" to appeal to the younger generations in China.[76] While some Protestant missionaries actually began to embrace the CCP, it seems that many others who were disillusioned with the KMT came to regard communism as acceptable, albeit undesirable. Above all they wanted to steer a pragmatic course that would enable them to maintain their work in China – regardless of the government under which that work took place.

V

Following the establishment of the "People's Republic of China" on October 1, 1949, debate within the American missionary community shifted to the question of diplomatic recognition of Mao's new government. The missionaries remained just as opinionated, just as determined to influence U.S. policy – and

---

[75] Anonymous author, "What's Happening in China," *The Messenger*, 13 September 1949, 14–15; Lucius C. Porter, "Another Angle on What's Happening in China," *The Messenger*, 6 December 1949, 16–18. See also William H. Daniels, "The Communists Have Taken Over in Yuanling," and Lewis S.C. Smythe, "Grounds for Hope in Communist China," 6 December 1949, 17–18.

[76] From "Notes on the Seminar," September 17, 1949. Harold S. Matthews Collection, Box 1, HIA.

just as divided as before. They all agreed, however, that the recognition decision held momentous import.

In 1949 Ambassador Stuart seemed quite conflicted, in contrast to the
adamant stance against recognition he later expressed in his 1954 memoirs.
Speaking to a group of current and former missionaries in November 1949,
he argued that recognition of the PRC should be extended only when Mao's
regime demonstrated adequate popular support and a commitment to international standards of governance. Yet he worried aloud that not recognizing
the new government could be counterproductive. Ostracizing China in such
a manner might accomplish little, he feared, while causing damage to U.S.
interests and diminishing U.S. influence.[77] Other missionaries, not saddled
with the delicate diplomatic burdens Stuart bore, were not so ambivalent.

The participants in the ABCFM seminar that autumn all agreed to support
recognition. Failure to establish official relations with the new regime, they
believed, would only drive China into closer allegiance with the USSR, whereas
maintaining diplomatic ties would preserve opportunities for the missionaries to "dilute" the appeal of communism.[78] In contrast, William Richard
Johnson, not surprisingly, barely paused to shift his agenda in response to the
communist victory. He soon subjected Capitol Hill and the White House to a
deluge of letters and telegrams opposing recognition.[79] Judd also immediately
declared his opposition to establishing relations with the PRC, connecting the
new Chinese government to America's principal Cold War foe. "We cannot
nurture the Chinese Communists who are the expeditionary forces of Soviet
Russia," he argued in an October 20 press release, "we cannot recognize them
as the rightful rulers of China."[80]

Several missionaries from Judd's former organization were upset by his
opposition and urged their missionary colleague-turned-Congressman to
support recognition. Some wrote from China, while others were serving as
mission board executives back in the United States. Their language was unusually frank, even harsh: "The game is up, Walter"; "Is [Judd] stupid?"; "How
on earth can you continue to advocate [for the KMT]?"; "This government
is going strong, with or without the recognition of the USA, and the longer
we put off such recognition, and the more we fight against the communists
in China, the worse for USA."[81]

---

77 From "Report of Conference with Ambassador J. Leighton Stuart," November 12, 1949. John
     Leighton Stuart Collection, Box 1, HIA.
78 From "Notes on the Seminar," September 17, 1949. Harold S. Matthews Collection, Box 1,
     HIA.
79 Letters, January 6, 7, 1950. WRJ Collection, RG 6, Box 20, folder 320, YDSA.
80 Press release, October 20, 1949. WHJ Collection, Box 37, HIA.
81 Letters to Judd, 1949, 1950. WHJ Collection, Boxes 160, 163, HIA.

The recognition controversy prompted soul-searching by missionary organizations as well, who felt acutely their stake in the situation in China. At its annual meeting in December 1949, Methodist Foreign Missions Board members found themselves deeply divided, and finally decided to abstain from taking any position because "this was something for individual judgment and not for a Board of Missions to consider."[82] Somewhat ironically, one of the strongest proponents of not adopting an official Methodist position was Frank Cartwright, who had been one of the principal authors of the "official" statement by the China Committee seven months earlier urging suspension of U.S. assistance to the KMT. Perhaps rather chastened by the disagreements over the previous statement, Cartwright and other missionary executives now sought to tread cautiously before speaking for the "official" missionary position.

Possessing no such hesitations was John Mackay, a Presbyterian and the President of the International Missionary Council. Following a two-month tour of China, in January 1950 Mackay publicly urged recognition. He cited the "excellent behavior" of the communist armies, the lack of disruption of missionary activity, a belief that the CCP would not ally with the Soviet Union, and the apparent support of the Chinese people for their new government.[83] Outraged by such assertions, other missionaries such as Charles Scott and Geraldine Fitch issued detailed rebuttals, citing communist persecution of missionaries and other Christians, as well as communist treachery in general.[84]

Missionary contentions over the recognition question amounted to more than intramural squabbling, however. Believing that the welfare of not one but two countries they cared about deeply was at stake, and realizing that for many their own future as missionaries in China was in question, a number of missionaries sought to influence the U.S. government as it deliberated how to respond. For example, Clarence Pickett, the head of the American Friends Service Committee (Quakers), which had long been active in China, wrote President Truman in January 1950. Moscow did not control the Chinese communists, Pickett argued, but rather the CCP reflected a natural development in China's ongoing economic revolution. Moreover, U.S. support for the KMT had only further alienated the Chinese people. "By treating Communist

---

[82] Letter to Johnson from Frank Cartwright, January 6, 1950. WRJ Collection, RG 6, Box 20, folder 321, YDSA.

[83] Statement in Johnson papers, January 16, 1950. WRJ Collection, RG 6, Box 34, folder 107, YDSA. This was the same John Mackay who later emerged as L. Nelson Bell's chief nemesis.

[84] See, for example, "Should We Recognize Communist China? No" by Geraldine Fitch, June 22, 1950. WRJ Collection, RG 6, Box 34, folder 107, YDSA.

China as an enemy and by refusing to recognize her," Pickett wrote, "we are not isolating China, we are isolating ourselves."[85]

It would be hard to conceive of a perspective more contrary to Pickett's than that of an Evangelical Foreign Mission Association bulletin issued on June 1, 1950. Written by one missionary who claimed to speak for several others throughout China, the bulletin described China as "looking more and more like a satellite country of central Europe" because of so many Soviet officials controlling the new government. Moreover, the letter reported "very wide resentment against the communist regime among all classes of Chinese," and said that "mass demonstrations... have been brutally suppressed," and poverty was spreading. The writer deplored "any attempt to bring pressure upon Washington to recognize the communist government" and even warned against American trade with the PRC, which only seemed to fuel the CCP's "war machine." Finally, the bulletin suggested that American missionaries ought to leave China, both because they were no longer welcome and, intriguingly, because it might be that "the Chinese Church is at last reaching the point we've all hoped and prayed for, where it can stand in its own right and push ahead."[86] In the speculation of at least this one evangelical missionary, China may have been "lost" politically, but "saved" religiously.

The recognition debate continued to divide missionaries throughout 1950. The China Committee of the mainline Foreign Missions Conference, strongly favoring recognition but wary of igniting further contention by taking an "official" position, prepared a memorandum urging recognition to be sent to Congressional leaders and senior officials at the State Department, including the Secretary of State. The letter was to be signed by missionaries "as individual American citizens."[87] The next month, 68 current and former missionaries and mission executives sent just such a letter to the State Department and Congress urging diplomatic relations with the PRC. While emphasizing that they spoke "as individuals," the signers referred to their missionary experience in China as "a fact which gives us the right to be heard on this issue and places on us an obligation to express our opinion." The letter invoked some of the conventional arguments – it referred to the PRC's support among the Chinese people and the need for the United States to maintain its relationship with China – but it also took the unusual step of addressing concerns particular to

[85] January 16, 1950 letter from Clarence Pickett to President Truman; OF 150, Box 758; HST Papers.

[86] June 1, 1950 "Bulletin of China"; EFMA Papers, Box 2, Folder 2; BGCA.

[87] Letter from Rowland Cross to members of the China Committee, March 31, 1950. Rowland Cross Collection, Box 1, HIA.

missionaries. Noting that "Christian missions . . . operate within the frame-work of the People's Republic," the signers worried that non-recognition would "militate against the carrying on of such work by Americans" and "delay in recognition would make still more difficult the continuance of even our present contacts."[88]

While concern for the viability of missionary work had always been at the forefront of missionary interest in United States–China relations, when addressing policy-makers, missionaries had generally refrained from refer-encing their own enterprise. Now, fearing that their very existence in China was jeopardized, the signers made clear the connection between the policy of the state and the work of the church. Rep. Judd, an official recipient of the letter as a member of the Foreign Affairs Committee, felt outraged and per-sonally betrayed. He scribbled furious margin notes all over his copy, taking issue with almost every point. He also noted with regret the 19 names of his former ABCFM colleagues who had signed the letter.[89]

Judd no doubt welcomed the statement issued in direct response later that year by a coalition of 230 Americans closely involved with missions work in China. This letter, sent to President Truman and Secretary of State Acheson, urged "non-recognition" of the PRC and continued support for the Nationalists. It mimicked the structure of the earlier statement favoring recognition with almost point-by-point rebuttals. The signers believed "it would be a moral compromise and a political mistake of great magnitude for our government to recognize the so-called People's Republic of China." Again, besides asserting some of the standard anticommunist concerns about the illegitimacy of the PRC and the communist threat to international security, this letter also made direct reference to missionary work. It warned that "Christian missions must compromise with a system which is atheistic in order to give diplomatic approval or recognition to the government they represent." Furthermore, the statement noted the number of missionaries and Chinese Christians killed by the communists in the past year and worried that "we see no greater hope for freedom of religion in Communist China than in other satellite countries." Finally, while promising their support for any missionaries staying in China who "feel they can continue Christian work without compromise and without endangering their Chinese colleagues," the signers suggested that the best way to maintain friendship with the Chinese people would be by continuing to support "Free China on Formosa."[90]

---

[88] Letter, April 26, 1950. WHJ Collection, Box 160, HIA.
[89] Ibid.
[90] From WHJ Collection, Box 38, HIA.

Like the opposing letter, this one made a direct link between government policy and missionary work. But while the first statement had hinged the missionary enterprise on the policy adopted by the United States Government (i.e., recognition would enable missions work to continue), this second statement connected missionary efforts to the policies of the communist Chinese Government (i.e., the communists were already eradicating any prospects for continued missionary efforts). Accordingly, the second letter implied that any missionaries hoping that a change in U.S. policy towards China would improve conditions for missionary work were deluding themselves.

The State Department followed the missionary argument with great interest, both because of its bearing on U.S.–China policy and because of how the new regime in Beijing would affect so many Americans working in China. In May 1950, the Department called a conference of missionary agencies, mostly to discuss missionary concerns over how, if at all, they could continue their activities in China. Walter McConaughy, former Consul General in Shanghai, gave the main presentation. McConaughy reported that while Mao's government did not necessarily intend to exterminate Christianity, it was moving to ban all foreign missionary activity. Nevertheless, the persecution Christians were suffering seemed to be provoking great religious interest among many Chinese, and churches were unusually full. McConaughy suggested that any new missionaries being sent to China should be trained in Marxism, to prevent gullible religious workers from falling for communist propaganda. He also advised missionaries to "have some trade or profession in addition to their ability to evangelize," which might make them more palatable in the eyes of the new regime.[91]

The debate among the missionaries was resolved not by either camp, but instead by the new government in China, which soon moved to expel all foreign missionaries. The paramount motivation behind the PRC's eviction notices lay more in suspicion of all things "foreign" than particular animus towards "missionaries." Hyper-nationalism superseded hostility to religion as the primary factor, and even some Chinese Christians supported the missionary expulsion. About the same time that the State Department was advising American missionaries on adapting to the changes in China, Premier Zhou Enlai was working with a group of Chinese Christian leaders in May 1950 to draft and publish "The Christian Manifesto: Direction of Endeavor for Chinese Christianity in the Construction of New China." Authorities

---

[91] Notes on May 22, 1950 "Conference on China" with Walter McConaughy; EFMA Papers, Box 2, Folder 2; BGCA.

circulated this document throughout China, and eventually 400,000 Chinese Protestants signed it, or about half of all those in China at the time.[92]

The "Christian Manifesto" opened with a rhetorical broadside against 140 years of Protestant missionary work in China. "Not long after Christianity's coming to China, imperialism started its activities here; and since the principal groups of missionaries who brought Christianity to China all came themselves from these imperialistic countries, Christianity consciously or unconsciously, directly or indirectly, became related with imperialism." While not explicitly restricting missionary activities, the Manifesto hinted that their days were numbered. "All Christian churches and organizations in China that are still relying upon foreign personnel and financial aid should work out concrete plans to realize within the shortest possible time their objective of self-reliance and rejuvenation." Tellingly, the Manifesto asserted a political agenda for the Chinese church in support of the "Common Political Program."[93] No significant events over the previous six months had caused this growing hostility towards missionaries. Rather, it was a natural outgrowth of the PRC's attempts to consolidate power, control religious groups, and draw sharp distinctions between China and the outside world.

Even at this time, the remaining missionaries who acquiesced to the new restrictions were still hopeful of a smooth evolution under PRC authority. But within a few months, the new regime's attitude towards missionaries became more severe. On Dec. 29, 1950, a state Council under Zhou Enlai issued a harsh pronouncement of "Regulations Governing All Organizations Subsidized With Foreign Funds." These measures clearly intended to further circumscribe missionary activities by targeting their operational lifeblood of funding from their home organizations.[94] The regulations did not expressly prohibit the receipt of outside funding, but instead sought to "control effectively the funds from foreign sources sent into China" through a series of onerous registration requirements.[95]

The primary cause of these new restrictions lay just over the border in war-torn Korea. Following a series of advances by the largely American-led United Nations forces, Mao had sent Chinese troops to enter the war on the side of the North Koreans. President Truman reacted to the Chinese invasion by issuing

---

[92] Cited in Donald MacInnis, *Religious Policy and Practice in Communist China* (New York: Macmillan 1972), 158.

[93] Cited in MacInnis, 158–160.

[94] Bob Whyte, *Unfinished Encounter: China and Christianity* (London: William Collins 1988), 220–221.

[95] Cited in MacInnis, 24–25.

an order on December 16 freezing all Chinese assets in the United States. Zhou responded in kind by targeting those few organizations in China that received funding from abroad, the majority of whom were mission agencies.[96] Events in the international arena thus accelerated the process, already in place, of forcing foreign missionaries out of China.

By the end of 1951, the vast majority of missionaries had left China. The PRC seized control of all medical, educational, and other missionary institutions, and had moved to place all Chinese Protestant activity under the authority of the government-controlled Three Self Patriotic Movement (TSPM) church. One historian describes what faced those who stayed:

> After 1951, of the remaining missionaries, practically all were at least under house arrest; many were imprisoned, and soon most were deported. A few were brainwashed, but by and large the missionaries were not attacked physically; rather the Communist authorities sought to denigrate the reputation of missionaries.... By early 1953 practically all missionaries, Protestant and Roman Catholic alike, had been forced out, "deported," and the Chinese Church was completely on its own.[97]

Another scholar notes that in the spring of 1953, only ten American Protestant missionaries remained in China – and eight of them were in prison.[98]

The effects on missionaries who had remained in China were demoralizing. While journeying home to the United States in 1951, missionary Laura Cross wrote to her brother Rowland of her vanquished hopes to stay. Under the new regime, "I thought as a Christian American I could be sympathetic and understanding. I could approve of some things and criticize others.... But the time came in the Communist state where we learned we must lean completely to their side or be considered an enemy. I felt then that I must leave."[99]

The eminent Sinologist John Fairbank has described one of the great ironies of the relationship between American missionaries and the Chinese revolution. The China of the late nineteenth century had been plagued by pernicious social, cultural, and economic ills, which many missionaries sought to redress. These efforts at reform had in turn revealed to many Chinese the yawning gap between their own aspirations and their trying existence. In Fairbank's

---

[96] Whyte, 221–222.
[97] William H. Clark, *The Church in China: Its Vitality; Its Future?* (New York: Council Press 1970), 121.
[98] Richard C. Bush, Jr. *Religion in Communist China* (New York: Abingdon 1970), p.48. No detail given of where the other 2 American missionaries were.
[99] Letter, May 18, 1951. Rowland Cross Collection, Box 1, HIA.

words, "The missionaries came as spiritual reformers, soon found that material improvements were equally necessary, and in the end helped to foment the great revolution. Yet as foreigners, they could take no part in it, much less bring it to finish. Instead, it finished them."[100] In at least one sense, these missionaries' very effort to save China had caused them to lose the country they loved.

VI

Missionaries in foreign lands soon learn to deal with the inevitable setbacks, failures, and disappointments, and Walter Judd had been no exception. The perseverance he learned during the hardship years of his medical service in rural China only stiffened his resolve as the China debate entered a new chapter. The PRC had consolidated power, expelled missionaries, and asserted itself in the international arena. Having failed in his crusade to save China from communism, Judd now dedicated himself to seeing that the international community shunned the new regime. He found a receptive ear in the new American president, Dwight D. Eisenhower. Judd also found some new allies from the ranks of his erstwhile adversaries.

On October 22, 1953, Judd led a small group to meet with Eisenhower and present a petition against admitting the PRC to the United Nations. The petition, sponsored by Judd, former president Herbert Hoover, Senator H. Alexander Smith, and four others, contained an impressive list of signatories, including those who had not always agreed with Judd on China policy such as General Marshall and Ambassador Stuart, both now retired. The petition's other signatories spanned the vocational spectrum, including more than 30 senators, 12 governors, eminent war heroes General Claire Chennault, General James Doolittle, and Admiral Chester Nimitz, missionary leader (and Nobel Peace Prize winner) John Mott, author John Dos Passos, publisher William Randolph Hearst, labor leaders Jay Lovestone and George Meany, and historian Arthur Schleslinger, Jr.. All affixed their names against admitting "the so-called Chinese People's Republic to the United Nations" for a litany of reasons, including the fears that "admission would destroy the purposes, betray the letter, and violate the spirit" of the UN, it would cause Chiang's Republic of China to be expelled, it would "destroy the prestige and the position of the United States and of the Free World in Asia," it would "restore the prestige and authority of the Soviet Government," it would "encourage subversive

---

[100] Fairbank, "The Many Faces of Protestant Missions in China and the United States," in Fairbank, ed., *The Missionary Enterprise in China and America*, 2.

totalitarian movements in the free nations of the world," and it would blithely ignore the PRC's intervention in Korea, in which it waged a war "against the very organization in which their supporters now claim membership for them."[101] Eisenhower indicated his fervent agreement, responding to Judd that "the Chinese Communist regime... seeks representation in the UN in order to promote the objectives of international Communism."[102]

Judd developed a close relationship with Eisenhower, and the former missionary regularly shared his insights with the president on Asian matters. Besides their own meetings, Judd arranged for some of his missionary colleagues to brief Eisenhower, including the Methodist Ralph Ward, longtime bishop of Shanghai until the revolution, and a fierce anticommunist.[103] In this way and others, Judd ensured that Eisenhower heard a missionary perspective that reinforced his Administration's generally stern Far Eastern policy. In the Eisenhower years, at least, America's containment policy came to include containing any further expansion by the People's Republic of China.

While theological conservatives generally opposed communism, theological tradition or even denominational affiliation did not always determine the political position that Protestant missionaries took towards the conflict in China. Numerous missionaries from within the same mainline Protestant tradition, even the same denominations, came to dramatically different conclusions over how the United States should relate to China. Other political and theological considerations aside, the fundamental factor determining missionary attitudes towards China was their generic assessment of communism. Those who regarded communism as either a progressive good or an unfortunate but tolerable error generally frowned on the Nationalists and advocated recognition of the PRC. Conversely, those missionaries who regarded communism as an unmitigated evil, antithetical in every way to Christianity, generally expressed much more patience and support towards the Nationalists and nothing but militant opposition to the PRC. Within this

---

[101] October 22, 1953 letter and petition to Eisenhower; White House Central File (WHCF): Confidential File, Subject Series, Box 99, Folder: United Nations (1); Dwight D. Eisenhower Papers, Eisenhower Presidential Library, Abilene, Kansas (hereinafter DDE Papers).

[102] October 24, 1953 letter from Eisenhower to Judd; WHCF: Confidential File, Subject Series, Box 99, Folder: United Nations (1); DDE Papers.

[103] See, for example, June 25, 1954 Memorandum For the Record; Ann Whitman File, Ann Whitman Diary Series, Box 2, Folder: ACW Diary June 1954; August 15, 1954 Memorandum For the Record; Ann Whitman File, Ann Whitman Diary Series, Box 3, Folder: ACW Diary August 1954; September 14, 1954 letter from Judd to Thomas Stephens; October 9, 1954 letter from Ralph Ward to Eisenhower; Official File, Box 856, Folder: 168-B; March 12, 1955 letter from Judd to Eisenhower; March 14, 1955 letter from Eisenhower to Judd; March 15, 1955 letter from Judd to Eisenhower; March 18, 1955 letter from Eisenhower to Judd; Official File, Box 856, Folder: 168-B-1; DDE Papers.

framework, all missionaries believed they were following God's plan for both China and America – a bedrock assumption so foundational that they rarely felt the need to articulate it. Ironically, in light of their explicitly religious vocations – and in contrast with the public theologies of Truman and Eisenhower – missionaries seem to have been the least inclined to use explicitly religious language in contesting American foreign policy. Yet virtually all of them couched their convictions at least partially in terms of what they believed was best for China, and almost every missionary based his or her opinion on personal experiences with the Communists, the Nationalists, and the Chinese people. In that sense, they all desired to "save" China.

5

~

Guided by God: The Unusual Decision-Making
of Senator H. Alexander Smith

I

Senator H. Alexander Smith began December 3, 1948, in the same way that he began every other day. He arose early, washed, dressed, ate breakfast, and waited to hear from God. On this particular day, God revealed, in Smith's words, "that I have a special message for this Congress and God will guide me."[1] It was not unusual for Senator Smith to hear such things. God's instructions, according to Smith's daily prayer journal, often addressed affairs of state – just as often as God spoke to him about more mundane matters such as what to wear, where to vacation, or how to deal with Mrs. Smith's temper. Smith's journal, in which he recorded these revelations, provides more insight into his efforts to shape Cold War foreign policy than any volume of the *Congressional Record* or any piece of legislation.

H. Alexander Smith served as a Republican Senator from New Jersey from late 1944 until the beginning of 1959. Previously a New York City lawyer and a lecturer in the department of politics at Princeton University, during his time in the Senate Smith focused primarily on foreign affairs and domestic labor issues.[2] From his seat on the Senate Foreign Relations Committee, and particularly as sometime chairman of the Subcommittee on East Asian

---

[1] HAS journal entry, December 3, 1948. Box 282, HAS papers.
[2] "Smith, Howard Alexander," in *Biographical Directory of the United States Congress 1774–1989* (Washington, DC: United States Government Printing Office 1989), 1830–1831. Senator H. Alexander Smith has received remarkably little, if any, scholarly attention. No biography of him exists, and he makes only episodic appearances in scholarly treatments of the foreign policy issues that attracted his involvement. This neglect becomes especially surprising considering that Senator Smith left the type of source material that historians dream of: a detailed daily journal of his life, particularly focused on his time in the Senate and the divine guidance he believed he received. This journal is available in the collection of Smith's papers at the Seeley G. Mudd Manuscript Library, Princeton University, Princeton, NJ.

Affairs, Smith both observed keenly and participated actively in the formation of American foreign policy during the formative years of the Cold War.

In terms of his foreign policy convictions, Senator Smith himself always remained ambivalent about the containment doctrine. Though he decried what he regarded as its cold realism, he nonetheless arrived at essentially the same diagnosis of the international situation as containment's advocates. The world was separated into two antagonistic, irreconcilable blocs, divided most fundamentally by their contrasting theologies. On the one side, the Soviets denied the existence of God and the inherent dignity of man, and held the Marxist dialectic as the supreme engine of history and the communist state as the supreme authority on earth. On the other side, the Americans worshipped God, and believed he had endowed all human beings with inalienable rights and freedoms, and that he authored history and reigned over all human governments. Moreover, God had given the United States a special calling to resist communist advances and to protect the world from further communist malevolence. Smith embraced this calling, and dedicated his Senate career to seeing it fulfilled. In this respect, Smith vividly personifies the Congressional dimension of Cold War public theology.

Smith's role in shaping American policy admittedly does not approach the stature of figures such as Truman and Acheson, or Eisenhower and Dulles. His importance lies elsewhere, in at least three ways. First, perhaps more vividly than any other public figure of the day, Smith offers a case-study in how religion – not just as a belief system, but as a set of practices such as prayer – can directly influence the actions of policy-makers. In this way his diaries provide nearly incomparable material for scholars wrestling with the methodological question of accounting for how generally intangible factors such as prayer and supernatural guidance inform decision-making. Second, as a foreign policy leader in the Senate, Smith demonstrates how the diplomatic theology developed by the Truman and Eisenhower Administrations both influenced and was influenced by Congress. Third, within the United States Government, Smith was the most eager disciple and enthusiastic advocate for Moral Re-Armament.

Smith's worldview received its strongest formation from his long-standing and deep involvement in the shadowy, quasi-religious movement known as Moral Re-Armament (MRA).[3] MRA defies easy categorization. Founded

---

[3] Though MRA's apologists and detractors have over the years spilled much ink alternately defending or defaming the movement, a comprehensive scholarly analysis is still needed. For one academic case study on MRA, see Luttwak, Edward, "Franco-German Reconciliation: The Overlooked Role of the Moral Re-Armament Movement," in Douglas Johnston and Cynthia Sampson, eds., *Religion: The Missing Dimension of Statecraft* (New York: Oxford

in the 1920s by an American Lutheran minister named Frank Buchman and known variously as the "Oxford Group," "Buchmanite movement," and most commonly as "MRA," it attracted a considerable international following during its heyday from the 1930s to the 1950s. Characterizing itself as an "ideology," MRA offered an intellectual and spiritual basis for living, both to navigate life's daily challenges and to give transcendent meaning to human existence. MRA consisted of an international network of individuals, many of them prominent political and business leaders, who met regularly for prayer and discussion. The group claimed, rather immodestly, to be "God's supreme offer to this generation" and hoped to "bring in the Golden Age, the new civilization built here and now on enduring foundations." As if those aspirations were not ambitious enough, MRA audaciously and without irony proclaimed its goal of "a fear-free, hate-free, greed-free world."[4]

MRA developed its own distinctive vocabulary. Adherents committed themselves to the almost Maoist-sounding "Four Absolutes": "absolute honesty, absolute purity, absolute unselfishness, absolute love." Those who converted to a new, MRA-inspired outlook on life were pronounced "changed." Followers engaged in a daily morning ritual, either alone or in groups, known as the "quiet time" in which they would pray and then wait attentively for God's "guidance" for the day's events. Logically enough, they described a good decision or a desired outcome as "guided." In other words, MRA believed and taught that God gave direct and unmediated instructions to his followers, who needed only to listen – and obey.

MRA deliberately played on theological ambiguity. On the one hand it had unmistakably Christian roots. Buchman himself declared the strongest need of the age to be "the greatest revolution of all time whereby the Cross of Christ will transform the world."[5] Yet MRA frequently eschewed Christian distinctives and embraced a sort of syncretism, evidenced by Buchman's description of MRA as "the good road of an ideology inspired by God upon which all can unite. Catholic, Jew, or Protestant, Hindu, Muslim, Buddhist and Confucianist – all find they can change, where needed, and travel along this good

University Press 1994). For more general background, though from a partisan perspective favoring MRA, see Piquet, Charles, and Michel Sentis, *The World At the Turning: Experiments With Moral Re-Armament* (London: Grosvenor 1979), Austin, H.W., *Frank Buchman As I Knew Him* (London: Grosvenor 1975), and Marcel, Gabriel, *Fresh Hope for the World: Moral Re-Armament in Action* (London: Longmans 1960). For a much more critical view of MRA, see Driberg, Tom, *The Mystery of Moral Re-Armament* (London: Secker and Warburg 1964).

4 Quoted in Entwistle, Basil, and John Roots, *Moral Re-Armament: What is It?* (Los Angeles: Pace Publications 1967), 125–126.

5 Quoted in Howard, Peter, *Frank Buchman's Secret* (New York: Doubleday 1961), 18.

road together."[6] Although MRA may have affirmed religious pluralism, it did not embrace political diversity to the same degree. Its followers united around a firm, impassioned anticommunism. MRA frequently characterized communism, because of its atheism and materialistic view of reality, as the most pernicious threat facing the world, and the worst of the bad "ideologies" in opposition to MRA's good "ideology." Beyond its anticommunism, however, MRA received support from a broad array of political interests around the world. It attracted many followers and attained significant influence in the United States Government, particularly in Congress, where numerous Senators and Representatives participated in weekly prayer groups based on MRA principles. Besides its relevance as a religious factor in American foreign policy, MRA also offers a fascinating example of how a secretive movement or network can attain significant sway with decision-makers. For some leaders who embraced MRA, customary influences such as political parties, lobbyists, finances, and regional interests paled in comparison with the opportunity MRA offered to receive guidance from God.

Not surprisingly, MRA attracted its share of comment and criticism. Will Herberg saw it as more intriguing than offensive: "a curious upper-bracket revivalistic movement . . . [that] cultivates a kind of sophisticated pietism in a house-party atmosphere."[7] But Reinhold Niebuhr found it simply galling. What he perceived as MRA's idealism, moralism, naiveté, and pretension offended his deepest sensibilities. In the late 1930s Buchman had commented favorably about Hitler, to the effect that while the Nazi dictator's anti-Semitism was regrettable, his anticommunism was commendable, and if Hitler would only believe in God he might accomplish some good. This outraged Niebuhr. Buchman's remarks, he argued, revealed at last MRA's "Nazi social philosophy." MRA's belief that converting powerful individuals would produce a greater impact on the world indicated "a simple and decadent individualism" and a failure to understand "that the man of power is always to a certain degree an anti-Christ." Even MRA's "quiet times" did not escape Niebuhr's scorn. He found "not the slightest indication that the prophetic spirit of the Bible has ever entered into this pollyanna religion by way of the quiet hour." Instead, "the increasingly obvious fascist philosophy which informs the group movement is in other words not only socially vicious but religiously vapid."[8]

---

[6] Quoted in Entwistle and Roots, 13.
[7] Will Herberg, *Protestant, Catholic, Jew: An Essay in American Religious Sociology* (New York: Doubleday and Company 1955), 133.
[8] Niebuhr, "Hitler and Buchman," *Christianity and Power Politics* (New York: Scribners 1940), 159–165.

Buchman's sympathy, if not quite support, for Hitler severely damaged
MRA's credibility. But the group was eminently adaptable, and with the advent
of the Cold War a few years later it saw a new opportunity for restoring its stature and influence as crusaders against communism. This was not enough to
win over most evangelicals, however. *Christianity Today* editorialized in 1958
that while it appreciated MRA's anticommunism, any Christian distinctives
were sorely missed. "The centrality of Christ's atoning work and the unique
authority of Scripture are not to be found. So syncretistic is the message, in fact,
that neither Moslem nor Buddhist need change his religion to join the ranks.
[MRA] is spectacular and flashy . . . but it still lacks spiritual discernment and
depth."[9]

MRA's new focus hardly placated Niebuhr, either. In a 1955 *Christianity and
Crisis* article, he observed that MRA had shifted its "emphasis from 'changing'
individual lives to providing an 'ideology' for the salvation of the world from
communism and wars." Niebuhr found MRA "akin to the perfectionist sects of
all Christian ages," though when MRA became involved in politics, "it is in this
realm that this kind of perfectionism becomes either irrelevant or dangerous."
He noted approvingly that a Church of England commission had just issued a
report highly critical of MRA's beliefs and methods. Besides finding MRA in
serious error theologically, socially, and politically, the report also expressed
considered skepticism at MRA's "quiet times." In the absence of any reference
to Jesus Christ, do MRA members "have sufficient means for distinguishing
between the genuine guidance of the Holy Spirit and the deliverances of their
own subconscious minds masquerading as God's voice"?[10] An important
question, though one that Senator Smith may not have asked himself.

II

Perhaps no Member of Congress was more involved in MRA than Senator
Smith. He seems to have first embraced MRA as a young lecturer at Princeton
in the 1920s, and soon made the "quiet time" to seek divine "guidance"
his most important daily ritual, which he followed with religious devotion.
Smith's son-in-law, H. Kenaston Twitchell, served full-time as a senior MRA
staff member, and Twitchell (known to Smith as "Ken") emerged as one
of Smith's closest advisors and confidants during his time in the Senate.
Inspired by the change he had experienced in his own life, Smith professed
high hopes that MRA could change the world as well. Writing in his journal
on New Year's Day, 1936 (several years before he became a Senator), Smith

⁹ "Moral ReArmament and the Biblical View," *Christianity Today*, 29 September 1958, 22.
¹⁰ Niebuhr, "Buchmanism Under Scrutiny," *Christianity and Crisis*, 16 May 1955, 62–64.

lamented the moral decay he saw afflicting the United States and the world, and expressed his belief that the "Oxford Group" (as MRA was then known) offered a remedy for these ills. He described MRA as "a collective advance to change the way of life and the thinking of a diseased world."[11]

As a Senator, Smith continued to apply MRA practices and principles to his political responsibilities. Over decades of journal entries, Smith comes across as a man of simple, even at times somewhat simplistic, faith. Rather than wrestling with theological conundrums or ruminations on the nature of God and human existence, Smith practiced his faith only as it connected to his daily life. He often recorded in his diary the sentiment that "I need the guidance and inspiration of God in these coming days," and believed he needed to seek direction from God for all of life's matters, large and small.[12] In this way, Smith sacralized the otherwise mundane. Not infrequently, his daily journal entries contain a "to do" list of the day's activities suffused with a quasi-religious character. Smith prefaced each task with the phrase "It comes to me to . . . ," indicating his unambiguous conviction that God spoke intimately and directly to his daily activities. The phrase "it comes to me" may have been passive, but Smith resolutely believed in God's active presence in his life.

Smith does not seem to have regarded God as merely a source of guidance at Smith's behest. Rather, he believed in his responsibility to serve and submit to God's will, whatever it might be. Anticipating the new year of 1949, he recorded his prayer: "O God, during the year make me true to thine principles which are true and guided by thee and not those which are merely expedient or vote-getting."[13] As a Senator, Smith felt acutely the tensions between the temptations and exigencies of political life and his own sense of religious calling. He declared repeatedly his hope to stay true to the latter. Even when a potential difference arose between his own convictions and his sense of divine guidance, he evidently relegated his conscience to the second tier. Reflecting on one such situation, he wrote: "Ken was right when he said that guidance should overrule conscience if there was a conflict. This happened yesterday. My conscience said go down and do my work. My guidance said stay home and rest there four days. I saw Dr. (illegible) and I feel better this morning."[14] This exchange raises all manner of interesting epistemological questions

---

[11] H. Alexander Smith (hereinafter HAS) journal entry, January 1, 1936. Box 281, H. Alexander Smith papers, Seeley G. Mudd Manuscript library, Princeton University, Princeton, NJ (hereinafter HAS papers).

[12] HAS journal entry, January 7, 1947. Box 281, HAS papers.

[13] HAS journal entry, January 2, 1949. Box 282, HAS papers.

[14] HAS journal entry, February 6, 1948. Box 282, HAS papers. "Ken," of course, refers to H. Kenaston Twitchell, Smith's son-in-law, who was very active with Moral Re-Armament and also served as one of Smith's closest advisors and confidants.

concerning the sources of knowledge and moral guidance. Religious liberty advocates often speak of the "right to worship God according to the dictates of one's conscience," but Smith sought instead to submit his conscience to the dictates of God. While many people might regard fidelity to conscience as the highest personal calling, and many religious thinkers consider personal conscience to be informed by divine guidance, Smith instead experienced an apparent conflict between his own human "conscience" and his belief in how God was guiding him. This particular matter concerning the question of whether to work or rest may have been quotidian, but its implications are profound. Smith here reveals himself as so single-mindedly devoted to God's directions for his life that he was willing to lay even the claims of his own conscience on the divine altar.

A sensitive, introspective man, Smith struggled continually between trying to maintain control in his own life and relying on divine sustenance. Insomnia frequently afflicted him. A typical journal entry from 1947 reads, "It is 4 a.m. I am trying to break a bad habit that am in of waking about this time and being troubled. So I am putting down what troubles me now and then leaving it to God."[15] At another time, Smith summarized his own understanding of the balance between God's assistance and Smith's responsibility. "God is with me and will guide me or I will make a failure in a big (illegible). Of course God will not fail me but I must be consecrated."[16] Smith's mild neuroses and simplistic pietism gave rise to moral quandaries that may appear somewhat humorous to readers but caused him no small amount of distress. Smoking stands as one example. Smith perpetually struggled with the temptations posed by his beloved cigars and pipes, and early in 1947 he observed that "I have had bad days because I am tired and I need God. I have been smoking my pipe which I do enjoy, but I wonder if it has meant that I am not getting that feeling of guidance that I so much need."[17] A couple of months later he complained of "not being up to my normal spiritual vigor" and noted "it comes to me to make an experiment: 'Does my smoking keep me from God's guidance?' I will try for this week and see what the effect is."[18] Smith's guilt-ridden angst over the occasional cigar persisted over the next few years, and he often diagnosed his smoking as the cause of more profound spiritual and emotional maladies. A journal entry in early 1949 notes, "I must record a depression these days that is heavy because I seem to lack God's guidance. Try no smoking for two days.

---

[15]   HAS journal entry, January 17, 1947. Box 281, HAS papers.
[16]   HAS journal entry, January 27, 1947. Box 281, HAS papers. Emphasis original.
[17]   HAS journal entry, February 9, 1947. Box 281, HAS papers.
[18]   HAS journal entry, April 19, 1947. Box 281, HAS papers. Emphasis original.

God will not let us down."[19] Nothing seems to have bothered Smith more than the feeling that he might be alienated from divine counsel and comfort, and when such feelings overtook him he tried frantically to diagnose the cause, be it smoking or stress or political complications.

The question remains whether Smith's prayer life and religious convictions were merely "private" matters, recorded faithfully in his diary but exercising no influence on his public life. To the contrary, even a casual glance at Smith's self-understanding reveals an integrated individual whose religious life profoundly informed his public actions. Senator Smith saw himself bearing a special message from God – one intended for his colleagues in Congress, the American people, and the world. In the Senate he believed that he represented not just the people of New Jersey, but also the will of God.

III

Suffering from one of his periodic bouts of guilt and self-doubt in early 1947, Smith offered a telling insight into his own mind. "My entire illness is due to the fact that I have not had God and Christ right in the center of my work. This is fundamental. . . . Be patient. The truth will come. You have a message."[20] Yet as another journal entry written just a few days later indicates, Smith's perception of himself as God's messenger was more than mere hubris or self-delusion. "My message to this Congress must be one of hope and inspiration. The world is in a desperate condition and we sorely need the guidance of God. Am I sufficiently consecrated to get that guidance and inspiration? I pray God that in these days here I may see it all clearly."[21] He was, in fact, a relatively conflicted man, who both eagerly sought divine counsel and yet only hesitatingly embraced his role in bearing it.

Alternatively triumphant and timid, Smith saw himself playing the part of a prophet or even an oracle. The content of the message originated with God, not with him, and yet Smith had to maintain a certain standard of personal piety in order to hear and communicate this divine mandate. He believed this message from God spoke particularly to the place of the United States in the world. He prayed fervently and frequently for divine guidance on the pressing foreign affairs issues of the day, and possessed strong convictions on how the United States should seek to lead and shape a troubled world. In 1947 he recorded his prayer that

---

[19] HAS journal entry, January 11, 1949. Box 282, HAS papers.
[20] HAS journal entry, February 17, 1947. Box 281, HAS papers.
[21] HAS journal entry, February 26, 1947. Box 281, HAS papers.

> God grant that in these days I may find my truth and speak it into my speech in the Senate on this Greek and Turkish aid bill. Can that be an expression of the war of ideas? Can I now develop my overall philosophy of the American Way? Freedom and opportunity with God the guiding hand? And with opportunity comes responsibility. God help me to tell truth and not merely theorize. Help me to show the place of the United Nations in this picture and my relation to it all.[22]

Smith here hints at what he soon revealed to be a full-blown vision of Wilsonian idealism for the United States in the world. Though in his message to Congress Truman had proposed aid to the governments of Greece and Turkey as a rather straightforward measure to stall communism's advance, Smith supported the assistance package out of a much more grandiose dream. It was a first step in creating an entirely new world.

The stakes were alternatively apocalyptic or utopian: "Our foreign policy today will mean World War III or the end of all wars," he wrote in early April 1947.[23] And in articulating this policy, Smith seemed to believe his words could be divinely inspired, if not dictated. The next day's journal entry contains this revealing passage:

> I have gotten up early for the inspiration of the mornings and God. I am making my notes for this foreign relations speech. It must be God or it will fail. It comes to me that I will be guided. Start now.
>
> 7:30. The guided note was that America's destiny is to unite the world. We oppose Russia, not because we want the material things that Russia wants but because communism is divisive and is not the protagonist of freedom. We believe in the dignity and sanctity of the individual human being.
>
> God will help me in my dictation.[24]

And God ostensibly gave Smith a specific mandate for America's role in the world, a mandate that resembled idealistic multilateralism, rejecting *realpolitik* and even the nation-state model. As Smith himself described it, echoing MRA's lexicon, he saw the world in very "ideological" terms, in which good and bad ideologies competed with each other for the allegiances of mankind. In a 1947 radio address, he warned that "the danger of World War III comes primarily from the fact that we are living in an age when ideas are warring with each other. The next war . . . will be a conflict of ideologies and it may fairly be said that that conflict is with us today."[25]

---

[22] HAS journal entry, April 5, 1947. Box 281, HAS papers.
[23] HAS journal entry, April 7, 1947. Box 281, HAS papers. Emphasis original.
[24] HAS journal entry, April 8, 1947. Box 281, HAS papers. Emphasis original.
[25] Transcript of "NBC University of the Air" broadcast, January 11, 1947. Box 92, HAS papers.

Smith firmly believed in the "American ideology," which, as he articulated it, "is built around the conception of equality of opportunity, economic and political, for all our people without regard to race, creed and color, and it is this idea which the little nations of the world are looking to us to take the leadership in establishing."[26] Although a liberal idealist who believed in a special role for the United States, Smith resisted hyper-nationalism or parochialism. In the midst of his acute concern over apparent communist gains in Greece in 1947, Smith recorded in his journal that "the United States has to face the issue of accepting responsibility of leadership in world affairs or of letting the world drift into Civil War and chaos.... We must help the world help itself back to sanity and back to God." However, in this same passage he also clarified, "but this should not mean that we must get into a pattern of building antagonisms with Russia. We must make Russia an ally to rebuild the world – but it must be one world under the United Nations and not two spheres of influence. There must not be any balancing of power."[27] Two years later, Smith elaborated on this vision:

> I need a one great purpose... a world at Peace built upon understanding human relationships. Peace cannot be maintained by military force because that means domination. Peace can only come through eager voluntary coop-eration. This may mean the resistance to evil by the policeman but it must be the policeman of limited authority and not the balance of power.[28]

Though many realists believed the balance of power to be an effective system for maintaining international peace and stability, Smith found it utterly distasteful. To his mind – and, he believed, to God's mind – *realpolitik* represented a crass capitulation to the basest of human inclinations. True peace would be possible only when people pursued their highest ideals instead of their lowest instincts. In the meantime, the use of force was a regrettable, and, he hoped, a temporary measure to be employed as little as possible.

Smith found the existence of the United States, like the use of force, to be only a proximate step on the path to glory. He affirmed American exceptionalism insofar as America should take an active role in leading the world and exporting its "ideology." But Smith seems to have sought ultimately for America's leadership role, perhaps even its very existence as a nation, to be subsumed eventually into a utopian one-world community. In 1948, following

---

[26] Transcript of "NBC University of the Air" broadcast, January 11, 1947. Box 92, HAS papers.

[27] HAS journal entry, March 3, 1947. Box 281, HAS papers. Emphasis original.

[28] HAS journal entry, September 5, 1949. Box 282, HAS papers.

a meeting with leaders from Princeton urging support for "world government," Smith recorded his skepticism towards nationalism and his thought
that "perhaps we should be willing to merge ourselves to save civilization.
I hope for guidance on this."[29] On another occasion, he recorded a curious
guidance. "It comes to me that George Kennan is an important member of
State Department to get close to. What we want is not our own prestige but
a better America. America must lead in the right way – not as a dominant
political and 'great power' – but in sharing her heritage of freedom."[30] Smith
seemed unaware of the irony that his guidance directed him both to work
more closely with Foggy Bottom's most articulate advocate of *realpolitik* and
to urge America to improve the world instead of its own standing. Or perhaps
the guidance hinted that Smith should try to convert Kennan to this sense of
American mission. For while Smith and Kennan shared similar convictions
about the spiritual stakes of the Cold War, they differed on just how God was
calling America to respond.

In short, while the Truman Administration was developing its own theology
of containment, Smith attempted to develop an *eschatology* of containment.
For him, containing Soviet expansion was only a distasteful near-term measure on the way to working with Russia to create a new world entirely. While
sharing the anticommunist zeal of many of his Republican colleagues, he
rejected hostility towards Russia *qua* Russia. And while trumpeting the glories
of American ideals and the unique responsibilities of America in the world, he
simultaneously entertained notions of a one-world government based on the
"natural brotherhood of man" in which national identities would virtually
cease to exist.[31]

Smith's idealism was not borne out of a dispositional optimism. He occasionally suffered from acute bouts of self-doubt and spiritual malaise. After
a particularly arduous day in March 1947, he wondered "can it be that I am
doing something wrong and that God is warning me? Do we need a different
approach to these terrible world problems? I just don't know the answers at
the moment but I know that God has some good purpose in it all."[32] The
next month, while continuing to fret over his difficulties in drafting a major
foreign policy speech, Smith confessed, "I was troubled and confused. It was
unguided and I do not quite know why unless it was because I smoked a cigar
and lost my guidance." But he maintained his faith that "in my heart I feel
that America has a great message for the world and this may be the chance

---

[29] HAS journal entry, February 18, 1948. Box 281, HAS papers.
[30] HAS journal entry, January 3, 1950. Box 282, HAS papers.
[31] HAS journal entry, April 8, 1947. Box 281, HAS papers.
[32] HAS journal entry, March 5, 1947. Box 281, HAS papers.

to give it."[33] Such were the complexities of Smith's inner world. Convinced of both his country's special calling and his own responsibility to help carry it out, Smith's tortured spiritual conscience nonetheless continued to plague him over matters from the epic (the American destiny) to the comic (his own weakness for cigars).

As for Smith's prayers, they should not be dismissed or minimized as merely reinforcing decisions he had already made on his own. He often seemed bewildered and overwhelmed at the responsibilities he faced, and only after praying did he seem able to move forward with any confidence. Yet an important picture emerges here of Smith as a Senator who did not confine his prayers for divine guidance merely to private concerns. He sought divine guidance on matters both mundane and momentous, believing God to be involved in every one of life's last details. His foreign policy was merely an extension of his personal commitments. Smith possessed a coherent, expansive ideology about how the world should work – and regular prayer was just one component of this entire spiritual framework.

And God, in turn, seemed to be telling Smith how to defeat communism and reshape the world. One night in early 1951, Smith received a guidance that President Truman and Myron Taylor would certainly have appreciated. "It comes to me that we must unite all our forces that believe in Christ to meet this world menace. I will be able to be a great leader of spiritual strength if I can find the key to the door of Christian unity."[34] Christian unity, however, had proven quite elusive for other American leaders who had tried to forge a Christendom allied against communism, and later in the year Smith found himself opposing Truman's signature initiative in this regard. "I am seeking guidance about . . . the Vatican matter. Perhaps see the President and suggest the appointment of a representative committee with the State Department but not an Ambassador to the Vatican."[35] Though Smith may have shared Truman's goal of uniting Christian leaders around the world against the Soviets, God seemed to be telling him that recognizing the Vatican was not the way to do it.

IV

The growing crisis in China, as Mao Zedong's communist forces continued to advance against Chiang Kai-shek's Nationalists, provided Senator Smith a challenging opportunity to implement his ideals. His efforts in crafting

[33] HAS journal entries, April 10–11, 1947. Box 281, HAS papers.
[34] HAS journal entry, January 25, 1951. Box 282, HAS papers.
[35] HAS journal entry, November 23, 1951. Box 282, HAS papers.

U.S. policy towards China and Taiwan beginning in the closing months of 1948 illustrate just how Smith attempted to apply his idealistic philosophy to practical politics, in a real time and a real, troubled place. Not surprisingly, Smith's interest in China was fueled by Moral Re-Armament.

Smith's attention seems to have been drawn towards China only in 1948. He did not possess much of a background or previous interest in Chinese affairs, and hardly mentions China in his journal throughout 1947. In 1948, two MRA staff began warning him of what they perceived as a looming crisis in China, as Chiang Kai-shek's forces suffered loss after loss to Mao Zedong's troops. John Roots, who had grown up in China as the son of a prominent missionary and who had known Chiang since 1926, was MRA's leading China specialist.[36] On January 10, 1948, Smith recorded his belief that God might be directing him to become involved in China. "It comes to me this morning to call John Roots re: his excellent summary of the Chinese situation. He is suggesting that the U.S. could get a special group of Chinese together – who he names – to lay the foundation for a new ideology. It is a fine thought."[37] The other MRA staff member who encouraged Smith's involvement in China policy was his son-in-law and close advisor, Ken Twitchell. On July 26, 1948, Twitchell alerted Smith that "the time has come for us to enter wholeheartedly into a business of aid-to-China exactly as we have done with Greece and Turkey . . . we ought to take the risk and begin to deal with that side of the world as we are dealing with every other part."[38] Like Walter Judd and William Richard Johnson, MRA thought that the United States needed to oppose communist expansion anywhere in the world – not just at the perimeters of the Soviet bloc.

Two months later Twitchell wrote Smith that "Asia is still the Number 1 treasure of the Communist heart. So very much hangs on the support we give to China. If China goes, half the world will go."[39] In what soon amounted to a personal lobbying campaign, Twitchell followed up in October, warning Smith that "every day that goes by without our wholehearted help is a day which we will live to regret bitterly in later years."[40] In this early, grandiose incarnation of the "domino theory," Twitchell appealed to the sensibilities he shared with Smith about a global ideological struggle posing communism against Christian democracy.

---

[36]   For more on Roots, see the memo sent by his father, Bishop Logan Roots, to President Truman on May 30, 1945. Harry S. Truman Papers, Official File 150, Box 758, Folder: Miscellaneous; Harry S. Truman Presidential Library, Independence, MO (hereinafter HST Papers).
[37]   HAS journal entry, January 10, 1948. Box 282, HAS papers.
[38]   July 26, 1948 letter from Twitchell to Smith. Box 251, HAS papers.
[39]   September 17, 1948 letter from Twitchell to Smith. Box 251, HAS papers.
[40]   October 21, 1948 letter from Twitchell to Smith. Box 251, HAS papers.

Smith began to reveal his own interest in China in November 1948. He observed in his diary that "the Chinese situation is very critical. It may be right to go there and see what we can do to help practically." He was unsure of how to proceed, however. Early December found Smith worrying that "we certainly need guidance . . . there seems to be a complete collapse of Chinese morale and any money sent there appears to get into [the] wrong hands."[41] Smith had been intensively studying the Chinese situation, conferring with many China experts in the State Department and Congress, and seemed bewildered after hearing "absolutely divergent viewpoints from men who ought to know." He wrote to Twitchell detailing the standard litany of complaints against the Nationalists – corruption, ineptitude, waste – and tentatively concluded in a December 9, 1948, letter that "it would be very difficult in a practical way to support the Chiang government."[42]

Roots and Twitchell fervently sought to disabuse Smith of his negative assessment of Chiang. On December 20, Twitchell sent a lengthy response to his father-in-law. He began by reminding Smith that "your position and potential influence is of God-given importance right now" and offered detailed reasons for why the United States ought to bolster its support of the Nationalists. Twitchell concluded that there "is . . . no alternative to Chiang's leadership" and "if there ever was a time for action it is certainly now."[43] One week later, John Roots sat down with Smith for three hours. Smith recorded in his diary that Roots "felt that we should give full support to Chiang. It comes to me to see [General Albert] Wedemeyer about this." Smith and Roots soon after met with Wedemeyer, after which Smith recorded a turnabout in his perspective. "I fear that Marshall has been wrong in his position. I must follow this up because we must not let the Christian General Chiang down."[44] Besides offering some of the more conventional reasons for supporting the KMT, both Roots and Twitchell appealed to Smith's sense of divine calling and Christian kinship with Chiang. The guidance he received from God, the exhortations from Roots and Twitchell, and his own research into the situation all combined to produce in Smith within one month a significant change in his position towards China. He had been converted to the Nationalist cause.

---

[41] HAS journal entries, November 13, December 2, 1948. Box 282, HAS papers.
[42] December 9, 1948 letter from HAS to Twitchell. Box 251, HAS papers.
[43] December 20, 1948 letter from Twitchell to HAS. HAS papers (courtesy of J.L. Gaddis).
[44] HAS journal entries, December 30, 1948 and January 5, 1949. Box 282, HAS papers. General Wedemeyer, following significant experience in China, had become known as a strong supporter of the Nationalists following his 1947 fact-finding trip to China. Marshall refers, of course, to General George Marshall, who had served as Secretary of State under Truman and had sought to distance the United States from the Nationalist cause.

And as new converts are wont to do, he pursued his calling with unfettered zeal.

The fact that Chiang Kai-shek himself professed Christian faith in many ways enhanced the appeal to Smith of the Nationalist cause. While Twitchell grudgingly conceded some of Chiang's shortcomings – offering the disclaimer that Chiang's "wife may have been largely responsible" for some of the KMT mistakes – Roots unapologetically presented Chiang as a veritable saint. Roots wrote Smith describing Chiang's expressions of piety, and said that Chiang's "conversion in 1927 has been compared to the conversion of Constantine." Furthermore, Chiang's "personal faith burns with a fiercer zeal than can be said for any other chief of state." Roots concluded with a flourish: "in Chiang the West has an Eastern leader who, with all his faults, will in the final count stand like a rock for the traditional values of Christendom and for those moral concepts at the heart of Christian democracy." Smith, impressed with this description of Chiang's piety, circulated Roots' report on Chiang to several other Senators and Representatives as well as to the new Secretary of State, Dean Acheson.[45]

Twitchell and Roots' enthusiasm for China derived not only from their estimation of China's strategic importance or of Chiang's piety, but also from their growing involvement with certain KMT leaders in spreading the message of Moral Re-Armament. Twitchell excitedly informed Smith in October 1948 that two senior Nationalist officials had apparently embraced MRA. Ho Ying-chin, who had earlier met in Washington with Smith and Twitchell, had become the Nationalist Minister of Defense. Ho had turned down the premiership because he "felt the greatest need was to get across the ideas of moral regeneration to the Nationalist troops." Chen Li-fu, Vice-President of the Chinese Parliament, following a sojourn at the MRA retreat center in Caux, Switzerland, reported that "I have come back to China with a stronger conviction than ever, that MRA is the very remedy to cure sickness of all kinds – economic, political, social, and international." Chen then appealed for "substantial military aid from the United States" and urged Twitchell to "exert your best influence to convince responsible persons in your Government of the threatening of world Communism to peace and security of all mankind, and of the urgency and necessity of helping China in her struggle."[46]

---

[45] December 20, 1948 letter from Twitchell to Smith; January 31, 1949 letter from Roots to Smith; January 31, 1949 letter from Smith to Representative James Wadsworth. HAS papers (courtesy of J.L. Gaddis).

[46] October 21, 1948 letter from Twitchell to HAS, and September 30, 1948 letter from Chen Li-fu to Twitchell. Box 251, HAS papers.

Chen's enthusiasm for MRA may well have been genuine, but it also served as a convenient basis for making a strategic appeal for increased assistance from the United States. Twitchell used Chen and Ho's MRA involvement in a similar way. Twitchell's exhortation to Smith to support the KMT included the argument that "we have seen the necessary elements of change in men like Chen Li-fu and Ho Ying-chin that could cure the division and dishonesty at the heart of Nationalist circles."[47]

J. Leighton Stuart, the American missionary-turned-Ambassador to China, wrote to John Roots in March 1949 describing Ho and Chen's ongoing interest in MRA (Ho by this time had accepted the position of Premier). Apparently upon returning to China they had spoken enthusiastically to Stuart about MRA. "Both men have been very much helped by coming in touch with MRA," said Stuart, noting that Chen "was more than ever convinced of the supreme importance of moral and spiritual values" and Ho had a new vision "of the need for moral character in sharp contrast with his experiences hitherto in China."[48] The Nationalist leaders also continued to press their case – and their MRA connections – for more American aid. In 1949 Ho wrote to MRA leader Hanford M. Twitchell requesting his assistance in securing more funding from the United States, to "prevent the Communists from complete domination of China and later, perhaps, the whole of Asia."[49] Twitchell in turn contacted John Steelman, one of Truman's senior aides, described the moral reforms that Ho seemed to be implementing in the notoriously corrupt Nationalist government, and urged the Administration not only to increase its support for the KMT, but to take "a new stand" on China as well. Steelman responded that while the United States would maintain a modicum of funding for Chiang's government, after it had already given over two billion dollars to the cause, "the economic and military position of the Chinese government has deteriorated to such an extent" that future aid would be futile. Undaunted, Twitchell responded with two more letters appealing not only for more financial assistance, but also for "the training of a nucleus of positive Chinese citizens in ideological warfare."[50]

By this Twitchell meant MRA, and he specifically mentioned the desire he shared with Ho to bring KMT leaders to the upcoming MRA conference in

---

[47] December 20, 1948 letter from Twitchell to AS. HAS papers (courtesy of J.L. Gaddis).

[48] March 14, 1949 letter from John Leighton Stuart to John Roots, copy sent to HAS. Box 98, HAS papers.

[49] It is not clear whether Hanford M. Twitchell was H. Kenaston Twitchell's father or brother.

[50] April 4, 1949 and June 20, 1949 letters from Ho Ying-Chin to Hanford M. Twitchell; April 21, 1949, June 30, 1949, and July 12, 1949 letters from Twitchell to John Steelman; May 13, 1949 letter from John Steelman to Twitchell; Official File (OF) 150, Box 759; HST Papers.

Caux. Twitchell suggested to Steelman, none too subtly, that the United States consider funding the Nationalist's attendance as an "investment ... in the training of citizens for inspired democracy in other lands. It is the way ... to make our Marshall Plan investment effective."[51] The White House apparently disagreed, and the KMT leaders, doubtless preoccupied with their impending defeat on the mainland, did not make it to Switzerland. They did make a further appeal, however. Attendees at the MRA "World Assembly" were read an address from the absent Chen Li-fu, declaring "the tragic events which you see taking place in China today are a preview of what will surely happen in nation after nation all over the world, unless the inspired ideology of Moral Re-Armament takes hold quickly and effectively." Chen even announced his own personal conversion of sorts, using the favored MRA jargon: "The change began in me. I have brought this message of change to some of my colleagues in the leadership of China." Not wanting to miss any opportunity, Chen also included his appeal for "America and China, and the other democracies, to work together with moral courage to save this country from disappearing behind the Iron Curtain."[52]

Having successfully enlisted Senator Smith in support of the Nationalists, Ken Twitchell and Roots now focused more directly on policy towards China itself. In February 1949, Twitchell and Roots composed a memo on "U.S. Policy in China," which Smith endorsed and circulated among leaders in the State Department and Congress. Repeated almost as a mantra throughout the nine-page memo is the MRA cardinal tenet that American efforts towards China need to be "ideological." Dismissing economic and military aid alone as insufficient, the memo urged an "ideological approach" that "assumed that the decisive element in world affairs is the battle for the minds of men." Religious language permeated the memo. It encouraged the United States to "regenerate" China's leaders, hoped for the "redemption" of China, and referred repeatedly to the "democratic faith."[53] Smith's enthusiasm for the MRA approach to China policy, which only became more evident as the months went on, reveals that his quest for divine guidance was not an isolated, private discipline, but was just one element in a comprehensive view of how the world should be ordered that was neither exclusively political nor solely religious. If anything, his whole approach to foreign relations in general and China in particular was, indeed, heavily "ideological."

[51] July 12, 1949 letter from Hanford M. Twitchell to Steelman; OF 150, Box 759; HST Papers.
[52] August 30, 1949, Message from Chen Li-fu. Box 98, HAS papers.
[53] Undated memo "U.S. Policy in China." Box 98, HAS papers.

Not surprisingly, this approach was not without its critics. An anonymous State Department official composed a detailed and not altogether flattering reply to the MRA memo. Adopting a slightly defensive tone, the State Department memo offered a firm defense of the United States posture towards China, and in conclusion described the MRA proposal as containing "little that is new," as well as having "a number of inaccuracies and apparent internal contradictions." Smith, who by this point realized he faced an uphill battle in convincing Foggy Bottom of the MRA approach, jotted numerous marginal notes on the State Department memo indicating his displeasure with the response, which he believed "completely lacks vision."[54]

But Smith did not believe that by himself he possessed perfectly clear vision. He recorded in his journal in January his prayer for "guidance" in meeting with the new Secretary of State Dean Acheson on China policy, and lamented that "these are hard days and I must be close to God if I am to win in this confusion." Three days later, reflecting on what he saw as Soviet efforts to woo China, Smith saw divine intervention as the most effective solution. "Almighty God may take it in hand and make it impossible for agnostic Russia to win these people to the communist view. It will take concerted prayer."[55] While some American policy-makers believed basic national differences and strategic imperatives would prevent the Soviet–Chinese relationship from becoming too close, Smith's religious convictions and ideological predilections caused him to fear that the common bonds of irreligion and Marxism would join these two nations together. And what communist-atheism brought together, only God could tear apart.

V

The spring and summer of 1949 found Smith still mulling over events in China, convinced of the need to oppose the communists but unsure of how to do so. Twitchell and Roots continued to exhort Smith, using increasingly apocalyptic rhetoric. In one letter, Twitchell, urging Smith to push for immediate consideration of a Senate bill supporting the KMT, warned that "the Nationalists are fighting for the life of free China and may be fighting for ours as well.... I pray you may be led to take hold of this crisis with both hands. It may well be the greatest reason why God put you there."[56] Roots

[54] Undated memo "Comments on Memorandum Regarding United States Policy in China Transmitted by Senator Smith." Box 98, HAS papers.
[55] HAS journal entries, January 15, 18, 1949. Box 282, HAS papers.
[56] April 22, 1949 letter from Twitchell to HAS. Box 251, HAS papers.

excitedly shared with Smith the details of his lengthy meeting with senior
State Department China specialists, who had apparently taken an interest in
the MRA philosophy. Explaining how this information could assist Smith's
prayers, Roots said he hoped Smith would now "have a more intelligent basis
for guidance regarding your part in the future of Asia and the development
of an overall ideological policy for the American Government."[57] A frustrated
Roots later complained that "our policy-makers are either fools or knaves"
for not adopting the MRA approach of "ideological training." Roots encouraged Smith to appeal to Secretary Acheson on the basis of a shared religious
identity: "Acheson is a Christian man.... He will know what you are talking
about when you speak of an ideology capable of redirecting human nature
and regenerating Cabinets."[58]

Smith, Roots, and Twitchell viewed their highest allegiance not to the
United States but to God. Yet while some Americans may at times have confused their country with their God, the MRA advocates sometimes muddled
the distinction between their "ideology" and their God. Smith, for his part,
wanted to make clear that he finally followed God and not MRA. He certainly appreciated, and was profoundly influenced by, the input of Roots and
Twitchell. In one journal entry Smith noted that Roots "sees the 'rat race' in
Washington and he wants to help me get away from it through guidance. He
suggests that I give up everything except Foreign Relations and just concentrate on the development of a Foreign Policy (under God)."[59] Two weeks later
found Smith feeling more despondent, about China and about MRA. "I am
much depressed over the China situation and am not clear how to move.... I
need real guidance in dealing with [John Roots] as he seems to be trying
to work the MRA's into my office. I am grateful to them all and are fond
of them but the 'push in' is difficult to deal with."[60] Having been taught by
"the MRA's" to handle life's issues by seeking divine guidance, the pupil now
sought "guidance" on how to handle his teachers.

Smith's frustrations mounted. A few days later, he scheduled a lunch with
several State Department China experts and John Roots. Smith complained
that "I am greatly troubled by John because he is trying to 'move in' and run
me and my office.... It is the great tragedy of this group but this may be the

---

[57] April 12, 1949 letter from Roots to HAS. Box 98, HAS papers. "Guidance," of course, is MRA
jargon for prayer.
[58] August 27, 1949 letter from Roots to HAS. Box 98, HAS papers.
[59] HAS journal entry, April 5, 1949. Box 282, HAS papers.
[60] HAS journal entry, April 23, 1949. Box 282, HAS papers. Note also the irony that Smith prays
for "guidance" in dealing with the very same group that taught him to seek "guidance" in
such a manner.

chance to clear it up. It comes to me to have a talk with John after the lunch. I believe that God will not make the Senate debate today of such importance as to prevent the full consideration by us of the China situation and John's problem."[61] These entries in many ways encapsulate Smith's view of life. He did not draw sharp lines between faith and practice, public and private, but saw existence as one complete, interconnected whole, all maintained by God. In this way he could express his confusion over a massive foreign policy issue such as the Chinese Civil War and also a vexing personal problem involving a pushy colleague, and then look for God to orchestrate the schedule of the (self-proclaimed) "world's greatest deliberative body" in a way that allowed Smith's concerns to be addressed.

Not that Smith's concerns about MRA necessarily diminished. After praying with his daughter and son-in-law, who urged him to work even more closely with MRA adherents, Smith believed that God was leading him in a different direction. "[Ken and Marian] may be right but my guidance seems to be that there are many people to deal with of varied faiths and outlooks and all cannot be brought into the MRA world."[62] Here again was an irony: the "guidance" techniques through which MRA had taught Smith to seek God's will seemed to tell him that God did not will all people to follow the MRA model. Meanwhile, Smith continued to feel the several pulls of divided loyalties. On another occasion Twitchell urged Smith to invite the Nationalist leader K.C. Wu to visit Washington ostensibly to discuss conditions on Taiwan; Twitchell's deeper purpose seems to have been persuading Wu to attend an upcoming MRA assembly in Michigan. Smith saw this as a rather manipulative ploy. "It seems to me that it is not quite <u>honest</u> to use the argument that we want him about Formosa just to get him to the [MRA] meeting. But I want to do all that I can to help the children and be close to God in these hard times."[63]

As 1949 went on Smith began to believe that God directed him to focus more and more on events in China. In July he noted in his journal that "it may be that God wants me to concentrate on [China].... I must watch all these signs."[64] Despite his periodic frustrations with MRA, he continued to rely heavily on Twitchell and Roots for counsel. Roots wrote Smith in June encouraging him to push Acheson on certain points, including not recognizing the impending new communist government in China and also

---

[61] HAS journal entry, April 27, 1949. Box 282, HAS papers.
[62] HAS journal entry, December 23, 1949. Box 282, HAS papers.
[63] HAS journal entry, May 28, 1951. Box 282, HAS papers. Emphasis original.
[64] HAS journal entry, July 26, 1949. Box 282, HAS papers.

granting "full liberty" to Christian activities in China. Roots made clear his agenda: "this would enable us to infiltrate communist China, provided that our teachers, technicians, missionaries, and traders were themselves ideologically equipped." Furthermore, Formosa "could be developed as a springboard for the eventual ideological redemption of the Chinese mainland."[65]

Smith seems to have taken this advice, for he met with Acheson the next month and reported back to Twitchell and Roots that he addressed many of these points with the Secretary of State. Acheson apparently confirmed to Smith that he did not intend to recognize communist China, leading Smith to report that "I was very happy over what seemed to be a very definite statement of policy on this point." Smith also suggested to Acheson (as per Roots' idea) that the United States should use its existing missionary organizations in China for infiltration of the emerging communist society. Smith noted that Acheson agreed "that we should develop in every possible way the use of our educational and religious organizations . . . in improving the ideological relationship between the Chinese and the United States."[66]

In August 1949, Smith summarized his perspective on the status of China and U.S. policy in two lengthy memos. Besides his conventional calls for more attention to China from the Truman Administration and more military and economic aid to the Nationalists, Smith urged, "special emphasis should be placed on so-called ideological aid in the form of educating the people in the non-Communist areas . . . to the Western tradition and what the anti-Communist groups of nations are trying to do in order to preserve human freedoms."[67] Smith reiterated this plan when he met in September with Ambassador Stuart. He reported that Stuart "is convinced that no further military aid can properly be given to Chiang Kai-shek and the Nationalist Government, but he agrees with me that there is an enormous area of aid of other kinds . . . to at least indicate to the Chinese people that we have not abandoned them."[68] In this way Smith distinguished himself from some of the more vocal Congressional members of the "China lobby" such as Representative Walter Judd (whom Smith respected but believed was prone to hyperbole). While the "China Lobby" focused primarily on military and economic aid to the KMT, Smith always believed such assistance was insufficient, even ill-conceived. Smith's unique contribution to the debate on China policy came in his ongoing insistence on the "ideological" dimension of the struggle.

---

[65] June 28, 1949 letter from Roots to HAS. Box 98, HAS papers.
[66] July 15, 1949 letter from HAS to Twitchell. Box 98, HAS papers.
[67] August 1, 1949 "Memorandum re Far Eastern Situation" and August 15, 1949 letter from HAS to Twitchell. Boxes 204 and 98, HAS papers.
[68] September 2, 1949 letter from HAS to Twitchell. Box 251, HAS papers.

It may have been at times vague, naïve, or just disregarded, but Smith at least attempted to articulate what he saw as the larger clash in China between two worldviews.

As his involvement with China grew, Smith believed God directed him to take an investigative trip to the Far East. He recorded this guidance in his journal on September 24, 1949: "it comes to me to . . . find out about Formosa and perhaps go there. This will be a thrilling guided trip. God grant that we may save Asia to Christianity. It is a wonderful challenge – the Western tradition and our spiritual heritage. . . . Have no fear or hesitation God will guide this trip step by step."[69] Smith viewed the situation in China as a clear confrontation between good and evil. And he believed that the hand of God favored one side over the other. While traveling elsewhere in Asia and anticipating his visit to Formosa, Smith wrote, "God has guided us all this trip and I know that He will guide us now. Our going to Formosa will show the Nationalists there that there are those of us who still believe in a free China and want to help."[70] And after meeting with Chiang Kai-shek, Smith concluded the discussion was "very impressive and we can see no reason for [Chiang's] being a political leper." Smith reported that he avoided any discussion of military aid with Chiang, but instead asked Chiang "what kind of a program he was offering to the Chinese people to offset the vicious propaganda of the Chinese communists against the United States." Although Chiang responded rather vaguely to Smith's equally vague query, Nationalist official K.C. Wu informed Smith the next day that "our visit meant more to [Chiang] than anything that had happened during the last year and he felt we had challenged the Gimo to a definite program to meet the communist propaganda."[71]

As Smith reflected on his visit, he concluded that the United States had not been supportive enough of the Nationalist cause, and that God had subsequently revealed some of the American errors. Voicing his disgust with certain "China hands" in the State Department, Smith complained that "it is a disgrace to our great nation to be controlled by a lot of 'pink [illegible] young men'!. . . . I thank God that we were guided to come here and see this on the ground."[72] For his part, Smith became more than ever convinced of the imperative of supporting the Nationalist outpost. Mainland China itself had officially come under the rule of the communists just weeks before, as Mao founded the "People's Republic of China" on October 1. Smith, meanwhile,

[69] HAS journal entry, September 24, 1949. Box 282, HAS papers.
[70] HAS journal entry, October 15, 1949. Box 282, HAS papers.
[71] October 24, 1949 letter from HAS to Sen. William Knowland. Box 98, HAS papers. "Gimo," shorthand for "Generalissimo," refers of course to Chiang.
[72] HAS journal entry, October 17, 1949. Box 282, HAS papers.

began to seek guidance on how the United States ought to remain involved in Asia. In this regard, he recorded an intriguing suggestion from the end of his Asia trip. Before his departure from Formosa he "was waited on by two American missionaries and a native Tiwanian [sic] who presented to me the case against the Chinese occupation of Formosa, and who urged that either the United States take over and occupy the Island and run it, or that the Island be put under the trusteeship of the UN with the U.S. as a trustee."[73]

Smith seized on this possibility and on his return began to promote it in Washington. He met with Ambassador Stuart for two hours, and Smith recorded that while he emphasized to Stuart "no recognition of Communist China and keep Formosa out of hostile hands," the Ambassador seemed "tired" and torn between competing factions.[74] Smith also met again with Acheson to report on his trip. According to Acheson's record of the meeting, as usual Smith pressed strongly against recognizing Mao's new government, since "any commercial advantages that might be gained . . . would not compensate for the psychological defeat that would be ours as a result of recognition." Acheson assured the senator that, absent dramatic improvements in Mao's behavior and democratic support for his government, America would not extend recognition. Besides the question of diplomatic relations, nothing related to China divided American policy-makers more than the vexing question of the KMT leader himself. "At this point in the conversation a complete difference of opinion arose between the Secretary and the Senator as regards Chiang Kai-shek's 'absconding' with the Chinese Government funds." Acheson and others had long accused the generalissimo, not without plausibility, of personally profiteering from American largesse, and at the considerable expense of the Nationalist cause. Smith disagreed, but "after a valiant but completely unsuccessful effort on the part of the Senator to convince the Secretary that he should modify his view on Chiang," he moved on to the question of Formosa itself. Not mentioning that he had heard the idea from the missionaries, Smith nonetheless urged Acheson to keep the island out of the PRC's control either by turning it into a UN trusteeship or by occupying it with American military forces. A noncommittal Secretary of State only responded that all options remained under consideration.[75] For his part, Smith noted in his journal, "Had a good talk with Acheson, afraid that he is very much prejudiced against Chiang Kai-shek. . . . Believe that we may get . . . no immediate recognition of the Chinese Commies – also possibly a

---

[73] October 24, 1949 letter from HAS to Sen. William Knowland. Box 98, HAS papers.
[74] HAS journal entry, November 6, 1949. Box 282, HAS papers.
[75] November 30, 1949 Memorandum of Conversation; Dean Acheson Papers, Memorandum of Conversations, Box 65, Folder: October–November 1949; HST Papers.

formula to hold Formosa."[76] Smith at least could take solace in being faithful
to his calling. His "guidance" had directed his travels, and had revealed to him
the imperative of supporting Chiang and protecting Formosa. The senator, in
turn, had obediently passed on these revelations to his government colleagues.
Now they were responsible for how they would respond.

One month after returning to the United States, Smith issued a formal
report on his trip to Asia, which he circulated widely to every member of
Congress and just about every American government official and media leader
with even a remote interest in China. The report neatly encapsulates Smith's
entire approach to foreign relations. He introduced the report by emphasizing his consistent support for anticommunist initiatives in Europe such as the
Marshall Plan and NATO, and sought to place recent events in China in such
a global context. "I . . . felt completely frustrated because it seemed to me that
while we were barring our front door (the Atlantic area), the back door (by
which I mean the door to the Far East) was being left unlocked. The iron
curtain is quietly being lowered over Asia." Smith proceeded from echoing
Churchill to invoking Christian themes. He wrote of his "privilege to talk
with American-trained Chinese who have the vision of the Western Christian
tradition and who, I believe, would sincerely make any personal sacrifice to
save China from the dangers that now threaten it." He singled out Chiang as
one "who still has much to contribute to the *salvation* of his country." Smith
offered a series of policy recommendations, including the now familiar calls
for no American recognition of the PRC, an "ideological program of reform
and rehabilitation," and the protection of Formosa, possibly including American occupation or turning the island into a "United Nations trusteeship."[77]
He concluded the report with a remarkable distillation of his foreign policy
vision:

> People were meant by the great design to be free and to live together. It
> was never meant that any people on this globe should be subjected to the
> domination and control of any other people. The yearnings in the Far East
> and in other parts of the world for freedom is [sic] an expression of the
> recognition of these eternal truths. The sympathy of the United States for
> these yearnings, and the determination of our people to aid in this eternal
> quest for freedom must continue to be the foundation of our foreign policy.[78]

Rooted in God's very creation of the world (the "great design"), and universally affirmed by all men and women ("any people on this globe"), Smith's

---

[76] HAS journal entry, December 1, 1949. Box 282, HAS papers.
[77] December 1, 1949 "Far Eastern Problems Facing the United States: Report on Visit to the Far
East, September and October 1949." Box 98, HAS papers. Emphasis added.
[78] *Ibid.*

diplomatic theology drew a direct connection between God's will and America's role.

The last month of 1949 saw Smith engrossed in further activity on behalf of the Nationalist cause. He brought Twitchell to a meeting with Madame Chiang and her nephew in New York, and noted Madame Chiang's "bitterness" towards the United States for reducing its support of the KMT. Regarding Formosa, "she was clearly scornful of the Formosan people" but "agreed that we need a Christian foundation" for the country.[79] After much prayer and consultations with Twitchell, Smith sent a letter to Truman and Acheson stressing that he did "not imply the sending of American troops in force to Formosa, but simply the establishment of a joint political authority and responsibility there between ourselves and the Nationalists."[80] Elsewhere Smith clarified his hope for the United States to "occupy as we occupy Japan and help work out a plan of government which will be an example for the (Eastern?) Mainland."[81] Just as his New England ancestors centuries earlier had hoped to establish a community in the "new world" to serve as an example of renewal to corrupted England, Smith now sought to establish a Christian democracy on Formosa as a shining witness to the growing darkness on the mainland.

The mainland may have fallen, but Smith did not despair, as God revealed to him a new policy, and a new hope. "Non-recognition and Formosa are the two keys we must follow up on to retain a base for ideological advance. All is well. God is guiding us."[82] Just before Christmas, Smith met with Kennan for an hour "and was very much pleased with his attitude. He is against recognition of the Chinese Commies and favors finding a formula to take over Formosa."[83] The end of the year brought the welcome report that General MacArthur and another senior American official had recommended an increased American presence on Formosa, leading Smith to conclude, "it is wonderful news and is the hand of God."[84]

VI

Into the 1950s, Senator Smith continued his efforts to maintain American support for Taiwan. After Twitchell and his MRA colleague Basil Entwistle visited

---

[79] HAS journal, December 10, 1949. Box 282, HAS papers.
[80] December 27, 1949 letter from HAS to President Truman and Secretary Acheson. Box 98, HAS papers. On Smith's prayer and consultations with Twitchell, see his journal entries throughout December, 1949.
[81] HAS journal, December 20, 1949. Box 282, HAS papers.
[82] HAS journal, December 6, 1949. Box 282, HAS papers.
[83] HAS journal, December 21, 1949. Box 282, HAS papers.
[84] HAS journal, December 29, 1949. Box 282, HAS papers.

Taiwan in 1950, Smith eagerly circulated their report – which urged maintaining U.S. assistance to the Nationalists – to Acheson, Dulles, and Smith's
colleagues on the Senate Foreign Relations Committee.[85] He also expanded
his spiritual focus from Asia to Europe, which he hoped to see united in
peace and against communism. In this he worked closely with another ally
on China matters. Walter Judd recalled that Smith was his best, and often
his only, Senate comrade in working "to get Western Europe together politically as well as economically and militarily." The two, bonded by Protestant idealism, Republican internationalism, and fervent anticommunism,
organized a Congressional delegation to the First Consultative Assembly
of the Council of Europe in 1951. They labored thereafter with both European and American leaders to forge closer ties among the Western European
nations.[86]

Not surprisingly, Smith sought divine guidance over which Republican to
support for president in the 1952 election. November 19, 1951, found Smith
noting "it comes to me early this morning that I must think of my candidate for
President. Is it Eisenhower or Taft? Or someone else?"[87] The next week Smith
thought God seemed to favor the Ohio Senator and leader of the GOP's isolationist wing. "It comes to me that Taft may well be the best candidate and that
I must seriously consider his support."[88] The nation's growing enthusiasm for
Eisenhower restrained Smith from making any formal announcement, however, and Smith's work with John Foster Dulles on the peace treaty with Japan
left him frustrated with Taft's political base. After meeting with Dulles in January, Smith wrote, "we must guard against the isolationist Republicans trying
to put conditions on ratification."[89] This, in turn, led Smith to reconsider his
man for president. Before meeting with Taft on February 1, Smith wrote "I
must make it clear that I have not lined up with anybody and that I may find it
right to support Eisenhower. Make it clear that I am gravely concerned over our
foreign policy."[90]

As international affairs ascended on Smith's priority list, so did his interest in Eisenhower. In March, as Smith pondered the upcoming election, he
distilled the most important factor. "The moral issue, which is closely tied

---

[85] May 17, 1950 letters from Smith, with copy of report; Box 100, Folder: Twitchell Report on
Formosa 1950; HAS Papers.
[86] Walter Judd, oral interview, April 22, 1969, Washington DC, conducted by Paul Hopper.
Dwight D. Eisenhower Oral History Project, Dwight D. Eisenhower Presidential Library,
Abilene, Kansas (hereinafter DDE Papers).
[87] HAS journal, November 19, 1951. Box 282, HAS papers.
[88] HAS journal, November 27, 1951. Box 282, HAS papers.
[89] HAS journal, January 13, 1952. Box 282, HAS papers. See also entries for January 7, 8, and
11.
[90] HAS journal, February 1, 1952. Box 282, HAS papers.

to 'freedom and independence,' must be stressed from now on. 'Unless man is ruled by God, he will be ruled by a dictator'."[91] Smith's concern over the spiritual stakes of the Cold War led him to take another look at Eisenhower, who also saw the conflict with the Soviets in religious terms. On March 15, Smith recorded "I have been praying for guidance ... my personal judgment is that we should support Ike."[92] God's answer was not yet clear, however, and questions persisted. The next day Smith wrote "in guidance about Ike, certain things have come to me: Will he be for our side of the Far East policy? ... Will he adequately consider the fiscal situation or will he have the extreme military attitude? ... Would Ike be the only man who can save the Republican Party from another defeat and possibly extinction? ... God will guide us today."[93] Election day seemed to alleviate Smith's concerns; after Eisenhower's resounding victory, and Smith's own overwhelming re-election, he noted happily "God has been good."[94]

After the Eisenhower Administration took office in January, 1953, Smith felt particularly sanguine that his old friend Dulles had become Secretary of State. He and Dulles shared much: Republican internationalism, Princeton, the Presbyterian Church, and the firm conviction that God had ordained a special role for America in reshaping the world. Dulles, in turn, highly esteemed Smith, and privately hoped that Smith would become the chairman of the Senate Foreign Relations Committee.[95] Not everyone in the new White House thought fondly of Senator Smith, however. Notes of a 1954 meeting between Eisenhower and Smith on the problem of McCarthyism reveal that the president's aide General Wilton B. Persons held Smith in very low regard. Persons cautioned Eisenhower that while "Smith fancies himself a fixer, a negotiator," the senator had a poor track record. Persons mentioned in particular some earlier legislation on military deployment that the White House had asked Smith to guide through the Senate. Instead, the senator "messed it up and it took about four weeks to get it back on the rails." Moreover, Persons warned the president not to reveal anything of importance to Smith, since "he is the Senate's biggest gossip ... he goes back to the Cloak Room and talks and talks and talks – and is dangerous."[96] Such a reputation no doubt hampered

---

[91] HAS journal entry, March 7, 1952. Box 282, HAS papers.
[92] HAS journal entry, March 15, 1952. Box 282, HAS papers.
[93] HAS journal entry, March 16, 1952. Box 282, HAS papers.
[94] HAS journal entry, November 6, 1952. Box 282, HAS papers.
[95] HAS journal entry, November 12, 1952. Box 282, HAS papers. See also November 22, 1952, and other November entries.
[96] August 12, 1954 notes from Eisenhower "Conference with H. Alexander Smith, Senator from New Jersey"; Ann Whitman File, Ann Whitman Diary Series, Box 3, Folder: ACW Diary Aug. 1954 (3); DDE Papers.

Smith's effectiveness, and hindered his hopes of translating his "guidance" into political action.

Moral Re-Armament's reputation also continued to suffer, at least in certain circles. While MRA still enjoyed strong influence with many members of Congress, in the 1950s it began to attract closer scrutiny – and skepticism – from some in the executive branch.[97] For example, after attending an MRA theatrical production in Washington in 1951, Smith commented "I regret to note that there seems to be a prejudice against the MRA here in Washington. I do not know what it is due to unless it is the old Princeton prejudice which is represented here in the State Department."[98] Smith himself continued to have his own misgivings. The next year, after his daughter Marian Twitchell informed him that she planned to sell a valuable family necklace to help finance her and her husband's travels with MRA, Smith agonized over what to do.

> I am trying to be guided. Marian has the idea that this is the great revolution that MRA is putting on and she wants to give her all as the American revolution did. Are they right? Or is there room for all groups who love God and believe in His guidance? . . . What is the right answer? I am happy that my children see their value and I cannot oppose them. But I hope God will guide me to guide them correctly. It is difficult because Dearest [Mrs. Smith] is so negative. She was very angry with me yesterday.[99]

Despite its message of unity, here MRA was the cause of family division, leaving Smith distanced from his children and wife, and leading him to ask whether only MRA spoke for God, or if God spoke for himself aside from MRA.

MRA soon caused another division on a grander scale. It still enjoyed much support in Congress, and in 1952 the chairmen and ranking members of the Senate Foreign Relations and House Foreign Affairs Committees invited White House Psychological Strategy Board (PSB) representatives to attend the MRA World Assembly at Mackinac Island, Michigan, held to "answer

---

[97] For more documents revealing MRA's influence in Congress, see the lengthy list of Senators and Representatives who sponsored MRA's 1951 World Assembly in Los Angeles; OF, Box 1672, Folder: 1600; See also the letters and reports from Rep. Charles Deane to President Truman describing at length and with great enthusiasm MRA's many activities; August 21, 1951 letter from Deane to Truman; November 5, 1951 memo from Deane to Truman; OF, Box 1672, Folder: 1600; September 27, 1951 letter from Deane to Truman; OF, Box 197-C, Folder: 686; HST Papers.

[98] HAS journal entry, January 3, 1951. Box 282, HAS papers. Smith's mention of Princeton refers to a controversy while he was teaching at Princeton two decades earlier, when MRA's activities among Princeton undergrads drew much unfavorable comment.

[99] HAS journal entry, November 8, 1952. Box 282, HAS papers.

the ideological threat of world communism" and "to proclaim to the world an inspired experience of democracy, based on moral standards and the guidance of God, which is the greatest bulwark of freedom."[100] In particular, MRA leaders boasted to PSB officials that MRA had succeeded in converting many communists to believe in God and freedom, and suggested that the PSB should partner with MRA in its Cold War initiatives. Intrigued, PSB officials undertook a classified study of MRA.

MRA did not receive a good assessment. The PSB first consulted a confidential background paper on MRA prepared two years before by the State Department Office of Intelligence and Research. The State Department study dismissed MRA's pre-war activities in England as "a campaign to promote a policy of appeasement with Germany, perhaps with overtones of approval for the Hitler regime." When the war came, MRA "opportunistically shifted . . . [to] thoroughgoing support of the war effort." After describing MRA's doctrinal vacuity and operational secrecy, the report concluded that MRA's "claims to great success in a variety of undertakings . . . are not borne out by the available facts and are in many instances quite improbable." Moreover, the "least convincing of these claims . . . is its alleged or prospective inroads made into the Communist movement." The report noted that MRA's own literature mentioned only the "conversion" of two dozen communists, and "with one exception, their importance in the ranks of the party is a minor one and the sincerity of their conversion is open to some doubt." All of this meant that the U.S. government had little to gain from working with MRA. "Its own pretensions notwithstanding, MRA's effectiveness as an anti-Communist force is negligible, and its potentials for the future are limited."[101] The PSB's own study in 1952 reached a similar conclusion. Many of the "communists" that MRA purported to have converted either never had been communists, had not left communism, or had left it for reasons besides MRA's influence. A senior PSB official concluded that for these reasons, as well as "the obvious host of problems in trying to deal with an amorphous organisation of this sort, it would . . . make it quite impracticable to make any attempt to 'harness' MRA under our plans."[102]

---

[100] May 20, 1952 letter from Dubois Morris to John Sherman, enclosing May 7, 1952 letter from Senate and House Chairmen; Staff Member and Office Files (SMOF), Psychological Strategy Board Files (PSB), Box 1, Folder: 000.3; HST Papers.

[101] "MRA Background," from Department of State OIR Report No. 5109, March 3, 1950; White House Office (WHO) File, NSC Staff, OCB Central File, Box 2, Folder: OCB 000.3 File #1 (3); DDE Papers.

[102] April 25, 1952 memo from CIA/OCB official [name classified] to Peter Craig; May 13, 1952 memo from John Sherman to Mallory Brown; May 23, 1952 memo from John Sherman to

Though rebuffed by the Truman White House, with the election of Eisenhower MRA redoubled its efforts to gain influence with the Executive branch. An impressive collection of public figures, including President Konrad Adenauer of West Germany, Vice-President Richard Nixon, Speaker of the House Joseph Martin, Senate Foreign Relations Committee Chairman Alexander Wiley, and of course Senator Smith, now Chairman of the Senate Labor and Welfare Committee, all joined with Admiral Richard Byrd, famed Antarctic explorer and fervent MRA proponent, in endorsing MRA to the new administration. MRA's precise agenda remained unclear. Its appeal to the White House noted "the President has declared that a great issue of the day is the preservation of liberty" and described MRA's desire "to help the President with this tremendously difficult task," but exactly how MRA could help was not spelled out. Skittish White House officials remained non-committal, and seemed to hope that MRA would just go away.[103]

This was hardly what MRA had in mind, as "absolute persistence" seemed to be the group's unofficial "Fifth Absolute." Admiral Byrd especially continued to push MRA on the administration, repeatedly urging Eisenhower and his staff to attend MRA conferences and theatrical productions. Growing frustrated with this badgering, Walter Scott, a senior State Department official, sent a memo to the White House warning against MRA. He criticized the group's murky financial arrangements and outlandish claims, and complained "it is virtually impossible to attempt to define its doctrine, estimate its strength or evaluate its future potentialities." Scott was also skeptical of the many apparent endorsements of MRA from prominent leaders. MRA "has a reputation for putting officials who have shown any interest and given any credence to the 'movement' under undue pressure to assist it." Furthermore, "the many published tributes to M.R.A. from leaders in government, trade unions, and business do not in many instances imply knowledge of the 'movement' or close affiliation with it." Scott did note, however, that two senators – Wiley of Wisconsin, and of course Smith of New Jersey – actually were quite involved.[104]

Mallory Brown; July 27, 1952 memo from S.D. Cornell to P.C. Putnam; SMOF, PSB Files, Box 1, Folder: 000.3; HST Papers.

[103] April 24, 1953 letter and enclosures from Byrd, et al. to Eisenhower; February 3, 1954 memo from Charles Masterson to Sherman Adams; February 5, 1954 letter from Byrd to Adams; February 5, 1954 memo from Masterson to Adams; OF, Box 737, Folder: OF 144-F; DDE Papers.

[104] May 26, 1955 letter from Byrd to Eisenhower; May 28, 1955 letter from Byrd to Bernard Shanley; June 7, 1955 memo from Walter Scott to Arthur Minnich and Col. A.J. Goodpaster; OF, Box 737, Folder: 144-G; DDE Papers.

One particularly revealing controversy occurred during the summer of 1955, when MRA put on a play in Washington titled *The Vanishing Island*. As with all MRA dramatic productions, this one contained a not very subtle "ideological" message, purporting to display the problems with both communism and decadent capitalism. Smith initially loved the play. The day after seeing it, he wrote "it was beautifully done and they are starting on the trip around the world. God be with them and help the message."[105] Not everyone shared this review. After Byrd persuaded Eisenhower's Chief of Staff Sherman Adams to attend the play, a sheepish Byrd wrote to apologize. Apparently the drama's message had seemed too critical of democracy. Byrd told Adams that he and an aide had "analyzed the play and we feel that it would hurt our country and hurt the MRA to show it all over the world, especially to the Asiatic and African peoples. We do not believe, however, that it would do any harm in the United States." Byrd also reported that Senators Karl Mundt and Smith shared this concern, and "they are prepared to help us in a very friendly way to persuade MRA to make some correction" (sic). In a very revealing criticism, Byrd then allowed that while MRA did much good, its spiritual practices rendered its leaders immune from any questions. "The great trouble is that some of us who are sinners are at a great disadvantage because they [MRA] get their word directly from the Lord; and when we sinners disagree with them, they think it is our bad conscience interfering."[106]

This, of course, touched on the perennial problem with unmediated divine revelation. How can it be evaluated or verified and what does it mean if two or more people seem to receive differing messages? Even as devoted a believer in MRA as Byrd found himself frustrated not only with the intransigence of MRA leaders, but with their smug insistence that only they enjoyed unfettered access to the divine will. Smith, for his part, soon realized the play's problems. One journal entry records his bewilderment over the growing controversy. "Newspapers are asking me about MRA. Hope I have answered them properly. God was guiding me. But can't tell what reporters do."[107] Two days later, Smith met with Byrd and noted "we are both concerned over the play but both desire to help the members of the group in their dedication."[108] Neither of them could persuade MRA to modify *The Vanishing Island*. As Byrd wrote Adams, "we cannot prevent their showing the play.... Smith's daughter and son-in-law, who are with the play, have gotten peeved at him and they are peeved

---

[105]   HAS journal entry, June 9, 1955. Box 282, HAS papers.
[106]   June 15, 1955 letter from Byrd to Adams; OF, Box 737, Folder: 144-G; DDE Papers.
[107]   HAS journal entry, August 2, 1955. Box 282, HAS papers.
[108]   HAS journal entry, August 4, 1955. Box 282, HAS papers.

at me too."[109] Between the complexities of familial ties and the confidence of divine revelation, MRA's leadership could not be persuaded to yield their own mission to the U.S. Government's Cold War agenda.

For many in the American government, this was beyond the pale. Having seen the play, Adams wrote Byrd that "it is my rather firm impression that the entertainment which I saw, produced by MRA, ought not to be shown abroad in its present state."[110] Alerted to these concerns, Eisenhower's Operations Coordinating Board (OCB), which replaced the PSB to handle the National Security Council's intelligence and propaganda work, began to put MRA under closer scrutiny. Curious OCB officials attended a production of *The Vanishing Island*, which apparently attempted to present "even-handed" criticism of both American and Soviet societies. The OCB staff did not view it that way. "The show ridicules the ideals of the Free West and promotes an acceptance of Communism," wrote one. "It could not have been done better if it had been produced in Russia." Another complained that "the attack upon Western thinking, upon freedom as we understand it, upon business, politics, and statesmanship of the West, was savage and unrelenting" until the final scene, by which point the damage had been done.[111] If MRA hoped to convince American leaders of the value of its "ideology" in fighting communism, *The Vanishing Island* was not the way to do it.

An amateurish play in Washington, DC, was only the least of the U.S. Government's concerns, however. Preventing or minimizing its public relations damage with international audiences was another matter entirely. A distressed OCB reluctantly concluded it "had no authority or means to stop the play and that it was the responsibility of the Department of State to take whatever action remained to minimize the effects of the play." Foggy Bottom immediately contacted every U.S. Embassy in countries scheduled for the MRA tour and warned that the "play has been criticized for ridicule of Western democracy, emphasis on neutralism and over-all net gain for Soviet concept." The State Department cable also stressed that the MRA "group has no (repeat no) official U.S. sponsorship."[112]

This warning proved as warranted as it was ineffective, as this itinerant group of amateur thespians soon provoked great consternation for American diplomacy around the world. A combination of MRA manipulation,

[109]   August 22, 1955 letter from Byrd to Adams; OF, Box 738, Folder: 144-G; DDE Papers.
[110]   June 18, 1955 letter from Adams to Byrd; OF, Box 737, Folder: 144-G; DDE Papers.
[111]   October 25, 1955 Confidential OCB Memorandum and Staff Study (including several attachments); WHO, NSC Staff, OCB Central File, Box 2, Folder: OCB 000.3, File #1 (3); DDE Papers.
[112]   *Ibid.*

Congressional pressure, and Defense Department acquiescence produced a
bizarre situation that completely undermined State's efforts to distance the
U.S. Government from the play. In the words of a recently declassified OCB
report, upon arriving in Manila, the MRA group

> cabled the Secretary of Defense that they were stranded. Under Defense
> regulations, the use of military planes to carry "stranded" persons is per-
> mitted. Their plea was fortified by a request from a number of United States
> Congressmen . . . who proclaimed that to carry MRA representatives around
> Asia . . . was a worthy assignment for the Air Force. Secretary [of Defense
> Charles] Wilson told Secretary Talbott to "take care of this." The use of three
> USAF C-119 aircraft and crews, despite all Embassy assurance to the contrary,
> gave rise to the speculation that the play enjoyed United States sponsorship.
> Their use, in fact, countered the Department of State's cable advising the
> Embassies to make it clear that the United States was not sponsoring the
> play.[113]

Even a "guided" message from Smith had failed to wean the MRA troupe from
its military transports. On learning of the Pentagon's growing frustrations that
its airplanes were being used for such an outlandish mission, Smith sought
a solution. Since the group would soon be arriving in Cairo and would have
access to commercial airlines, he noted "it has come to me to send Ken a
cable to voluntarily switch planes there." Whether because of bureaucratic
inertia or MRA intransigence, this proposal did not work, and the Air Force
continued to shuttle its renegade passengers around the globe.[114]

Traveling to numerous countries throughout the Middle East and Asia,
the *Vanishing Island* production left a trail of bewilderment, frustration, and
resentment almost wherever it went – and all apparently at the behest of the
U.S. government, since the performers arrived at every stop in three large
United States Air Force transports. Every American Embassy in countries
visited, including India, Iran, Iraq, Thailand, Taiwan, Egypt, and Japan, was
"unanimous in their condemnation of the play's theme." Some foreign governments had a similar response. For example, the Prime Minister of Pakistan,
who had previously welcomed the group because of its ostensible anticommunism, after viewing the play angrily told MRA that it was "pro-communist and
injurious to the West." Even more damaging were a litany of complaints from
foreign leaders of the "high pressure tactics of the MRA apostles," especially
MRA's aggressive solicitation of endorsements before their group's arrival.

---

[113] *Ibid.*
[114] HAS journal entry, August 9, 1955. Box 282, HAS papers.

Unsuspecting government officials were exhorted to offer words of praise based only on, as the OCB report put it, "the MRA principles of truth, love, unselfishness, and purity – principles few would dispute."[115] But if the value of such principles was difficult to contest, how MRA tried to implement them left much to be desired.

VII

The OCB report on MRA claimed its purpose was to make American leaders "aware of the possibilities of exploitation," and to make "the MRA a case study for a warning to government officials of the pitfalls which lie in Congressional cooperation."[116] After all, many in the executive branch had grown weary and frustrated with what they perceived to be congressional whimsy and ineptitude under the influence of quasi-religious groups like MRA. The report illustrated a larger dynamic in America's spiritual campaign to contain – and defeat – the Soviet Union. Religion is very difficult to control. Both the Truman and Eisenhower Administrations defined the Cold War as a religious conflict, pitting the "spiritual values" of a Judeo–Christian worldview and American democracy against the materialist–totalitarian–atheist threat of communism. Most Americans, both clergy and laity, seemed to agree with their political leaders. Yet enlisting religion in the Cold War cause proved to be a much more challenging task. MRA activists, for example, while agreeing on the theological nature of the conflict, called for a very different strategy and very different tactics than either the Truman or Eisenhower White Houses. And since MRA believed it received its "guidance" in this matter and all matters directly from God, its followers were not easily disabused of their course of action – even when it differed with the U.S. Government.

Senator Smith's life illustrates this conflict, both internal and external. Smith's importance lies more in the questions he provokes than the answers he provides. While his influence in creating U.S. foreign policy should not be overdetermined, he displays the complications of competing loyalties – between MRA and the Senate, between family and country, between his American identity and his hope for one world unity, and even between the perceived voice of God and Smith's own conscience – that characterized much of the Cold War. He raises pointed questions on how foreign policy is made, and how history ought to be written.

[115] *Ibid.*
[116] *Ibid.*

Specifically, how do historians comprehend a motive for decision-making that we cannot see, hear, or perhaps even understand? Political leaders frequently receive guidance and input for their policy decisions based on relatively conventional – and relatively accessible – factors such as the desire to increase power, territory, wealth, or prestige, or the needs to satisfy a particular domestic constituency or meet a particular international obligation. Even less tangible but nonetheless not unusual factors such as ideology, ideals, the bonds of personal relationships, or the vagaries of personality often directly influence the decision-making of political leaders. But what to do when a political leader seems to believe he is spoken to by God? And how should we account for when that political leader appears deliberately to seek guidance from God on decisions of considerable gravity, affecting not just him but his nation and even the entire world?

Many of the devoutly religious might find consolation in knowing that a political leader grounded his decisions in such guidance from the divine. Others might find it merely odd but certainly unobjectionable. Still others, however, would be deeply troubled to learn that one of their leaders believed he received guidance from God. And historians – beyond those who study explicitly religious history and thus encounter such phenomena on a regular basis – tend to shift uncomfortably in such cases and either shirk the subject or else probe ever deeper, and often in ever more futility, for the "real" motivation.

Yet this scenario may not be as radical as it first appears. For one, much of the prayer "guidance" that Senator Smith records in his diary appears to inform relatively mainstream, rational decisions – certainly well within the bounds of credibility and credulity. This is not to pronounce one way or another on the validity or veracity of his prayers, but only to observe that the "guidance" he believed he was receiving did not prompt him to act in dramatically unusual or irrational ways.

Senator Smith emerges as a significant figure not necessarily for what he accomplished, but for *how* and *why* he tried to accomplish it. Many American leaders, and many world leaders, for that matter, have expressed their reliance on prayer and divine guidance in matters of state. However, rarely in the annals of twentieth-century American diplomatic history will we find a figure who made such explicit connections between his spiritual view of the world, his regular prayers, and his decision-making. When faced with such an unusual combination, historians ought to employ what has been described as "epistemic humility." Absent our own direct divine revelation, we are hard-pressed to establish with certainty one way or another whether someone like Smith did or did not receive guidance from God. We must, however, be fair to the subjects of our study, and seek as accurately as possible both to provide "voices" for them to tell their own stories as well as to interpret those stories for our contemporaries. In Smith's case, the most important factor is what he believed informed his decision-making. And as Senator Smith himself would say, he did not act alone.

6

∾

Chosen by God: John Foster Dulles and America

I

John Foster Dulles faced the same problem that had troubled his Puritan forefathers three centuries before. As Edmund Morgan memorably posed it, the "Puritan dilemma" of the seventeenth century entailed trying to live virtuously in a fallen world without in turn falling to the corruptions of that world.[1] Though Puritanism as a movement eventually disappeared, the Puritan dilemma persisted – at least for all successive religious Americans who refused either to conform to the world or to separate from the world. Dulles encountered the same dilemma in a different guise. He envisioned a world governed by God. In this world, all people shared bonds as members of one human family, enjoyed peace, liberty, and goodwill, and honored the divinely ordained universal moral law. When Dulles looked at the world he lived in, however, he confronted a jarring reality that bore little resemblance to his idyllic vision. War and conflict, nationalism and division, and pernicious ideologies such as atheistic communism combined to tarnish his utopian ideal. In one sense, his entire foreign policy career can be understood as a series of continuing efforts to reconcile the dreams he held with the reality he faced.

Many biographers of John Foster Dulles try to resolve his dilemma by describing Dulles as not one, but two men. The "early Dulles," they say, worked to promote global ideals such as peace, dialogue, and the spiritual brotherhood of man. The "later Dulles" embraced a hardened, nationalist worldview as a calculating Cold Warrior. At some point, the argument goes, most likely in the late 1940s, Dulles underwent a political conversion of sorts – and perhaps

---

[1] Edmund S. Morgan, *The Puritan Dilemma: The Story of John Winthrop* (New York: Longman Press 1999, 2nd edition).

a religious one. One author describes this as a change from a "prophet of realism" to "priest of nationalism."[2] Though it has some insight, this view ignores many important continuities in Dulles' thought. And the changes he did undergo are better understood as an evolution than as a conversion. He maintained the same utopian vision throughout his career. The changes came as he adopted different means of pursuing and implementing his world order. The combination of new threats emerging abroad as the Cold War escalated, and new responsibilities arising at home as Dulles left his work as an ecumenical lawyer to take up prestigious government positions, forced him to reconsider just how his ideals could be realized.[3] He withdrew his dreams from transnational bodies like the United Nations, and shifted them instead to his beloved America. By the time he became Secretary of State, he saw the United States as God's chosen instrument to accomplish divine purposes in the world.

Diplomacy and devotion were intertwined in Dulles' world from the earliest years. Dulles biographers invariably emphasize that his maternal grandfather John W. Foster served as Secretary of State in the Harrison administration. And his uncle, Robert Lansing, was Secretary of State under President Wilson. The clear implication, largely warranted, is that Dulles' lineage prepared him for a lifetime of statesmanship. However, less often noted is that his paternal grandfather, John Watson Dulles, was a career missionary to far-flung locales such as India. And his father, the Rev. Allen Macy Dulles, was a prominent Presbyterian minister in New York.[4] This religious legacy figures just as much in the life of the man memorably described by Churchill as a "dour Puritan, a great white bespectacled face with a smudge of a mouth."[5]

Unlike his seventeenth-century theological ancestors, this "dour Puritan" stood squarely, and comfortably, in the theological tradition of Protestant liberalism. He was a longtime member of a mainline flagship, New York's venerable Brick Presbyterian Church. While in Washington, Dulles maintained an associate membership at National Presbyterian Church, even occupying the same pew as had his maternal grandfather and uncle, who had preceded

---

[2] Mark Toulouse, *The Transformation of John Foster Dulles: From Prophet of Realism to Priest of Nationalism* (Georgia: Mercer University Press 1985). Though Toulouse's biography is the only sustained scholarly analysis of Dulles' religious convictions, he confines his analysis to Dulles' years before becoming Secretary of State.

[3] For a more sympathetic interpretation of Dulles that argues along these lines for essential continuity in his thought, see the essay/lecture by his son Avery Dulles, "John Foster Dulles: His Philosophical and Religious Heritage," the 1994 Flora Levy Lecture in the Humanities at the University of Southwestern Louisiana.

[4] Toulouse, 4.

[5] Quoted in Henry Kissinger, *Diplomacy* (New York: Touchstone 1994), 535.

him at the church as well as at State.[6] Dulles' Presbyterian affiliation seemed to arise as much from custom as from conviction, for in his family and in the popular mind, to be a Dulles was to be a Presbyterian.[7]

On those rare occasions when he did notice doctrinal questions, Dulles took the liberal side. Amidst the many theological debates roiling American Protestantism in the 1920s, Dulles served as a legal advisor in ordination disputes defending ministers who denied doctrines such as the Virgin birth or the bodily resurrection of Christ. This advocacy at one point even placed him in direct opposition to former Secretary of State William Jennings Bryan, who vigorously supported theological conservatives.[8] Though perhaps uncomfortable with certain Christian doctrines, Dulles felt even more discomfort with those who would police doctrinal rigor. The theologian John Mackay, a longtime friend of Dulles, described him as a "liberal Protestant" who lacked "a very deep theological understanding of the Christian faith."[9] Henry Van Dusen, the president of Union Theological Seminary and also a close friend of Dulles, observed that Dulles seldom if ever referred to the Old Testament or the Pauline epistles, but rather focused almost exclusively on the ethics of Jesus and the Gospels since "the heart of Dulles' religion was ethical."[10] Dulles believed in the Christianity of the Sermon on the Mount – not the Hill of Calvary.

Though liberal in his theological beliefs, Dulles was not lax in his spiritual life. One friend recalled that Dulles read the Bible regularly, always keeping a copy of it on his desk in the State Department.[11] Dulles even boasted at one point that "nobody in the Department of State knows as much about the Bible as I do."[12] Senator H. Alexander Smith, one of Dulles' closest friends in

---

[6]   Dr. Edward Elson oral interview, February 8, 1968, Washington DC, 126. Conducted by Paul Hopper, Dwight D. Eisenhower Oral History Project, Dwight D. Eisenhower Presidential Library, Abilene, KS (hereinafter DDE Papers). Also March 25, 1954 letter from Dulles to National Presbyterian Church Board of Trustees, Box 85, John Foster Dulles Papers, Public Policy Papers, Department of Special Collections, Princeton University Library, Princeton, NJ (hereinafter JFD Papers).

[7]   This heritage reveals just how much shocking it was when in the 1940s Dulles' son Avery announced his conversion to Roman Catholicism and subsequently became a Jesuit priest.

[8]   Toulouse, 17–24. See also Avery Dulles, "John Foster Dulles: His Philosophical and Religious Heritage." For more on the debates and divisions within Presbyterianism at this time, see Bradley J. Longfield, *The Presbyterian Controversy: Fundamentalists, Modernists, and Moderates* (New York: Oxford University Press 1991).

[9]   Dr. John Mackay, oral interview, January 9, 1965. Conducted by Dr. Philip A. Crowl. JFD Papers, John Foster Dulles Oral History Project.

[10] Dr. Henry P. Van Dusen, oral interview, 1965. Conducted by Dr. Richard D. Challener, JFD Papers, John Foster Dulles Oral History Project.

[11] Dr. O. Frederick Nolde, oral interview, June 2, 1965. Conducted by Dr. Richard D. Challener. JFD Papers, John Foster Dulles Oral History Project.

[12] Quoted in Kissinger, 534.

the Senate, remembered "the deeply religious nature that Foster Dulles had in everything he did. He was always very deeply spiritual."[13] Yet ironically, this same man known so widely for proclaiming publicly the importance of Christian morality and spiritual values seems to have been reticent to speak about his own faith in personal terms. Senator Smith also observed that Dulles largely kept his faith to himself, and didn't "recall his ever talking religion to me in his life."[14] Van Dusen concurred that Dulles kept his personal spiritual life intensely private.[15]

Even Dulles' public expressions of his Christian faith had a calculated ambiguity about them. Because of his own discomfort with doctrinal rigor, Dulles did not articulate his spiritual creed with much theological precision. But ambiguity is not the same as ambivalence. For all of his dogmatic uncertainty, Dulles maintained a firm resolve in the spiritual stakes of the Cold War. Nor did his uncertainty produce apathy. If anything, the opposite held true. Had Dulles believed in God's intimate intervention or specific plan for world affairs, the Secretary of State might have traded in his diplomatic credentials for a clerical collar. Instead, he saw himself as a necessary co-laborer in re-ordering the world according to divine mandate, if not a divine blueprint. He knew that God was at work on the side of the United States. He just was not always sure how or why.

II

The basic framework of Dulles' spiritual worldview coalesced in the years immediately preceding his appointment as Secretary of State in late 1952. While the foundations had been poured and reinforced throughout his entire lifetime, the rise of Cold War tensions immediately following World War II provided a crucible that refined his perspective on the world. To those familiar with Dulles' hardening convictions in the late 1940s and early 1950s, his pronouncements and policies as Secretary of State would offer few surprises.

Like so many other American leaders, Dulles defined the international crisis in theological terms. He believed the world divided along a spiritual fault-line into two irreconcilable and competing spheres. This division would appear on a map as the line between the nations in the Western bloc and the nations in the Eastern bloc, but in Dulles' mind the real demarcation existed on a cosmic

---

[13] Senator H. Alexander Smith, oral interview, April 16, 1964. Conducted by Dr. Philip A. Crowl, JFD Papers, John Foster Dulles Oral History Project.
[14] Smith, oral interview, JFD Oral History Project.
[15] Van Dusen, oral interview, JFD Oral History Project.

level. In a June 4, 1950, commencement address at Vanderbilt University, Dulles proclaimed that "the big difference, indeed the only vital difference" between the two realms "relates to ideas, not things. . . . Our people, as a whole, believe in a spiritual world, with human beings who have souls and who have their origin and destiny in God. As put in the Declaration of Independence, all men are endowed by the Creator with certain unalienable rights." Drawing a stark ideological contrast, Dulles declared that "Russia, on the other hand, is run by communists who deny the existence of God, who believe in a material world where human beings are without souls and without rights, except as government chooses to allow them."[16]

The sheer magnitude of the confrontation raised the stakes in Dulles' mind. He estimated that about 750 million people, or fully one-third of the world's population, had come under communist domination, and "the Russian Communists have their plans for making that one-third become three-thirds." And he did not believe compromise or negotiated settlement to be viable options in this apocalyptic clash. "Certainly we are not prepared to compromise, by one iota, our belief in the spiritual nature of man and our insistence that political institutions must respect that belief. . . . On the Russian side, there is no particle of evidence to suggest that their leaders are yet prepared to compromise, by one iota, their belief that world peace and world order depend upon their subjecting the whole world to their particular pattern."[17] His own firm resolution aside, Dulles feared that this sense of compromise and apathy still lingered at America's door. "Our greatest need is to regain confidence in the supreme value of our spiritual heritage. . . . We need to have that burning conviction and carry it into daily life if we are to combat successfully the methods and practices that derive from a materialistic creed and if we are to achieve leadership in a world that desperately craves spiritual sustenance."[18]

Though Dulles and George Kennan shared the same analysis of the world – two sides irreconcilably divided along spiritual and ideological lines – they shared little affection for each other. Kennan dismissed Dulles as a sour, stubborn moralizer.[19] And Dulles reserved a particular antipathy for the "realist"

---

[16] Dulles, "Our International Responsibilities," June 4, 1950 speech; Box 50, JFD Papers.
[17] *Ibid.*
[18] *Ibid.*
[19] George Kennan, *Memoirs 1925–1950* (Boston: Little, Brown, and Company 1967), 496 and *Memoirs 1950–1963* (Boston: Little, Brown, and Company 1972), 182–186. Also interesting is Kennan's comment that Dulles "had the reputation of being a pious man; but I, a fellow Presbyterian, could never discern the signs of it in his administration of the State Department," 184.

school of foreign policy, and especially for Kennan's containment doctrine, which struck Dulles as heresy. "It assumes," he complained, "that we should be willing that the Kremlin should continue to rule its 800 million captive peoples, provided it will leave us alone."[20] The dictates of containment may have permitted such a status quo for a season, but Dulles believed that he and his nation had a higher, more urgent calling. The spiritual, moral, and physical welfare of those languishing behind the Iron Curtain could not be so callously disregarded.

Dulles denounced containment in the strongest terms his lexicon afforded: it was "non-moral diplomacy." He warned America against professing such an erroneous doctrine. "First, it inevitably makes for a break between our government and our people. . . . We do not feel happy to be identified with foreign policies which run counter to what we have been taught in our churches and synagogues and in our classes on American history." Dulles maintained that the legitimacy of American foreign policy rested on its popular domestic support, and he believed that the average American did not, indeed could not, support containment. Moreover, "a second reason against divorcing diplomacy from morality is that this strikes at the heart of free world unity."[21] If the nations opposing communism shared a common allegiance based on liberty, the viability of the alliance depended on fidelity to that ideal. Each nation's pursuit of self-interest would only erode their collective bonds. Dulles elaborated on this in a 1955 meeting with the British Ambassador, Sir Robert Scott. Scott commented that although he found American moralism "aggravating, particularly in relation to colonial matters, nevertheless he was convinced that the US was guided by moral principles in its foreign relations and that this was of immense value to the rest of the world." A gratified Dulles responded that "there was a school of thought, represented by Kennan and Hans Morgenthau, who claimed that we should always act in terms of direct national expediency and not of morality. I did not see how, if that were the case, other countries could count on what the US would do and coordinate their policies with ours. If we were guided by moral principles, then they could know where we would stand."[22]

Thus it was all the more ironic that when it came to actual policy, Dulles did not depart much from containment. Instead, he took the strategic architecture of containment and sacralized it. To Kennan's dispassionate analysis of Soviet

[20] Dulles, "Principle versus Expediency in Foreign Policy," September 26, 1952 speech; Box 65, JFD Papers.
[21] Dulles, "Principle versus Expediency in Foreign Policy"; Box 65, JFD Papers.
[22] Dulles, September 19, 1955 Memo of Conversation with Sir Robert Scott; Eisenhower Library files, General Correspondence, Box 1, Folder 16, JFD Papers.

weaknesses and calculated call for calibrated pressure in response, Dulles added the heat of spiritual fervor and the righteous certainty of a religious conflict. America would contain the Soviet Union not just because it made tactical sense, but also because doing so would bring the eventual triumph of God's plan for world order.

The tragedy of the world's division into two hostile spheres was exacerbated, in Dulles' mind, by the fact that it ran contrary to the created order. God had designed a unified world governed by a set of universal ethical principles which Dulles described as the "moral law." This moral law, he believed, had been revealed in the Bible and was to order the affairs of all people – even those living under the dominion of communist tyranny. Communism, of course, denied the existence of a divinely revealed higher moral law, and also denied its subjects any recourse to such convictions. To Dulles, this constituted a moral and religious travesty.

Dulles explained the origins and purpose of this moral law in a 1950 "Universal Bible Sunday" radio broadcast to the United Nations troops serving in Korea. He praised the "moral principles which we find in our Bible" and described this "moral law" as "a natural law imbedded [sic] in the conscience of all men." He continued, asserting

> that so many soldiers of different races and nations are today reading and studying the same Bible means a great deal not only in terms of their own individual lives, but in terms of bringing the whole human race to a unifying determination to live up to a moral law which is just as real as are the laws of physics. As we learn God's holy purpose, and as we make ourselves into means for its fulfillment, then we shall be in the way of replacing man's disorder with God's design.[23]

Dulles elaborated on these convictions in an early 1952 address to the Princeton Alumni Association. "There is a moral or natural law not made by man which determines right and wrong and conformity with this law is in the long run indispensable to human welfare."[24]

He believed that as a *universal* norm, this moral law was certainly not unique to Christianity. Speaking of the earlier Japanese peace treaty conference in San Francisco, Dulles reflected on his success in leading the negotiations. "All of the delegates at San Francisco who accepted a religious view of the world, whether Christian, Buddhist, or Moslem, found inspiration from the fact

---

[23] Dulles, radio broadcast for "Universal Bible Sunday," November 28, 1950; Box 50, JFD Papers.
[24] Dulles, Address to Princeton National Alumni Luncheon, February 22, 1952; Box 65, JFD Papers.

that the Treaty invoked the principles of the moral law, and the Conference became the expression of dynamic and righteous faith."[25] While Christianity provided the particular lens through which Dulles understood these universal principles, he believed other religions provided similar lenses for their own followers. As did Truman and Eisenhower, Dulles seemed to value religion in general for its social utility as much if not more than he valued the particular doctrines of his own Christian tradition.

The 1951 peace treaty negotiations with Japan also brought Dulles an opportunity to put his religious ideals into practice. He recalled this process in a March 1952 article titled "A Diplomat and His Faith" for the venerable Protestant journal *The Christian Century*. Dulles stated explicitly his hope that "here, if ever, was the occasion to try to make a peace which would invoke the principles of the moral law." After all, the treaty "invoked the spirit of forgiveness to overcome the spirit of vengefulness; the spirit of magnanimity to overcome the spirit of hatred; the spirit of humanity and fair play to overcome the spirit of competitive greed; the spirit of fellowship to overcome the spirit of arrogance and discrimination; and the spirit of trust to overcome the spirit of fear."[26] Others shared in this glowing assessment. Methodist Bishop G. Bromley Oxnam later described Dulles' role as "the first time in the history of American diplomacy that a responsible statesman deliberately took the Christian principle of reconciliation and tried to write it into a treaty, instead of the pagan principle of revenge."[27] Even accounting for some of Oxnam's fulsome hyperbole, Dulles' oversight of the treaty negotiations came to be regarded by many observers as a model of Christian statesmanship.

No doubt the escalating tensions of the Cold War also played a role in the terms of the treaty's ratification, given the need for the United States to ensure an alliance with Japan and resist Soviet designs on America's sphere of influence. But Dulles' Christian idealism seems to have contributed significantly to the relatively balanced final form that the treaty took, and gained plaudits

---

[25] Dulles, Address to Princeton National Alumni Luncheon, February 22, 1952; Box 65, JFD Papers. See also Avery Dulles, "John Foster Dulles: His Philosophical and Religious Heritage."

[26] Dulles, "A Diplomat and His Faith," *Christian Century*, 19 March 1952, 336–338. While the Japanese Peace Settlement has not attracted considerable scholarly attention, those scholars who have studied it seem to pay little, if any, attention to the influence of Dulles' religious convictions on his role as negotiator. This neglect is ironic, given that Dulles himself regarded the Peace Settlement as a cardinal example of his faith influencing policy. See for example Seigen Miyasato, "John Foster Dulles and the Peace Settlement with Japan" in Richard H. Immerman, ed., *John Foster Dulles and the Diplomacy of the Cold War* (Princeton, NJ: Princeton University Press 1990), 189–212. This otherwise solid analysis makes no mention of the role of religious belief in Dulles' negotiations.

[27] G. Bromley Oxnam, Introduction of John Foster Dulles at World Order Study Conference, November 18, 1958; Box 133, JFD Papers.

from many other participating nations. He believed it justified his conclusion that "what was done showed that moral principles are not something to be relegated to Sunday services in our churches. They can be brought boldly and unashamedly into the arena of world affairs. There *is* a moral law which, no less than physical law, undergirds our world."[28]

Like Truman and Eisenhower, Dulles discovered this vision in the very origins of America. The "Founders," he declared, "believed that men had their origin and destiny in God, that they were endowed by Him with inalienable rights, that they had responsibilities and duties prescribed by moral law, and that man's job on earth was to build the kind of a society that would help men to develop their God-given possibilities." Most important, he believed, through the propagation of these ideals "our nation got security during its early years... out of the moral quality that our people had put into their effort." The moral idealism inherent in the American founding provided not just domestic benefits to the early citizens, but actually constructed the international security structure that would protect the nascent nation from any foreign threats. This was because, in a theme Dulles would repeat throughout his public career, the United States incarnated the ideals to which the rest of the world aspired. At the founding, "no leaders in other countries, however hostile and ambitious, could have brought their people to try to crush out that experiment because it carried the hopes and aspirations of all the peoples of the world."[29] Some found this conviction inspiring, and others found it arrogant and triumphalistic, but it formed a bedrock principle of Dulles' worldview. In so reasoning, he linked the fate of the United States with the fate of the world. If America remained faithful to its ideals and promoted them abroad, America would remain secure and the rest of the world would be blessed. If America shirked these principles, it would jeopardize not only its own security but also the welfare of the rest of creation.[30]

Dulles interpreted American history in light of these ideals. Having secured them at the nation's birth, Americans had led the Western world in spreading

---

[28] Dulles, "A Diplomat and His Faith," 338. Emphasis original.

[29] Dulles, "The Importance of Spiritual Resources," January 27, 1950 speech; Box 47, JFD Papers.

[30] In equating America's welfare with the welfare of the rest of the world, and thus universalizing America's fate, Dulles stood in a long American tradition. Thomas Jefferson, for example, had held a similar conviction. See Robert W. Tucker and David C. Hendrickson, *Empire of Liberty: The Statecraft of Thomas Jefferson* (New York: Oxford University Press 1990), 251. And Woodrow Wilson, whose foreign policy convictions exerted a strong influence on Dulles, likewise drew a close connection between America's interests and the interests of the world. See, for example, N. Gordon Levin, *Woodrow Wilson and World Politics: America's Response to War and Revolution* (New York: Oxford University Press 1968).

the virtues of Christian morality abroad. This accounted for Dulles' explanation for why Soviet Communism had not been embraced by more of the developing world.

> That was the saving power of the religious influence that had spread from the Western nations into all the world. Wherever their flags went, the missionaries had gone too – and much farther. And the missionaries carried to subject peoples, and implanted in Western policy, the Christian conception of a universal God who was as much concerned with Indians and Chinese and Koreans as with Englishmen and Americans, and who had endowed each of them with the right to develop freely in accordance with the dictates of his individual reason and conscience.

Christian missionaries figured prominently in Dulles' grand design. He believed "what the missionary men of God have done in the past gives our political leaders of today at least the *opportunity* to avoid total disaster."[31] No doubt his own paternal grandfather's missionary career loomed large in Dulles' mind. Christians in American history had both cultivated the moral law in the United States and planted it in nations abroad. American statesmen had the responsibility to build on this legacy, and to implement it in America's foreign policy.

Dulles could play the part of the stern prophet, and, troubled and provoked by the state of affairs in 1950, he issued a dire warning against declining American virtue. "Now our generation is not drawing dynamic power out of its Christian beliefs. It is Communist beliefs that are spreading like a green bay tree." If America engaged in the Cold War struggle only on the basis of material strength, it would be doomed to lose the ideological battle to the Communists. "We can see that our great national weakness is that we are trying to win [the] cold war and to win lasting peace without any sense of seeking great spiritual or moral goals." He called instead for a "moral offensive" in the Cold War, and predicted that rather than leading to violent conflict, such an effort would only illuminate the contradictions within the Soviet system. "Peace depends upon the increasing internal difficulties of Soviet Communism and their inability to consolidate their present and prospective areas of conquest." Embracing Christian virtues, the United States could hasten the Soviet demise. "In the face of faith and hope and peaceful works, the rigid, top-heavy and over-extended structure of Communist rule can readily be brought into a state of collapse."[32] Despite their differences and mutual dislike, Dulles stands alongside George

---

[31] *Ibid*, emphasis original.
[32] *Ibid*. See also Avery Dulles, "John Foster Dulles: His Philosophical and Religious Heritage."

Kennan as one of the few public figures of the day to predict the eventual
disintegration of Soviet Communism along the fault-lines of its own internal
contradictions and moral failures.

Meanwhile, having preached his lofty vision for American foreign policy,
Dulles turned to the means of implementing this vision. He singled out
America's Christian community for particular attention. "It is up to the
churches to shake the American people out of a materialistic mood that is a
suicidal mood," he warned. "There is a broken connection between religious
faith and national works. To repair that breach is a great and urgent task
of our churches." Dulles called for a religious revival with implications far
beyond religion. "A spiritual renewal can win the cold war peacefully. It can
make the United Nations a growing power for peace. It can give us security
by dedicating us to goals beyond security."[33] God may have been at work in
the world, but Dulles believed that God's people must embrace with vigilance
their calling to carry out God's purposes, particularly in America.

Despite his fervent rhetoric, Dulles was far from an unsophisticated theocrat
seeking to conflate God and Caesar. Just a few months after delivering the
speech described above, he gave an intriguing address to a Jewish audience
in Cleveland. He offered a vigorous defense of freedom of conscience and
inter-faith cooperation, averring that "there can be peace where men think
and believe differently provided each man respects the right of his fellowman
to follow the dictates of his reason and his conscience. This is the kind of
world peace our nation seeks." In the tradition of classical liberalism, Dulles
presented two contrasting visions. "The Soviet Communist world is built
on the obligation to be alike and subservient. The free world is built on
the right to be different and independent." He rejected any sort of religious
qualifications for membership in the United Nations and warned that "it
is dangerous business to mix politics and religion and to seek to impose
a religious test upon membership in a world organization or government."
Instead, Dulles saw the different faiths represented in his audience as "a source
of basic strength in our own society, namely the combination of a political
order that is tolerant of difference and a citizenry which is strong in faith
and sense of mission. Let us make it clear that that is the goal of our foreign
policy."[34]

This paean to tolerance, diversity, and inclusiveness may seem to stand in
stark contrast to Dulles' strident calls for a "moral offensive" and a "spiritual
renewal," and in some ways it does. He muted these tensions, however, by

[33] Dulles, "The Importance of Spiritual Resources"; Box 47, JFD Papers.
[34] Dulles, "The Strength of Diversity," May 18, 1950 speech; Box 47, JFD Papers.

employing deliberately vague spiritual language designed to appeal to the broadest spectrum of adherents to the American civil religion. He made frequent use of relatively inoffensive terms like "moral," "spiritual," "faith," and "mission." He also sought to reduce this creed to a lowest common denominator of religious faith, to which only the most hardened atheist or cynical skeptic could object. In a 1952 address to the Military Chaplain's Association, he spoke of his desire to find a basis for unity amidst America's diversity. "When we seek to identify the framework capable of containing the differences which are healthy, we find that love of God and love of country must be our great dependence." In the same speech he made a similar appeal to a somewhat different formulation. "The only unity which can be adequate to comprehend the degree of difference we should welcome, is the unity which is compelled by the two great Commandments, which summarize the law and the prophets – love of God and love of neighbor." Not surprisingly, Dulles located these values in the American founding. "Our founders represented many creeds, but most of them took a spiritual view of the nature of man. They believed in a Divine Creator who had endowed all men with certain inalienable rights. . . . They believed that this nation had a mission to help men everywhere to get greater opportunity to be and to do what God designed. So they had a foreign policy that was dynamic."[35]

Dulles connected each element of his worldview to another. Personal piety led to corporate unity, which contributed to national strength and security, which in turn translated into a moral foreign policy, which accorded with the divine plan for the world. Any weakness in this scheme put the whole enterprise in jeopardy. Any threat to it, such as the depredations of Soviet totalitarianism, materialism, and especially atheism, demanded a comprehensive response. In short, the basic outlines of Dulles' diplomatic theology were firmly in place when he took office as Secretary of State at the beginning of President Eisenhower's first term in 1953.

III

Dulles in many ways served as a theological bridge between Truman and Eisenhower. Though not a political supporter of Truman, Dulles for many years had articulated a similar spiritual interpretation of the Cold War as the Democratic president. Dulles' convictions, in turn, helped develop and reinforce Eisenhower's own growing understanding of the world crisis. Dulles had served as a foreign policy advisor to Eisenhower during the presidential

[35] Dulles, "On Unity," February 29, 1952 speech; Box 65, JFD Papers.

campaign and was regarded widely as the leading candidate for Secretary of State. On November 20, 1952, Eisenhower officially offered the post to Dulles, who in turn quickly accepted.[36] Three weeks later, Dulles gave a nationally broadcast address to the General Assembly of the National Council of Churches, in which he sketched out his broad vision of foreign policy for the new administration. He could now put in to practice what he had been preaching for years.

Dulles began by posing a foreign policy challenge to his fellow Americans: "If we have a righteous purpose, then our future will match our glorious past." He emphasized what he regarded as the democratic nature of America's foreign policy, ultimately owned by the American people and therefore informed by the American people. "We can rejoice that at this juncture our churches are vigorous and that they recognize a responsibility to influence our national conduct. . . . Our foreign policies, too, have been influenced by religious beliefs. Our people have wanted their government, in its international conduct, to do what was right and to redress what was wrong."[37]

Freedom, which Dulles regarded as the "dominant American theme," provided the ideological centerpiece to his vision for a democratic, moral foreign policy. But freedom required a "noble purpose." "Freedom is not license to self-indulgence. It is the right to live under the compulsions of the moral law." With this in mind, Dulles pointed to the previous century as a model of how American ideals of freedom could reinforce each other both home and abroad. "As missionaries, doctors, educators, scientists, engineers and merchants, Americans spread their ideas throughout the world. The result of all this was that our own land became an area of spiritual, intellectual and material richness the like of which the world had never seen and the world environment became one of friendliness and goodwill." Dulles called for a return to that vision, for "the need today is to rekindle faith in freedom, and to make it contagious, by a fresh demonstration of what to do with freedom."[38]

The Secretary of State–designate then suggested three particular areas of focus, both for church members and for his foreign policy. First, Americans needed to "intensify their determination to perfect an organization for world peace and justice." While he believed the United Nations had experienced some successes and continued to offer great potential, unrealistic expectations had combined with structural flaws and Soviet opposition to curtail

---

[36]   Richard H. Immerman, *John Foster Dulles: Piety, Pragmatism, and Power in U.S. Foreign Policy* (Wilmington, DE: Scholarly Resources Books 1999), 39–45.

[37]   Dulles, "Freedom and its Purpose," December 11, 1952 speech; Box 62, JFD Papers.

[38]   *Ibid.*

severely the world body's effectiveness. Nevertheless, the effort to perfect such a transnational organization should not be abandoned. Second, Dulles urged a stronger "determination to respect human rights and fundamental freedom." He saw a close link between racial discrimination in America and eroding respect for human rights abroad, and he exhorted Americans to get their own proverbial house in order – if there were to be any hope of improved conditions abroad. "Throughout the world, there are myriad souls that suffer in humiliation and bitterness because of the white man's assumption of racial superiority. If freedom is to seem worthwhile, then our people, who profess to be the champions of liberty, must voluntarily practice human fellowship." The Eisenhower Administration may have failed initially to take significant measures on behalf of civil rights, but Dulles can at least be credited with progressive rhetoric, if not action. Finally, Dulles called on Americans to "more bountifully dispense aid and comfort to those who are materially less fortunate." Pointing out that foreign nations often viewed direct governmental aid with suspicion, he argued that charitable giving overseas by churches, individuals, and private organizations had "in the past won us great goodwill and, as a by-product, great security." American goodness, in short, could serve both to spread America's ideals and to protect America's borders.[39]

Dulles concluded by defending his use of the term "liberation" in the previous months of the presidential campaign to describe the American objective towards people living under communist rule. "Liberation" had engendered much controversy, inciting fears that the Eisenhower–Dulles team would provoke Cold War tensions and ignite new hostilities. Dulles responded in this speech that America had always stood for liberation, and that while military force could provide defense against further tyranny, true liberation could be accomplished only by a spiritual offensive. "If our free people will dramatically show that freedom provides the qualities of spirit, of mind and of action needed to lead the way to world order, to observance of human rights, to practice of the Golden Rule, then freedom will again become the force that puts despotism to rout. Then a new era of liberation will be ushered in."[40] America's new Secretary of State made clear that he intended not just a new policy but a new mission for America to the world.

While Dulles enjoyed considerable authority as Secretary of State, his influence extended only so far as his President permitted.[41] The next chapter will

---

[39] *Ibid.*
[40] *Ibid.*
[41] For more on the working relationship between Eisenhower and Dulles, see John Lewis Gaddis, *Strategies of Containment: A Critical Appraisal of Postwar American National Security Policy* (New York: Oxford University Press 1982), 129, 162–63.

explore Eisenhower's diplomatic theology in greater detail. For now, it is
enough to note that Dulles fortunately found in Eisenhower a kindred spirit.
Eisenhower used language very similar to Dulles' in describing the worldwide
conflict "between a civilization that is firmly based in a religious faith, and
atheism or materialism."[42] Eisenhower also agreed with Dulles that morality
provided a basis for popular support of foreign policy. He showed Dulles
a draft of a 1954 letter to Prime Minister Winston Churchill concerning
American opposition to the admission of the People's Republic of China to
the United Nations. In the letter, Eisenhower wrote "I have heard it said
that America makes a mistake in attempting to introduce moral codes into
international relationships and that morals and diplomacy have nothing in
common . . . the fact remains that the American people like to think that they
are being just and fair in these matters and therefore they will not be brow-
beaten into accepting something that they consider completely unfair, unjust,
and immoral."[43]

In short, when Dulles articulated his spiritual worldview, he spoke in a
language his President understood – and affirmed. And together, they sought
to convert America's strategic allies to its spiritual cause. For example, in
early 1956, Dulles played a significant part in formulating the "Declaration of
Washington," a statement jointly issued by President Eisenhower and Great
Britain's Prime Minister Anthony Eden, along with Secretary Dulles and
British Foreign Secretary Selwyn Lloyd. The Declaration's opening sentence
framed its purpose, and revealed Dulles' unmistakable influence. "We are
conscious that in this year of 1956, there still rages the age-old struggle between
those who believe that man has his origin and his destiny in God and those
who treat man as if he were merely designed to serve a state machine."
Dulles seemed particularly proud of the Niebuhrian tenor of this statement,
emphasizing it in a letter to his son Avery later that month.[44]

As Secretary of State, Dulles maintained numerous relationships with
prominent Christian leaders. Their previous work together and their shared
spiritual convictions provided the foundation for continuing cooperation
once Dulles took office at Foggy Bottom. At their best, these contacts provided Dulles with valued spiritual counsel and theological insight. At their
worst, the relationships between Dulles and the churchmen were characterized by mutual manipulation, even verging on exploitation. Either way, during

---

[42] *Ibid*, 198.
[43] July 8, 1954 letter from Eisenhower to Churchill; Ann Whitman File, Eisenhower Library files,
Dulles–Herter Series, Box 3, Folder 3; JFD Papers.
[44] Dulles, "Declaration of Washington" statement, February 1, 1956; Box 102, JFD Papers.

his tenure as Secretary of State Dulles experienced a growing alienation from some members of the American Protestant leadership. He still professed to share their grand ideals, but found implementation much more difficult and far messier. Dulles himself admitted the difficulty in applying religious principles to foreign policy. In a rare but revealing moment of introspection, he confessed in a 1953 letter to Bishop Oxnam that foreign policy challenges posed significant problems for his own spiritual convictions. "Surely, the problems are, as you say, complex and baffling. I try to meet them in the light of Christian principles, but sometimes these principles seem to get in each other's way."[45]

One severe trial, which occurred with the Suez Canal crisis midway through the Eisenhower Administration, richly illustrates the complicated web of relationships enmeshing America's Protestants, Catholics, and Jews. In April 1956, the prominent American Rabbi Hillel Silver met with Dulles and Eisenhower at the White House to urge the United States to sell arms to the nascent state of Israel. Dulles suspected that the Israeli government had dispatched Silver to make the pitch on its behalf. Expressing the Administration's concern of further inflaming Middle East tensions, Dulles and Eisenhower demurred. Further, Dulles feared that taking a strong pro-Israel stance might make the United States appear too beholden to Jewish interests. "We do not want our policy to seem to be made by the Zionists," he warned Rabbi Silver.[46] Two months later, Dulles met with New York's powerful Cardinal Francis Spellman. The Catholic leader complained "that the Jewish activities were becoming excessively arrogant and demanding." Dulles agreed that "that was one of my problems, that I felt it very important to try to demonstrate that the Jews did not in an election year dictate the foreign policy of the United States."[47] Despite the still significant cultural animus between Protestants and Catholics, Dulles realized that support from Catholics in general and Cardinal Spellman in particular was vital for the Eisenhower Administration.[48]

---

[45] November 9, 1953 letter from Dulles to Oxnam; Box 73, JFD Papers.

[46] Dulles, April 16, 1956 Memo of Conversation at White House; Eisenhower Library files, General Correspondence, Box 1, Folder 16; JFD Papers.

[47] Dulles, June 16, 1956 Memo of Conversation; Eisenhower Library files, General Correspondence, Box 1, Folder 16; JFD Papers.

[48] For example, earlier in 1956 Dulles had spoken of contacting Cardinal Spellman, in Rome consulting with the Pope, to ensure that a forthcoming Vatican statement on nuclear weapons would not be perceived as too negative towards American policy. See January 5, 1956 memo; Eisenhower Library files, Telephone conversations, Box 4, Folder 9; JFD Papers. Spellman and Dulles seem to have regarded each other warily, sharing a strong anticommunism but also significant religious differences. As one of Spellman's aides noted, Dulles "certainly would do nothing if he thought it would benefit the Church." (quoted in John Cooney, *The American Pope: The Life and Times of Francis Cardinal Spellman* (New York: Times Books 1984), 232.).

And Catholics and Protestants, whatever their own differences, could at least agree that they did not want Jews determining American foreign policy. Such attitudes on Dulles' part, hinting at a veiled anti-Semitism, stood in marked contrast to the relatively progressive and tolerant views he had expressed in his speech to the Jewish audience several years earlier.

The plot thickened in early 1957, as the United States considered economic sanctions against Israel in response to its aggressive actions in the Suez Canal crisis. Congressman John Vorys complained to Dulles of the pressure Congress was receiving from Jewish groups opposed to sanctioning Israel. Vorys expressed his hope that Christian organizations, both Protestant and Catholic, would be more vocal in backing the Administration's policies.[49] A few days later, Dulles contacted his close friend Dr. Roswell Barnes, a prominent New York Presbyterian minister and leader with the World Council of Churches. Dulles asked Barnes to encourage Protestant ministers to include support for the Administration's stance in the Middle East in their sermons that upcoming Sunday. Dulles griped that "it was impossible to hold the line because we got no support from the Protestant elements of the country. All we get is a battering from the Jews." Barnes informed Dulles that he had already been "working on priming some comments" from prominent pastors in their sermons that week, and would continue to do so.[50]

That same day Dulles phoned his own pastor, Dr. Edward Elson of National Presbyterian Church, and informed Elson that President Eisenhower, himself an active member of National Presbyterian, had become discouraged by the criticism from Jewish organizations of the Administration's policy. Dulles asked Elson to generate "pulpit support" from other churches for Eisenhower, and also to include some favorable remarks in his own sermon that Sunday. Elson, generally an enthusiastic backer of the administration's foreign policy and certainly no supporter of Israel, readily assented. Dulles went on to warn that "if the Jews have the veto on US foreign policy, the consequences will be disastrous. The future of the UN is at stake."[51] Though by this time

---

[49] February 13, 1957 telephone call from Dulles to Vorys; Eisenhower Library files, Telephone conversations, Box 6, Folder 2; JFD Papers.

[50] February 19 and 22, 1957 telephone calls from Dulles to Barnes; Eisenhower Library files, Telephone conversations, Box 6, Folders 1, 2; JFD Papers.

[51] February 22, 1957 telephone call from Dulles to Elson; Eisenhower Library files, Telephone conversations, Box 6, Folder 1; JFD Papers. Also, Pierard and Linder, 203. Perhaps one reason for Elson's eagerness to offer pulpit support for the Administration's Middle East policy came from his own reservations about Israel. In an oral history interview conducted in 1968 that evinces hints of "polite anti-Semitism," Elson still maintained that Truman's recognition of the new state of Israel in 1948 "could be the one dark spot on his decisions in foreign relations. We will be many many years recovering from that action." Rev. Edward Elson oral interview,

he had serious reservations about the efficacy of the UN, Dulles knew that the organization still commanded broad respect among mainline Protestant clergy. Appeals to its welfare were sure to command the attention of Protestant ministers.

Some Christian leaders willingly placed themselves and their organizations at the service of the Secretary of State. Oxnam wrote Dulles of his efforts to expound on "the fundamental principles upon which your policy is based" in sermons and lectures around the country. But Oxnam wanted to provide even more assistance in generating public support. "To mobilize an expression of opinion upon the part of the Church for principles is one thing. To secure support for concrete proposals is another.... We want to help." He believed Dulles had been divinely ordained for his role, rejoicing "that you were finally charged with the responsibility of translating the ideals of religion into the actualities of international life."[52] Two years later Oxnam again wrote Dulles, telling of his efforts to mobilize Methodist support for the Administration's foreign policies. Oxnam in particular noted the Methodist Church's public relations campaign in support of Dulles' foreign aid proposals, including a notice sent to 40,000 Methodist congregations. Even in the midst of these efforts, Oxnam lamented that "I wish the Church could be more effective."[53] Dulles, of course, profoundly appreciated such religious support.

Beyond his own lofty moralizing about the divine order of the world, Dulles realized the utility of enlisting religious leaders, particularly Protestant pastors, behind his foreign policy agenda. These clerical relationships served several purposes. Dulles used these literal "bully pulpits" to cultivate and mobilize popular support for the Administration's policy decisions. He also sought the bestowal of pastoral blessings on his agenda in order to soothe his Presbyterian conscience. After all, Dulles' own spiritual justifications for his policies would have a greater resonance both in his own mind and among the American people if American pulpits echoed in agreement. Finally, when these clergymen traveled overseas or met with foreign dignitaries, they could serve as both ambassadors of American values and intelligence agents, reporting what they learned back to Dulles.

Billy Graham became a prime example of this last category. Graham began cultivating a relationship with Dulles shortly after the Secretary of State took

January 19, 1968, Washington DC. Conducted by Paul Hopper. Dwight D. Eisenhower Oral History Project, DDE Papers. For more on Elson's views on the Middle East, see chapter seven of this book.

[52]   March 24, 1955 letter from Oxnam to Dulles; Box 96, JFD Papers.

[53]   January 18, 1957 and May 27, 1957 letters from Oxnam to Dulles, Box 120, JFD Papers.

office. In 1953 he solicited Dulles' counsel concerning a possible evangelistic trip to England. Dulles' reply was encouraging. "I feel that your trip can accomplish much good," he wrote. "The most basic ties that bind our two nations together are religious ties. The political institutions and political thinking of our two peoples derive from the same Christian view of the nature of man. . . . It is gratifying that you should have been asked to go to England, and I hope that your mission there will be a blessed one."[54] Dulles also arranged for American consulate offices in England to provide the necessary assistance to Graham and his entourage. Two years later, Graham received an invitation to preach in the Soviet Union, and consulted with Dulles as to whether or not he should accept. Dulles encouraged Graham to make the trip, though he cautioned the evangelist to make sure he had a good interpreter for his messages and meetings, since Dulles had not found Soviet interpreters trustworthy.[55]

The early months of 1956 found Graham and Dulles each preparing to travel through Asia. Before departing, Graham wrote Dulles that "to hundreds of thousands of people I will in one sense represent America. . . . If a trip such as this can contribute to building better relations and good will for the United States, then I shall be very grateful."[56] Dulles, for his part, invited Graham to Foggy Bottom for an hour-long personal briefing and gave the evangelist a specific diplomatic commission: to facilitate better relations with India's notoriously prickly Prime Minister, Jawaharlal Nehru, who had been moving his nation away from the American orbit and towards "non-alignment" between the Cold War blocs. Graham's trip timing was particularly auspicious, given that only weeks earlier Soviet leader Nikita Khrushchev had received a warm diplomatic embrace from Nehru during a visit to India. At Dulles' personal request, Nehru agreed to meet with Graham during the India leg of the tour. Their meeting began poorly. During Graham's opening discourse describing America's great affection for India's leader and people and the evangelist's own glowing impressions of India, Nehru alternated between staring impassively at the ceiling and playing with a letter opener. Only when Graham, in one biographer's words, "cut loose from State Department cant" and shifted to his own personal testimony of Christian faith did Nehru respond. The Prime Minister told Graham he appreciated the Christian presence in India as long as missionaries avoided politics, and encouraged Graham in his spiritual

---

[54]   September 1, 1953 letter from Dulles to Graham; Box 70, JFD Papers.
[55]   August 12, 1955 Memo of phone conversation; Eisenhower Library files, Telephone conversations, Box 4, Folder 2, JFD Papers.
[56]   January 7, 1956 letter from Graham to Dulles; Box 103, JFD Papers.

endeavors.[57] Though failing his diplomatic mandate from Dulles, Graham succeeded in his own religious mission.

On his return, Graham provided a briefing to Eisenhower, Vice President Richard Nixon, and Dulles. The evangelist observed that people in Asian nations felt reluctant to accept or appreciate American economic assistance, whereas Khrushchev's gift to Nehru of a white stallion had received wide acclaim in India. Graham suggested that American foreign aid would be more effective if it included such symbolic gestures. Yet, perhaps remembering his meeting with Nehru, Graham believed that Asia's problems were primarily of a spiritual nature. He concluded that "I tried not only to be an ambassador for Christ but also a good ambassador for America."[58] Dulles informed Graham that "I ran across your trail in Asia with consistently good reports" and shared with the evangelist a report on his own Asia trip.[59]

The aftermath of Graham's Asia mission brought its own curious episode and caused no small commotion. In an address to the United States Chamber of Commerce upon his return, media reports quoted Graham complaining that an American diplomat in Asia who hosted him "threw a party and got dog-drunk; his wife also got drunk.... US relations couldn't be lower, and we as taxpayers paid the bill." These purported accusations of debauchery in the diplomatic corps, coming as they did from such a prominent minister, immediately seized the attention of official Washington. The Senate Foreign Relations Committee announced plans to hold an investigative hearing into licentious misbehavior in the Foreign Service, and invited Graham as the marquee witness. A senior State Department official, saying he had been "deeply pained" to learn of Graham's concerns, requested a meeting to initiate a thorough investigation. Graham, deeply embarrassed by the whole episode, wrote a contrite letter to Dulles and the others protesting that he had been wildly misquoted in relating a story he had heard second-hand.[60]

While Dulles was cultivating closer ties with the evangelical Graham, his relationships with his longtime friends in the Protestant mainline became more and more ambivalent. The churchmen did not hesitate to press their own agenda with their erstwhile colleague. When Dulles agreed and could help, he did. When he did not agree or would not help, tensions ran high.

---

[57] This anecdote comes from William Martin, *A Prophet With Honor: The Billy Graham Story* (New York: William Morrow and Company 1991), 191–197, and from Nancy Gibbs and Michael Duffy, *The Preacher and the Presidents: Billy Graham in the White House* (New York: Center Street 2007), 64–65.

[58] Gibbs and Duffy, 64–65. Also April 2, 1956 letter from Graham to Dulles; Box 103, JFD Papers.

[59] March 28, 1956 letter from Dulles to Graham; Box 103, JFD Papers.

[60] May 4, 1956 letter from Graham to Dulles, with enclosures; Box 103, JFD Papers.

One example of the former came early in the Eisenhower Administration. In planning its 1954 assembly to be held in the United States, the World Council of Churches wanted to invite clerical delegates from Soviet bloc countries. American immigration law, however, barred known communists from entry into the United States. Dr. O. Frederick Nolde, Director of the WCC's Commission of the Churches on International Affairs, wrote to Dulles of his concern that "there would be very great difficulty under present law and the present state of public opinion in bringing to this country private persons from behind the Iron Curtain, who presumably would not be allowed to leave unless the authorities there felt that that was in their interest." Nolde then requested assistance from Dulles in waiving the prohibition and granting travel visas to the communist officials.[61] Dulles responded favorably, and recommended to the Attorney General that the Soviet bloc ministers be admitted to the United States, which they were.[62] Hard-line anticommunist though he was, Dulles showed himself to have a soft spot for appeals from his clergy friends.

A curious development in Colombia afforded Dulles the opportunity both to address the concerns of American Protestants and to promote his own spiritual vision for the world. The Colombian government in 1954 began taking legislative measures to sharply restrict Protestant activities in the predominantly Catholic country. In response to appeals from American Protestant leaders and at least one U.S. Senator, Dulles turned his attention to the situation. Besides instructing State Department staff to monitor closely the treatment of Protestants in Colombia, over the next several years Dulles himself kept up a personal involvement, sharing his concerns in meetings with the Colombian Foreign Minister and the Colombian Ambassador.[63] His own son's Catholicism and his sometime cooperation with Cardinal Spellman notwithstanding, Dulles still desired a world largely modeled after his mainline Protestant vision. Universal human rights and religious liberty, while goals in their own right, were also intended to create ideological room for the further growth of Protestantism. Any encroaching Catholic hegemony needed to be resisted, particularly in the Western hemisphere. Advocating on

---

[61] March 21, 1953 letter from Dr. O. Frederick Nolde to Dulles; Box 73, JFD Papers.

[62] June 25, 1953 and November 9, 1953 letters from Dulles to Nolde; Box 73, JFD Papers. For more on this episode, and the public relations use the Eisenhower Administration made of it, see chapter two of this book.

[63] July 2, 1954 letter from Dulles to Senator Irving Ives; Eisenhower Library files, Special Assistant Chronological Series, Box 8, Folder 16; Also June 16, 1958 Memorandum of Conversation with Colombian Foreign Minister Sanz de Santamaria; Eisenhower Library files, General Correspondence, Box 1, Folder 16, JFD Papers.

behalf of Protestant rights in Colombia allowed Dulles to further his own vision and placate some key supporters at the same time.

Dulles welcomed the embrace of the clergy when they agreed with the administration's policies, but the Protestant leadership seldom offered its affections without condition. And at times the idealism of the clergy diverged from the constraints of office – and the personal convictions – that informed Dulles' policies. Foreign assistance provided one such example. The Secretary and the ministers both supported significant increases in U.S. foreign aid, though Dulles emphasized more the utility of foreign aid to advance American ideals and security interests, while the churchmen saw foreign aid as a corporate manifestation of Christian charity. In meeting with Eisenhower and Dulles in 1957, Roswell Barnes and Eugene Blake of the Commission of the Churches on International Affairs (CCIA) urged the administration to distinguish more clearly between economic development assistance and military aid, and to emphasize the former. Barnes and Blake also pressed for giving the UN a greater role in determining and disbursing foreign aid. Finally, they hoped "that our government's programs of technical and economic aid can increasingly be planned and administered in relation primarily not to political and military considerations but to economic and social needs and opportunities."[64] In other words, Eisenhower and Dulles needed to do what was right, and not just what seemed best for America.

Of course, in Dulles' mind, these two motives were one and the same. And while the UN still remained worthy of support, it could hardly be trusted to administer American foreign aid dollars as efficiently or effectively as the United States. Nevertheless, Dulles eagerly welcomed the mobilization of the churches to support increased foreign aid. An excited Barnes and Blake informed the president and Secretary of the massive publicity campaign generated by the NCC and CCIA, including mobilizing thousands of local churches and pastors and distributing thousands of brochures, all to increase popular support for the generally unpopular foreign assistance program.[65] Dulles, for his part, saw to it that the campaign did not get hoodwinked by legislative arcana. Later that summer, he wrote the NCC encouraging it not to rest on its laurels but to keep the pressure on Congress. Though in an apparent victory the Senate had passed the authorizing legislation

---

[64] April 2, 1957 memo from Richard Fagley to Roswell Barnes and Kenneth Maxwell; April 3, 1957 internal memo on NCC meeting with Eisenhower and Dulles; National Council of Churches Collection (hereinafter NCC Papers), Record Group 4, Box 17, Folder 25; Presbyterian Historical Society, Philadelphia, PA (hereinafter PHS).

[65] April 3, 1957 internal memo on NCC meeting with Eisenhower and Dulles; NCC Papers, Record Group 4, Box 17, Folder 25; PHS.

for increased foreign aid, both branches of Congress still needed to pass the appropriating legislation – a more secretive stage when many an unsuspecting bill had met its demise.[66] By the next year, Dulles and the Protestant leadership seemed to move closer together on the foreign aid question. A CCIA official attended Dulles' Senate testimony on the administration's foreign aid proposal and noted approvingly that Dulles now drew a sharper distinction between developmental and military aid. Dulles argued for economic development on several grounds, including American interest, the universal brotherhood of man under the moral law, and the need to extend freedom. In closing, the CCIA memo revealed the churchmen's own growing realism – on this matter at least. "While the proposal as a whole falls far short of an adequate program, it represents I suspect about as much as can be achieved at the present time."[67] Perhaps Dulles thought he was succeeding in bringing his former colleagues around to a more realistic understanding of the constraints of his position.

If so, other differences would soon enough disabuse him of such optimism. The arms race, for one, revealed a persistent divide. As maneuvering between the United States and the USSR over the question of nuclear testing continued through 1957, a delegation of Protestant clerics led by Nolde met with Dulles and urged on him their position that, even if negotiations with the Soviets failed, America should still unilaterally cease its atomic tests for at least a "trial period." The church leaders suggested this position "in the hope that [other nations] will do the same, a new confidence will be born, and foundations laid for reliable agreements."[68] What to the churchmen sounded bold and principled, to Dulles sounded more naïve and almost reckless.

At times Dulles simply found himself at odds with the mainline denominational leadership. He gave a major address at the 1958 conference of the National Council of Churches during which, among other things, he argued against the admission of the People's Republic of China to the United Nations. Many conference participants strongly disagreed with the Secretary of State, and the Conference then released a report recommending that the PRC be admitted to the UN. One church leader recalled that "it was strong and bitter medicine to Mr. Dulles, because word came back almost at once to us

---

[66] June 17, 1957 letter from Dulles to Kenneth Maxwell; NCC Papers, RG 4, Box 17, Folder 35; PHS.

[67] April 9, 1958 memo from Richard Fagley to Kenneth Grubb, et al; NCC Papers, RG 4, Box 17, Folder 25; PHS.

[68] September 10, 1957 letter from Nolde to Dulles; September 16, 1957 letter from Nolde to Dulles; NCC Papers, RG 4, Box 17, Folder: 25; PHS.

all that he really felt it a personal blow and a repudiation."[69] Dulles' sister Eleanor later described the resolution as a "real and deeply felt hurt" for her brother.[70]

In some respects the bad feelings were mutual. Many Protestant leaders wondered, with a sense of bemusement and even betrayal, what in the air at Foggy Bottom had so clouded the mind of their erstwhile colleague. That same year, in the midst of one of the periodic Taiwan Strait crises, NCC President Edwin Dahlberg rather audaciously reminded the Secretary of State of his own views in his previous incarnation as an ecumenical lawyer. Dahlberg sent Dulles a quote from a 1940s report by the Commission on a Just and Durable Peace, which Dulles had chaired, cautioning that maintaining military forces far from a nation's own territory and near the borders of an adversary might be "incompatible with a policy designed to dissipate distrust and to increase goodwill." Lest Dulles miss the clear implication, Dahlberg thanked Dulles for "such clear thinking as this which was done by you and your colleagues on the Commission," and encouraged Dulles to apply such principles to the present tensions.[71] Dulles and Eisenhower, of course, believed displaying American strength against the PRC to be a vital measure of American credibility, and reiterated their support for the Nationalist regime on Taiwan.

Dr. John Mackay, president of Princeton Theological Seminary and long-time colleague of Dulles', later worried that Dulles' advocacy of "massive retaliation" had symbolized a larger, more troubling shift. Mackay believed that "massive retaliation" did not produce "a constructive approach in our American foreign policy at the present time. And I cannot but feel that in this, Mr. Dulles was not really true to his deepest self and to insights which he had formerly expressed."[72] Henry Van Dusen, president of Union Theological Seminary, recalled that when calling on Dulles in his office at Foggy Bottom, "the church representatives . . . usually went to criticize him."[73] As Dulles felt his support wither from the mainline church organizations, some clerical leaders in turn began to see the Secretary of State as a prodigal son who had sold his birthright of a new international order for the pottage of nationalism.

But Dulles had not converted so profoundly. He had indeed transferred his hopes for promoting universal law and morality from transnational bodies

---

[69] Ernest A. Gross, oral interview, November 5, 1964. Conducted by Richard D. Challener, JFD Oral History Collection.

[70] Quoted in Toulouse, 235.

[71] September 9, 1958 letter from Dahlberg to Dulles; NCC Papers, RG 4, Box 17, Folder 35; PHS.

[72] Mackay, oral interview. JFD Oral History Project.

[73] Van Dusen, oral interview, JFD Oral History Project.

like the UN to his beloved America. And as he came to perceive the Soviet Union and international communism as truly apocalyptic threats, he adopted harder-line positions on issues like nuclear arms and China. But longtime UN official and Dulles colleague Andrew Cordier pointed out that Secretary of State Dulles merely became more realistic about the responsibilities of power. Dulles was simply not as free to pursue his idealistic hopes of the 1940s. He did grow increasingly distant from his friends at the National Council of Churches, but Cordier attributed this in part to the incredible demands on his position as Secretary of State. Additionally, Dulles "had a responsible position, and he had to take positions which were not altogether in line with some of the conclusions of the National Council in those earlier years."[74]

Of course, clergy, not unlike academics, have the relative luxury of holding opinions or issuing pronouncements that cannot be implemented in practice. Nolde, of the Commission of the Churches on International Affairs, realized as much. He acknowledged that there were "many clashes" between Dulles and the churchmen. "They were based on misunderstanding, or they failed to reckon with the difference between a leader of the opposition and a leader of the party in power. In a sense, the churches were always in tension with the government. . . . But they have to keep in mind that the government has a responsibility and cannot take certain risks that the critical opposition calls upon them to take."[75] And as Avery Dulles points out, his father always maintained a vital distinction between the role of churches and the role of individual Christians.

> An enlightened and universal religion, my father believed, lays the moral foundations on which sound political structures can be built. But to make specific applications is not the task of the churches. . . . Christians should involve themselves in the world, but without committing their churches to the particular position they adopt. My father was quite conscious that many of his own negotiations in the realms of politics and international affairs were practical compromises that fell far short of the ideal.[76]

This distinction sometimes eluded Dulles' critics, many of whom preferred to level accusations of hypocrisy against the Secretary of State instead of appreciating the distinctions between pulpiteer and diplomat.

---

[74] Andrew Cordier, oral interview, February 1, 1967. Conducted by Dr. Richard D. Challener, JFD Oral History Project.
[75] Nolde, oral interview. JFD Oral History Project.
[76] Avery Dulles, "John Foster Dulles: His Philosophical and Religious Heritage."

IV

In the midst of their periodic rifts, Dulles on occasion still sought input from the Protestant hierarchy. In 1957, he solicited assistance from Roswell Barnes, then NCC General Secretary, in preparing a major foreign policy address. After meeting to go over a draft of the speech, Barnes told Dulles it "is one of your best." If anything, Barnes encouraged Dulles to focus even more on "freedom" as the cornerstone principle of American policy, and not merely "justice." "This is the point at which I believe we most effectively put the propaganda from Moscow on the defensive.... Insistence upon freedom is more welcome to the people we want to influence than insistence upon justice. Communists and imperialists both talk justice as an evasion of the issue of freedom."[77] Though voices in the mainline church leadership often advocated some degree of accommodation with communism, at least in this instance, Barnes' actually bolstered the contrast Dulles drew between communism and the free world. The speech's final version bore Barnes' influence. As Barnes had suggested, Dulles enumerated three core principles governing American foreign policy: peace, justice, and liberty. In more practical terms, he believed these translated into self-determination for all peoples, the need for a strong national defense, collective security, free trade, and cooperation with the United Nations. Dulles concluded his speech with a flourish, once again returning to the spiritual themes that he believed inspired these priorities. "Americans are a people of faith. They have a sense of mission in the world and are willing to sacrifice to achieve great goals.... If we are faithful to our task, no one can doubt that the present danger, great as it is, can be overcome."[78]

Several years into his tenure, Dulles returned to a favorite forum to deliver another major address on America's role in the world. His November 18, 1958, speech to the NCC's World Order Study Conference gave him the opportunity to emphasize some familiar themes, clarify certain distinctions, and apply his spiritual grand strategy to current foreign policy challenges. It demonstrates, in many ways, that Dulles had changed his views very little during his time as Secretary of State. To begin with, he reiterated how the church community should – and should not – participate in international affairs. "The churches do not have a primary responsibility to devise the details of world order. They do have a responsibility to proclaim the enduring moral principles by

---

[77] April 3, 1957 letter from Barnes to Dulles; NCC Papers, RG 4, Box 17, Folder 35; PHS.
[78] Dulles, April 19, 1957 draft of speech to Associated Press luncheon; Ann Whitman file, Eisenhower Library files, Dulles–Herter series, Box 6, Folder 12, JFD Papers.

which governmental action as well as private action should constantly be inspired and tested." Dulles emphasized the "interdependence" of the world, that America's actions did not just affect itself but had ramifications the world over. And since America was good, this would bring good to the world. "The normal requirement that a government serve its own nation must, under present conditions, include concerns which are world-wide. Success in our national goals requires that we have the vision to see, the hearts to understand, and the minds to resolve the problems of the world in which we live." He proposed nothing less than making "the world one that measures up more closely to Christian ideals."[79]

While Dulles' convictions had not changed, the world and the institutions around him had. Descending from the rhetorical throne of lofty spiritual idealism, he proceeded to identify several foreign policy issues of particular concern. First, he turned to the transitions away from colonial rule taking place in the developing world, and placed the United States firmly on the side of self-determination. "The United States supports political independence for all peoples who desire it and are able to undertake its responsibilities." He committed the United States to providing direct aid and expanding free trade with these emerging nations, and urged the private charities administered by churches to expand their assistance as well. Dulles claimed self-determination as an ideal for its own sake, but quickly warned of the designs that "International Communism" had on countries with newfound independence. If the United States did not step in and ally itself with these post-colonial nations, then he feared that communism would "move in to 'amalgamate' the newly independent peoples into the Communist bloc."[80]

Dulles also lauded the Eisenhower Administration's "Atoms for Peace" program. In line with his emphasis on the "interdependence" of the world, he sought to ameliorate fears of nuclear holocaust by constructing a community of nations benefiting from nuclear energy. "We continue to develop and to spread knowledge of the peaceful uses of atomic energy," he claimed, citing bilateral arrangements with 42 nations and plans to supply nuclear reactors to 16 nations. "In such ways we propose to reverse the trend which now is building up atomic and nuclear power to proportions that endanger all humanity."[81]

The most acute danger to humanity, Dulles continued to believe, came from "International Communism." The nuclear threat posed the significant

[79] Dulles, "Principles and Policies in a Changing World," November 18, 1958 speech; Box 137, JFD Papers.
[80] *Ibid.*
[81] *Ibid.*

problem of physical destruction, of course, but that paled in comparison with the apocalyptic spiritual threat of communism. In words he could have uttered a decade before, he proclaimed again that "we oppose International Communism because its creed and practices are irreconcilable with the principles of our faith.... Nothing could be more dangerous than to operate on the theory that if hostile and evil forces do not readily change, it is always we who must change to accommodate them. Communism is stubborn for the wrong; let us be steadfast for the right." Dulles then offered glimmers of hope. Though his analysis of communism's malevolence had not changed, his diagnosis of its prospects had. He detailed a litany of Soviet retreats and weaknesses he had observed in recent years, but observed that it was pressure from the free world, combined with communism's own internal weaknesses, that would bring communism to its final demise. "So it is that the free world's effective resistance to International Communism will bring nearer the day when" the Soviet Union would cease to be an international threat.[82]

Dulles continued to hope that the United Nations would further this purpose as well. His optimism had been tempered, however, by years of experience. Throughout his tenure as Secretary of State, Dulles had become increasingly frustrated at the limits of the UN's effectiveness. In a private address the year before to the Council on Foreign Relations, Dulles complained that "a good many of the members of the United Nations do not, I think, advocate very seriously the basic concept of the United Nations.... There is a great deal of talk about justice and international law, but unhappily very few people want to have recourse to it. They are greatly interested in principles so long as they operate in their favor."[83] He praised the UN Charter as "an expression of sound principles upon which peace might be based." Furthermore, "we have repeatedly sought to have the United States move in this direction. But this is persistently opposed by the Soviet Union." By his count, the USSR had used its veto power as a Permanent Security Council member at least 85 times to "obstruct the will of the majority in relation to matters of world security." In the face of such Soviet intransigence and UN ineffectiveness, America had no choice but to shoulder the burden of securing peace and morality in the world. As Dulles put it, "never before has a nation possessed of great military power so dedicated that power to be the shield of all who, having freedom, would retain it."[84] Some would consider this smug self-righteousness, and others would regard it as noble self-sacrifice. In Dulles' mind, it simply reflected the connection between the welfare of America and the welfare of the world.

---

[82] *Ibid.*
[83] Dulles, June 7, 1957 speech to Council on Foreign Relations; Box 122, JFD Papers.
[84] Dulles, "Principles and Policies in a Changing World"; Box 137, JFD Papers.

To those who accused him of ignoring America's national interests while embracing visions of lofty ideals, Dulles had a ready response. Idealism was one of America's national interests. In a 1958 speech he identified the goals of American foreign policy as defending three particular interests: the physical safety of America, the American economy, and "the integrity of the principles for which our nation was founded." He argued that "these ideals are an integral part of America, to be defended and promoted by our foreign policy."[85] To stand for anything less would be a betrayal of America.

V

Dulles' spiritual grand strategy sought to transcend the nation-state system. As much as he saw the United States as a divine instrument, he earnestly hoped that the United Nations could eventually establish and maintain his aspirations for a spiritual world order. But Dulles could not escape the concept of irony. Much as he knew how he wanted the world to be, he never figured out quite how to bring it about. His vision of a world community governed by international law and characterized by comity and goodwill continued to rise up and seize his fancy. But the reality of human sin and international disorder always snared this vision and brought it back down to earth.

The warnings of Reinhold Niebuhr and other Christian realists against unbridled utopianism echoed through Dulles' world. Though the two occasionally had worked together on church commissions during the 1940s, Dulles and Niebuhr did not enjoy a close relationship. They had joined together at the World Council of Churches planning conference in July 1946 to push strenuously for a resolution promoting a policy of forgiveness towards the defeated Axis powers, to the consternation of the British delegates. And that same year, Allen Dulles, Foster's brother, nominated Niebuhr for membership in the Council on Foreign Relations.[86]

During Dulles' tenure as Secretary of State, however, he increasingly found himself on the receiving end of Niebuhr's withering criticisms. Ideologically Niebuhr's disagreements seemed to come from both the right and the left. For example, Niebuhr, a persistent and impassioned supporter of the state of Israel, denounced Dulles and Eisenhower for their policy of relative non-intervention during the Suez Canal crisis. Niebuhr feared that while the United States passively stood aside and mouthed moral platitudes, the Soviets gained further influence and Israel clung precariously to its very

---

[85] Dulles, May 2, 1958 speech at University of New Hampshire; Box 136, JFD Papers.
[86] Richard Fox, *Reinhold Niebuhr: A Biography* (San Francisco: Harper and Row 1985), 227, 238.

existence. Commenting on the situation to a friend, Niebuhr caustically observed that "the one [Ike] is amiable and the other [Dulles] is not, but the stupidity is equal."[87] Two years later Niebuhr wrote a critical review of Dulles' foreign policy in *The New Republic*. He particularly singled out Dulles' view of morality, which he regarded as dangerously simplistic. "Mr. Dulles' moral universe makes everything quite clear, too clear. Yet . . . it does complicate our relations with our allies, who find our self-righteousness very vexatious. For self-righteousness is the inevitable fruit of simple moral judgments, placed in the service of moral complacency."[88] Dulles, Niebuhr believed, had grown too confident of America's rightness and too smug in trumpeting America's vision to an ambivalent world community.

Niebuhr also took a rather jaundiced view towards what he saw as Dulles's glib appeals to the "objective moral law" and denunciations of "atheistic communism" as the lines defining the adversaries in the Cold War. Not that Dulles was entirely wrong. "The one true element in [Dulles's] conception is the assertion that the struggle between communism and the free world is a moral and religious one," conceded Niebuhr. And it was true that "atheism robs communism of a transcendent point of reference for its moral calculation." But this was letting communism off too easily and too simply. "Communism is dangerous," Niebuhr held, "not so much because of its atheism but because of its idolatry, its worship of a false god . . . defined as the 'dialectical principle' which is supposed to explain the processes of both nature and history." And communists were not evil because they denied the "objective moral law," but "because they are fierce moral idealists who ruthlessly sacrifice every decency in human relations in obedience to one wholly illusory value: the classless society."[89] Niebuhr's cardinal objection to communism was not so much that it replaced God with the State, but that it replaced God with Man in guiding history and in governing humanity. And Niebuhr feared that in missing the root of communism's evil, Dulles was also climbing too high in the tree of American virtue.

In reflecting on Dulles' life, his theologian colleague John Mackay reluctantly concluded that Dulles sublimated Christian principles to the American national interest. Dulles "ended up, not so much as a crusader . . . for the Christian faith, but for the national self-interest. . . . It was our faith, the

---

[87] *Ibid*, 265.

[88] Reinhold Niebuhr, "The Moral World of Foster Dulles," *The New Republic*, 1 December 1958, 8.

[89] Reinhold Niebuhr, "Christianity and the Moral Law," *The Christian Century*, 2 December 1952, 1386–1388. For more of Niebuhr's critique of communism along these lines, see also Reinhold Niebuhr, *The Irony of American History* (New York: Scribners 1952), 67, 173.

American faith."[90] This seems to approach the truth of how Dulles came to see the world. During his tenure as secretary of state, Dulles gradually conflated the ideals of Christendom with the identity of the United States. As America went, so went the kingdom of God. He developed a civil–religious vernacular that, perhaps because it was often so deliberately vague, he employed to great effect. The Christian faith became not merely a crude ideology to advance his nationalism, but rather became intertwined with the "American faith." To protect the security and advance the fortunes of America was to do the same for Christianity. Dulles never became anything close to a Christian fundamentalist, but, confronted with the evil of communism, he did become an American fundamentalist of sorts. His earlier hopes for a world community governed by divine principles had not been completely dashed – they had just been transferred to America.

Dulles hardly stood alone, however. As a totalizing conflict, the Cold War threw the fundamental contrasts between the two sides into sharp relief. Forged in this crucible was a new ideological synthesis of international idealism, American nationalism, and religious devotion. And presiding over the refining of this new faith was Dulles' fellow church member, friend, and president, Dwight D. Eisenhower.

[90]   Mackay, oral interview, JFD Oral History Project.

7

ↄↄ

Prophet, Priest, and President: Dwight D. Eisenhower and the New American Faith

I

On February 1, 1953, at the National Presbyterian Church in Washington DC, the Rev. Edward Elson baptized the newest member of his congregation. Elson also made history, of a sort. The person baptized was Dwight D. Eisenhower, newly inaugurated as president of the United States – and the only president to be baptized while in office.[1] Besides its spiritual significance for Eisenhower's faith, his baptism also represented a new era of public religiosity in American life. The signs could be seen and heard everywhere. From Eisenhower's unprecedented offering of his own prayer before his inaugural address, to his decision to open Cabinet meetings with prayer, to the creation of the National Prayer Breakfast, to adopting "In God We Trust" as the United States' motto and printing it on the nation's paper currency, to adding "one nation, under God" to the Pledge of Allegiance, to the new highs in church membership throughout the land, the Eisenhower Administration oversaw the establishment of a new American civil religion.

The reasons behind this public piety were not hard to discern. They lay as near as the home fallout shelters American families had begun to construct, and as far away as the menacing walls of the Kremlin. The United States faced a foe of an unprecedented nature, an enemy whose cardinal ideology enshrined not only atheism but also active hostility to any and all religious faith. And this enemy was armed with the most destructive weapons ever to threaten the

---

[1] Edward Elson, *Wide Was His Parish* (Wheaton, IL: Tyndale House 1986), 115–118. Note that William Martin erroneously describes Billy Graham as performing Eisenhower's baptism, in the White House no less. See Martin, *A Prophet With Honor: The Billy Graham Story* (New York: William Morrow 1991), 151. There is no evidence for this; even Graham's own memoirs attribute Eisenhower's baptism to Elson. See Graham, *Just As I Am: The Autobiography of Billy Graham* (New York: HarperCollins 1997), 200.

planet. The more fervently the Soviets proclaimed their communism, the more zealously Americans rallied to their own faith. To be sure, factors other than just Cold War contingencies helped to inspire the American religiosity of the 1950s. Exhaustion in the aftermath of World War II, along with repulsion at the manifest evils it unleashed, may have prompted a renewed spiritual yearning among a previously complacent people. The American tradition of revivalism may have been at a top arc of its periodic ebb and flow. Other influences indiscernible to the modern historical method may have been in play. But no doubt the specter of an atheistic foe unleashing a global apocalypse prompted Americans to prayer – in pews and pulpits, and also in the public square.

This chapter will consider a series of examples that illustrate the importance of religion in the Eisenhower Administration's foreign policy. Taken together, these factors demonstrate the pervasiveness of religion as both cause and instrument of Eisenhower's version of containment. In short, religious faith helped define for Eisenhower – as it did for Truman – the line of division between the free world and the communist world. And it appealed as a powerful device to bolster domestic support for anticommunism while also undermining communist regimes abroad.

Even as a presidential candidate, Eisenhower had begun to outline the spiritual stakes of the conflict. With one eye towards his impending campaign, he wrote a letter on March 27, 1952, to newspaper columnist Drew Pearson describing the means needed to defeat communism. "The more intimately I become familiar with the desperate difficulties that abound in the world today, the more convinced I am that solutions must be firmly based in spiritual and moral values." Moreover, Americans needed to search their own collective soul. "[We must] first carefully determine what it is that we are trying to protect against the Communistic threat." Eisenhower defined this as the "American system," which "means the entire fabric of man's moral and spiritual aspirations woven together with the kind of political and economic arrangements that will best support and advance those aspirations." This shared anthropology linked the United States with the rest of the "free world," by which Eisenhower meant "all areas that still lay outside the Iron Curtain and, of course, all those inside it that want to get out." He closed with a warning, and an exhortation. If "we lose sight of our true strength and try to measure both cooperation and results in material values only, then we are right down with the Communists, who uphold the materialistic dialect. We must not lose faith."[2] And if anyone still failed to grasp his meaning, a

---

[2]   March 27, 1952 letter from Eisenhower to Pearson; Personal Files of General of the Army, Principal Files, Name Series, Box 92, Folder: Pearson, Drew; Dwight D. Eisenhower Papers,

few months later candidate Eisenhower made this point explicit. "What is our battle against communism if it is not a fight between anti-God and a belief in the Almighty? Communists know this. They have to eliminate God from their system. When God comes in, communism has to go."[3]

These convictions were vintage Eisenhower. Earnest yet vague, fervent yet non-dogmatic, they spoke in tones designed to appeal to the broadest possible audience – while still isolating the Soviet Union from the United States, and from the rest of the world. Yet Eisenhower's sentiments should not be dismissed as mere platitudes. He seems genuinely to have believed in a core set of principles based on a rather simple natural theology. These he had expressed in a private letter in 1947 to his close friend Swede Hazlett. "I believe fanatically in the American form of democracy, a system . . . that ascribes to the individual a dignity accruing to him because of his creation in the image of a supreme being."[4]

It was such a creed that in part prompted Eisenhower's most infamous, yet revealing, comment on religion. On December 22, 1952, president-elect Eisenhower met in New York with his old counterpart and friend from World War II, Marshal Grigori Zhukov of the Soviet army. Describing their discussion at a press conference afterwards, Eisenhower delivered fodder for critics of civil religion – and of his own intellect – for generations thereafter. After quoting the Declaration of Independence's recognition that "all men are created equal" and "are endowed by their Creator with certain unalienable rights," Eisenhower offered this interpretation: "In other words, our form of government has no sense unless it is founded in a deeply felt religious faith, and I don't care what it is. With us of course it is the Judeo-Christian concept but it must be a religion that all men are created equal. So what was the use of me talking to Zhukov about that? Religion, he had been taught, was the opiate of the people." Taken out of context, of course, this statement could seem to reveal a cynical manipulation of faith and a callous, even ignorant disregard for religious doctrine. And for the likes of Will Herberg, Sydney Ahlstrom, Robert Bellah and many other interpreters, it did indicate just that. But even taken in context, Eisenhower's sentiment reveals much.[5] He did see

Eisenhower Presidential Library, Abilene, Kansas (hereinafter DDE Papers). See also Stephen Ambrose, *Eisenhower: Soldier and President* (New York: Simon and Schuster 1990), 266, for more on the letter's political context.

[3] Quoted in Richard V. Pierard and Robert D. Linder, *Civil Religion and the Presidency* (Grand Rapids, MI: Academie Books 1988), 198.

[4] Quoted in Ambrose, 232.

[5] Quoted in Patrick Henry, " 'And I Don't Care What It Is': The Tradition-History of a Civil Religion Proof-Text," *Journal of the American Academy of Religion*, vol. XLIX, no.1, 35–49. Henry's article, a witty demonstration of the pretensions and assumptions that often distort

religious faith – or at least a religious faith that affirmed human equality – as indispensable for democratic government. Within these parameters, he cared little about the particulars of religious doctrine, as long as that religion served its necessary social function. And perhaps most important, he regarded this religiously grounded belief in God and man as a crucial difference separating the "free world" from the Soviet bloc. Unless and until the Soviets could see that religion was not a narcotic, but a necessary foundation for a good society, conflict would be unavoidable.

Eisenhower's efforts to use religion to enhance national unity and strengthen an anticommunist consensus reflect his broader worldview. Described by Robert Griffith as the "corporate commonwealth," this worldview derived from Eisenhower's belief that

> the inevitable conflicts produced by the short-sighted and self-interested actions of classes and interest groups could be resolved only through the leadership of public-spirited and professionally skilled managers such as himself, who could exercise the disinterested judgment necessary to avoid calamities such as war or depression and achieve long-range goals such as peace and high-productivity. The task of such leadership was to quell the passion of the masses, to encourage self-discipline on the part of business, labor, and agriculture, and to promote the pursuit of long-term, enlightened self-interest rather than immediate gain.[6]

Eisenhower's efforts to adapt and expand the institutions of the American civil religion to meet the challenges of the Cold War reflect his broader concern to reconcile the various social and economic tensions and fissures that he saw fraying his nation. In all of these areas, he believed that government had an indispensable though carefully circumscribed role to play. Specifically, the president's duties often would be hortatory rather than coercive. He would suggest, encourage, and convene, rather than regulate and mandate. He would bridge divisions – whether economic, social, political, or religious – rather than exploit them. He would enlist the support of leading private citizens as often as he would use the instruments of government. He would employ public relations as a vital strategy, for building domestic consensus and for undermining the international credibility of communism.

Confident in these convictions, on the cold Tuesday morning of January 20, 1953, Eisenhower attended a special service at National Presbyterian Church,

---

historical scholarship, also exhaustively investigates what others have said Eisenhower said, what Eisenhower actually said, and what Eisenhower likely meant.

[6] Robert Griffith, "Dwight D. Eisenhower and the Corporate Commonwealth," *American Historical Review*, February 1982, vol. 87, no. 1, 93.

and then traveled down Pennsylvania Avenue to take the oath of office and deliver his inaugural address. That morning he spontaneously decided to begin his speech with a prayer that he had just composed. While past presidents had usually invited clergy to deliver an inaugural prayer, no president had ever before given his own prayer.[7] After asking those assembled to bow their heads as their new president prayed to "Almighty God" for aid "that all may work for the good of our beloved country and Thy glory," Eisenhower began his speech on an apocalyptic note. "Forces of good and evil are massed and armed and opposed as rarely before in history. This fact defines the meaning of this day." Part sermon, part call to arms, and part appeal for peace, the address was devoted entirely to foreign policy. As he had done before and would so often do throughout his presidency, Eisenhower professed the convictions he expected his nation to live by. "We who are free must proclaim anew our faith. This faith is the abiding creed of our fathers. It is our faith in the deathless dignity of man, governed by eternal moral and natural laws. This faith defines our full view of life. It establishes, beyond debate, those gifts of the Creator that are man's inalienable rights, and that make all men equal in His sight." This creed stood unalterably opposed to atheistic communism. "The enemies of this faith know no god but force," which was really no god at all. Eisenhower sought to disabuse any appeasement-minded listeners of the notion that the battle lines in this crusade could be glossed over. "Here, then, is joined no argument between slightly different philosophies... freedom is pitted against slavery; lightness against the dark." Finally, he clarified the relationship of this American faith to the rest of the world. While "the faith we hold belongs not to us alone but to the free of the world... destiny has laid upon our country the responsibility of the free world's leadership."[8] Here was the American paradox: while the American creed was universal, God had given the United States as a nation a particular calling to lead the world and protect and promote this faith.

In proclaiming this global paradox, Eisenhower could not escape a personal paradox. He affirmed the same sense of a divine mandate for America's role in the world, and the same belief in the spiritual nature of the Cold War, as his detested predecessor Harry Truman. If anything, Eisenhower refined, expanded, and institutionalized the civil religion that Truman had proclaimed. For all of their apparent differences, not to mention personal

---

[7] Ambrose, 295–296. See also Eisenhower, *The White House Years: Mandate for Change, 1953–1956* (New York: Doubleday 1963), 100–101.

[8] Eisenhower, Inaugural Address in Washington, DC, January 20, 1953. *Public Papers of the Presidents: Dwight D. Eisenhower, 1953* (Washington: United States Government Printing Office 1960), 1–8.

enmity, Presidents Harry Truman and Dwight Eisenhower pursued remarkably similar foreign policies, as much from common theological convictions
as from strategic necessity.[9] Containment continued to reign as the governing strategic doctrine, albeit with certain modifications. And Eisenhower
shared Truman's beliefs in the religious roots of human rights and freedoms, the spiritual evil of atheistic communism, and the divine mandate for
America to save the world. The two presidents also shared certain particulars, from ambivalent relationships with the Protestant church leadership,
to interest in forging an alliance of religious leaders united against communism, to efforts to use religion in American propaganda, and even to Myron
Taylor.

It should come as no surprise that a shadowy figure well traveled in the
halls of power such as Taylor would appear in the Eisenhower Administration, albeit in a much-reduced role. Although advanced in years and failing in
health, Taylor could not resist at least a dash of further ecumenical intrigue.
Shortly after Eisenhower's inauguration, Taylor sent him two bound volumes containing copies of the correspondence between Presidents Roosevelt
and Truman and the Pope, along with a letter in which Taylor described his
covert activities for the two presidents. Taylor closed by asking to meet with
Eisenhower in order to brief him on Taylor's previous efforts with "interfaith
activities in the cause of peace." Because "this is a subject which has been
very difficult to undertake," Taylor wanted the new president to understand
what had already been done, should Eisenhower decide to pursue the initiative further.[10] Before meeting with Eisenhower a few weeks later, Taylor also
informed the president about Lutheran Bishop Otto Dibelius' anticommunist activities in Berlin, about Truman's previous meetings with Dibelius, and
about Dibelius' ongoing need for financial assistance from the U.S. Government. Eisenhower instructed CIA Director Allen Dulles to look into Dibelius'
request, and it appears likely that the CIA continued to provide some amount
of funding to the German Bishop.[11]

---

[9] For more on the complex, tumultuous relationship between Truman and Eisenhower, see
Steve Neal, *Harry and Ike: The Partnership that Remade the Postwar World* (New York: Scribner
2001).

[10] March 31, 1953 letter from Taylor to Eisenhower; White House Confidential File (WHCF),
Confidential Subject Series, Box 83, Folder: Taylor; DDE Papers.

[11] April 16, 1953 letter from Taylor to Eisenhower; WHCF, Confidential Subject Series, Box 83,
Folder: Taylor; April 22, 1953 letter from Eisenhower to Allen Dulles; April 25, 1953 letter from
Eisenhower to Taylor; Ann Whitman File, Subject Series, Box 83, Folder: Taylor, Myron (1);
Note that an April 25, 1953 letter from Dulles to Eisenhower re: funding for Dibelius remains
classified, having been reviewed by the CIA as recently as May 15, 2001 and not released. DDE
Papers. Unfortunately, no description or transcript of Eisenhower's meeting with Taylor in
late April, 1953 could be found.

The next year Taylor met with Eisenhower again and presented him with two more volumes detailing Taylor's efforts with Truman to forge a world religious coalition against communism. Taylor also informed Eisenhower that he would be traveling soon to the Vatican, and suggested that the president send along with Taylor a letter of greeting for the Pope. After the State Department affirmed the idea, Eisenhower agreed to do so, giving Taylor a perfunctory letter for Pius XII that lauded "your accomplishments as a great leader of the world's moral forces." On the eve of Taylor's departure for Europe, however, he came across an Associated Press article describing his meeting with Eisenhower. The White House press office had obviously prompted the report. Obsessed with secrecy, nothing nettled Taylor more than unsolicited media coverage. He sent a sharp, somewhat disrespectful letter to Eisenhower, reminding the President that he had asked for confidentiality, and concluding "I regret exceedingly that my request was not observed."[12]

Satisfied that he had made his point, Taylor still delivered the president's letter to the Pope. Pius XII saw this as an opportunity to raise two issues that had been concerning him, and responded to Eisenhower in his customary florid language. First, referring to the protest that had greeted Truman's failed effort in late 1950 and early 1951 to establish formal diplomatic relations with the Vatican, Pius XII lamented "the campaign of injurious attacks against this Apostolic See." Moreover, in a not-so-veiled complaint against Truman, he wrote "we would have expected, on that occasion, that qualified persons would have recalled certain elements of public opinion to a due respect by noting the absolute correctness of the Holy See, from whom there was not the slightest suggestion of interference in the matter." Notwithstanding the fact that the Vatican had urged Truman to extend recognition, the point was clear. The Pope believed the White House had not defended him sufficiently against the heated anti-Catholicism of the day. Trust had been damaged. Moreover, Pius XII complained that he no longer had an effective channel to the White House. In response, Eisenhower and Dulles directed the State Department to communicate with the Vatican through the Apostolic Delegate in Washington.[13] In the face of the threat of atheistic communism, Washington and Rome realized they still needed each other.

[12] May 13, 1954 letter from Taylor to Eisenhower; May 17, 1954 letter from Eisenhower to Taylor; May 18, 1954 letter from Taylor to Eisenhower; WHCF, Confidential Subject Series, Folder: Taylor; May 14, 1954 memorandum from Bernard Shanley, Counsel to the President, to Robert Murphy, Deputy Under Secretary of State; May 18, 1954 letter from Eisenhower to Pope Pius XII; Ann Whitman File, International File, Box 54, Folder: Vatican; DDE Papers.

[13] June 19, 1954 letter from Pope Pius XII to Eisenhower; August 2, 1954 memorandum from Dulles to Eisenhower; August 3, 1954 letter from Eisenhower to Pope Pius XII; Ann Whitman File, International File, Box 54, Folder: Vatican; DDE Papers.

II

Eisenhower developed an unusually close relationship with Dr. Edward Elson, his pastor at National Presbyterian Church. Dapper, winsome, polished, relatively conservative in his politics and loosely evangelical in his theology, in 1952 Elson had only recently taken the pastorate at National Presbyterian, but immediately showed himself comfortable, and adept, in ministering to persons of prominence and power. Very soon after Eisenhower's election victory, Elson held little back in courting the president-elect. Billy Graham had already recommended National Presbyterian to Eisenhower. Elson encouraged eminent members of his congregation to contact the president-elect, and he himself wrote and called Eisenhower to extend a church invitation. He had one elder in his church tell Eisenhower of Elson's lecture tour through the Middle East for the purpose of "pointing out that our participation in world affairs is not prompted by selfish motives." The pastor, in other words, was also a patriot, eager to advance American interests abroad. Elson even contacted Eisenhower's wife Mamie, and brother Milton, one of the president-elect's closest confidants, inviting them to speak well of National Presbyterian to their husband and brother, respectively. In Elson's appeals, he emphasized his previous service as an Army chaplain who had been General Eisenhower's emissary to the German Protestant Church after the war's end in 1945, boasting that "I am the only Presbyterian pastor in Washington having personally served you in the past." Elson also advertised his availability for any of Eisenhower's particular needs. "On the morning of the Inauguration I am at your service for such private devotions as you would like to have conducted and for whatever other service I may render. Thereafter the President's Pew is awaiting your use each Sunday." Finally, Elson did not hesitate to drop the names of his famous parishioners, who included the likes of Henry Luce and others. "In company with Mr. J. Edgar Hoover and Lt. General Willard S. Paul, two officers of our Church, I should like to call upon you to present our invitation personally."[14]

If this display of clerical obsequiousness bothered Eisenhower, he did not reveal it. Never in his life having been a regular churchgoer, he had only begun to consider the question of church attendance. His family had belonged to an

---

[14] November 13, 1952 letter from Paul Wooton to Eisenhower; November 23, 1952 letter from Elson to Eisenhower; December 2, 1952 memorandum from Anne Wheaton to Mamie Eisenhower; Central File (CF), President's Personal File (PPF), Box 913, Folder: 53-B-1 National Presbyterian Church; DDE Papers. Also Graham, 192. For more on Elson's ministry and thought, see his book *America's Spiritual Recovery* (Westwood, NJ: Fleming H. Revell 1954); Elson dedicated the book to Eisenhower, and had Hoover write the introduction.

obscure Mennonite sect known as River Brethren, whose congregations were so few and far flung that in his youth the Eisenhowers had only worshipped in their home because their town of Abilene, Kansas, had no River Brethren church. Nonetheless, his boyhood years had been steeped in domestic piety, including family Bible readings twice daily. After departing Abilene for West Point and an army career that spanned the globe, Eisenhower had never acquired the habit of regular church attendance. According to both Elson and Billy Graham, Eisenhower later complained that the few churches he did visit during these years had preached only liberal politics instead of biblical sermons. By several accounts, Eisenhower's decision to resume churchgoing related closely to his campaign for the presidency. Claire Booth Luce – former Connecticut Congresswoman, wife of Henry Luce, and eventually Eisenhower's Ambassador to Italy – claimed that in 1952 she encouraged him to begin attending church. He protested that while he possessed deep faith, religion was strictly "a matter between himself and God" and it "would be an unbearable piece of hypocrisy" to join a church only to gain votes. She retorted that his non-attendance would set an iniquitous example to American children, who would most certainly protest to their parents that if the president of the United States did not go to church, why should they? Billy Graham likewise encouraged Eisenhower to join a church, and apparently received a similar response as Luce had: Eisenhower would join a church, but only after the election.[15]

Into this milieu came Elson's campaign to win Eisenhower's membership. Mamie had grown up Presbyterian, and in the words of one of her assistants, as the denomination's flagship, National Presbyterian "would seem a logical choice." Moreover, Elson "has one of the most outstanding churches in Washington, is personally popular, and conducts an excellent church program." By mid-December, the Eisenhowers agreed, and informed Elson they would make his church theirs as well. Elson, in turn, promised "to serve your spiritual needs in every way possible" and insisted "that this relationship will never be allowed to be exploited for any other purpose."[16] Elson's baptismal waters also brought a shower of publicity, though whether by accident or by design remains unclear. Eisenhower's diary for the day records how the

<hr/>

[15] Ambrose, 16; Dr. Edward Elson oral interview, volume 3, February 8, 1968, Washington DC. Conducted by Paul Hopper; Claire Booth Luce oral interview, January 11, 1968, New York City. Conducted by John Luter; DDE Papers, Dwight D. Eisenhower Oral History Project. Also Graham, 191–192 and Martin, 148.

[16] December 2, 1952 memorandum from Anne Wheaton to Mamie Eisenhower; December 21, 1952 letter from Elson to Eisenhower; CF, President's Personal File (PPF), Box 913, Folder: 53-B-1 National Presbyterian Church; DDE Papers.

sweet moment turned sour. "Mamie and I joined a Presbyterian church. We were scarcely home before the pact was being publicized, by the pastor, to the hilt. I had been promised, by him, that there would be no publicity. I feel like changing at once to another church of the same denomination. I shall if he breaks out again."[17] Elson, for his part, claimed that no one in his church had "released a news story," but rather a flock of reporters just arrived, unannounced and uninvited.[18]

Regardless, both pastor and president soon smoothed over this turbulence, and Eisenhower did not leave the church. Shortly after Eisenhower joined National Presbyterian, Graham wrote Elson a letter of encouragement. "I do not know of anybody in the entire world that could help him like you can.... I am absolutely certain that God has placed you in this place of responsibility in being a spiritual helper to this man."[19] Despite its rocky start and its roots in what appears as opportunism on both sides – Eisenhower's initial resumption of churchgoing as much for public relations as from personal conviction, and Elson's desperation to secure the most prominent parishioner in the land – the relationship that developed between Eisenhower and Elson grew to be abiding and meaningful. Moreover, Eisenhower became an active member at National Presbyterian, and appears to have become a practicing Christian.

Elson encouraged his new congregant to develop a public ministry of his own. Telling Eisenhower that he symbolized "a moral resurgence and spiritual counter-offensive in our world," Elson suggested that Eisenhower have each Cabinet meeting begin in prayer, which "would have a tremendous effect upon the Cabinet and the Country." Elson offered to coordinate these prayers, including "occasionally to have the prayer offered by representatives of other faiths." Eisenhower himself gave the prayer to open his first Cabinet meeting – a gesture that moved Secretary of Agriculture Ezra Taft Benson to request that every meeting begin thus.[20] This also represented a significant development in American civil religion. Still rooted in Protestant culture, American public piety began to take on a much more ecumenical, even interfaith dimension. Most remarkably, this pluralism grew out of an intentional campaign on the part of public officials such as Truman and especially Eisenhower, with the eager cooperation of clergy such as Elson, to craft a more doctrinally inclusive public religion. Or perhaps not so much

---

[17] Quoted in Pierard and Linder, 203.
[18] Elson, 117.
[19] Quoted in Elson, 133.
[20] January 14, 1953 letter from Elson to Eisenhower; January 28, 1953 letter from Benson to Eisenhower; February 2, 1953 letter from Eisenhower to Benson; OF Box 401, Folder: 101 P Cabinet; DDE Papers.

"doctrinally inclusive" as doctrinally minimalist, as Protestants, Catholics, Jews, and Mormons were asked to leave their theological distinctives at home and embrace a common public faith based on basic tenets such as prayer, God, the divine origins of human rights and freedoms, and the unique blessings and responsibilities bestowed on America. So it was that in a Cabinet predominantly composed of Presbyterians, Benson the Mormon most enthusiastically endorsed opening in prayer.[21] To be sure, many Americans would resist this latest incarnation of civil religion. Protestant intransigence, after all, had frustrated Truman's attempt to recognize the Vatican and forge a pan-religious anticommunist alliance. And as discussed earlier, the 1950s witnessed anything but irenic unity within a Protestantism rent by increasingly violent divisions. Nevertheless, many Americans sought to consign this religious upheaval to the margins of public life. Probably a majority of American religionists desired more unity around God and country than disunity on doctrinal matters deemed less essential. From the White House pulpit they heard great encouragement.

It is hardly rhetorical license to refer to the "White House pulpit" in the Eisenhower years. The Administration seems to have seen itself that way. One of Eisenhower's senior aides, the former Congregational minister Frederic Fox, who had been appointed to a special position to coordinate religious affairs, wrote an internal memo to White House press secretary James Hagerty asserting that "the President has a new responsibility. He is not only the Upholder of the Constitution; he is the 'Defender of the Faith'." Fox distinguished between the Queen of England, who "only defends the faith of the Church of England," and Eisenhower, who "defends faith generally – faith in all its American variety." In another memo to his White House colleagues on "The Pastoral Duties of the President," Fox declared "in his role as 'Pastor' of the Nation, the President encourages worthy pursuits, promotes charity, strengthens the moral fibre."[22] Even the Republican National Committee got into the act. In 1955, the RNC adopted a resolution declaring Eisenhower to be "not only the political leader, but the spiritual leader of our times."[23] Eisenhower's repeated public tributes to God and to the divine origins of human rights and freedoms, along with his perpetual exhortations to Americans to pray and to maintain their spiritual faith, were not mere bromides casually tacked on to presidential

---

[21] Benson eventually became the President of the Church of Jesus Christ of the Latter Day Saints, the Mormon equivalent to the Pope.

[22] August 11, 1956 memorandum from Fox to Hagerty; November 5, 1959 memo by Fox; OF Box 286, Folder: 72-A-2 Fox; DDE Papers. See also Pierard and Linder, 204.

[23] Quoted in Will Herberg, *Protestant, Catholic, Jew: An Essay in American Religious Sociology* (New York: Doubleday and Company 1955), 265.

remarks. Rather, they revealed a coherent civil religion intentionally developed and maintained by a President who believed it had tremendous social utility – and that is was true, besides.

Eisenhower's convictions in this regard were more conventional than exceptional by the standards of the day. Perhaps inspired by their president, or perhaps influencing him, or perhaps just reflecting the spirit of the age, many of Eisenhower's contemporaries sent him copies of speeches they had given on a similar theme. For example, Milton Eisenhower, President of Penn State University, shared with his brother an address he gave in 1954 on "The Spiritual Foundations of Democracy." The speech described the Cold War as at its core "a conflict of ideas – the evil, cynical, materialistic idea that Man is but a creature of the State versus the Judaic-Christian idea that Man is a child of God and that *all* men are equal in His sight and in the eyes of the law."[24] Henry Luce, a close friend of the president, sent Eisenhower a speech that Luce gave in 1955 along with a note that he had "leaned very heavily" on Eisenhower's ideas in composing it, particularly "the foreign policy principles that you and your extraordinary Secretary of State have hammered out." Luce's speech, on America's "Public Philosophy and the Spirit of Geneva," lauded Eisenhower's performance at the Geneva summit earlier that summer, where he had unveiled his audacious "Open Skies" proposal for unlimited reciprocal aerial inspections by the United States and USSR. The United States, which Luce described as "the clearest example of Providence working in history" because of its founding "on the premise that there is a universal moral law," had been perfectly represented by its president in Geneva. Luce contended that Eisenhower's foreign policy had transcended crass "real-politik" because it was inspired by the president's faith in God and in a universal morality "written somewhere in the hearts of all men." Not surprisingly, Eisenhower loved Luce's speech, and sent a copy to Dulles as well.[25]

In a curious illustration of just how widely this ethos was shared, even Henry Wallace spoke fervently of the importance of religious faith in the life of his nation and its leaders. The Wallace of the 1940s may have known more for his efforts to downplay the threat of communism and accommodate the Soviet Union's rising power, but the Wallace of the 1950s gave a speech – which he proudly sent to Eisenhower – comparing Eisenhower with George

---

[24] Milton Eisenhower speech, "The Spiritual Foundations of Democracy," March 10, 1954, Pittsburgh, PA; MSE Collection, Box 5, Folder: 1954 [Speeches, Articles]; DDE Papers. Emphasis original.

[25] November 19, 1955 letter from Luce to Eisenhower, with copy of Luce speech "The Public Philosophy and the Spirit of Geneva"; November 22, 1955 letter from Eisenhower to Luce; Ann Whitman File, Administration Series, Box 25, Folder: Luce, Henry; DDE Papers.

Washington, especially their common faith. After cataloguing Washington's many virtues, Wallace told his audience of Episcopalian church members that "America today is again led by a General with deep faith in God and a strong sense of America's destiny in a world of great perils. Never has America been so feared, hated and envied by godless men with greedy eyes."[26] Curiously, it seems to have been Soviet communism's atheism that had come to disturb Wallace most.

As pervasive as this civil religion may have been, Eisenhower never quite figured out just how far he could extend it. Almost as revealing as his role as "pastor to the nation" are some of the religious initiatives that he did not pursue, for reasons both ideological and practical. Just as the Cold War created unprecedented challenges and shifting alliances, so also did the civil religion that America developed in response possess its own complications. For example, Congressman Herbert Zelenko wrote Eisenhower suggesting that since "our most effective skirmishes with atheistic communism have been won by men of the cloth of every religion," the president ought to convene a meeting for world religious leaders "to organize a collective security pact for the protection of the souls of mankind." In a response that Harry Truman and Myron Taylor would have appreciated, Eisenhower aide Wilton Persons wrote that while the president agreed "that the greatest power against communism is spiritual force and a belief in God," such a convocation would not be practicable because "Governmental action in this area would be construed by many as an invasion of the prerogatives of the faiths."[27]

Not that Eisenhower gave up entirely. With a new pope came a new opportunity for a religious alliance against communism, or so it seemed in January 1959 after John XXIII succeeded Pius XII as Bishop of Rome. In a column Eisenhower said "interested me greatly," Cyrus Sulzberger of the *New York Times* described the new pope's plan to convene an ecumenical council to promote unity among Christendom's divided branches. Sulzberger contrasted this with Truman and Taylor's failed initiative, a failure that he attributed in part to Pius XII's insistence on the Catholic prerogative as the "only true church." Now, "even a slight success would have much political importance. For if all those who believe in divinity can in any way be drawn together, communism will suffer a serious setback." After reading the column, Eisenhower wrote to Sulzberger that if all religious leaders could be convened to

---

[26] February 19, 1957 letter from Wallace to Eisenhower, with copy of speech enclosed on "George Washington as a Statesman and Religious Man"; February 22, 1957 letter from Eisenhower to Wallace; Ann Whitman File, Name Series, Box 33, Folder: Wallace; DDE Papers.

[27] May 29, 1957 letter from Zelenko to Eisenhower; June 12, 1957 letter from Persons to Zelenko; OF, Box 660, Folder: 133-E-1; DDE Papers.

direct their attentions to a single main point – namely that of insisting
upon the supremacy of spiritual values and thus developing clear kinship
among themselves – there would develop a more unified and stronger purpose among free peoples to yield no single inch or advantage to atheistic
communism.... Such a declaration, I believe, would do much to alert us to
the threat posed by Communist imperialism, and to unite us better in the
search for peace.

Eisenhower's experience with some religious leaders tempered his hopes. "My
fear would be that zealots would introduce so many questions and argumen-
tative subjects into a convocation of such a kind that most of the discussion
would revolve around relatively unimportant points." Many religious leaders
would no doubt differ with the president, and hold that their serious differences over the nature of God and man were hardly "relatively unimportant."
But the president's perspective was clear: the Soviet peril demanded a new set
of priorities in interfaith relations.[28]

He continued to ponder what tangible steps he might take in this regard.
Two months before reading of the new pope's plans, Eisenhower had written
to his former speechwriter Emmet Hughes, now returned to working for
Luce at Time-Life, Inc. The president informed Hughes that he had been
pondering "an attempt to center greater attention in our country, and so
far as possible the free world, on the predominant influence of spiritual
values in our lives, and to do this in some rather well organized way so as
to get maximum effect." One specific step Eisenhower mentioned involved
gathering support and involvement from the heads of state in other free
countries. He did not want to frame this initiative only "in the terms of the
freedom-communist struggle," but argued that "it should be an effort of the
affirmative kind because of a conviction that we have been woefully neglecting
the field in which the democracies and, indeed, all civilizations based upon a
religious faith, should be particularly strong.... We have too much thought
of bombs and machines and gadgets as the arsenal of our national and cultural
strength." Eisenhower said he had "a long conversation" with Dulles about
the proposal, who in turn had directed the State Department staff to prepare
a memorandum on it. And he asked Hughes for his input as well. Despite
his uncertainty about the details, Eisenhower concluded "the only thing I am

---

[28] Cyrus L. Sulzberger, "The Political Implications of Pope John's Move," *New York Times*, 28
January 1959; January 31, 1959 letter from Eisenhower to Sulzberger. Note that Eisenhower also
sent a shorter letter expressing similar sentiments to NYT publisher Arthur Hays Sulzberger;
see January 28, 1959 letter from Eisenhower to Arthur Sulzberger; Ann Whitman File, DDE
Diary Series, Box 38, Folder: DDE Dictation – January 1959; DDE Papers.

completely sure of... [is that] sometime, somewhere, and by someone the effort *must* be made."[29]

Two things stand out about Eisenhower's letter to Hughes. First, he continued to sound the same themes from almost seven years before, when he had written to Drew Pearson about the primacy of "spiritual values" in the Cold War conflict, and had told a New York press conference about the necessity of religion for democracy. Second, that he continued to lament the free world's focus on "material values" indicated his frustration over his inability as president to achieve more changes in this area. Perhaps Eisenhower had come to share a frequent complaint from clergy for almost 2,000 years: no matter what is said from the pulpit, the congregation does not always respond.

Eisenhower did not confine these hopes to his own advisors and cabinet. A week after writing to Hughes, he pressed his case in a private meeting with Queen Frederika of Greece. He shared with her his desire to persuade all allied governments to focus on "spiritual values," on speaking of "the dignity of man rather than of man as a fixture of the state." While assuring the Queen of his continued commitment to maintaining a strong military presence in Europe, he told her he "wants to see whatever usefulness [there is] in a real crusade, to get an understanding of the spiritual values adopted."[30]

Yet as with Truman and Taylor's initiative, nothing seems to have come of this one either. A few months later, the White House allowed *Life* magazine to publish Eisenhower's letter to Hughes, along with numerous other letters the president had written, for a profile on his personal correspondence. Noticing the letter in *Life*, the prestigious Chicago Sunday Evening Club invited Eisenhower to develop his ideas in an address in their religious lecture series – whose previous speakers that year had included Walter Judd, Martin Luther King, Jr., Abraham Joshua Heschel, and Paul Tillich. Eisenhower declined the invitation, with the reason that "I simply do not see where I could salvage the time to prepare such an address. I could not possibly delegate any part of it to anyone else and, even though the idea has been in my mind for some time, my thoughts are far from crystallized."[31] Though it may have

[29] November 20, 1958 letter from Eisenhower to Hughes; Ann Whitman File, DDE Diary Series, Box 37, Folder: DDE Dictation, November 1958; DDE Papers. The memo Dulles had prepared for Eisenhower on the subject could not be found in either the Dulles Papers or the Eisenhower Papers.

[30] Transcript of Eisenhower's December 9, 1958 meeting with Queen Frederika, "STRICTLY OFF RECORD"; Ann Whitman file, DDE Diary Series, Box 38, Folder: Staff Notes – December 1958; DDE Papers.

[31] "The Private Letters of the President," *Life*, 20 November 1958, 104. April 9, 1959 letter from Chicago Sunday Evening Club to Eisenhower; April 11, 1959 letter from Eisenhower to Fred Gurley; CF, PPF, Box 490, Folder: 1-EE Illinois 1959; DDE Papers.

been out of politeness, Eisenhower's response was rather disingenuous. The president's letter proposing the idea had been addressed to one of his favorite speechwriters, after all, so "delegation" was hardly out of the question. And he certainly had regarded his thoughts as developed enough to discuss them with the Queen of Greece. More likely, Eisenhower had simply grown frustrated with the complications of his proposal, and decided to set it aside.

Failing to spark a worldwide spiritual revival, he found it easier to help build a local church. The complications that had crippled his efforts to forge a religious coalition against communism did not discourage him from helping Elson construct a new sanctuary for National Presbyterian Church, as the current building in downtown Washington had outgrown its utility. Eisenhower also saw this as another opportunity to bolster his Cold War agenda. He embraced the project with vigor and verve, teaming with Henry Luce to contact wealthy donors, holding fund-raising dinners at the White House, and endorsing the project in a financial appeal brochure. Besides Luce, J. Howard Pew and his brother Joe, and Eisenhower friends Sid Richardson and George Allen all contributed substantial sums of money towards the projected $20 million project.[32] Eisenhower even contacted Secretary of the Navy Thomas Gates to inquire if the Navy would sell a portion of its Naval Observatory property – some of the most desirable real estate in Washington, and current site of the Vice-Presidential mansion – to the church for a site to build its new sanctuary. After Secretary Gates somewhat sheepishly informed his boss that the Navy "for valid technical reasons" did not want to part with its observatory land, the church finally found an adequate plot in Northwest Washington.[33]

Shortly thereafter, Eisenhower appeared at a meeting with church leaders and donors to review the proposed architectural plans. Invited to give some impromptu remarks, which were soon transcribed and widely circulated by the White House and the media, he connected the new church building with the Cold War, particularly the unfavorable gap between Soviet and American technology apparently revealed by Sputnik. "We hear a lot of talk about the accomplishments of atheistic communism," he began, but then noted how

---

[32] See January 26, 1957 letter from Luce to Eisenhower; January 29, 1957 letter from Eisenhower to Luce; February 20, 1957 letter from Luce to Eisenhower; April 17, 1957 letter from Luce to Eisenhower; Undated (April 1957) letter from Eisenhower to Luce, enclosing endorsement for brochure; April 29, 1957 letter from Luce to Eisenhower; Ann Whitman File, Administrative Series, Box 25, Folder: Luce, Henry; August 9, 1957 memorandum on Eisenhower meeting with Elson; August 9, 1957 letter from Eisenhower to Luce; Ann Whitman File, DDE Diary Series, Box 26, Folder: August 1957 – DDE Dictation; DDE Papers.

[33] January 15, 1959 letter from Eisenhower to Gates; February 27, 1959 letter from Gates to Eisenhower; April 27, 1959 letter from Luce to Eisenhower; April 30, 1959 letter from Eisenhower to Luce; OF, Box 736, Folder: 144-B-1-A; DDE Papers.

the "strength and beauty" of the church blueprint "contrasts sharply with some of the material that comes off the drawing boards of the communists. In Moscow they seem to worship only the achievements of science and glorify their moon searching rockets." Americans, in contrast, "put our faith in love of God and neighbor. This faith provides the indispensable basis for true self-government; on it is based our dedication to the rights and dignity of man."[34] Eisenhower had received much criticism in the wake of Sputnik, out of fears that Soviet military and scientific technology was surpassing that of America, and the purported "missile gap" would become a major issue in the upcoming 1960 presidential campaign. Partly out of defensiveness for his own fiscal austerity, and partly out of personal conviction, Eisenhower returned to a favorite theme. American strength should not be measured against Soviet strength only in material and scientific terms, but also by spiritual standards. Here, America reigned supreme.

III

For all of its enthusiasm about religion as a powerful instrument to undermine communism around the world, the Eisenhower Administration did not always fully understand the religious people in its own backyard. The Administration's efforts to promote "spiritual values" coincided with the desire of evangelicals to achieve mainstream recognition – and to distinguish themselves from their embarrassing fundamentalist relatives. The Administration did not always recognize this difference, however, and found evangelicals confusing. To Eisenhower's staff, it seemed that on the one hand, their rather strident, narrow theology was matched by an equally narrow constituency; on the other hand, they appeared reliably patriotic, and anticommunist – and besides, they had Billy Graham, whom the president considered such a nice man, and a good friend.

So it was that when the National Association of Evangelicals (NAE) wrote Eisenhower in 1953 thanking him for his inaugural prayer and his "simple, unabashed public stand" of belief in God, and asking Eisenhower to sign the NAE's "Declaration of Freedom" in honor of the approaching July 4th, the Administration did not know quite what to do. White House aides contacted the Library of Congress to find out who exactly these evangelicals were. After hearing back from the Library's diligent researchers, a White House

---

[34] January 26, 1960 letter from Thelma Livingston to Frederic Fox, with transcript of Eisenhower remarks, and copy of article from *Time*, 18 January 1960, 14; OF, Box 736, Folder: 144-B-1-A; DDE Papers.

staff member reported that the NAE comprised "bible-believing Christians" numbering some 10 million, and that while organizationally it somewhat resembled the National Council of Churches (NCC), the NAE differed "in that it does not include 'liberal' or 'modern' Christians – only 'fundamentalists'." However, "the organization is considered to be thoroughly reputable and has some of the finest preachers in the country included in its membership."[35] This assessment from 1953 mirrors later evaluations by the Administration's Frederic Fox, who described the NAE to inquiring White House colleagues as, variously, "a good group but considerably smaller than the National Council of Churches," and "a highly determined group of Biblical Fundamentalists."[36]

If the Eisenhower White House was lukewarm towards evangelicals, it was downright cold to fundamentalists. Not that the fundamentalists did much to help their cause. In 1958, the American Council of Christian Churches (ACCC), a fundamentalist organization formed by Carl McIntire to oppose the NCC, passed resolutions denouncing Eisenhower for appearing at a mass in Washington for Pope Pius XII, and for appearing at a dedication ceremony for a new NCC building in New York.[37] Just a few weeks later, the ACCC's international division, known as the International Council of Christian Churches (ICCC), rather audaciously requested that Eisenhower meet with an ACCC delegation, a request soon amended to include meeting with five Chinese Christians who had ostensibly fled communist persecution in their native land and wanted to present the president with a silver shield to express appreciation from "the people of Free China . . . for the unswerving stand the United States has taken on their behalf." This initiated a bewildering, almost comic exchange of letters, telegrams, phone calls, and memos over the next ten months, as the White House steadfastly refused the meeting, and the ACCC/ICCC just as tenaciously refused to drop the subject. A few internal, confidential State Department and White House memos were candid, and revealing. "Extreme caution should be exercised in dealing with leaders of [the ICCC] . . . this organization does not command the confidence of other religious councils and associations." Frederic Fox described the group as "about 230,000 humorless souls" and noted "STATE is dead set against this outfit. Its leader, Dr. McIntire, is a discredited Presbyterian minister with a

[35] April 10, 1953 letter from Clyde Taylor to Eisenhower; April 10, 1953 letter from Clyde Taylor to Thomas Stephens; May 19, 1953 White House Memorandum on NAE; CF, PPF, Box 830, Folder: 47 National Association of Evangelicals; DDE Papers.

[36] January 7, 1958 memo from Fox to Bob Gray; March 10, 1959 memo from Fox to Tom Stephens; CF, PPF, Box 830, Folder: National Association of Evangelicals; DDE Papers.

[37] American Council of Christian Churches press release, October 30, 1958; OF, Box 736, Folder: OF 144B; DDE Papers.

big log in one eye and a beam on his shoulder." Internal deliberations aside, the official White House line to the ICCC availed of the perennial excuse: "scheduling complications." This only caused more and more frustration to the ICCC, which responded with several sputtering letters complaining that Eisenhower's schedule somehow allowed him time for meetings with leaders from the NCC, NAE, and the Greek Orthodox and Methodist Churches.[38] The real meaning was clear enough: as anticommunist as they may have been, American fundamentalists were too strident, too divisive, and too marginal to be included in the Eisenhower Administration's Cold War civil religious program.

Having by this time himself been virtually excommunicated by most fundamentalists, Billy Graham symbolized not only the growing divide between evangelicals and fundamentalists, but also the growing acceptance of evangelicals by the White House.[39] As evangelicalism's foremost representative, Graham found much favor in the Oval Office. Even before developing his relationship with Dulles, Graham had taken an interest in Eisenhower's life, both spiritually and politically. The two had first met in early 1952, when after exchanging letters, their mutual friend Sid Richardson had arranged for Graham to travel to France and visit with General Eisenhower at the Supreme Headquarters of the Allied Powers in Europe (SHAPE). Richardson, a crafty Texas oil baron, had his own designs. He enlisted Graham in the campaign to urge Eisenhower to run for president. Graham, though as always disavowing partisanship, happily observed that "the American people have come to the point where they want a man with honesty, integrity, and spiritual power. I believe [Eisenhower] has it." Meeting with Eisenhower, the evangelist added his voice to the chorus of those urging the General to run. Eisenhower, in turn, took a significant interest in Graham, inviting him to spend a few days together at a Denver hotel during the campaign. Cautious to avoid an official endorsement of Eisenhower, Graham gladly offered personal spiritual counsel in addition to his own insights into religious and moral conditions in the

---

[38] March 2, 1959 letter from Ronn Spargur to Frederic Fox; March 10, 1959 memo from Fox to John Calhoun; March 17, 1959 memo from John Calhoun to Fox and General Andrew Goodpaster; March 13, 1959 State Department memo on ICCC/ACCC, marked "Limited Official Use"; March 18, 1959 letter from Fox to Spargur; April 8, 1959 letter from Spargur to Wilton Persons; April 9, 1959 and May 8, 1959 notes from Fox to Ferne Hudson and Helen Colle; May 7, 1959 letter from Spargur to Fox; September 9, 1959 letter from Fox to Spargur; September 15, 1959 letter from Spargur to Fox; Also included in file, "Three Oriental Protestants Here to Oppose Red China," *New York Times*, 18 March 1959; OF Box 736, Folder: OF 144B; DDE Papers.

[39] For more on Graham during this time, particularly his break with fundamentalism and his growing national prominence, see Martin, 210–224, and Silk, 54–69, 101–107.

country.[40] Graham also gave Eisenhower a Bible, annotated by Graham with margin notes and highlighted passages, which the president would keep by his bedside throughout his years at the White House.[41]

James Hagerty, Eisenhower's press secretary, described Graham and Eisenhower as "very close," and recalled that Eisenhower invited the evangelist to the White House on just about every occasion that he visited Washington.[42] The two also carried on a regular correspondence. Eisenhower came to see Graham as an agent of spiritual and moral renewal at home and an ambassador for American goodwill abroad. Graham gladly reinforced this assessment; following his widely acclaimed evangelistic crusade in England in 1954, he reported to the president that both the American Ambassador and the British Home Secretary had praised Graham as the single most effective agent of improved Anglo–American relations since the war.[43] In 1957, Eisenhower congratulated Graham on the success of his crusade meetings in New York, and observed that "I have always agreed with you that human beings – especially Americans – do have an underlying spiritual hunger which from time to time manifests itself markedly. I believe that we are now experiencing such a period."[44] Graham, for his part, realized the potency of a presidential endorsement to enhance his domestic and international cachet. At the outset of a five-month evangelistic campaign in Australia in 1959, Graham asked Eisenhower for a letter of greeting to the Australians, because "it would help more than anything I can think of to intensify the Australian friendship for America." Graham closed with characteristically effusive praise: "You are a courageous, honest, and faithful President. I believe that history will say that you were among our greatest."[45]

Eisenhower's response reveals some of the aforementioned constraints he felt in religious matters. While he told Graham "you may, of course, convey to the citizens of Australia the good wishes of all American citizens, including myself," Eisenhower also added a note of caution. "You recognize, of course, that if anything further were said, you might give the impression that your efforts had some official connection with our government. I might add privately that I have had to lean over backward, in the last six years, to draw a

[40] Martin, 146–149 and Graham, 188–192.
[41] Nancy Gibbs and Michael Duffy, *The Preacher and the Presidents: Billy Graham in the White House* (New York: Center Street 2007), 39.
[42] James Hagerty oral interview, April 17, 1968, New York City. Conducted by Ed Edwin. DDE Papers, Dwight D. Eisenhower Oral History Project. See also Martin, 207–208.
[43] Martin, 185.
[44] August 9, 1957 letter from Eisenhower to Graham; Ann Whitman File, DDE Diary Series, Box 26, Folder: August 1957 – DDE Dictation; DDE Papers.
[45] February 19, 1959 letter from Graham to Eisenhower; OF, Box 868, Folder: 183-A; DDE Papers.

distinction between my official position and myself as a private individual."
Both Graham and Eisenhower continually chafed against the cords of propri-
ety and even legality in how far their respective offices would permit them to
support each other. While still disclaiming any official endorsement, Graham
assured Eisenhower after the 1956 Republican convention that "I shall do all
in my power during the coming campaign to gain friends and supporters
for your cause." As the generally sympathetic Graham biographer William
Martin describes it, while in public Graham claimed his apolitical neutrality,
"in private he continued to act like a Republican strategist."[46]

Graham's foreign ministry sometimes rendered him a foreign minister, of
a sort. Following a 1960 evangelistic campaign throughout Africa, he spent
several hours at the White House giving a briefing to Eisenhower, Nixon,
Secretary of State Christian Herter, and several other top aides on conditions
throughout the continent, capped off by Graham's recommendation that
Eisenhower travel to Nigeria soon to forestall a slide towards communism.
Nor did Graham hesitate to offer his input to Eisenhower on relations with
the Soviets. In 1959, no doubt mindful of the current confrontation prompted
by Kruschev's threat to close access to West Berlin, Graham wrote:

> I am delighted that you are standing up to the Russians! I think that it is time
> we called their bluff. We cannot afford to allow them to continue nibbling
> at the Western World until we are too weak to withstand. They must be
> stopped now. Please do not allow extreme Liberal churchmen to advise you
> that war is the ultimate evil. There is absolutely no foundation in the Bible
> for such a Pacifist view. The Scripture teaches that good government is from
> God. When we stand on the side of moral justice we can be assured that God
> is with us ... [quotes Joshua 1:9] Take this as your Biblical promise as you
> prepare for a showdown.[47]

Eisenhower certainly welcomed such encouragement from his good friend,
especially since, unlike most pronouncements from mainline Protestant

---

[46] March 2, 1959 letter from Eisenhower to Graham; March 16, 1959 letter from Graham to
Eisenhower, and enclosed clippings from Australian newspapers; OF, Box 868, Folder: 183-A;
DDE Papers. Also Martin, 209, 244. Note that Eisenhower wrote his March, 1959 letter at
about the same time that he shelved his plans to unite America's world allies in a spiritual
initiative against communism. Note also that, as widely reported in the Australian media,
Graham read Eisenhower's letter to a gathering of almost 144,000 Australians in Melbourne,
the largest crowd to which he had ever preached, and reportedly the largest gathering for a
single event in Australian history.
[47] March 16, 1959 letter from Graham to Eisenhower; OF, Box 868, Folder: 183-A; DDE Papers.
Also Martin, 269.

organizations, Graham's views on national security supported the Administration's positions. On a political level, the president knew that the endorsement of a prominent clergyman like Graham could only strengthen his own position with the American people. On a personal level, Eisenhower, wanting to think of himself as a man of faith who followed the "Christian" position, no doubt found spiritual comfort in the evangelist's words.

Political and diplomatic calculations notwithstanding, Eisenhower relied on Graham as a spiritual counselor, even away from the public limelight. While on vacation at his Gettysburg farm in 1955, a crisis of faith seized the president. He had his staff locate Graham and drive him immediately to Eisenhower's home. The president unburdened himself and his spiritual questions to Graham, who stayed well beyond his allotted schedule in reassuring Eisenhower of the Christian gospel message. Eisenhower then had one of his presidential airplanes urgently fly Graham to Charlotte, lest he miss an evangelistic meeting he was scheduled to address that night. Years later, shortly before Eisenhower died, he summoned Graham once again to his hospital bedside and asked, "Billy, you've told me how to be sure my sins are forgiven and that I'm going to heaven. Would you tell me again?"[48] The old Cold Warrior may have enlisted generic "faith" and broad "spiritual values" in his diplomacy, but in his own twilight days, he turned to traditional Protestant evangelicalism for solace.

IV

In 1953, on taking office in hopes of using his religious vision to strengthen America's Cold War fibers, Eisenhower encountered a significant problem. He could not find a major national religious organization able and willing to cooperate in promoting this campaign. Mainline Protestantism, exemplified by the National Council of Churches, faced growing division within its own ranks over questions of theology and politics, as a less anticommunist liberalism became more and more predominant. Evangelicalism, though politically reliable enough, lacked the institutional and cultural stature to be a major influence. And theologically, evangelicalism would be resistant to Eisenhower's hopes to blur confessional lines and promote close cooperation with mainline Protestants, let alone Catholics and Jews. Fundamentalist organizations – seen as obscurantist, divisive, and hopelessly marginal – were not even considered. Nor would they have wanted to be.

Just two months after Eisenhower's inauguration, Elson approached him with an idea that soon grew into a significant new organization. In light of

---

[48] Graham, 203–206.

the president's convictions, Elson proposed convening a "White House Conference on Moral and Spiritual Recovery," whose purposes would include proclaiming "an official desire on the part of government to achieve the moral and spiritual rehabilitation of our nation" and "inculcating basic American convictions within our people in order to strengthen character and launch a spiritual counter-offensive to Communism." Eisenhower responded enthusiastically, though his aides, particularly Chief of Staff Sherman Adams, cautioned that such an event would be more effective if it began "where it belongs, namely, with the American clergy." Adams offered Elson the use of a White House staff assistant, "officially or unofficially as you prefer," for help with logistics, and promised that once the project gained momentum, Eisenhower would extend more visible support. This gave Elson the green light that he needed. He quickly enlisted his friend and colleague Charles Wesley Lowry, and together they founded what became the Foundation for Religious Action in the Social and Civil Order (FRASCO).[49]

One of the more curious and colorful figures of the day, Lowry brought tremendous energy and enthusiasm to the new organization. He became its chairman and executive director, while Elson, still attending to his primary duties as senior pastor of National Presbyterian, became co-chairman. A native of Oklahoma, Lowry had earned his doctorate at Oxford, a degree that gave him considerable pride throughout his life, to judge by its prominence in his letterhead and correspondence. After two decades as a theology professor and Episcopalian minister, Lowry's biographical profile noted that in 1953 he resigned from his rectorate "to devote full time as a prophetic voice in the crusade against Communism." He was just the sort of clergyman that Eisenhower and Elson had been looking for. Stern, dour, indefatigable, dogmatic though given to flashes of brilliance, Lowry had a penchant for grand dialectical flourishes in the Niebuhrian tradition, albeit without Niebuhr's nuance or profundity. If John Foster Dulles had followed his mother's wishes and become a clergyman, he might well have closely resembled Lowry. In short, Lowry married a penchant for ideas with a nose for publicity and a zeal for battle. Allied with Elson's more irenic disposition and access to Eisenhower, they made an intriguing team.[50]

[49] July 7, 1953 letter from Elson to Eisenhower; November 25, 1953 letter from Elson to Sherman Adams, with attached memo; December 23, 1953 letter from Adams to Elson; OF, Box 738, Folder: 144-G-1; DDE Papers. Note also that in choosing a name for their organization, Elson and Lowry seemed to share mainline Protestantism's predilection for verbosity.

[50] Lowry biographical sheet; Evangelical Foreign Missions Association Collection (hereinafter EFMA), Box 68, Folder 11; Billy Graham Center Archives, Wheaton, IL (hereinafter BGCA); March 23, 1954 letter from Lowry to Sherman Adams, and enclosed brochure; OF, Box 738, Folder: 144-G-1; DDE Papers.

Lowry and Elson moved ahead with dispatch. Within a few months, they had lined up an impressive advisory board, including figures such as Herbert Hoover, Billy Graham, Norman Vincent Peale, former Psychological Strategy Board director (and Eisenhower's future National Security Advisor) Gordon Gray, and prominent Rabbi Norman Gerstenfeld. Elson and Lowry also received commitments of support from Bishop Fulton J. Sheen and Harold Ockenga. Pleased with this progress, Eisenhower sent a congratulatory letter, declaring that "our government has logically been described as a translation into the political field of a deeply held religious faith." He also gave permission for his letter to be publicized to generate further support for FRASCO. Backed by this endorsement, along with financial support from the Rockefeller family, Elson and Lowry announced to the world their organization and its core purposes: "to pin-point the religious issue in the crisis of our time . . . to unite all believers in God in the struggle between the free world and atheistic communism which aims to destroy both religion and liberty," and "to overthrow the big lie by the bigger Truth."[51]

Besides organizing FRASCO's upcoming national conference, Lowry immediately began working on more covert initiatives to undermine communism at home and abroad. He sent to Vice-President Richard Nixon and National Security Advisor Robert Cutler copies of an article by prominent American communist William Z. Foster advocating "co-existence" with the Soviet Union, along with the suggestion that Nixon "could make good campaign use" of it in the upcoming mid-term elections. Lowry also warned that the "unaltering world strategy of International Communism" included defeating Eisenhower and the Republicans, laying "the foundations for a farmer-labor party to replace after 1956 the Democratic party" and advancing "faith in the peaceful co-existence of Communism and Capitalism." Cutler, outraged by the article, forwarded it to FBI Director J. Edgar Hoover, asking "how this type of domestic propaganda should be dealt with."[52]

Recently declassified documents reveal that in 1954 Lowry engaged in detailed discussions with Eisenhower Administration officials over emergency measures to "use the religious factor to intensify local anti-communism" in

---

[51]   March 5, 1954 and March 8, 1954 memos from Elson and Lowry to Adams; April 12, 1954 letter from Elson to Eisenhower; April 15, 1954 memo from Adams to Eisenhower; April 17, 1954 letter from Eisenhower to Elson; May 11, 1954 letter from Elson to Adams; May 25, 1954 letter from Lowry to Eisenhower; June 10, 1954 FRASCO press release; OF, Box 738, Folder: 144-G-1; DDE Papers.

[52]   October 4, 1954 letter from Cutler to Lowry; October 4, 1954 letter from Cutler to Hoover, October 8, 1954 letter from Lowry to Cutler; WHCF, Confidential File, Subject Series, Box 62, Folder: Russia (5); DDE Papers.

Vietnam. Eisenhower's Operations Control Board (OCB), which coordinated covert intelligence and propaganda activities, considered funding FRASCO to send two representatives, including a Catholic priest, on a secret mission to Vietnam to generate "a spiritual offensive movement directed against Communism and for a new democratic order in which the active agents will be native Buddhists, Cao-Daiists, Catholics, and other men and women of conviction." This proposal drew the attention of Nixon, who forwarded it to former CIA director and current Under Secretary of State Walter Bedell Smith. Telling Smith of his "deep and continuing interest in the peoples of Southeast Asia" and his hope of convincing them "that their ideals and aspirations" are common with those of America, Nixon assured Smith of his "high regard for and considerable confidence in Dr. Lowry" and his strong endorsement of the proposal. Unfortunately other documents related to this proposal, particularly on the question of whether or not it was actually implemented, have not yet been declassified. Nevertheless, this provides a revealing window into FRASCO's cooperation with the Administration, Nixon's very early interest in Vietnam, and the ideological uses of religion against communism.[53]

Cloak and dagger intrigue aside, Lowry and Elson's main focus remained FRASCO's upcoming November conference. Eisenhower agreed to deliver a keynote address at the conference, thus boosting its profile immeasurably. But the White House remained leery of blurring the boundaries between religion and politics too overtly, and still tried to keep its organizational distance. It insisted, for instance, that the conference be held at a local hotel instead of in the White House's Executive Office Building, as Elson and Lowry wished. This reticence did not prevent one White House official from privately describing the conference as providing "excellent material for propaganda" for United States Information Agency (USIA) broadcasts.[54] As indeed it did; the USIA recorded the entire conference, so that, as Elson informed the White House, "the most salient and persuasive features may be exported abroad." Elson made clear the conference's purposes in a letter to Eisenhower. "We have worked toward and planned for a consolidation of the religious forces of the nation in support of your spiritual objectives."[55] Here was a candid,

---

[53] September 10, 1954 letter from Nixon to Walter Bedell Smith, and attached proposal; White House Office Collection (WHO), NSC Staff File, OCB Central File Series, Box 2, Folder: OCB 000.3 File #1(1); DDE Papers.

[54] July 15, 1954 memo from Paul Stephens to Sherman Adams and Thomas Stephens; July 23, 1954 letter from Elson to Eisenhower; OF, Box 738, Folder: 144-G-1; DDE Papers.

[55] October 3, 1954 letter from Elson to Adams; October 3, 1954 letter from Elson to Eisenhower. See also September 29, 1954 letter from Lowry to Adams; OF, Box 738, Folder: 144-G-1; DDE Papers.

shorthand acknowledgement of a complex reality. The country's existing religious organizations, particularly Christian ones, were too divided, within themselves and from each other, to mount a unified religious campaign against communism. Rather than try to sift through such a spiritual morass, Eisenhower and his pastor just decided to form their own organization.

FRASCO made the deliberate decision to be interfaith, consistent with Eisenhower's own views on the social utility of religion. Updating the president on the planning, Elson noted proudly, "we are especially grateful for the active and generous support of the Roman Catholic hierarchy and men of substance from the Jewish faith, together with representative Protestants. At last we have the instrument for marshaling our spiritual forces and launching a spiritual counter-offensive of worldwide proportions."[56] In this regard, FRASCO, in its name and activities, tried to distinguish between what it did and did not intend. It gathered together "religious" people, for the purpose of "religious action," but only in the "social and civil order" – not in the churches and synagogues. Thus, as Catholic priest and FRASCO board member Fr. John Cronin reminded conference participants, FRASCO did not aim to "accomplish religious unity" or promote interfaith dialogue on matters of doctrine. Nor was it a forum for proselytizing. It expected religious leaders to maintain their doctrinal differences while joining together "in the social and civil order to combat Communism and secularism."[57] To some, these purposes were decidedly grandiose; to others, they were too limited.

Regardless, especially by the standards of the day, FRASCO's inaugural conference from November 8 to 10, 1954 presented a remarkable display of religious diversity, at least in the spirit of "Protestant, Catholic, and Jew." In this regard, attendees heard Jewish intellectual Will Herberg present a paper on "The Biblical Basis of American Democracy," in which he contended

---

[56] October 3, 1954 letter from Elson to Eisenhower; OF, Box 738, Folder: 144-G-1; DDE Papers.

[57] January 13, 1955 letter from Lowry to FRASCO members, enclosing summary of conference; See also FRASCO brochure, which disavows "discussions of dogma or church unity" as well as "evangelism with a view to making converts for any sect or doctrine"; OF, Box 738, Folder: 144-G-1; DDE Papers. Note that a FRASCO press release describing the participation of the "three major faiths" drew the ire of a representative of the Greek Orthodox Church in America, which sent the White House a telegram protesting that there were in fact "four major faiths [:] Catholic, Greek Orthodox, Protestant, Jewish" and that "seven million orthodox in America will not have three faiths slogan go unchallenged." Lowry apologetically informed the Orthodox that the American Bishop Athenagoras had been prominent at the conference, and had in turn brought encouragement and greetings from the Ecumenical Patriarch Athenagoras. This seemed to assuage any hurt or hard feelings. November 1, 1954 telegram from Peter Chumbris to Eisenhower; November 27, 1954 letter from Chumbris to Eisenhower; OF, Box 738, Folder: 144-G-1; DDE Papers.

"the conflict between Soviet Communism and the free world is a religious conflict . . . a struggle for the soul of modern man." As such, Americans must understand and affirm the roots of their political system grounded in the biblical tradition. The Bible teaches individual human dignity grounded in the divine image, the sinfulness of humanity and consequent need for restraints, and the final sovereignty of God over all political systems, necessitating both popular participation in government and also popular criticism of government.[58]

Theodore Hesburgh, president of the University of Notre Dame and a leading American Catholic, spoke on "The Necessity of Faith in a Living Democracy," and delivered the now standard theological critique of communism. Drawing on Pascal, Lincoln, Niebuhr, Jacques Maritain, and Charles Malik, he asserted that Marxism is "evil, first and foremost because it is atheistic," and "all of the other errors of Communism stem from this basic atheism." Moreover, it "sneers at [the] objective moral order" instituted by God, and replaces God with the State as the supreme authority over humanity. The free world's only hope, he averred, is not to have "faith in democracy," but rather to base its democracy on a transcendent religious faith.[59] Lowry, representing Protestantism, gave a third plenary address on "Democracy's Answer to the Marxian Dialectic." At times profound, at times pretentious, and at times barely intelligible, Lowry attempted to both explain and refute Marxist doctrine, concluding that "it is in a rekindled and resurrected democracy, child of a Jewish father and a Christian mother, and not in a totalitarian materialism, stripped of soul and mind, of mercy and pity, of freedom and love, that man's hope lies."[60] Besides these keynote addresses, the 250 political and religious leaders in attendance also heard from panelists or speakers such as Catholic intellectual John Courtney Murray, U.S. Senator Stuart Symington, Thomas Murray of the Atomic Energy Commission, and Dr. Elton Trueblood of USIA.

President Eisenhower, whose political and religious convictions provided FRASCO with its main impetus, delivered a plenary address. The importance of Eisenhower's speech, essentially the reiteration of his now familiar thoughts on the spiritual conflict between democracy and communism, paled in comparison with his mere presence, which significantly enhanced the conference's profile and legitimacy. He called for a renewed commitment

[58] Herberg, "The Biblical Basis of American Democracy," paper delivered at FRASCO conference, November 8–10, 1954, Washington DC; EFMA Collection, Box 68, Folder 11; BGCA.
[59] Hesburgh, "The Necessity of Faith in a Living Democracy," paper delivered at FRASCO conference, November 8–10, 1954; EFMA Collection, Box 68, Folder 11; BGCA.
[60] Lowry, "Democracy's Answer to the Marxian Dialectic," paper presented at FRASCO conference, November 8–10, Washington DC; EFMA Collection, Box 68, Folder 11; BGCA.

at home to the "spiritual foundation" of democracy, and a renewed vigor abroad to defending against the "tremendous attacks" of communist ideology. He concluded with a pithy summation of Eisenhower-era civil religion: FRASCO must show Americans how to "take the Bible in one hand and the Flag in the other, and march ahead." Putting the best possible gloss on the president's remarks, Lowry described them as "notable for their depth and simplicity."[61]

Intellectually, conference speakers engaged in a rather crude project of natural theology. Given their confessional differences, they attempted to distill, and to unite around, common theological principles accessible to all persons, irrespective of a particular religious tradition or the need for particular revelation from a divine source. Natural theology can travel only a short journey, as it soon bumps up against serious and substantive theological distinctions and divisions between communions. Yet Eisenhower and FRASCO seemed quite happy with this first endeavor, as the few religious principles they did profess together were more than enough to draw a sharp contrast with communism. To keep the lines of containment clear and precise, Eisenhower knew he needed to define the distinctions between the United States and the Soviet Union not only in political and economic terms, but also – and perhaps especially – in spiritual terms.

Their confidence bolstered by the success of their first conference, Lowry and Elson moved ahead. Future plans for FRASCO included sponsoring a series of television broadcasts of panel discussions on faith and foreign policy, symposia on university campuses, and of course another conference. They announced that their 1955 gathering would center on the theme of "Civilization and Religion."[62] Such a broad topic merited a broad participation, and Lowry and Elson succeeded in securing a remarkable array of leaders. Religiously, besides the now customary Protestant, Catholic, Orthodox, and Jewish voices, representatives of the Buddhist, Muslim, and Hindu faiths were also invited, all affirming their common allegiance to "spiritual values" and opposition to communist materialism. Economically, leaders from the U.S. Chamber of Commerce, major corporations, and the Congress of Industrial Organizations all spoke, together affirming that business and labor united in affirming the shared "spiritual values" of America. Internationally, ambassadors or representatives from Israel, Egypt, India, and Pakistan all spoke

---

[61] Eisenhower, remarks at FRASCO conference, November 9, 1954, Washington DC; January 13, 1955 letter from Lowry to FRASCO members, enclosing conference summary; OF, Box 738, Folder: 144-G-1; DDE Papers.

[62] 1955 FRASCO brochure; OF, Box 738, Folder: 144-G-1; DDE Papers.

(West Germany's Chancellor Konrad Adenauer, who had hoped to give a keynote address, unfortunately had to send his regrets). Politically, the Eisenhower Administration was again well represented. The president's recent heart attack prevented his attendance, but he sent Vice-President Nixon to speak in his stead, in addition to Admiral Arthur Radford, Chairman of the Joint Chiefs of Staff, who spoke on "The Mind and the Spirit in National Security" and Lewis Strauss, Chairman of the Atomic Energy Commission, who spoke on "Spiritual Factors in National Security."[63]

Though little noticed then or since, in a way the conference participants also accomplished what President Truman and Myron Taylor had worked towards so hard and for so long, though in vain. The conference issued a statement on behalf of the different religious faiths against communism and for world peace. To be sure, though most major world religions were represented, these participants were not the authoritative leaders of their faiths. And the fact that the statement did not produce a dramatic shift in international consciousness may indicate the limits of such an endeavor, despite Truman and Taylor's grand hopes or Eisenhower's subsequent efforts to generate a more vigorous, visible coalition for "spiritual values." Nevertheless, the "conference message" unanimously approved by the participants still displayed a significant measure of unity and purpose. Calling for "a revival of faith in God and a fresh synthesis of faith and reason," the message renounced technological materialism as "a cardinal error of Marxism-Leninism, an error which we repel emphatically." The message then urged the leaders of the world's religions to work together "to bring about peace among men, unity and cooperation among nations. We issue this world-wide call, aware of the many differences of creed and worship among us, fully respectful of the rights and convictions of all men, yet fervent, in the name of God, our common Creator."[64] Despite years of dreams, negotiations, and effort, this seems as close as anyone came in the early Cold War years to producing a statement in the names of several religious

---

[63] September 22, 1955 letter from Lowry to Eisenhower; September 26, 1955 letter from Ann Whitman to Lowry; OF, Box 738, Folder: 144-G-1; October 25, 1955 letter from Elson to Eisenhower; CF, PPF, Box 913, Folder: 53-B-1 National Presbyterian Church; FRASCO brochure "Things You May Want to Remember From the Second National Conference on Spiritual Foundations," October 24–26, 1955; OF, Box 676, Folder: OF 133; DDE Papers.

[64] "Civilization and Religion Conference Message" in FRASCO brochure "Things You May Want to Remember From the Second National Conference on Spiritual Foundations," October 24–26, 1955; OF, Box 676, Folder: OF 133; DDE Papers. Note that the Buddhist representative, Ambassador R.S.S. Gunewardene of Ceylon, had to cancel his address to the conference because of the Geneva Foreign Ministers' Conference. Had he been present, it is not clear whether he would have signed the conference message, given the ambivalence of some Buddhists towards Western notions of "God."

faiths opposing communism. That in itself marks the FRASCO message as no mean achievement.

Statements and conferences alone could only accomplish so much, and lest it be accused of doing more "talk" than the "action" heralded by its name, FRASCO entered 1956 mindful of new initiatives. Lowry and John L. Sullivan, a FRASCO board member and Secretary of the Navy under Truman, proposed to Secretary of Defense Charles Wilson that FRASCO assist the Pentagon in "broadening and deepening... the meaning of Armed Forces Day and of the slogan 'Power for Peace'." Specifically, they suggested incorporating more spiritual language in the president's upcoming Armed Forces Day proclamation, encouraging American churches to pray for and honor members serving in the military, and enhancing the religious dimension in military ceremonies and proclamations. The Pentagon readily appreciated this proposal, and Eisenhower's proclamation reflected it, as he called for "participation by representatives of all religious faiths in [Armed Forces Day] ceremonies in order that the interdependence of our security and the deep and abiding religious faith of Americans may be recognized."[65]

Though Billy Graham was already a board member, FRASCO sought other ways to strengthen ties with evangelicals. To this end, Elson and Lowry contributed feature-length articles for *Christianity Today*; each in his typical fashion, Elson wrote on "Worship in the Life of the Nation" and Lowry on "Judgment on the Christian West."[66] Eager to do his part, Graham mailed a copy of Lowry's signature book *Communism and Christ* to every member of the U.S. Congress. Other major FRASCO initiatives of 1956 included organizing a "Freedom Rally" in Washington "on behalf of the Hungarians, Poles, and other Captive Peoples" and drafting an "Open Letter to Perplexed Communists." This letter, signed by more than sixty American leaders including clergy from the usual faiths, sought to exploit hints of communist misgivings in the wake of Josef Stalin's death in 1953. It urged communists "not to evade or silence these doubts and promptings of conscience" sparked by recent acknowledgements of Stalin's depredations, but instead "to admit that the sacrifices of a lifetime have procured not the heaven on earth you had expected from Communism, but a dictatorship of terror and slavery." The

---

[65] January 3, 1956 letter from Lowry and Sullivan to Charles Wilson; January 23, 1956 letter from Robert Tripp Ross to Lowry; "Excerpts from 1956 Armed Forces Day Proclamation"; NCC Papers, Record Group 4, Box 16, Folder 1; Presbyterian Historical Society, Philadelphia, PA (hereinafter PHS).

[66] Elson, "Worship in the Life of the Nation," *Christianity Today*, 12 November 1956, 10–11, 19; Lowry, "Judgment on the Christian West," *Christianity Today*, 7 January 1957, 17, 24–25.

USIA happily informed Lowry that it gave the letter "rather extensive dissemination overseas," including broadcasts in numerous languages by the Voice of America (VOA), Radio Free Europe, Radio Liberation, and publication in many European press outlets.[67] Among all religious organizations, FRASCO provided the Eisenhower Administration with the most fertile material for propaganda – just as it was intended.

Frustrated with lack of support for his Administration's foreign assistance programs, the president decided he needed to generate some domestic assistance. This was one area where, in Eisenhower's mind, the normally nettlesome NCC could actually be of genuine use. Meeting in 1957 with a delegation of NCC leaders, he asked for their help in raising awareness and enthusiasm about U.S. foreign aid programs. NCC president Eugene Carson Blake responded quite favorably, telling Eisenhower "we are mobilizing the concern of our churches for an improved, expanding, long-term program of foreign aid."[68] Later that year, Arthur Flemming, Eisenhower's friend and sometime Administration official, wrote on the same topic. Flemming reminded Eisenhower of remarks the president at one point had made spontaneously during a meeting with American business executives skeptical of foreign aid.

> You then made the point that we are not helping other peoples solely for the purpose of persuading them to join our military or our political alliance. You stated that we were helping other peoples because we believed in spiritual values to such an extent that we were willing to apply them to the practical situations of our day. You expressed the conviction that if we continued to follow such a policy, other peoples might be attracted to our spiritual values and might embrace them.

Flemming suggested that Eisenhower make such an appeal more broadly. "Many church people, for example, have not looked at our programs for assistance in this light.... When we are able to bring such people to the place where they see the relationship between the application of spiritual values and these programs, we are tapping a source of real power."[69]

---

[67] November 25, 1956 letter from Lowry to Eisenhower; OF, Box 738, Folder: OF 144-G-2; October 17, 1956 memo from William Elliott (Office of Defense Mobilization) to R.V. Mrozinski (OCB); WHO, NSC Staff, OCB Central File Series, Box 2, Folder: OCB 000.3 File #1(4); 1958 FRASCO brochures; OF, Box 890, Folder: OF 225 1958; DDE Papers. Also "Episcopal Leaders Join Others in Letter to 'Perplexed' Reds," *Episcopal Church News*, 2 September 1956, 10.

[68] April 4, 1957 memo from Gabriel Hauge to Ann Whitman; April 9, 1957 letter from Blake to Eisenhower; OF, Box 573, Folder: 116-B Foreign Aid; DDE Papers.

[69] December 20, 1957 letter from Flemming to Eisenhower; OF, Box 666, Folder: 133-L 1957; DDE Papers.

Eisenhower responded eagerly to Flemming's ideas. Admitting that the "spiritual values" angle had been neglected, the president suggested "perhaps we can use that approach more effectively than we have. Certainly I would like to enlist the confidence of the churchgoing people of the Middle and Far West in the programs that I believe to be so vitally important."[70] Two months later, Eisenhower oversaw just such a campaign. Supported by a White House appropriation of $25,000 and organized by Eric Johnston, President of the Motion Picture Association of America, on February 25, 1958, the White House sponsored a "Conference on Foreign Aspects of United States National Security." Designed to bolster popular and congressional support for foreign aid programs, the conference featured addresses by Eisenhower, Truman, John Foster and Allen Dulles, Dean Acheson, and Adlai Stevenson. It also made a decidedly spiritual appeal. An invocation by Lowry and a benediction by Episcopal Bishop Henry Knox Sherrill bracketed presentations by renowned Catholic Bishop Fulton J. Sheen, Rabbi Theodore Adams, and NCC leader Edwin Dahlberg on the religious imperatives behind foreign aid. Sheen, for example, called for "our belief in God" and "the dignity of the human person" to distinguish American financial assistance to impoverished nations from that offered by the materialistic Soviets. Adams, asserting that "the utilitarian motive of benevolence is not worthy of the United States," called on Americans of all religious persuasions to uphold "essential spiritual values in face of an unprecedented assault of materialist atheism" by sharing "our democratic faith as well as our material wealth." Following the conference, Lowry compiled and distributed a FRASCO publication containing testimonies from a wide array of religious leaders – including Norman Vincent Peale; Paul Rees, past president of the NAE; Congressman Brooks Hays, serving concurrently as President of the Southern Baptist Convention; as well as Orthodox priests, other Catholic leaders, and even a deceased Unitarian minister – all bearing witness to the importance of U.S. government Mutual Security Program of foreign assistance.[71]

FRASCO never attained the stature of organizations like the NCC or NAE, nor had it sought to. Born out of Eisenhower's desire to cultivate religious

---

[70] December 24, 1957 letter from Eisenhower to Flemming; OF, Box 666, Folder: 133-L 1957; DDE Papers.

[71] February 25, 1958 conference program; WHO, Office of the Staff Secretary, Subject Series, White House Subseries, Box 4, Folder: Eric Johnston; March 7, 1958 letter from Lowry to FRASCO members, including FRASCO brochure on foreign aid; June 26, 1958 FRASCO bulletin, including FRASCO brochure on foreign aid; OF, Box 676, Folder: OF 133-T; DDE Papers. Note that Eisenhower, still estranged from Truman, angrily rejected the possibility of appearing together with his predecessor. Instead, each spoke at different times. Neal, 291–292.

support for his Cold War foreign policy at home while using religion to undermine communism abroad, and out of Elson and Lowry's need for political support for their religious anticommunist campaign, FRASCO distilled a clear purpose, and then carried it out. It represented a tangible effort to put action behind Eisenhower's frequent words, to help the White House literally change the landscape of American religion by forging a new spiritual unity – of "Protestants, Catholics, Jews" – where only religious divisions had existed before. To the extent that Eisenhower succeeded – and to some measure he did – it is somewhat ironic that it took the political threat of Soviet communism to create a new religious unity among Americans. And yet, to the minds and souls of the faithful in America, Soviet communism posed much more than a political threat; it posed a religious threat as well. And a religious threat, of course, demanded a united religious response.

V

It was halfway around the globe that Eisenhower and Elson found their area of closest cooperation and greatest camaraderie. As the historic and geographic seat of three of the world's most formidable religions – Judaism, Christianity, Islam – the Middle East also demonstrated regularly that religion and politics were hardly separable. This applied not only to the peoples residing in the region, but also to the world leaders who ventured into the morass of Middle Eastern policy. Truman's Christian convictions had certainly exerted a considerable influence on his decision – against the vehement opposition of his own State Department, including Dean Acheson and George Marshall – to extend diplomatic recognition to Israel at the precarious moment of the new nation's birth.[72] In turn, Eisenhower's own faith, along with his relationship with his pastor, seems to have reinforced his own skepticism towards Israel and his relative affinity for Arab states. Here is a methodological curiosity. If religion is held to influence foreign policy, does this mean religion always would dictate similar policy positions? Not necessarily; for example, consider the dramatically opposing stances on China taken by American missionaries. Motivated by their missionary experience, both sides sought to "save China," and yet arrived at very different answers about what that meant. Likewise with the Middle East; while Truman and Eisenhower held similar religious

---

[72] For a persuasive argument in this regard, see Michael T. Benson, *Harry S. Truman and the Founding of Israel* (Westport, CT: Prager 1997). See also Michael Oren, *Power, Faith, and Fantasy: America in the Middle East, 1776 to the Present* (New York: W.W. Norton 2007), 483–502, for a portrayal of a more ambivalent Truman, whose religious convictions combine with political calculations to carry the day in his decision to support Israel.

convictions, and freely allowed that their faith informed their diplomacy, their faith did not always determine the same policies. In this case, it seems to have contributed to very different perspectives. This hardly means that religion did not matter – only that religion did not mean the same thing.

Early on in his Administration, Eisenhower made a deliberate effort to reach out to the Islamic world. In September 1953, the State Department, along with Administration propaganda specialists C.D. Jackson and Abbott Washburn, urged Eisenhower to meet with a delegation of fifteen Muslim leaders from various Middle Eastern nations. "In view of the President's deep convictions regarding the spiritual foundations of our democracy," the meeting would be especially relevant, argued Washburn. "The hoped-for result is that the Muslims will be impressed with the moral and spiritual strength of America." Thus persuaded, the Christian president took the unusual – and perhaps unprecedented – step of meeting with the Muslim leaders.[73] Mindful of Soviet attempts to make inroads in the Middle East, particularly by appealing to Arab nationalism and anti-colonialism, Eisenhower and his advisors sought to neutralize such overtures by emphasizing America's own "spiritual" connection with Islamic nations. The religious values shared between the West and the Middle East would, they hoped, prove stronger than any other connections that the Soviets might try to exploit.

Throughout the course of his presidency, the Middle East remained a region of constant concern for Eisenhower – a concern periodically punctuated by acute crises. Much of his focus stemmed from his fear of growing Soviet influence in such a strategic area, exemplified by the "Eisenhower Doctrine" of assisting any governments threatened by potential communist subversion. Reinforcing this, however, was the particular Christian perspective brought by Elson, whose longtime involvement in the region preceded his pastoral relationship with Eisenhower. Elson traced his interest to the history of American missionary activities in the Middle East, particularly by Presbyterians. "Most of the colleges and universities and cultural institutions created by Americans in the Middle East had been the result of Christian missionary endeavor . . . and I suppose this is how my interest in and attachment to this part of the world was strengthened and made rich very early in my life." He stressed these missions as a civilizing exercise, rather than an evangelistic one. "Instead of winning individual converts, which is very difficult for Muslims, the American Christian thrust himself into the life of the Middle East and penetrated its culture in a transforming way." Deeply sympathetic to the Arab

---

[73] September 8, 1953 letter from Abbott Washburn to Thomas Stephens; September 17, 1953 letter from Leonard Ware to Thomas Stephens; OF, Box 737, Folder: 144-B-4; DDE Papers.

peoples, he had been appalled at Truman's decision to recognize the new nation of Israel Elson later complained to Eisenhower that Truman's "action in the creation of Israel was the most colossal diplomatic debacle of our day." This, along with Elson's disagreement with "the dynamic world Zionist apparatus," had prompted him in 1948 to help found and lead the organization American Friends of the Middle East, a coalition of leading pro-Arab voices.[74]

Elson observed with great approval that Eisenhower came into office with similar predilections. He later recalled an incident in March 1953, when "some Zionist officials" met with the new president in the Oval Office and tried to persuade Eisenhower to be supportive of Israel. A perturbed Eisenhower "inquired whether they were visiting him as representatives of Americans or representatives of some other foreign interest." He then held forth on the strategic importance of the Middle East and the need for maintaining good relations with the Arab nations, and made clear he would not treat Israel as any sort of "favored nation."[75] To be sure, unlike Elson's Arab affinities, Eisenhower's initial sympathy towards the Arab nations seems to have been driven more by geo-strategic calculations than by a spirit of kinship grounded in the missionary tradition. And hints of the "polite anti-Semitism" somewhat prevalent in the 1950s seem to have possibly influenced both Eisenhower and Elson's skepticism towards Israel. Witness Elson's cavils against the "dynamic world Zionist apparatus," and Eisenhower's insinuation that American supporters of Israel were, at best, divided in their loyalties, and at worst, treasonous. Regardless of the reasons, a common affinity for the Arabs and a common distaste for the nation of Israel brought Elson and Eisenhower together.

The 1956 Suez Crisis, in which Eisenhower and Dulles surprised their traditional allies and the rest of the globe by forcefully opposing Great Britain, France, and Israel, generated a significant amount of goodwill towards America in the Muslim world. Several months later, Eisenhower sought to enhance these relations by giving an address at the dedication ceremony for the new Islamic Center in Washington. Lauding Islam's historic contributions to world civilization, he called for "the peaceful progress of all men under one God." And he assured Muslims of their freedom to worship, even if he could not keep straight *where* they worship: "America would fight with her whole

[74] Edward Elson oral interview #6, September 22, 1968, Washington DC. Conducted by Paul Hopper. Dwight D. Eisenhower Oral History Project; also August 4, 1958 letter from Elson to Eisenhower; OF, Box 589, Folder: 116-R; DDE Papers.

[75] Elson, oral interview. Also, in a conversation with the author, Ambassador Jeanne Kirkpatrick recalled that as a young State Department official in the 1950s, she and her colleagues at Foggy Bottom knew well of the president's pastor's anti-Israel opinions.

strength for your right to have here your own church and worship according to your own conscience."[76] To capitalize on this unprecedented gesture
by an American president towards Islam, the American propaganda apparatus kicked into high gear, broadcasting and distributing printed copies of
Eisenhower's remarks throughout the region. Egyptian newspapers proudly
published pictures of President and Mrs. Eisenhower removing their shoes
as they prepared to enter the Washington mosque.[77] In Iran, the media gave
extensive coverage to the speech, and leading mullahs contacted the American
Embassy to express their gratitude, with one imam singling out "America's
deep belief in religion" as a significant cause of American strength.[78] By this
measure, at least, Eisenhower's emphasis on "spiritual values" as an instrument to stifle – and contain – the spread of communism appeared to bear
fruit.

At the same time, Elson departed for a six-week trip to the Middle East.
Officially he journeyed in his capacity as Chairman of American Friends of
the Middle East, but the fact that this was the president's pastor was not lost on
the political leaders with whom he met. Nor was this opportunity for "back
channel" diplomacy lost on Eisenhower, who waited eagerly for a report from
his pastor-turned-ambassador. The president gave Elson a letter of greeting
for King Saud of Saudi Arabia, which likely played no small part in Elson
becoming the first American clergyman ever to visit Saudi Arabia openly.
Elson's meetings with Middle Eastern leaders, in turn, were hardly confined
to ceremonial niceties. He found the young King Hussein of Jordan quite
impressive, and saw him as a potential leader for the greater Arab world.
Elson also received a curious decoration from the Jordanian government.
On a visit to the country five years earlier, Elson apparently had identified a
certain Jordanian man as a communist. The Jordanians had imprisoned the
man, and on this visit, they honored Elson in gratitude for his contribution
to their country's domestic security.[79]

In Saudi Arabia, Elson discussed with King Saud the contested status of the
Gulf of Aqaba, which the Saudis wanted returned to their proprietorship, in

[76] Eisenhower, Remarks at Ceremonies Opening the Islamic Center, Washington DC, June 28,
     1957. *Public Papers of the Presidents: Dwight D. Eisenhower, 1957* (Washington: United States
     Government Printing Office 1958), 509–510.
[77] Elson, 157.
[78] "Reaction to President's Islamic Center Address"; Ann Whitman File, DDE Diary Series, Box
     26, Folder: August 1957 Memo on Appointments; DDE Papers.
[79] June 19, 1957 letter from Elson to Eisenhower; August 5, 1957 letter from Eisenhower to Elson;
     PPF, Box 913, Folder: 53-B-1 National Presbyterian Church; August 9, 1957 memo of meeting
     between Elson and Eisenhower; Ann Whitman File, DDE Diary Series, Box 26, Folder: August
     1957 Memo on Appointments; DDE Papers.

contrast to America's desire to keep it as an international waterway. Nevertheless, the King made clear his enduring bond with Elson's most prominent parishioner, based in large part on the King's recent visit to Washington. Elson also met at length with Egyptian President Gamal Nasser. This took place the day after Eisenhower's Islamic Center address, which gave Elson occasion to tell Nasser of Eisenhower's own deep spirituality as well as the religious awakening in America. Although personally charmed by Nasser, Elson noticed some troubling signs. Nasser intimated his growing ties with the Soviets, and all of the pictures in his office depicted only communist leaders, with nary a single Western official represented. And for the first time ever, the script of a sermon that Elson gave in a local church was inspected by Egyptian secret police, who also monitored the worship service. Nevertheless, Elson found that in almost every country he visited – Egypt, Saudi Arabia, Lebanon, Syria, Iran, Iraq, Pakistan, Yemen, and even Israel – Eisenhower was "exceedingly popular, particularly for his spiritual qualities and for his statesmanship."[80]

On returning to Washington, Elson met with Eisenhower to give a detailed report on his trip. The president also asked his pastor to provide the Assistant Secretary of State for Near Eastern Affairs with an account of what he had learned. Elson reported that throughout the region, besides enjoying high personal approval, the president's Eisenhower Doctrine had provided a new sense of security. Yet all was not well. "In the Arab world you find much emotionalism and historic hostilities, bordering on the pathological. Israel fears extinction; the Arabs fear expansion by Israel." Concerning the Jewish state, Elson then made a curious policy suggestion. Though he had found David Ben-Gurion a charismatic and inspiring leader, Elson's distaste for Israel had not diminished. Counseling against inviting Ben-Gurion to the White House for any meetings, Elson held that "it is more important to keep Arabs and Jews apart than it is to bring them together." Instead, "what we ought to aspire to is to have a guaranteed containment of Israel" and prevent Israel from any further expansion.[81] Here were Elson's predilections on full display. Though his analysis had distilled concerns with both Arabs and Jews, his policy prescription centered only on constraining Israel, and placed no corresponding burden on Arab states to recognize Israel or to refrain from aggression. Moreover, it is quite telling that he chose to apply America's cardinal strategic doctrine – "containment" – not just to the Soviet Union, but to Israel as well.

---

[80] *Ibid.*
[81] *Ibid.*

Eisenhower, for his part, looked to apply some of his pastor's insights to United States policy in the region. In the weeks after receiving Elson's report on his Middle East trip, Eisenhower convened a series of meetings with the members of his national security team in part to explore how to bolster the religious dimension of Islamic opposition to communism. In one meeting with Dulles, Rountree, the Joint Chiefs, and CIA clandestine chief Frank Wisner, Eisenhower declared "we should do everything possible to stress the 'holy war' aspect" of the Cold War to Arab leaders. Dulles in turn proposed a "secret task force" through which the CIA would provide arms, funding, and other means of support to the leaders of Saudi Arabia, Jordan, Lebanon, and Iraq.[82]

The next year saw the Middle East fraught with even more tension. Several fragile regimes, including Lebanon, Jordan, and Iraq, found themselves teetering precariously as proxies in the global stand-off between the United States and USSR. In the midst of these crises, Elson and Eisenhower engaged in a searching dialogue over religion, diplomacy, and the American role in the region. Elson began with a long letter of counsel to the president, drawing on his own considerable knowledge and experience in the Arab world. "The Arab respects strength; he honors force," Elson noted, but by themselves these did not suffice as policy principles. "Military firmness" was of course necessary, but not sufficient. "The Arabs will understand us if we communicate in spiritual terms. It will help to acknowledge our indebtedness to the Middle East for contributing to the world the three great religions of Semitic origin. Exploit the pride of Islam." Elson still regarded Israel as more a problem than a friend. "Keep Israel out of this crisis completely.... The Israeli reacts too easily by expansion ... assure the Arabs *we are as devoted to the containment of Israel as we are to order and stability of the Arab world.*" Additionally, the United States should sacralize Arab nationalism. "Assure the Arabs we share with them their aspirations for self-realization, for freedom under God, and for the achievement of a national destiny. Nationalism is good when spiritually disciplined." Of course, the Soviets would appeal to Arab sentiments as well. "It is the combination of unbridled nationalism, the drive toward unity, and the excessive preoccupation with Israel which gives communism its opportunity to disrupt, destroy, and colonize the Middle East." America must use a religious appeal to trump communism's ideological appeal. After all, "atheistic communism is as *hostile* to *Islam* as to Christianity."[83]

---

[82] Quoted and cited in Tim Weiner, *Legacy of Ashes: The History of the CIA* (New York: Doubleday 2007), 136–137, 575.

[83] July 24, 1958 confidential letter from Elson to Eisenhower; OF, Box 584, Folder: 116-R; DDE Papers. Emphasis original.

Sacralizing Arab nationalism was easier said than done, however, especially with a crafty figure like Nasser pursuing his intrigues in the region. Eisenhower responded appreciatively to Elson's letter, expressing his agreement with his pastor's main points. He complained, however, of "one very complicating factor . . . the obviously unbridled ambition of Nasser." Lamenting Nasser's vanity, Eisenhower ominously warned where it might lead. "To realize his ambitions he of course relies on Soviet help. As he gets deeper and deeper into debt to the Kremlin, the great danger is that he will set off an explosion of terrifying proportions."[84] Intensely preoccupied with the volatile region, three days later Eisenhower followed up with another letter to Elson, this one a remarkable six-page digest of the president's musings on the Middle East. The president agreed on the need to keep Israel out of the crisis. The problem, however, "is that in any conversation with an Arab, he is the one that brings up the subject of Israel." Arab intransigence on Israel aside, Eisenhower assured Elson that "I never fail in any communication with Arab leaders, oral or written, to stress the importance of the spiritual factor in our relationships. I have argued that belief in God should create between them and us the common purposes of opposing atheistic communism." But this strategy had its limits. Eisenhower related how King Saud once responded "that while it was well to remember that the Communists are no friends of ours, yet Arabs are forced to realize that Communism is a long ways off, [but] Israel is a bitter enemy in our own back yard."[85] Here was Eisenhower's greatest concern: perhaps communism was not so far from the Arab regimes.

He then described for Elson the extensive informational and economic programs being undertaken in the Middle East to promote American values and increase goodwill towards the United States, much of it incorporating "the religious approach" to appeal to "Arab interest." Curiously, Eisenhower complained that "some of our very able friends" remained too seduced by military power, and he singled out Charles Wesley Lowry in this regard. Lowry had just sent the president a letter and two articles, in which the FRASCO leader apparently criticized Truman and Franklin Delano Roosevelt for not having capitalized on America's disproportionate military hegemony by threatening a preemptive military strike on the Soviet Union. Eisenhower said that while "I respect and like" Lowry, such charges were "completely unsupportable." Moreover, Lowry's armchair quarterback hindsight irked the president. "For a man who has never had the responsibility of conducting

---

[84] July 28, 1958 letter from Eisenhower to Elson; Ann Whitman File, DDE Diary Series, Box 34, Folder: DDE Dictation July 1958; DDE Papers.

[85] July 31, 1958 letter from Eisenhower to Elson; OF, Box 584, Folder: 116-R; DDE Papers.

America's relationships with the remainder of the world to take it upon himself to make this sweeping criticism rather destroys my confidence in his judgment. This I say with some sadness because in his personal letter to me he expresses some thoughts that are more than appealing. They are in some instances very penetrating."[86] Lowry would no doubt have been severely disappointed to learn of Eisenhower's criticism, if Elson ever shared it with him. Somewhat lost in the wilderness of his own ideological zeal, Lowry had also lost sight of the very real practical, political, and moral constraints under which policy-makers must operate. This led in turn to his greatest loss: the president's confidence. Apprised of Eisenhower's frustrations with his colleague, Elson determined to keep his own counsel realistic, whether pastoral or political.

In his response to Eisenhower's letter, Elson conceded the president's criticism, while offering a partial defense of his partner. "Dr. Lowry's genius is in sharpening the ideological issue of our age and bringing to bear upon it all spiritual resources. He is less at home in Mid-East affairs." Turning to Eisenhower's other points, the pastor shared his concerns about Nasser. Elson recalled that in his last meeting with the Egyptian leader, Nasser had displayed a "total disregard of and lack of appreciation for" Eisenhower's support for Egypt during the Suez crisis. "He took all the credit for ending the conflict. . . . I was disappointed, shocked, and somewhat frightened by the way he handled the facts of history." Nor did the Arabs comprehend their greatest threat. "Every Arab leader with whom I have talked in recent years confirms King Saud's statement to you that while the Arabs cannot accept Communism, Israel is nearer and more menacing. Mr. Dulles was correct – the Arabs fear Zionism more than Communism." Finally, Elson agreed with his parishioner on the need to enhance domestic understanding of the Middle East, which focused too much on Israel. He noted that American Protestant churches would be paying more attention to the region, and increasing their support for American foreign aid programs. Moreover, "the Church press, both Protestant and Catholic, has been the most authentic interpreter of the entire Mid-East for it has been freer of the Zionist distortions than the secular press."[87]

Eisenhower seems to have applied much of Elson's counsel. The next week he gave a major address to an Emergency Session of the UN General Assembly. Beginning with a vigorous defense of his decision to deploy troops in

---

[86] *Ibid.* Also, July 20, 1958 letter from Lowry to Eisenhower; July 24, 1958 letter from Eisenhower to Lowry; OF, Box 597, Folder: 116-SS; DDE Papers.

[87] August 4, 1958 letter from Elson to Eisenhower; OF, Box 584, Folder: 116-R; DDE Papers.

Lebanon, Eisenhower repeatedly denounced "the fomenting of civil strife in the interest of a foreign power." No delegate present could miss his implication. Communist mischief designed to undermine or overthrow Middle Eastern governments would meet with a forceful American response, whether in Lebanon, or Jordan, or elsewhere in the region. Consistent with Elson's advice, the president then sought the political high ground by endorsing "Arab nationalism." "The peoples of the Arab nations of the Near East clearly possess the right of determining and expressing their own destiny." He called for increased assistance for economic development in the region, as well as the creation of regional institutions. Finally, Eisenhower paid homage to the contributions of Arab civilizations to world history, and "above all, we remember that three of the world's great religions were born in the Near East." Not once in the speech did he mention Israel.[88]

Elson, for his part, hardly confined his concerns about Israel to his private correspondence. Two months after this exchange, he led a group of prominent American Protestant leaders, including Harry Emerson Fosdick and Douglas Horton, Dean of Harvard Divinity School, in sending a letter and an analysis by Harvard philosopher William Ernest Hocking to Eisenhower and to almost every major political, media, academic, and religious leader in the country. The letter ominously warned "we are running a terrible risk – that of becoming involved in a war against Russia to defend the State of Israel." Elson and his cohort called on American leaders to pressure Israel for further concessions, and for America to increase its economic assistance to the entire region. For its part, the enclosed essay by Hocking attacked the very establishment of Israel. It denounced the Balfour Declaration as "devious" and "disingenuous," and it catalogued a litany of purported Israeli depredations against Palestinians.[89] Elson continued to hold that Israel was the primary source of instability in the Near East, and thus needed pressure instead of support from the United States.

Such views stirred the ire of Reinhold Niebuhr like little else. Generally more critical than supportive of Eisenhower's diplomacy, Niebuhr found the president's policies in the Middle East especially galling. He singled out the Eisenhower Doctrine – which promised both the carrot of economic aid to the region and the stick of military assistance to any Near East nation threatened by the Soviets – for pontificating on overly grandiose ambitions

[88] Eisenhower, Address to the Third Special Emergency Session of the General Assembly of the United Nations, August 13, 1958. *Public Papers of the Presidents: Dwight D. Eisenhower, 1958* (Washington: United States Government Printing Office 1959), 606–616.

[89] September 27, 1958 letter from Elson to Eisenhower, and attached form letter and essay; OF, Box 589, Folder: 116-R; DDE Papers.

while ignoring specific power realities. Regarding economic aid, "instead of offering unspecified and unvouchered aid" to a region awash in petroleum resources, the United States should link economic development to more equitable distribution of oil revenues and to the resettlement of refugees, while developing alternate sources of supply and delivery to European nations hamstrung by dependence on Arab oil. Regarding military assistance, the Administration ignored the region's greatest security issue: Israel's survival. "A small nation is fighting for its existence and is unaided because a fog obscures the vision of the greatest of the powers." Niebuhr called instead for a more assertive policy, at once pro-Israel and anti-Arab nationalism. "We ought both to guarantee Israel and to prevent the unity of the Arab world under Nasser." Undergirding this misguided regional policy lurked the Administration's greatest flaw: a "combination of Eisenhower's moralism, which expresses itself in universal benevolence without regard for strategic necessities, and Dulles's formalism, which makes simple distinctions between nations which obey the 'moral law' and those which do not." Such "moral sentimentality . . . is dangerous in any seat of power, particularly in the greatest center of power in the modern world."[90]

The only meager excuse that Niebuhr could summon on the president's behalf was his relative consistency. The Administration's "vagueness" just reflected "a perennial flaw in American foreign policy" going back to Woodrow Wilson. "When an idealistic Democratic internationalist with an academic background, reigning almost a half century ago, proves to have similarities with a current Republican President with a military background," it reveals a deeper problem in the American condition.[91] As potent as was Niebuhr's critique, it was not entirely fair, and it obscured a principal similarity between the theologian and the president. Niebuhr married a sentimental attachment to Zionism with the *realpolitik* calculation that a secure Israel served as the most effective bulwark against Arab nationalism and Soviet expansion. Eisenhower, on the other hand, combined his own sentimental attachment to the Arabs with a *realpolitik* calculation that Arab nationalism, relieved of the annoyance of Israel, provided the most effective bulwark against Soviet expansion. That both of them drew on the resources of the Protestant tradition for their differing positions was an irony that neither seemed to acknowledge.

Niebuhr's charge of "vagueness" notwithstanding, Eisenhower was willing to address specific problems on occasion. On the eve of a 1959 state visit to Afghanistan, Elson mentioned to the president that the country did not allow a

---

[90] Niebuhr, "The Eisenhower Doctrine," *The New Leader*, 4 February 1957, 8–10; "Eisenhower's Theory of Power and Morals," *The New Leader*, 11 March 1957, 3–4.
[91] Niebuhr, "The Eisenhower Doctrine," *The New Leader*, 4 February 1957, 8–10.

single church building, despite the request of a fledgling Afghan congregation pastored by a young American missionary named Christy Wilson. Elson asked Eisenhower to bring up this issue with the king. "The Moslems are especially responsive to the religious note and, if you emphasize the religious devotion of the American people, you will get through to them. If you could refer to your participation in the dedication of the Mosque in Washington and point out how fine it would be to have a Christian Church in Kabal, I am sure it would have good effect." Though he would only be in the capital for four hours, Eisenhower agreed to "mention the desirability of a church in Kabul, especially since we accent freedom of religion in America." He did raise the matter with the king, and permission to build the church was soon granted.[92]

VI

As with so many other religious aspects of American foreign policy, what Truman began, Eisenhower continued. For its part, the Psychological Strategy Board (PSB) – motivated in equal parts by Cold War fervor and the bureaucratic survival instinct – sought to demonstrate its relevance to the president-elect in December 1952, when it proposed that he send a Christmas gift of "one million copies of the Scriptures" to the USSR. A cautious State Department squelched this idea, amidst its ongoing bureaucratic struggle with the PSB over control of American propaganda efforts.[93] Frustrated with such conflicts, and with inheriting from Truman what he regarded as poorly organized, feuding agencies, Eisenhower immediately set out to overhaul the system. On January 26, 1953, the White House established the "President's Committee on International Information Activities" (PCIIA), chaired by William Jackson, to evaluate all government activities in this area, including the PSB. The eventual PCIIA report recommended abolishing the PSB and replacing it with an Operations Coordinating Board (OCB). The OCB would have a narrower, more refined focus, and would work within the National Security Council (NSC) to coordinate the propaganda efforts of the State Department, CIA, and USIA.[94]

---

[92] November 29, 1959 letter from Elson to Eisenhower; Ann Whitman File, Name Series, Box 14, Folder: Elson; DDE Papers. Also Elson, 157–158. Apparently the government did not allow Wilson to place a cross on the steeple, and a decade later the church was bulldozed during an upsurge in Islamic radicalism. Wilson eventually returned to the United States, where he became an eminent professor of world missions at Gordon-Conwell Theological Seminary.

[93] Scott Lucas, *Freedom's War: The American Crusade Against the Soviet Union* (New York: New York University Press 1999), 150.

[94] Edward P. Lilly, "The Psychological Strategy Board and Its Predecessors: Foreign Policy Coordination, 1938–1953" in Gaetano L. Vincitorio, ed., *Studies in Modern History* (New York: St. John's University Press 1968), 379–380.

Though its name and organizational chart changed, many PSB officials remained with the OCB and continued their work from the one to the other. Eisenhower's top propaganda specialists C.D. Jackson and Abbott Washburn joined with Truman holdover Edward P. Lilly to preach the American message abroad. Lilly, himself a Catholic, focused on the religious dimension. Further demonstrating the biblical adage that "there is nothing new under the sun," Lilly's first proposal under Eisenhower was a White House-sponsored "International Congress of Religious Leaders" who would issue a statement affirming the universal "Fatherhood of God and Brotherhood of Man" as part of a broader propaganda campaign "emphasizing the dignity of the human individual and the basis for Western concepts of human rights and freedoms."[95] Although there is little evidence that Lilly was aware of it, this idea almost replicated Truman and Taylor's special project, not to mention its similarity to FRASCO's eventual campaign and Eisenhower's own personal musings on the subject. Lilly had a penchant for intrigue, and under the guise of being an academic "observer," would on occasion infiltrate meetings of American religious leaders focused on international relations. At one such "confidential meeting" held on March 17, 1953, at Columbia University's faculty club, Lilly learned, to his frustration, that the assembled Protestant, Catholic, and Jewish leaders were more interested in defending the United Nations than lending religious support to American foreign policy. After covertly attending a similar meeting the next year, at which Niebuhr gave a major talk, Lilly reported back to his NSC colleagues that this gathering held promise for the "utilization of American religious groups along lines that are favorable to American objectives."[96] As with many other such proposals, however, nothing of significance seems to have come from this one either.

Recently declassified NSC documents reveal that the Eisenhower Administration's interest in religion went beyond the rhetorical level to the operational level as well. One NSC memo from early 1953 warned that Soviet efforts to control the Orthodox Church – through persecution of defiant clergy and through financial support of compliant clergy – were gaining ground, potentially giving the communists "another powerful weapon of thought control." Besides their almost complete domination of the Russian Church, the

---

95 Lilly, March 12, 1953 memo on "International Congress of Religious Leaders"; WHO, NSC Staff, OCB Secretariat Series, Folder: Moral Factor (4); DDE Papers.

96 March 13, 1953 memo from Lilly to Edmond Taylor; WHO, NSC Staff, OCB Secretariat Series, Box 5, Folder: Moral Factor (4); March 17, 1953 memo from Lilly to Edmond Taylor and George Morgan; WHO, NSC Staff, PSB Central File, Box 9, Folder: PSB 000.3 (1); October 26, 1954 memo from Lilly to Elmer B. Staats; WHO, NSC Staff, OCB Central File, Box 2, Folder: OCB 000.3 file #1 (1); DDE Papers.

Soviets were making inroads with Orthodoxy throughout the Middle East and Mediterranean. However, the memo highlighted the pro-American convictions of Athenagoras, the Oecumenical Patriarch in Istanbul and a former U.S. citizen, along with the Orthodox community in the United States as potential "weapons with which to combat the communists in this field." Athenagoras, of course, had been installed as Patriarch five years before with the active support – and perhaps involvement – of Truman and Taylor. The memo concluded that "we could and should recapture the Church from the communists." Five months later, the Administration began a program to do just that. On July 13, 1953, Director for Mutual Security Harold Stassen approved the PSB's "U.S. Program for Support of the Orthodox Church." Though its details remain classified, the program appears to have been a "multi-country operation" coordinated by the CIA, Pentagon, and State Department to bolster the anti-communist leaders within the Church, likely including significant financial support.[97]

Such support for the Orthodox Church to undermine communism grew out of the Administration's explicitly stated goals, which in turn came from the president's own convictions. "The policy of the Eisenhower Administration, if the statements of the President and the Secretary of State are to be considered as determining . . . [favors] greater emphasis upon the religious factor in the American program against Communism," noted one NSC memo.[98] Another NSC analysis, from September 4, 1953, began "President Eisenhower has declared repeatedly our need for reliance upon moral and spiritual force in dealing with our domestic problems and our foreign relations." The memo then stated that "basic United States foreign policy objectives" included "[encouraging] effective cooperation of peoples with us toward the realization of a world order based on the fundamental moral and spiritual values inherent in our Judeo-Christian tradition and shared by other Deistic faiths."[99] The next month, the Administration adopted a new official national security guidance, NSC 162/2, which declared "the need for

[97] February 19, 1953 memo "Recommendation for a study of the Orthodox Church"; WHO, NSC Staff, OCB Secretariat Series, Box 5, Folder: Moral Factor (4); July 13, 1953 memo from Stassen to PSB Director; July 27, 1953 memo re: PSB D-39 (author and recipients classified); WHO, NSC Staff, PSB Central File, Box 9, Folder: PSB 000.3 (2); DDE Papers.

[98] July 21, 1953 memo from Edward Lilly to C.D. Jackson; WHO, NSC Staff, OCB Secretariat Series, Box 5, Folder: Moral Factor (4); DDE Papers.

[99] September 4, 1953 memo "Planning and Programming in the Area of Moral and Spiritual Values"; WHO, NSC Staff, OCB Secretariat Series, Box 5, Folder: Moral and Religious; DDE Papers. See also July 15, 1953 letter from John Read Burr to Abbott Washburn and attached memo "The USIA Program for 1954," which describes the "faith" animating U.S. foreign policy and propaganda efforts. OF, Box 909, Folder: OF 247, 1953; DDE Papers.

mobilizing the spiritual and material resources necessary to meet the Soviet threat."[100]

Robert Johnson, who directed the International Information Administration (IIA), the USIA's predecessor, doubled the amount of broadcast time devoted to religious programs because "the strongest bond between freedom-loving peoples on both sides of the Iron Curtain is their *shared* faith in spiritual values."[101] By late 1954, Radio Free Europe was broadcasting Lutheran and Catholic "religious programs, services, sermons, and music to the five nations representing its major audience." The new OCB undertook a concerted effort to give traction to Eisenhower's emphasis on "spiritual values" in the Cold War, and used NSC 162/2 as its scriptural guide. One OCB official, Byron Enyart, saw NSC 162/2 as a seminal document on integrating religion into the American ideological offensive, despite previous bureaucratic resistance. "NSC 162/2 now furnishes the peg upon which we can hang our hat. The Departments almost universally used the absence of such a document as an excuse for not doing anything in this field. . . . If we are not able to accomplish something with a climate of opinion as generated by the present administration . . . than we are not deserving of the great many things that the Good Lord has given us."[102] In a March 3, 1954 proposal to increase "the religious factor in Government activity implementing national security policies," Lilly singled out NSC 162/2 as well as speeches by Eisenhower and Dulles on "the importance of religious values . . . in countering the threat of Soviet communism" as the basis for new policies. Moreover, argued Lilly, religious faith was vitally important to most people in the world, "with the exception of [Western] government officials." He cited the recent example of two Indian officials who "repeatedly emphasized that the Indian people recognized America's technological superiority but they knew nothing about America's philosophical or spiritual viewpoint. Because of this gap, Indians could not tell whether they really liked or sided with" the United States or the USSR, since both nations focused only on military and economic prowess.[103] Indian Prime Minister

[100] Foreign Relations of the United States (FRUS): 1952–1954, II, 590.

[101] "Report on Operations of International Information Administration" by Robert Johnson; WHCF: Confidential File, Subject Series, Box 99, Folder: USIA (1); Emphasis original. See also August 1, 1953 letter from Robert Cutler to Theodore Streibert; OF, Box 738, Folder: 144-G-1; DDE Papers.

[102] November 2, 1954 memo from Lilly to Elmer Staats; March 8, 1954 memo from Byron Enyart to Elmer Staats; WHO, NSC Staff, OCB Central File, Box 2, Folder: OCB 000.3 File #1 (1); DDE Papers.

[103] March 3, 1954 memo from Lilly to Elmer Staats; WHO, NSC Staff, OCB Secretariat Series, Box 5, Folder: Moral and Religious; DDE Papers. Lilly referred specifically to Eisenhower's Inaugural Address and Dulles' December 11, 1952 speech to the National Council of Churches;

Jawarhal Nehru's eventual doctrine of "non-alignment" may have been as much spiritual as strategic, it seemed.

The Eisenhower Administration turned to a Quaker college in a small Indiana town to find the man who could help implement NSC 162/2's mandate. Elton Trueblood – philosopher of religion, preacher, former Stanford chaplain, Republican, and dedicated anticommunist – was chosen to fill the newly created position of "Chief of Religious Policy" at USIA. A professor at Earlham College, Trueblood had been recommended to the White House by Congressman Walter Judd and had the enthusiastic support of C.D. Jackson as well. Trueblood also found a new outlet for one of his old vocations. Two months after he arrived in Washington, Elson invited Trueblood to fill the pulpit as a guest preacher at National Presbyterian, on a Sunday when Eisenhower was in attendance and enjoyed hearing one of his Administration's newest officials deliver the sermon.[104]

One can hardly mention "religion" and "policy" in the same sentence, let alone the same government job title, without stirring some controversy. Trueblood's appointment was no exception. His opponents came from a surprising quarter, however. Instead of Protestant liberals upset over government attempts to politicize religion, it was fundamentalists fearful of government control of religion who raised a fierce cry. Even after the White House changed Trueblood's title to the slightly less ominous "Chief of Religious Information," the angry letters continued to pour in, warning of the undermining of "separation of church and state" and denouncing what appeared to be a government endorsement of Trueblood's mildly conservative Protestantism – as opposed to the undiluted conservatism of the fundamentalists.[105] The American Council of Christian Churches adopted a resolution urging Eisenhower to remove Trueblood from his post and abolish the Office of Religious Information. The

for more on the latter, see chapter six of this book. See also Lilly's October 26, 1954 memo titled "Peace with Justice and Prosperity." In language that deliberately mimics the Declaration of Independence, Lilly laid out the core theological principles that animated the "Free World" in its conflict with communism. WHO, NSC Staff, OCB Secretariat Series, Box 5, Folder: Moral and Religious; DDE Papers.

[104] February 8, 1954 memo from Abbott Washburn to Charles F. Willis; Central File, GF, Box 736, Folder: 121 T Jan–March 1954; USIA Second Review of Operations, January–June 1954, 8; April 16, 1954 letter from C.D. Jackson to Thomas Stephens; April 16, 1954 memo from Arthur Minnich to Thomas Stephens; OF, Box 909, Folder: OF 247 1954; May 20, 1954 letter from Elson to Eisenhower; CF, PPF, Box 913, Folder: 53-B-1 Nat'l Pres Church; June 8, 1954 "Memorandum for the Record" by Paul Carroll; OF, Box 909, Folder: OF 247 1954; DDE Papers.

[105] June 22, 1954 letter from Abbott Washburn to Arthur Minnich; for an example of a protest letter, see June 5, 1954 letter from Rev. E. Finkenbeiner of Huntington, West Virginia to Eisenhower; CF, GF, Box 1301, Folder: 201 1954; DDE Papers.

ACCC resolution gave several reasons: the office violated the constitutional guarantee of religious liberty, Trueblood "has used his office both to discriminate against and to attack" the fundamentalist denominations, he had "promoted in public meetings . . . the welfare of the ecumenical movement," and he "is using his position to promote throughout the world" the "welfare state and principles for a socialist order" advocated by the NCC.[106] Numerous Members of Congress contacted the White House as well, both to pass on constituent concerns and to express their own reservations.

These were serious charges, and they attracted enough attention on Capitol Hill and in the nation's heartland to cause some heartburn at the White House. Wanting to maintain religious unity against communism, the Administration reassured its critics of its benign intentions. Eisenhower's Chief of Staff Sherman Adams sent virtually the same letter in response to all of the protests. The USIA, he promised, "does not direct information to the people of the United States nor does it undertake to give official recognition to any religious bodies in our nation." Adams then appealed to the complainants' sense of patriotism, and restated the Eisenhower creed. In the international information campaign, "we should seek to present America not merely as a nation of great material strength but also one of great spiritual strength. Our democratic freedoms have a solid religious foundation which must be adequately explained if the true story of America is to be told." To equip the White House to respond to any further criticisms, Abbott Washburn prepared an internal memo defending USIA's agenda. Besides explaining the religious foundations of American life, USIA needed to oppose communism's commitment "to the destruction of the moral and spiritual forces which undergird our and other civilizations . . . we must also deal with moral and spiritual matters in our broadcasts to the USSR, China, and other Communist areas to convince the people of the spiritual bankruptcy of Communism."[107] This religious assault on the ramparts of communism entailed enlisting allies beyond just Christendom and even the "Protestant, Catholic, Jew" axis. Eisenhower Administration strategy documents reveal over and over again an interest in

---

[106] November 26, 1954 letter from William Harllee Bordeaux to Eisenhower, and accompanying resolution; CF, GF, Box 1301, Folder: 201 1954; DDE Papers.

[107] June 28, 1954 letter from Adams to Rev. E.A. Finkenbiner; See also August 19, 1954 letter from Adams to Congressman Frank C. Osmers, Jr., and December 27, 1954 letter from Washburn to Congressman R.D. Harrison; December 10, 1954 memo from Washburn to Colonel A.J. Goodpaster; CF, GF, Box 1301, Folder: 201 1954; DDE Papers. Note also that the Trueblood controversy further illustrates one of the divisions between fundamentalists and evangelicals. For example, in 1955 Trueblood and L. Nelson Bell exchanged friendly letters commiserating at Carl McIntire's continuing attacks on Billy Graham. See April 29 and April 30, 1955 letters in Bell Papers, Box 52, Folder 26; BGCA.

all faiths as co-belligerents in the Cold War crusade. To take just one example, a 1956 USIA policy guidance declares, "the common ground of all religion is that man is subject to a higher law and that he must be guided by moral and ethical principles rooted deep in religious faith." Moreover, "communism is a contemporary form... of materialism in ancient and continuing conflict with religion... religion provides a health and strength that enable any people to resist and overcome whatever enemies would destroy the dignity of man."[108]

This was more than just rhetoric; the Administration took concrete steps to work with other faiths, particularly Buddhism and Islam. Recently declassified documents reveal a comprehensive OCB program, involving the CIA, USIA, and State Department, to work through Buddhist channels to undermine communism in East Asia. By early 1957, the NSC had learned that "Chinese Communists have devoted increasing attention to extending their influence in the Buddhist countries of Southeast Asia" and "have met with some success in enlisting Buddhist clerical groups in the World Peace Congress, which is a Communist front." To counter this, the OCB covertly implemented many projects, including distributing anticommunist literature through Buddhist groups in Thailand and Burma, producing and screening anticommunist films at Buddhist gatherings throughout the region, broadcasting "special Buddhist programs including daily prayers" in Laos, and issuing proclamations of goodwill from the United States on the 2500th anniversary of the Buddha's birth. One secret report noted proudly that "provincial priests in Thailand have been won over to participation in the country-wide anti-communist indoctrination program. They make speeches, participate in discussion, distribute materials, and lead the people in chants in which the spirit of Lord Buddha is invoked to save Thailand from the communists." All of this was done with the utmost secrecy, mostly to make the program as effective as possible with the Buddhists, but also because it "may encounter serious criticism within the American religious world," which could in turn jeopardize congressional funding.[109] For all of their spirituality and anticommunist fervor, many American religionists would not want either their tithes or their tax

[108] June 1, 1956 USIA Religious Information Policy; *Christianity Today* Collection, Box 15, Folder 11; BGCA. Of course, the fact that the leading neo-evangelical periodical had secured this USIA policy paper shows evangelicalism's keen interest in both public acceptance and the Cold War.

[109] January 16, 1957 OCB "Outline Plan Regarding Buddhist Organizations in Ceylon, Burma, Thailand, Laos, Cambodia"; WHO, NSC Staff, OCB Central File, Box 2, Folder: OCB 000.3 File #2(1); See also documents on Buddhist campaign in Folders OCB 000.3 File #1(3), (4), (5), and (7), and File #2(2); DDE Papers.

dollars supporting such an unfamiliar faith. The Eisenhower Administration
had not yet converted all Americans to its version of Cold War civil religion.

Given Eisenhower's particular interest in the Middle East, it should be
no surprise that the OCB targeted Islam for its covert activities as well. A
secret OCB memo warned that "the Soviet and Chinese Communists have far
surpassed the West . . . in making direct appeals to the Muslims as Muslims."
This should not be so, for Islamic values aligned much more closely with
American values, particularly along Cold War fault lines. "The present division
of the world into two camps is often represented as being along political lines
while the true division is between a society in which the individual is motivated
by spiritual and ethical values and one in which he is the tool of a materialistic
state. Islam and Christianity have a common spiritual base." As such, the OCB
implemented several efforts to improve ties between Islam and the West, and to
bolster Islamic anticommunism, including broadcasting on the VOA regular
Koran readings in Arabic, special events from the Washington Islamic Center,
and a series on "Islam under Communism" on Arabic, Turkish, Persian,
Pakistani, and Indonesian channels. The OCB also produced and distributed
films trumpeting ties between the United States and the Islamic world.[110] This
campaign met with limited success, as various Middle Eastern and South
Asian regimes teetered between the American and Soviet blocs, their Muslim
people wrestling with whether the common faith of the "People of the Book"
should trump the common ideology of "anti-imperialism."

Alongside its specific appeals to particular religions, the Eisenhower
Administration seized on one step that all spiritual people could take against
communism: prayer. Pray early, and pray often, the White House seemed to
urge; pray for world peace, and implicitly, pray against communism. In 1954,
Eisenhower issued a proclamation designating September 22 as a National
Day of Prayer. The USIA made much of this in its broadcasts to Iron Curtain countries, contrasting Soviet persecution of religious believers with the
freedom and even encouragement religion enjoyed in the United States. One
highlighted sermon distilled the West's position by quoting Abraham Lincoln:
"What matters is not that God is on our side, but rather that we are on God's
side."[111] Eisenhower did more than just display America's religiosity; he invited

---

[110]   May 3, 1957 OCB "Inventory of U.S. Government and Private Organization Activity Regard-
        ing Islamic Organizations as an Aspect of Overseas Operations"; March 13, 1957 OCB Mem-
        orandum of Meeting: Ad Hoc Working Group on Islam; WHO, NSC Staff, OCB Secretariat
        Series, Box 4, Folder: Islamic Organizations. Also see documents on Islam in OCB Central
        File, Box 2, Folder: OCB 000.3 File#1(7) and #2(1); DDE Papers.
[111]   USIA "Output Highlights" for August, 1954; WHO, NSC Staff, OCB Central File Series, Box
        2, Folder: OCB 000.3 File #1(1); DDE Papers.

the beleaguered believers in the Soviet orbit to join in. Senate Majority Leader William F. Knowland wrote the president urging him to "extend the invitation of the proclamation to all people enslaved behind the Iron Curtain." Eisenhower readily agreed. "The Soviet regime has not succeeded in extinguishing the religious faith and aspirations of the peoples behind the Iron Curtain," he wrote Knowland. "If the present oppressive regime were removed, we should probably quickly establish friendly relations" with the citizens of these countries. Eisenhower issued a statement, widely disseminated by the USIA behind the Iron Curtain, inviting

> the peoples of Iron Curtain countries to join Americans in prayer for peace on September 22, 1954. . . . May the many millions of people shut away from contact and communion with peoples of the free world join their prayers with ours. May the world be ringed with an act of faith so strong as to annihilate the cruel, artificial barriers erected by little men between the peoples who seek peace on earth through Almighty God.[112]

But it was not enough just to have Americans and perhaps a few intrepid souls in Eastern Europe pray. Eisenhower wanted the whole world to pray. He had urged just that in his speech at the World Council of Churches Assembly in Evanston that same summer. And again, the Administration's propaganda team made maximum effect of the proceedings. A secret OCB memo described the "heavy and comprehensive coverage" given to the conference, with special focus on the president's call for prayer. USIA broadcasts gave extensive attention around the world to Eisenhower's prayer proposal. Abbott Washburn and Trueblood enthusiastically began to follow up. "To be successful, the worldwide movement of prayer must embrace not just Christians but Mohammedans, Buddhists, and all major religions," Washburn noted. The political possibilities tantalized him. "It would give us and the Free World the initiative in the movement for peace. . . . It would reveal the true spiritual foundation of our Government and our society, in contrast to the Russian. (The one thing the USSR cannot promote is *prayer* for peace.)"[113] Though the NCC, as noted earlier, had sheepishly informed Eisenhower that it could offer little help with the day of prayer, given the many honorific days already encumbering its calendar, this was little hindrance. The Eisenhower Administration had already shown itself more than willing to pursue its own religious

---

[112] September 1, 1954 letter from Knowland to Eisenhower; September 20, 1954 letter from Eisenhower to Knowland, including text of proclamation; OF, Box 737, Folder: OF 144F; DDE Papers.

[113] November 2, 1954 memo from Washburn to Minnich; OF, Box 738, Folder: OF 144 H; DDE Papers. Emphasis original.

initiatives, whether or not the church organizations came along. Throughout the next year, a secret OCB subcommittee worked with Trueblood to develop Eisenhower's proposal. In 1955, the Day of Prayer, originally scheduled for September 28, was changed to October 26. Not coincidentally, this was the day before the Geneva Foreign Ministers' Conference.[114]

Many Americans from all walks of life shared their president's eagerness to display American spirituality and freedom to the communist world. On the eve of Soviet Premier Nikita Khrushchev's visit to the United States in 1959, numerous congressmen, clergy (including Elson and Graham), and ordinary Americans all urged Eisenhower to invite the Soviet leader to church, or at least to pray in front of him. Even Senator H. Alexander Smith, now retired in New Jersey but still receiving daily "guidance," shared a special message with Eisenhower. In light of the upcoming meetings with Khrushchev, "it has been coming to me that we should try and mobilize the leaders of our Churches throughout the country to urge their people to have prayers for you during your very important conferences." Believing that God had revealed this to him, Smith informed Eisenhower that he had sent a similar notice to many denominational leaders throughout the country. "It is coming to me strongly that all the Christian and moral forces in the United States should be united in praying earnestly for God's direction in these conversations."[115] What, if any, religious conversation transpired between Eisenhower and Khrushchev remains unknown. Regardless, the unofficial suggestions of many Americans and the official activities of the OCB reveal that prayer was as much an instrument of Cold War diplomacy as it was of religious devotion.

VII

Eisenhower left the Oval Office much as he had entered it. He remained as convinced as ever that the Cold War was a religious conflict, that it was a

[114] October 27, 1954 letter from Samuel McCrea Cavert to Eisenhower; November 3, 1954 letter from Eisenhower to Cavert; May 6, 1955 letter from Trueblood to Eisenhower; May 12, 1955 letter from Kevin McCann to Trueblood; OF, Box 738, Folder: OF 144 H; May 19, June 8, June 20, and July 20, 1955 Memoranda of Meetings, OCB "Ideological Subcommittee on the Religious Factor"; WHO, NSC Staff, OCB Central File Series, Box 2, Folder: OCB 000.3 File #1(2); October 18, 1955 Confidential "News Policy Note"; OF, Box 737, Folder: 144 F(2); DDE Papers.

[115] September 7, 1959 letter from Smith to Eisenhower; September 14, 1959 letter from Eisenhower to Smith; September 14, 1959 letter from Elson to Eisenhower; September 23, 1959 letter from Edwin Dahlberg to Eisenhower; September 25 letter from Eisenhower to Dahlberg; OF, Box 892, Folder: 225-E; August 20, 1959 letter from Congressman Richard Poff to Eisenhower; August 21, 1959 letter from Eisenhower to Poff; OF, Box 893, Folder: 225-E-1; DDE Papers. Also Martin, 258.

contest not just between two rival powers but between two ways of life, and that it could never be won only by "material" means. Though history focuses almost myopically on Eisenhower's warning in his Farewell Address against the "military-industrial complex," the rest of his parting words should not be overlooked. This was the same president, after all, who had perpetually cautioned against ignoring "spiritual values" while trying to match Soviet military might. Holding the nation's attention as president one last time, he denounced communism as a "hostile ideology – global in scope, atheistic in character, ruthless in purpose, and insidious in method" that threatened America because it denied God. His concern at the "total influence – economic, political, even spiritual" posed by an unchecked conglomerate of Pentagon and corporate interests came not just out of Midwestern frugality or Republican fiscal prudence. It came also from Eisenhower's own religious convictions. He feared that it was not only communism, but also perhaps the very effort to defeat communism, that now threatened his nation's soul.[116]

[116]   Eisenhower, "Farewell Radio and Television Address to the American People," January 17, 1961. *Public Papers of the Presidents: Dwight D. Eisenhower, 1960–61* (Washington: United States Government Printing Office 1961), 1035–1040.

Afterword

If George Kennan's theology of containment informed the beginning of the Cold War, then it seems fitting to return to Kennan at the end of this book. Kennan again assumed the pulpit to survey his world at the end of the 1950s, as he had near the start of the decade. In a 1959 sermon, reprinted in the *Atlantic Monthly*, he made clear that he still saw communist totalitarianism as an apocalyptic threat and an "abomination to God." But the Kennan of 1959 was much more chastened and much less certain of how to define the spiritual stakes of the Cold War. With the passing of Stalin and an apparent amelioration of Soviet depredations, the old dichotomies between faith and atheism, good and evil, no longer came so easily.[1]

The world still faced an apocalyptic threat, however. It no longer emanated from the walls of the Kremlin but from laboratories and military installations the world over – even in the United States. Kennan's only Christian certainty came when he viewed nuclear weapons and the burgeoning arms race. And this certainty terrified him, as he concluded that

> the truly apocalyptic dangers of our time, the ones that threaten to put an end to the very continuity of history ... represent for us not only political questions but stupendous moral problems, to which we cannot deny the courageous Christian answer. Here our main concern must be to see that man, whose own folly once drove him from the Garden of Eden, does not now commit the blasphemous act of destroying, whether in fear or in anger or in greed, the great and lovely world in which, even in his fallen state, he has been permitted by the grace of God to live.[2]

---

[1] George F. Kennan, "Foreign Policy and Christian Conscience," *The Atlantic Monthly*, May 1959. I am indebted to Eric Gregory for bringing this article to my attention.
[2] *Ibid.*

To Kennan, the spiritual divide in the world conflict now stood not between the United States and the Soviet Union, but between God and humanity.

By 1960, the great diplomatic and civil–religious consensus of the Truman and Eisenhower years began to fray. The public theology that had captivated and compelled the nation, so deliberately constructed by the two presidents, now threatened to turn in on itself. For some such as Kennan, the doctrine that had once defined the Soviet Union as the most dangerous threat to spiritual existence now revealed nuclear weapons to be the greatest threat to existence of any sort. The Providence that he had confidently invoked on America's side in 1953, he now feared held all of humanity in its judgment.

For many others who viewed the Oval Office as both symbol and sustainer of God's favor on America, November 8, 1960, ushered in a nightmare: a Roman Catholic president. Just days after the election, a distraught L. Nelson Bell sent his condolences to the defeated Richard Nixon. Bell hinted darkly at a more sinister reason for Nixon's loss to John F. Kennedy: "But for the behind-the-scenes organizations (political and religious) you would have won overwhelmingly." Bell's post-script made his reference clear, as he warned of "what is taking place . . . a slow, completely integrated and planned attempt to take over our nation for the Roman Catholic Church." This left Bell despondent: "I feel that the judgment of God hangs over a people to whom He has given so much and who have rejected spiritual values for those which are material."[3] The worst fears of Bell and many other Protestants seemed to be coming to pass. America faced spiritual defeat, not by an external atheistic threat, but at the hands of infidels within its own house.

Even Truman, for all of his efforts to forge a partnership with the Pope and to include Catholics in his Cold War religious coalition, blanched at the prospect of a Catholic – notwithstanding a fellow Democrat and anticommunist – actually occupying the Oval Office. Though not as alarmist as Bell, Truman in 1959 had voiced his opposition to a Catholic president. "The main difficulty with that situation has been that the hierarchy of the Catholic Church always wants to control the political operation of a government," he had warned. After failing to defeat Kennedy's nomination at the 1960 Democratic Convention, Truman grudgingly gave way to his party loyalties and supported Kennedy, even campaigning for him throughout the Bible Belt.[4]

Though Kennedy on occasion would invoke religious language to describe America's role in the world, he presided at the beginning of an era when

---

[3] November 11, 1960 letter from Bell to Nixon; L. Nelson Bell Papers, Box 39, Folder 15; BGCA.
[4] Truman quoted in Steve Neal, *Harry and Ike: The Partnership that Remade the Postwar World* (New York: Scribner 2002), 311–313.

many of the institutions of the American civil religion would be reinterpreted, undermined, or even dismantled. Successive Supreme Court decisions in 1962 and 1963 removed official prayer and Bible reading from public schools. Martin Luther King Jr. and other leaders of the civil rights movement effectively employed a public theology that invoked God's judgment for America's sins more than God's blessings for America's righteousness. And with the nation's growing involvement in the Vietnam War, the clerical voices of Protestants, Catholics, and Jews began to sound as much against American policy as for it. Finally, for those Americans in the "Silent Majority" who trusted President Richard Nixon's public displays of piety and friendship with Billy Graham as symbols of their nation's spiritual resilience, Watergate's revelations of deception and vulgarity in the White House turned even their faith sour.

Meanwhile, Kennedy's presidency saw the Cold War almost turn catastrophically hot. The Bay of Pigs, the confrontation over Berlin, and the Cuban missile crisis all demonstrated just how precarious was the balance of terror between the superpowers. After coming so close in October 1962 to worldwide conflagration, the United States and USSR then settled into two decades of an uneasy stand-off, of proxy wars, regional conflicts, sporadic negotiations, and sometime détente.

If religion helped define much of the beginning of the Cold War, religion played a large role in determining its end as well. To be sure, it was a unique, complex, and largely unanticipated convergence of factors that brought the Cold War to an abrupt resolution, and the events that led to the dissolution of the Iron Curtain in 1989 and of the Soviet Union itself in 1991 will continue to be debated for generations. But in ways consistent with the religious themes that Truman and Eisenhower promoted, yet that manifested themselves in some surprising places, the "Protestants, Catholics, and Jews" that Truman and Eisenhower sought to enlist in the first fifteen years of the conflict not only helped shape its final fifteen years – they played an instrumental role in bringing the Cold War to an end. In this cause they were joined by a fourth pillar: Islam. Protestants, Catholics, Jews, and Muslims each inspired or led defining Cold War moments or campaigns that together led to the demise of Soviet communism. Together they also vindicated the essential insight that Truman, Eisenhower, Dulles, and others had first grasped: Soviet communism's atheism was one of its greatest weaknesses, and would be one of the keys to its eventual collapse. At the same time, looking back it is clear that Truman and Eisenhower also misread a part of the religious factor. Unlike the hopes and plans of Truman and Eisenhower, the Protestants, Catholics, Jews, and Muslims of the 1970s and 1980s would not be forged into a unified religious alliance. Rather, they would each protect themselves and promote their values in their own ways – consistent with their own interests and identities, and common in their antipathy to Soviet communism.

For Jews, this meant highlighting the plight of their co-religionists in the USSR. In an oddity of history, an arcane technical provision on freedom of emigration added as an amendment to U.S. legislation on tariff rates and trade assistance soon displayed to the world communism's tyranny and hostility to religion. The Soviet Union had long included restrictions on emigration among the many freedoms that it denied its citizens. Following Israel's stunning victory in 1967's Six Day War, a growing number of Soviet Jews began attempting to emigrate to Israel, both to live in greater freedom and to help strengthen the only two decade–old Jewish state. As the numbers of Jewish émigrés increased, the USSR reacted by imposing an onerous exit tax on all aspiring emigrants, ostensibly to help reimburse the Soviet welfare state for its expenses in educating its citizens. The exit tax in practice severely restricted the numbers of Soviet Jews able to leave the country. Around this same time, President Richard Nixon and his National Security Advisor Henry Kissinger were crafting the different provisions of their "détente" policy designed to ease tensions in the U.S.–USSR relationship. This included promoting in Congress the "East-West Trade Relations Act of 1971" to increase trade between the two nations with lowered tariffs and lending subsidies. To the surprise and vexation of Nixon, Kissinger, and the Soviet leadership, for the next two decades this legislation also provided a visible platform for highlighting the Soviet Union's repression, and further undermining its legitimacy with its own citizens.

In a maneuver that may look simple in hindsight but was quite innovative at the time, Senator Henry "Scoop" Jackson and Congressman Charles Vanik offered an amendment to the trade bill prohibiting the extension of "Most Favored Nation" (MFN) trading status (i.e. trade relations at standard tariff rates) for any non-market economy nation that did not allow freedom of emigration. Jackson's Senate floor speech introducing his bill made clear the bold intentions and primary target of the Jackson–Vanik amendment: "We have received numerous reports of late about the intensification of state repression in the Soviet Union.... The most dramatic violation of human rights is the recent decision of the Politburo to demand a ransom from Jews wishing to leave the Soviet Union." In response, the American economy "can be pressed into service as an instrument of our commitment to individual liberty.... We must not now, as we did once, acquiesce to tyranny while there are those, at greater risk than ourselves, who dare to resist."[5] Though

---

[5] Jackson speech quoted in Dorothy Fosdick (ed.), *Henry M. Jackson and World Affairs: Selected Speeches, 1953–1983* (Seattle: University of Washington Press 1990), 179–184. For more on

its precise legislative provisions would evolve, the core principle of Jackson–Vanik – legally conditioning the Soviet Union's external relationship with the United States on its internal treatment of its own citizens – would endure throughout the rest of the Cold War. And Russian Jews were far and way the most visible subjects of this condition. As Anatoly Dobrynin, the longtime Soviet Ambassador to the United States, later lamented, "probably no other single question did more to sour the atmosphere of détente than the question of Jewish emigration from the Soviet Union."[6]

The USSR's oppression of Jews continued to be a major theme of the Reagan Administration's Soviet policy – and continued to be a major irritant in U.S.–Soviet relations. Secretary of State George Shultz recalled that almost every meeting that he or President Reagan held with their Soviet counterparts included the Americans raising the plight of Soviet Jews and the need to allow free emigration. The Reagan Administration also undertook more visible efforts to show support for Russian Jews. For example, when the U.S. Embassy in Moscow in 1987 hosted a Passover Seder, Shultz attended and met with Jewish dissidents. Or when Reagan learned that the U.S. Embassy was the only one that regularly posted staff outside the Moscow synagogue on Friday nights to support Jewish worshippers and monitor KGB harassment, he wrote letters to various European leaders urging them to have their embassies do the same.[7] In short, the Soviet Union's mistreatment of its Jews caused enormous headaches to the Soviet leadership for almost two decades. It mobilized Jews around the world to highlight Soviet repression, it drew many non-Jewish activists into the broader cause, it emboldened Jewish dissidents within the Soviet Union, and it provided the United States Congress and the Reagan Administration with a powerful ideological weapon in their efforts to undermine the USSR's legitimacy.

1978 witnessed the coming of a formidable new voice against communism. When the puff of white smoke emanated from the Vatican on October 16 signaling that the College of Cardinals had elected a new Pope, few observers had anticipated that Karol Wojtyla would become John Paul II – and even fewer anticipated that this formerly obscure Polish cardinal would become perhaps the most consequential pontiff in centuries. John Paul II brought to the papacy an unprecedented Slavic identity, profound theological learning,

Jackson-Vanik's background and impact on U.S.–Soviet relations, see also Gaddis, *The Cold War: A New History* (New York: Penguin Press 2005), 182–183.

[6] Dobrynin, 339.

[7] George Schultz, *Turmoil and Triumph: My Years as Secretary of State* (New York: Scribner's 1993), 121, 171, 886–887. Also Max Kampelman, "The Ronald Reagan I Knew," *The Weekly Standard*, 24 November 2003.

compelling personal charisma, and an abiding aversion to communism. In a display of Polish nationalism and Catholic faith that confirmed the worst fears of the Kremlin, some thirteen million Poles, fully one third of the population, turned out in person to see the Pope at various rallies during his 1979 visit to Poland. Watching television coverage in California of the Pope's visit was then-candidate Ronald Reagan who, upon his inauguration as President one and a half years later, forged an anticommunist alliance with John Paul II that was even stronger and more effective than Truman's partnership with Pius XII.[8]

This was in part because of the historical moment. The domestic religious culture in the United States, while still shaped by Protestantism, no longer sought to marginalize Catholicism as it had in Truman's day. Different factors in the ensuing decades – including Kennedy's presidency, the reforms of Vatican II, and the growing co-belligerence of American Catholics and evangelicals on issues such as opposition to abortion – had combined to create an environment much more hospitable to the American government cooperating with the Vatican. Meanwhile, years of economic stagnation and political repression had left the Soviet bloc itself more fragile and vulnerable internally. Communist leaders themselves recognized this. One Communist party directive declared that "the Pope is our enemy" soon before his Poland trip. Soviet Premier Leonid Brezhnev warned the Polish leadership "don't give [the Pope] any reception. It will only cause trouble." A few months later, the Soviet Central Committee issued a directive titled "Decision to Work against the Policies of the Vatican in Relation to Socialist States" which outlined a series of action plans for the foreign ministry, KGB, and other arms of the Soviet government to counter growing Catholic influence.[9]

Reagan, meanwhile, oversaw the forging of a relationship between his Administration and the Vatican that was almost unprecedented in its substance and scope. In April 1981 he sent CIA Director William Casey on a mission to the Vatican, followed in December by Special Vatican Envoy (and retired General) Vernon Walters. These were the first of what would be numerous trips to Rome by Casey and Walters, to share sensitive intelligence with the Pope on Soviet military, espionage, and political developments, to coordinate covert American and Vatican support for Poland's Solidarity movement, and to strategize on their common interests in opposing communism elsewhere around the world, particularly Latin America. The Vatican also provided

---

[8]   See John O'Sullivan, *The President, the Pope, and the Prime Minister: Three Who Changed the World* (Washington DC: Regnery 2006), 52–55, 100–105, and Gaddis, 192–194.

[9]   Gaddis, 192–193, and O'Sullivan, 111.

Casey and Walters, both devout Catholics, with information and insights from the Vatican's extensive clerical network across the globe. Reagan himself paid his first visit to the Vatican in June 1982. In a trip itinerary full of symbolism of religious and political anticommunism, following his meeting with John Paul II, Reagan traveled to London to predict communism's inevitable demise on the "ash heap of history" in his speech at Westminster. Finally, in a gesture that Truman would have both appreciated and envied, Reagan in 1984 succeeded in granting official diplomatic recognition to the Vatican. Though this attracted some criticism both from secularist voices such as the *New York Times* editorial page and conservative Protestants such as Jerry Falwell, a Gallup poll showed that 57% of Americans supported the move, and the Senate confirmed Reagan's ambassadorial nominee William Wilson by a vote of 81–13. Truman had just been ahead of his time. Thirty-three years after the crush of domestic opposition had sunk his similar effort, the combination of improved Catholic–Protestant relations at home and the continued communist threat abroad had produced an entirely new climate.[10]

As for Protestantism, the most salient Protestant voice in ending the Cold War resided in the Oval Office itself. It was Reagan, a devout though idiosyncratic Protestant, who most deliberately and most emphatically resurrected the diplomatic theology of the Truman and Eisenhower years. While defining Reagan's personal beliefs with any precision remains an elusive exercise – his words and practices variously range from Emersonian mysticism to conventional evangelicalism to apocalyptic dispensationalism – he did bring an explicitly religious framework to his Cold War policy.[11] He took office in 1981 confident in the convictions that God had blessed Americans with their rights and liberties, that Soviet communism was not just evil *and* atheistic, but it was evil *because* it was atheistic, and that God had called the United States to play a special role in protecting and promoting freedom in the world. In words that Truman or Eisenhower could well have uttered, just months after his inauguration Reagan told an audience at the University of Notre Dame – and any others listening across the globe – that "it is time for the world

[10] O'Sullivan, 176–182; Paul Kengor, *God and Ronald Reagan: A Spiritual Life* (New York: Harper Collins 2004), 208–212,; Jim Nicholson, *The United States and the Holy See: the Long Road* (Rome, Italy: 30 Days Books 2002) 57–60.

[11] For two recent and quite divergent interpretations of Reagan's faith, see Kengor and also John Patrick Diggins, *Ronald Reagan: Fate, Freedom, and the Making of History* (New York: W. W. Norton 2007). Kengor depicts Reagan as an evangelical Protestant, while Diggins treats Reagan as an Emersonian mystic who sacralized American patriotism. Though Diggins' argument is much more sophisticated, neither Kengor nor Diggins is entirely persuasive. It seems most accurate to characterize Reagan's faith as sincere and fervent, rooted in the Protestant tradition yet embracing at various times divergent and even contradictory theological views.

to know our intellectual and spiritual values are rooted in the source of all strength, a belief in a Supreme Being, and a law higher than our own."[12]

This foundation gave the United States a special calling. In a 1983 speech to the National Association of Religious Broadcasters, Reagan proclaimed a favorite theme. "I've always believed that this blessed land was set apart in a special way, that some divine plan placed this great continent here between the two oceans to be found by people from every corner of the Earth – people who had a special love for freedom."[13] This "divine plan" included a particular mandate. He believed that, having blessed the United States, God had also ordained this chosen nation to lead the great crusade against communism. One of Reagan's favorite quotations, which he repeated often in public and in private, came from Truman's old ally Pius XII: "into the hands of America, God has placed an afflicted mankind."[14] It is no coincidence that Reagan made some of his most dramatic pronouncements on the spiritual stakes of the Cold War before religious audiences. For example, he delivered perhaps his defining words of the conflict, denouncing the Soviet Union as the "evil empire," before the annual conference of the National Association of Evangelicals. In context, this speech is even more remarkable. Reagan's jeremiad against the Soviet government began first with an appeal for the souls of the Soviet people. "Let us pray for the salvation of all of those who live in that totalitarian darkness – pray they will discover the joy of knowing God. But until they do, let us be aware that while they preach the supremacy of the state, declare its omnipotence over individual man, and predict its eventual domination of all peoples on the Earth, they are the focus of evil in the modern world."[15]

It was in part Reagan's affinity for individual stories of faith that also led him to realize the potency of religious persecution as a symbol of communism's tyranny, and his advocacy on behalf of religious believers included Protestants as well as Jews and Catholics. Nor did Reagan hesitate to link these cases to the Cold War's overall strategic framework. While the first two years of his Administration saw escalating tension and hostility between the United States and the Soviet Union, early in 1983 Reagan agreed with

---

[12] Ronald Reagan, address at University of Notre Dame, South Bend, IN, May 17, 1981. *Public Papers of the Presidents: Ronald W. Reagan, 1981* (Washington: United States Government Printing Office 1982), 434.

[13] Reagan, address to NRB convention, Washington DC, January 31, 1983. *Public Papers of the Presidents: Ronald W. Reagan, 1983* (Washington: United States Government Printing Office 1984), 154.

[14] Kengor, 140.

[15] Reagan, address to NAE convention, Orlando, FL, March 8, 1983. *Public Papers of the Presidents: Ronald W. Reagan, 1983* (Washington: United States Government Printing Office 1984), 359–364.

Shultz to seek quietly for the possibility of an opening. To test Soviet intentions – and to demonstrate in turn his own sincerity – Reagan seized on the case of seven Russian Pentecostal Christians who for five years had been living in a diplomatic exile of sorts in the basement of the U.S. Embassy in Moscow. The "Siberian Seven" originally had sought refuge in the Embassy to seek both relief from persecution and also the right to emigrate abroad. A stalemate had ensued: the United States would not release the Pentecostals to the Soviet police, and the Kremlin would not allow the Pentecostals to leave the country. Now Reagan had agreed to Shultz's suggestion for a clandestine meeting with Dobrynin, and in their discussion, Reagan focused on the plight of the Pentecostals as a key indicator for both sides. According to Shultz, Reagan told Dobrynin "if you can do something about the Pentecostals or another human rights issue, we will simply be delighted and will not embarrass you by undue publicity." This spurred six months of intensive diplomacy over the Pentecostals that involved other senior American officials including Shultz, Vice-President George Bush, and arms control negotiator Ambassador Max Kampelman, and resulted in the Soviets allowing all of the Siberian Seven to emigrate by July. Reagan in turn kept his word and kept quiet. Both sides later described the good faith displayed in resolving the Pentecostal issue as a key factor in advancing the Soviet–American relationship. In Dobrynin's words, it was "a small gesture that was to figure with unusual symbolism in the turn in our relations." Shultz remembered it as "the first successful negotiation with the Soviets in the Reagan Administration" which in turn "encouraged President Reagan and me to continue to pursue our efforts to turn the superpower relationship into something far more positive."[16]

If Jews, Catholics, and Protestants each did their parts to undercut the credibility and legitimacy of Soviet communism, it fell to Islam to deliver the most damaging battlefield blows. The USSR's invasion of Afghanistan in 1979 drew much of the Muslim world into the fight against communism. It also fulfilled Eisenhower's original dream of enlisting Islamic leaders in the Cold War, though in a way that he likely did not imagine. Rather than a pan-religious alliance of Protestant, Catholic, Jewish, and Muslim clerics joining together peacefully to denounce communism, Afghan and Arab *mujahadeen* launched a *jihad* – soon to be supported generously by Pakistani guidance,

---

[16] Shultz, 163–171, and Dobrynin, 523–524. For more on the roles that Catholic and Protestant churches played in the demise of communism in Soviet Bloc countries, see Barbara von der Heydt, *Candles Behind the Wall: Heroes of the Peaceful Revolution that Shattered Communism* (Grand Rapids, MI: Eerdmans 1993).

Saudi dollars, and American weapons – that led to a decade of bloodshed and eventual defeat of the Soviet army.

Though Afghanistan had been an Islamic nation for centuries, the more direct antecedents to the coming clash between Islam and communism were forged in the ideological ferment of the 1960s. Just as that decade saw Soviet-backed proselytism of Marxism flourishing among some Afghan professors and students in Kabul, other Afghan intellectuals were embracing the works of Islamist scholars such as Sayyid Qutb and Muslim Brotherhood founder Hassan el Banna. Afghanistan's previous traditions of tribal loyalties and a more syncretistic, tolerant Islam began to be eclipsed by the foreign (and mutually antagonistic) ideologies of communism and Islamism. By the late 1970s, Afghan communists and Afghan Islamists struggled for control of the nation. For a short time in 1979 an Afghan communist named Nur Mohammed Turaki held power. Even his Kremlin supporters, hardly attuned to religious matters, worried that in his Marxist zeal Turaki was trying to push his Muslim country too far, too fast. Notes from a March 18, 1979 Politburo meeting reflect Moscow's ironic concern about communism's limits. Defense Minister Dmitri Ustinov worried that "the leadership of Afghanistan did not sufficiently appreciate the role of Islamic fundamentalists." KGB chief Yuri Andropov saw formidable obstacles to the march of the Marxist historical dialectic. "Afghanistan is not ready at this time to resolve all of the issues it faces through socialism. The economy is backward, the Islamic religion predominates, and nearly all of the rural population is illiterate. We know Lenin's teaching about a revolutionary situation. Whatever situation we are talking about in Afghanistan, it is not that type of situation." Increasingly worried about Taraki's overreach, the ostensibly anti-religious Soviet leadership even pressured Taraki to ease up his repression of Islam and include more Muslim leaders in his government.[17]

These sensitivities notwithstanding, in the end the Kremlin underestimated the strength of Islam. As Turaki grew more and more erratic in his rule, and the Soviets saw their hoped-for client state slipping from their control, they decided to intervene in force on Christmas day, 1979. The Russian invasion of Afghanistan, driven in part by a misperception of the willingness of Muslims to fight in defense of their faith and their lands, contributed directly to the fall of the Soviet empire. The U.S. Government, starting under President Carter and accelerating under Reagan, exploited this opportunity as well. Though modest

---

[17] Quotations and background information cited in Steve Coll, *Ghost Wars: The Secret History of the CIA, Afghanistan, and bin Laden, from the Soviet Invasion to September 10, 2001* (New York: Penquin 2004), 38–46, 111–114.

at first in scale and scope, American aid to the Afghan fighters eventually reached the hundreds of millions of dollars annually. Most importantly, this support came to include the portable, potent Stinger missiles, which enabled otherwise primitive tribesmen on horseback to destroy the most advanced Soviet jets and helicopters, and decisively turned the battle. CIA director Casey, a devout Catholic, exemplified one strain of American enthusiasm for the Muslim warriors. In Steve Coll's words, "as his Muslim allies did, Casey saw the Afghan jihad not merely as statecraft, but as an important front in a worldwide struggle between communist atheism and God's community of believers." And in a 1980s version of the Truman Administration's covert support for the distribution of Bishop Dibelius' sermons in East Berlin, Casey agreed to have the CIA print and distribute thousands of Uzbek-language copies of the Koran among Uzbek-speaking Afghans in the northern part of the country – and even in Uzbek-speaking areas across the Soviet border.[18] This peculiar combination of American and Saudi funding, Stinger missiles, Islamic piety, Afghan ferocity, and CIA-printed Korans proved too much for the Kremlin. The Soviet army's withdrawal from Afghanistan early in 1989 was soon followed by the collapse of the Iron Curtain that same year, and the demise of the Soviet Union itself two years later.

Viewed through how it ended, and particularly through the roles played by Jews, Catholics, Protestants, and Muslims in bringing about its end, the Cold War's conclusion confirms the essential insight of Truman, Eisenhower, and other American leaders such as Dulles, Smith, and Judd. The Cold War was a religious war. Religion helped define the nature of the conflict, delineate the different sides, and determine the outcome. And yet how these various faiths played their roles in the Cold War's final decades reinforces the challenges and complexities of its first decades. Different religious leaders and groups never did come together in a unified alliance against communism. Even within each faith, serious divisions emerged. Just as Protestants in the 1940s and 1950s fought fiercely among themselves to define who they were and what they stood for and against, so in the 1980s did many mainline Protestant leaders oppose evangelicals and Reagan himself in part over Cold War policy. This is not to mention the debates within American Judaism over whether to work for peace or against Soviet communism – and whether those two goals were incompatible, or identical. Or the various voices that continued to emerge within Catholicism, from the Marxist-sympathies of Latin American libera-tion theologians, to the U.S. Catholic Bishops' Conference and its challenges to the Reagan Administration's nuclear policy, to the fierce anticommunism

[18] Coll, 90–93, 104–105.

of Polish priests. Rather than religious unity, what these various traditions brought to the Cold War was religious diversity – within themselves, and between each other. Yet even this religious diversity still had something that communism did not, and that was religious belief itself. This proved sufficient to help define the terms of the conflict and, in turn and in time, to help end it.

Bibliography

Abrams, Elliott, ed. *The Influence of Faith: Religious Groups and U.S. Foreign Policy.* Lanham, MD: Rowman and Littlefield, 2001.

Acheson, Dean. *Present at the Creation: My Years in the State Department.* New York: Norton, 1969.

Allitt, Patrick. *Catholic Intellectuals and Conservative Politics in America, 1950–1985.* Ithaca, NY: Cornell University Press, 1993.

Ambrose, Stephen E. *Eisenhower: Soldier and President.* New York: Simon and Schuster, 1990.

Arend, Anthony Clark. *Pursuing a Just and Durable Peace: John Foster Dulles and International Organization.* New York: Greenwood Press, 1988.

Bailey, Thomas A. *A Diplomatic History of the American People.* Englewood Cliffs, NJ: Prentice Hall, 1980.

Beisner, Robert L. *Dean Acheson: A Life in the Cold War.* New York: Oxford University Press, 2006.

Benson, Michael T. *Harry S. Truman and the Founding of Israel.* Westport, CT: Prager, 1997.

Boyer, Paul. *By the Bomb's Early Light: American Thought and Culture at the Dawn of the Atomic Age.* Chapel Hill, NC: University of North Carolina Press, 1994.

————. *When Time Shall Be No More: Prophecy Belief in Modern American Culture.* Cambridge, MA: Harvard University Press, 1992.

Brands, H. W. *What America Owes the World: The Struggle for the Soul of Foreign Policy.* New York: Cambridge University Press, 1998.

Brown, Robert McAfee, ed. *The Essential Reinhold Niebuhr: Selected Essays and Addresses.* New Haven, CT: Yale University Press, 1986.

Bush, Richard C., Jr. *Religion in Communist China.* New York: Abingdon Press, 1970.

Carpenter, Joel. *Revive Us Again: The Reawakening of American Fundamentalism.* New York: Oxford University Press, 1999.

Carpenter, Joel, and Wilbert R. Shenk, eds., *Earthen Vessels: American Evangelicals and Foreign Missions, 1880–1980.* Grand Rapids: Eerdman's 1990.

Chace, James. *Acheson: The Secretary of State Who Created the American World.* New York: Simon and Schuster, 1998.

Challener, Richard D. "The Moralist as Pragmatist: John Foster Dulles as Cold War Strategist," in Gordon A. Craig and Francis L. Lowenheim, eds, *The Diplomats, 1939–1979*. Princeton: Princeton University Press, 1994.

Chambers, Whittaker. *Witness*. Washington, DC: Regnery, 1980.

Christensen, Thomas J. *Useful Adversaries: Grand Strategy, Domestic Mobilization, and Sino-American Conflict, 1947–1958*. Princeton: Princeton University Press, 1996.

Clark, William H. *The Church in China: Its Vitality; Its Future?* New York: Council Press, 1970.

Cohen, Warren I. *America in the Age of Soviet Power, 1945–1991*. New York: Cambridge University Press, 1993.

Craig, Campbell. *Destroying the Village: Eisenhower and Thermonuclear War*. New York: Columbia University Press, 1998.

Diggins, John Patrick. *The Proud Decades: America in War and Peace, 1941–1960*. New York: W.W. Norton, 1988.

Divine, Robert. *Second Chance: The Triumph of Internationalism in America During World War II*. New York: Atheneum, 1967.

Dobrynin, Anatoly. *In Confidence: Moscow's Ambassador to America's Six Cold War Presidents, 1962–1986*. New York: Random House, 1995.

Dudziak, Mary L. *Cold War Civil Rights: Race and the Image of American Democracy*. Princeton, NJ: Princeton University Press, 2000.

Dulles, Eleanor Lansing. *Chances of a Lifetime: A Memoir*. Englewood Cliffs, NJ: Prentice-Hall, 1980.

Dulles, Foster Rhea. *American Foreign Policy Toward Communist China, 1949–1969*. New York: Thomas Y. Crowell, 1972.

Edwards, Lee. *Missionary for Freedom: The Life and Times of Walter Judd*. New York: Paragon House, 1990.

Eisenhower, Dwight D. *The White House Years: Mandate for Change, 1953–1956*. New York: Doubleday, 1963.

——. *The White House Years: Waging Peace, 1956–1961*. New York: Doubleday, 1965.

Fairbank, John K., ed. *The Missionary Enterprise in China and America*. Cambridge: Harvard University Press, 1974.

Federal Council of the Churches of Christ in America, Commission on the Relation of the Church to the War in the Light of the Christian Faith. *Atomic Warfare and the Christian Faith*. New York, 1946.

Fox, Richard. *Reinhold Niebuhr: A Biography*. San Francisco: Harper and Row, 1985.

Gaddis, John Lewis. *We Now Know: Rethinking Cold War History*. Oxford: Clarendon Press, 1997.

——. *The United States and the End of the Cold War: Implications, Reconsiderations, Provocations*. New York: Oxford University Press, 1992.

——. *The Long Peace: Inquiries Into the History of the Cold War*. New York: Oxford University Press, 1987.

——. *Strategies of Containment: A Critical Appraisal of Postwar American. National Security Policy*. New York: Oxford University Press, 1982.

——. *The United States and the Origins of the Cold War, 1941–1947*. New York: Columbia University Press, 2000, revised edition.

Gamble, Richard M. *The War for Righteousness: Progressive Christianity, the Great War, and the Rise of the Messianic Nation*. Wilmington, DE: ISI Books, 2003.

Gibbs, Nancy and Michael Duffy. *The Preacher and the Presidents: Billy Graham in the White House.* New York: Center Street, 2007.

Gilbert, James. *Redeeming Culture: American Religion in an Age of Science.* Chicago: University of Chicago Press, 1997.

Gilkey, Langdon. *Shantung Compound: The Story of Men and Women Under Pressure.* New York: Harper and Row, 1966.

Glendon, Mary Ann. *A World Made New: Eleanor Roosevelt and the Universal Declaration of Human Rights.* New York: Random House, 2001.

Graham, Billy. *Just As I Am: The Autobiography of Billy Graham.* New York: HarperCollins, 1997.

Hamby, Alonzo L. *Man of the People: A Life of Harry S. Truman.* New York: Oxford University Press, 1995.

Henry, Carl F. H. *Confessions of a Theologian: An Autobiography.* Waco, TX: Word Books, 1986.

Herberg, Will. *Protestant, Catholic, Jew: An Essay in American Religious Sociology.* New York: Doubleday, 1955.

Hero, Alfred O., Jr. *American Religious Groups View Foreign Policy: Trends in Rank-and-File Opinion, 1937–1969.* Durham, NC: Duke University Press, 1973.

Herzstein, Robert E. *Henry R. Luce: A Political Portrait of the Man Who Created the American Century.* New York: Scribners, 1994.

Hogan, Michael J. *A Cross of Iron: Harry S. Truman and the Origins of the National Security State, 1945–1954.* New York: Cambridge University Press, 1998.

Hollinger, David. *Science, Jews, and Secular Culture: Studies in Mid-Twentieth Century American Intellectual Historyi.* Princeton, NJ: Princeton University Press, 1996.

Hopkins, C. Howard. *John R. Mott, 1865–1955.* Grand Rapids, MI: Eerdmans, 1979.

Hulsether, Mark. *Building a Protestant Left: Christianity and Crisis Magazine, 1941–1993.* Knoxville, TN: University of Tennessee Press, 1999.

Hunt, Michael H. *Ideology and U.S. Foreign Policy.* New Haven, CT: Yale University Press, 1987.

Hutchison, William R, ed. *Between the Times: The Travail of the Protestant Establishment in America, 1900–1960.* New York: Cambridge University Press, 1989.

Hutchison, William R. *Errand to the World: American Protestant Thought and Foreign Missions.* Chicago: University of Chicago Press, 1987.

Immerman, Richard H. *John Foster Dulles: Piety, Pragmatism, and Power in U.S. Foreign Policy.* Wilmington, DE: Scholarly Resources Books, 1999.

Immerman, Richard H., ed. *John Foster Dulles and the Diplomacy of the Cold War.* Princeton, NJ: Princeton University Press, 1990.

Isaacson, Walter, and Evan Thomas. *The Wise Men: Six Friends and the World They Made.* New York: Simon and Schuster, 1986.

Jian, Chen. *China's Road to the Korean War: The Making of the Sino-American Confrontation.* New York: Columbia University Press, 1994.

Keegan, John. *Winston Churchill.* New York: Viking Penguin, 2002.

Kennan, George F. *Memoirs: 1925–1950.* Boston: Little, Brown, and Co., 1967.

———. *Memoirs: 1950–1963.* Boston: Little, Brown, and Co., 1972.

Korda, Michael. *Ike: An American Hero.* New York: HarperCollins, 2007.

Kunz, Diane B. *Butter and Guns: America's Cold War Economic Diplomacy.* New York: The Free Press, 1997.

Kurth, James. "The Protestant Deformation and American Foreign Policy." *Orbis*, (Spring 1998), 221–239.

Lefever, Ernest W. *The Irony of Virtue: Ethics and American Power.* Boulder, CO: Westview Press, 1998.

———. "Protestants and United States Foreign Policy, 1925–1954," Ph.D. diss., Yale University, 1956.

Leffler, Melvyn P. *The Specter of Communism: The United States and the Origins of the Cold War, 1917–1953.* New York: Hill and Wang, 1994.

———. *A Preponderance of Power: National Security, the Truman Administration, and the Cold War.* Stanford, CA: Stanford University Press, 1992.

Levin, N. Gordon, Jr. *Woodrow Wilson and World Politics: America's Response to War and Revolution.* New York: Oxford University Press, 1968.

Lilly, Edward P. "The Psychological Strategy Board and Its Predecessors: Foreign Policy Coordination, 1938–1953," in Gaetano L. Vincitorio, ed., *Studies in Modern History.* New York: St. John's University Press, 1968, 337–382.

Longfield, Bradley J. *The Presbyterian Controversy: Fundamentalists, Modernists, and Moderates.* New York: Oxford University Press, 1991.

Loveland, Anne C. *American Evangelicals and the U.S. Military, 1942–1993.* Baton Rouge, LA: Louisiana State University Press, 1996.

Lucas, Scott. *Freedom's War: The American Crusade Against the Soviet Union.* New York: New York University Press, 1999.

MacInnis, Donald. *Religious Policy and Practice in Communist China.* New York: Macmillan, 1972.

Marsden, George. *Reforming Fundamentalism: Fuller Seminary and the New Evangelicalism.* Grand Rapids, MI: Eerdmans, 1995.

———. *Fundamentalism and American Culture: The Shaping of Modern Evangelicalism, 1870–1925.* New York: Oxford University Press, 1980.

Martin, William. *A Prophet With Honor: The Billy Graham Story.* New York: William Morrow and Company, 1991.

May, Ernest R. *The Truman Administration and China, 1945–1949.* New York: J.B. Lippincott, 1975.

May, Ernest R., ed. *American Cold War Strategy: Interpreting NSC-68.* Boston: Bedford Books, 1993.

McDougall, Walter A. *Promised Land, Crusade State: The American Encounter with the World Since 1776.* New York: Houghton Mifflin, 1997.

Mead, Walter Russell. *God and Gold: Britain, America, and the Making of the Modern World.* New York: Alfred A. Knopf, 2007.

———. *Special Providence: American Foreign Policy and How It Changed the World.* New York: Alfred A. Knopf, 2002.

Merkley, Paul. *Reinhold Niebuhr: A Political Account.* Montreal: McGill-Queen's University Press, 1975.

Miscamble, Wilson D. *George F. Kennan and the Making of American Foreign Policy, 1947–1950.* Princeton, NJ: Princeton University Press, 1992.

Morgan, Edmund S. *The Puritan Dilemma: The Story of John Winthrop.* New York: Longman, 1999, 2nd edition.

Morison, Samuel Eliot. *By Land and By Sea: Essays and Addresses.* New York: Alfred Knopf, 1953.

Neal, Steve. *Harry and Ike: The Partnership that Remade the Postwar World*. New York: Scribners, 2001.

Newby, James R. *Elton Trueblood: Believer, Teacher, and Friend*. San Francisco: Harper and Row, 1990.

Nichols, J. Bruce. *The Uneasy Alliance: Religion, Refugee Work, and U.S. Foreign Policy*. New York: Oxford University Press, 1988.

Nicholson, Jim. *The United States and the Holy See: The Long Road*. Rome, Italy: 30 Days Books, 2002.

Niebuhr, H. Richard. *Christ and Culture*. New York: Harper and Row, 1951.

————. *The Kingdom of God in America*. New York: Harper and Row, 1937.

Niebuhr, Reinhold. *The Irony of American History*. New York: Scribners, 1952.

————. *The Children of Light and the Children of Darkness: A Vindication of Democracy and a Critique of its Traditional Defense*. New York: Scribners, 1944.

————. *Christianity and Power Politics*. New York: Scribners, 1940.

————. *Moral Man and Immoral Society: A Study in Ethics and Politics*. New York: Scribners, 1932.

Neils, Patricia, ed. *United States Attitudes and Policies Toward China: The Impact of American Missionaries*. Armonk, NY: M.E. Sharpe, Inc., 1990.

Ninkovich, Frank. *The Wilsonian Century: U.S. Foreign Policy Since 1900*. Chicago: University of Chicago Press, 1999.

————. *Modernity and Power: A History of the Domino Theory in the Twentieth Century*. Chicago: University of Chicago Press, 1994.

Noll, Mark. *A History of Christianity in the United States and Canada*. Grand Rapids, MI: Eerdmans, 1992.

Oren, Michael. *Power, Faith, and Fantasy: America in the Middle East, 1776 to the Present*. New York: W.W. Norton, 2007.

Pach, Chester J., Jr., and Elmo Richardson. *The Presidency of Dwight D. Eisenhower*. Lawrence, KS: University Press of Kansas, 1991.

Patterson, James T. *Grand Expectations: The United States, 1945–1974*. New York: Oxford University Press, 1996.

Perlstein, Rick. *Before the Storm: Barry Goldwater and the Unmaking of the American Consensus*. New York: Hill and Wang, 2001.

Pierard, Richard V., and Robert D. Linder. *Civil Religion and the Presidency*. Grand Rapids, MI: Academie Books, 1988.

Pruessen, Ronald W. *John Foster Dulles: The Road to Power*. New York: The Free Press, 1982.

Robert, Dana L. "From Missions to Mission to Beyond Missions: The Historiography of American Protestant Foreign Missions Since World War II." *International Bulletin of Missionary Research*, October 1994, 146–162.

Rotter, Andrew J. *Comrades at Odds: The United States and India, 1947–1964*. Ithaca, NY: Cornell University Press, 2000.

————. "Christians, Muslims, and Hindus: Religion and U.S.—South Asian Relations, 1947–1964." *Diplomatic History* (September 2000).

Shaw, Yu-Ming. *An American Missionary in China: John Leighton Stuart and Chinese-American Relations*. Cambridge, MA: Harvard University, 1992.

Shewmaker, Kenneth E. *Americans and Chinese Communists, 1927–1945: A Persuading Encounter*. Ithaca: Cornell University, 1971.

Silk, Mark. *Spiritual Politics: Religion and America Since World War II*. New York: Touchstone, 1988.

Smith, Tony. *America's Mission: The United States and the Worldwide Struggle for Democracy in the Twentieth Century*. Princeton, NJ: Princeton University Press, 1994.

Spalding, Elizabeth Edwards. *The First Cold Warrior: Harry Truman, Containment, and the Remaking of Liberal Internationalism*. Lexington, KY: University Press of Kentucky, 2006.

Spence, Jonathan. *The Search for Modern China*. New York: W.W. Norton, 1990.

Stephanson, Anders. *Manifest Destiny: American Expansion and the Empire of Right*. New York: Hill and Wang, 1995.

Strong, Josiah. *Our Country*. Cambridge, MA: Belknap Press, 1963.

Stuart, John Leighton. *Fifty Years in China: The Memoirs of John Leighton Stuart, Missionary and Ambassador*. New York: Random House, 1954.

_____. *John Leighton Stuart's Diary (Mainly of the Critical Year 1949)*. Palo Alto: Yenching University Alumni Association of USA, Inc., 1980.

Suri, Jeremi. *Henry Kissinger and the American Century*. Cambridge, MA: Belknap Press, 2007.

Tanenhaus, Sam. *Whittaker Chambers: A Biography*. New York: Random House Modern Library, 1998.

Thomson, James C., Jr. *While China Faced West: American Reformers in Nationalist China, 1928–1937*. Cambridge: Harvard University Press, 1969.

Toulouse, Mark G. *The Transformation of John Foster Dulles: From Prophet of Realism to Priest of Nationalism*. Macon, GA: Mercer University Press, 1985.

Trachtenberg, Marc. *A Constructed Peace: The Making of the European Settlement, 1945–1963*. Princeton, NJ: Princeton University Press, 1999.

Truman, Harry S. *Memoirs: Year of Decisions*. New York: Doubleday, 1955.

_____. *Memoirs: Years of Trial and Hope*. New York: Doubleday, 1956.

Tsou, Tang. *America's Failure in China, 1941–1950*. Chicago: University of Chicago Press, 1963.

Tucker, Nancy Bernkopf. *Patterns in the Dust: Chinese-American Relations and the Recognition Controversy, 1949–1950*. New York: Columbia University, 1983.

Tucker, Robert W., and David C. Hendrickson. *Empire of Liberty: The Statecraft of Thomas Jefferson*. New York: Oxford University Press, 1990.

United States Department of State. *The China White Paper: August, 1949*. Volumes 1, 2. Stanford, CA: Stanford University Press, 1967.

Van Dusen, Henry P., ed. *The Spiritual Legacy of John Foster Dulles*. Philadelphia: Westminster Press, 1960.

Varg, Paul. *Missionaries, Chinese, and Diplomats: The American Protestant Missionary Movement in China, 1890–1952*. Princeton, NJ: Princeton University Press, 1958.

Warren, Heather. *Theologians of a New World Order: Reinhold Niebuhr and the Christian Realists, 1920–1948*. New York: Oxford University Press, 1997.

Weiner, Tim. *Legacy of Ashes: The History of the CIA*. New York: Doubleday, 2007.

Whitfield, Stephen J. *The Culture of the Cold War*. Baltimore, MD: The Johns Hopkins University Press, 1991.

Whyte, Bob. *Unfinished Encounter: China and Christianity*. London: William Collins, 1988.

Wills, Gary. *Under God: Religion and American Politics.* New York: Simon and Schuster, 1990.

Winks, Robin. *Cloak and Gown: Scholars and the Secret War, 1939–1961.* New Haven, CT: Yale University Press, 1996.

Wuthnow, Robert. *The Restructuring of American Religion: Society and Faith Since World War II.* Princeton, NJ: Princeton University Press, 1988.

Index

ABCFM, 178, 179, 183
  decision to support PRC recognition, 180
Abernathy, John
  support for aid to China, 173
Acheson, Dean, 25, 23–25, 215, 288
  address to the National Conference of
    Christians and Jews, 24
  address to the National Council of
    Churches, 55
  and Israel, 289
  as Secretary of State, 23, 204
  decision not to grant China diplomatic
    recognition, 210, 212
  description of the Cold War, 24
  meeting with Senator Smith, 207, 212
  on divine calling of America, 25
  on threat of the international communist
    movement, 56
  Present at the Creation, 24
  realism of, 24
  speech on "the Role of the Bible in Our
    National Life," 24
Adams, Sherman
  as Eisenhower Chief of Staff, 220, 279, 304
Adams, Theodore, 288
Adenauer, Konrad, 125
  and FRASCO, 285
  endorsement of MRA, 219
Afghanistan, 320
  Eisenhower state visit to, 298
  Soviet invasion of, 319
  U.S. military aid to, 321
Africa
  and Billy Graham, 277
Air Force
  provision of transportation for MRA The
    Vanishing Island troupe, 222

Allen, George, 272
American Board of Commissioners for
  Foreign Missions. *See* ABCFM
American China Policy Association, 164, 169
American Council of Christian Churches,
  274
  and Eisenhower meeting, 274
  letter to Truman in support of Nationalists,
    170
  opposition to Trueblood, 303
American Friends of the Middle East
  and Elson trip, 292
  establishment of, 291
American Friends Service Committee, 181
American Legion
  "Back to God campaign" of, 20
Amsterdam conference. *See* World Council of
  Churches
Andropov, Yuri
  and Afghanistan, 320
Anglican Church
  statement on the Catholic Church, 151
Arbella, 6
Archbiship Spyridion
  meeting with Myron Taylor, 141
Archbishop Damaskinos
  death of, 140
Archbishop Eidem, 135
Archbishop Germanos, 135
Archbishop of Canterbury, 134, 150, 152
  letter to Myron Taylor, 146
  meeting with Myron Taylor, 124
Archbishop of Sweden, 150
Archbishop of York, 152
Archbishop Spyridion
  appointment as Patriarch of the Orthodox
    Church in Athens, 141

9 780521 156301